War by Other Means

.

War by Other Means

GEOECONOMICS AND STATECRAFT

Robert D. Blackwill and *Jennifer M. Harris*

• A COUNCIL ON FOREIGN RELATIONS BOOK •

THE BELKNAP PRESS OF
HARVARD UNIVERSITY PRESS

Cambridge, Massachusetts
London, England

First Harvard University Press paperback edition, 2017
Second printing

The Council on Foreign Relations (CFR) is an independent, nonpartisan membership organization, think tank, and publisher dedicated to being a resource for its members, government officials, business executives, journalists, educators and students, civic and religious leaders, and other interested citizens in order to help them better understand the world and the foreign policy choices facing the United States and other countries. Founded in 1921, CFR carries out its mission by maintaining a diverse membership, with special programs to promote interest and develop expertise in the next generation of foreign policy leaders; convening meetings at its headquarters in New York and in Washington, D.C., and other cities where senior government officials, members of Congress, global leaders, and prominent thinkers come together with CFR members to discuss and debate major international issues; supporting a Studies Program that fosters independent research, enabling CFR scholars to produce articles, reports, and books and hold roundtables that analyze foreign policy issues and make concrete policy recommendations; publishing *Foreign Affairs,* the preeminent journal on international affairs and U.S. foreign policy; sponsoring Independent Task Forces that produce reports with both findings and policy prescriptions on the most important foreign policy topics; and providing up-to-date information and analysis about world events and American foreign policy on its website, www.cfr.org.

The Council on Foreign Relations takes no institutional positions on policy issues and has no affiliation with the U.S. government. All views expressed in its publications and on its website are the sole responsibility of the author or authors.

Library of Congress Cataloging-in-Publication Data

Names: Blackwill, Robert D., author. | Harris, Jennifer M., 1981- author.
Title: War by other means : geoeconomics and statecraft / Robert D. Blackwill and Jennifer M. Harris.
Description: Cambridge, Massachusetts : The Belknap Press of Harvard University Press, 2016. | "A Council on Foreign Relations Book." | Includes bibliographical references and index.
Identifiers: LCCN 2015037690 | ISBN 9780674737211 (cloth : alk. paper) | ISBN 9780674979796 (pbk.)
Subjects: LCSH: Economic sanctions—Political aspects. | International economic relations— Political aspects. | United States—Foreign economic relations—21st century. | Geopolitics.
Classification: LCC HF1413.5 .B545 2016 | DDC 327.1/110973—dc23 LC record available at http://lccn.loc.gov/2015037690

Contents

Acknowledgments

We would like to express our gratitude to the many people who helped make this book a reality. To begin, we thank Council on Foreign Relations president Richard N. Haass, director of studies James M. Lindsay, and director of the Maurice R. Greenberg Center for Geoeconomic Studies Michael A. Levi for their support of this project and insightful feedback throughout the drafting process.

We owe a debt to the CFR 2012–2013 and 2013–2014 study groups on geoeconomics for their comments and critiques, all of which improved the ideas underlying the book. The text also benefited from interviews conducted with current and former U.S. government officials, as well as insights from researchers and journalists immersed in issues of economics and foreign policy.

Our work builds upon the scholarly expertise of David Baldwin, Alan Dobson, and David Singh Grewal, three authors who pioneered a necessary trail in the study of geoeconomics in their respective work. We are equally grateful to have received comments at various stages of this project, forcing us to rethink, clarify, and improve our text. These valuable commentators were Graham Allison, Richard Danzig, John Deutch, Andrew Erdmann, Martin Feldstein, Ellen Frost, Peter Harrell, Sasha Post, Sarah Stillman, Ali Wyne, Philip Zelikow, Rachael Ziemba, and Robert Zoellick. None of them, of course, bears any responsibility for the final product.

We are deeply indebted to our executive editor from Harvard University Press, Thomas LeBien, who was masterly in guiding us to a more polished and incisive text. We are also grateful to our agent, Andrew Wylie, as well as to Patricia Dorff and the team in CFR's Publications Department, and to Iva Zoric and the CFR Global Communications and Marketing team for their valuable assistance. Most important, we thank our three research associates at CFR whose contributions to this book were indispensable: Lauren Dickey, our gifted sinologist, Allison Dorey, and Matthew Lester, a supporting force behind the final manuscript.

We save for last our families—Karen, Ken, Ashley, and Sasha for Jennifer, and Vera Hildebrand for Robert. It is to you that this book is dedicated.

War by Other Means

Introduction

D ESPITE HAVING the most powerful economy on earth, the United States too often reaches for the gun instead of the purse in its international conduct. America has hardly outgrown its need for military force, which will remain a central component of U.S. foreign policy. But Washington in the past several decades has increasingly forgotten a tradition that stretches back to the founding of the nation—the systematic use of economic instruments to accomplish geopolitical objectives, what we in this book term geoeconomics. This large-scale failure of collective strategic memory denies Washington potent tools to accomplish its foreign policy objectives.

To compound matters, as economic techniques of statecraft have become a lost art in the United States, the rest of the world has moved in the opposite direction. Russia, China, and others now routinely look to geoeconomic means, often as a first resort, and often to undermine American power and influence. In ignoring the ever-greater role of geoeconomics in the international system, the United States squanders opportunities and dilutes its own foreign policy outcomes. It weakens the confidence of America's Asian and European allies. It encourages China to coerce its neighbors and lessens their ability to resist. It gives China free rein in vulnerable African and Latin American nations. It allows Russia to bend much of the former Soviet space to its will without serious answer from the United States. It reduces U.S. influence in friendly Arab capitals. It insufficiently acknowledges the economic roots of much of Islamic radicalism. These costs weigh on specific U.S. policy aims. But they also risk accumulating over time into a structural disadvantage that Washington may find hard to reverse. In short, the global geoeconomic playing field is now sharply tilting against the United States, and unless this is corrected, the price in blood and treasure for the United States will only grow.

Should Washington send lethal weapons to Ukraine? Should the North Atlantic Treaty Organization (NATO) reestablish a permanent presence in Eastern Europe? Should the United States directly arm the Iraqi Kurds in the fight against the Islamic State of Iraq and al-Sham (ISIS)? Should it intervene militarily in the Syrian civil war? Should America deploy boots on the ground in Iraq? Was an attack on Iran's nuclear facilities really an option for President Obama? What should be the military components of the Obama administration's pivot toward Asia? How many U.S. combat forces should remain in Afghanistan over the long term?

In the current era and across the political spectrum, the United States instinctively debates the application of military instruments to address all of these complex challenges. There is no comparable discussion in Washington of returning Ukraine to economic viability as a way to check Vladimir Putin's designs for a Novorossiya, or "New Russia"; of prioritizing economic and financial denial strategies in the fight against ISIS; of making reform of the Egyptian economy a primary U.S. foreign policy objective; of strengthening Jordan to withstand the effects of the Syrian conflict; of building a Middle East coalition to blunt the economic transmission lines Iran relies upon to project influence in the region; of mounting a major, patient effort to bolster the faltering Afghan economy, a prerequisite for defeating the Taliban over the long run; of building into the Trans-Pacific Partnership agreement or into the Asia pivot more broadly, defenses to help U.S. allies steel themselves against economic bullying from China.

Thomas Jefferson would have regarded this as exceedingly odd. He did not send the newly minted American army to conquer French territory between the Mississippi River and the Rocky Mountains; rather, in exquisite geoeconomic enterprise, he bought it (from Paris, France, at least; true to the colonial arrogance of that time, the native residents of these territories received no such offer). To help prevent London from supporting the Confederacy, the Lincoln administration threatened Britain with the loss of billions of dollars invested in U.S. securities. Government support for overseas private investment drove both American engagement with Latin America and the rebuilding of Europe in the 1920s. The Roosevelt administration in the 1930s deployed trade to preempt German encroachment in the Western Hemisphere and attempted to use the Export-Import Bank to blunt the rise of Japan.

A year and a half after the outbreak of World War II in Europe, the Lend-Lease policy of 1941 enabled the United States to supply Great Britain, France, the Republic of China, and later the USSR and other Allied nations with defense materials needed to win that war. In July 1944 delegates from the Allied countries, led by the United States, signed the Bretton Woods Agreement, which was explicit in its hopes that strengthened international economic cooperation, built on U.S. and British terms, could help to avoid the horrors of another global war. Secretary of State George Marshall in June 1947, delivering commencement remarks at Harvard University, famously declared an archetypal geoeconomic proposition: "The United States should do whatever it is able to do to assist in the return of normal economic health in the world, without which there can be no political stability and no assured peace."

In 1956, President Dwight Eisenhower, in one of the most brazen geoeconomic actions in the past century, forced Britain to end its invasion of Egypt and withdraw from the Suez Canal by threatening to instigate a collapse of the British pound. Soon after, he established the Commission on Foreign Economic Policy, the charter purpose of which was to put U.S. economic policy to work for the country's foreign policy and national security aims. "The national interest in the field of foreign economic policy is clear," said Eisenhower. "It is to obtain . . . the highest possible level of trade and the most efficient use of capital and resources. That this would also strengthen our military allies adds urgency. Their strength is of critical importance to the security of our country." In 1960, a task force commissioned by President-elect Kennedy argued for liberalization in East-West trade to produce a more reasonable and open Soviet Union, and economic assistance to developing nations as a geopolitical means of meeting the Soviet challenge in these regions.

By the Johnson and Nixon years, however, geoeconomics had noticeably begun to wane. The war in Vietnam pushed geoeconomics off the U.S. policy stage. It was perhaps inevitable that the outbreak of armed conflict and hundreds of thousands of U.S. troops on the ground in Southeast Asia would shift policy makers' attention in the direction of military use of force. But this continued through the 1979–1981 Iranian hostage crisis and the failed rescue attempt. It gained momentum with Washington's military responses to the Soviet invasion of Afghanistan; the interventions in Angola, Lebanon, Grenada, and Panama; the first Gulf War; the Clinton administration's air campaign in the Balkans; 9/11 and the wars in Afghanistan and Iraq; U.S.-led NATO intervention in Libya; the American drone and combat air attacks across the greater Middle East; and the re-introduction of U.S. ground forces in Iraq.

Even when policy makers' attention turned from waging conflict to deescalating it, the parameters of discussion stayed largely confined to conventional political-military concerns: arms control negotiations, détente with the Soviet Union, and diplomatic openings with Soviet allies, all assisted by largely political factors. And even in the rare cases when the United States did take on a geoeconomic project of some magnitude during this period—bringing Russia and China into the Western economic order is far and away the most important example—these tended to remain geoeconomic attempts only briefly, before morphing into more straightforward commercial and purely economic ones. Geopolitical factors have not disappeared from these efforts, but they have become secondary if not tertiary considerations.[1]

This is decidedly not so for the world's other major and lesser powers, for whom geoeconomics is a major, often primary instrument of their foreign policies. More and more states are waging geopolitics with capital, attempting with sovereign checkbooks and other economic tools to achieve strategic objectives that in the past were often the stuff of military coercion or conquest.

China curtails the import of Japanese autos to signal its disapproval of Japan's security policies. It lets Philippine bananas rot on China's wharfs because Manila opposes Chinese polices in the South China Sea. It rewards Taiwanese companies that march to Beijing's cadence, and punishes those that do not. It promises trade and business with South Korea in exchange for Seoul rejecting a U.S. bid to deploy the Terminal High-Altitude Area Defense (THAAD) missile defense system. It reduces economic benefits to European governments that host the Dalai Lama. It initiates the creation of the BRICS group, consciously excluding the United States. It promotes the Chinese-led Asian Infrastructure Investment Bank to rival the Washington-based World Bank. In its economic assistance to Africa, it privileges nations that vote with China at the United Nations. It provides more loans to Latin American nations than the World Bank and International Monetary Fund (IMF) combined. It reportedly plans to lend around $10 billion to Venezuela, the most anti-American regime in Latin America. The United States has no coherent polices to deal with these Chinese geoeconomic actions—many of which are aimed squarely at America's allies and friends in Asia and beyond.

Russia periodically shuts off energy to Ukraine in the winter to try to bring Kiev back within Moscow's orbit. It intends to shift all natural gas flows crossing Ukraine to alternative routes circumventing the country to deprive Kiev of crucial transit payments. It threatens to reduce energy supplies to the European Union (EU) if Europe joins the United States in responding to Russia's aggressive external behavior. It promises massive economic assistance to the newly annexed Crimea. It entices former EU leaders with lucrative contracts with Russian companies. It establishes the Eurasian Economic Union to tie countries in former Soviet space closer to Russia's policy preferences. It writes off the majority of Uzbekistan's debt to Russia. After Warsaw's strong reaction to Russia's intervention in Ukraine, Moscow suspends imports of Polish cheese due to alleged irregularities in "normative requirements." It bans the import of Georgian wine because of Tbilisi's determination to protect Georgia's territorial integrity. It offers financial aid to Greece while EU leaders are attempting their own bailout package. It dangles the prospect of an economic bailout before Cyprus in return for military port and airfield access, forcing EU leaders to choose between coming through with a sufficiently attractive bailout of their own or living with a Russian military presence inside the European Union. It bribes the weaker, cash-strapped members of the EU in hopes of provoking a defection from the U.S.-EU sanctions against Russia. For all of the readiness drills and commitments being undertaken by NATO leaders, the United States has no consistent polices to deal with Russia's resurgent geoeconomic coercion.

The Gulf states pledge $12 billion in 2015 as aid to Egypt, adding to the more than $20 billion already contributed since the military ouster of former President Morsi. Oman commits $500 million in aid and investment to Egypt. Saudi Arabia provides economic support to Iraqi Sunni tribes fighting ISIS. Saudi Arabia and the United Arab Emirates together supply Jordan with more than $2 billion in annual aid, leveraging Amman to contain and dismantle the Muslim Brotherhood. Riyadh approves millions to underwrite the budget of the Palestinian Authority. With sums like these, the Gulf states have essentially set off a new great game in the region; the rules are geoeconomic, and once again, the United States does not appear to have any policy to respond.

India intensifies its "Act East" initiative with a decidedly geoeconomic overhaul targeted at India's neighbors, extending new credit lines to Nepal and Mauritius, new high-speed data links to Myanmar, and new rail rinks to Sri Lanka, among others—all in clear response to China's own encirclement strategy around India's periphery. The European Union responds to Russian bullying in Ukraine by providing Ukraine an on-ramp to EU membership and Western investment. It pledges $15 billion in loans and grants over the next several years to help get the shattered Ukrainian economy back on its feet (not coincidentally, $15 billion is the precise sum that Putin offered and then later withdrew as the country's popular uprising proved itself). Turkey and Azerbaijan launch construction of the TANAP pipeline, a link in the EU-backed Southern Gas Corridor, a patchwork of pipelines intended to diversify Caspian energy export routes and reduce European dependence on Russian gas. After years of economic patronage to Hamas and Hezbollah, Iran adds Yemen's Shi'a Houthi rebels to its list of clients with an economic package to overhaul Yemen's ports, help construct power plants, and provide Yemen with a year's worth of oil stocks. Israel signs a deal to supply Egypt with 5 billion cubic feet of gas anually, beginning in 2018—an insurance policy in case its uneasy friendship with Egypt's military leaders turns out to be insufficient or short-lived.

So it is for many countries—the theater of foreign policy engagement has for some time been predominantly markets. Many states today are as likely or more likely to air disagreements with foreign policies through restrictions on trade in critical minerals or through the buying and selling of debt than through military activities. "Most nations beat their foreign policy drums to largely economic rhythms," as an astute early observer of this phenomenon put it.[2]

The decline of geoeconomics in American foreign policy making in recent decades proves to be a complicated story, with lots of variables, subplots, and nuances. But the short version is a combination of neglect and resistance. American economists tend to resist putting economic policies to work for geopolitical purposes, in part because the notion of subjugating economics in this way challenges some of their deepest disciplinary assumptions. As Michael Mandelbaum put it in his latest book, "The heart of politics is power; the aim of economics is wealth. Power is inherently limited. The quest for power is therefore competitive. It is a 'zero-sum game' . . . Wealth, by contrast, is limitless, which makes economics a 'positive-sum game.'"[3] Because many U.S. economists and economic policy makers tend to see the world through this positive-sum logic and have little appreciation for the realities of power competition among nations, they tend to be skeptical of using economic policies to strengthen America's power projection vis-à-vis its state competitors.

The notion has also encountered ambivalence from foreign policy strategists. Although they are steeped in traditional geopolitics and are not averse to viewing economic instruments of statecraft within a zero-sum logic, most strategists fail to recognize the power and potential of economics and finance as instruments of national purpose.

Thus embraced by neither most economists nor most foreign policy strategists, the use of economic and financial instruments as tools of statecraft has become an orphaned subject. For a time, it seemed of no great consequence. In the years following the Cold War, the United States faced no serious geopolitical rival, no real struggle for international influence or in the contest of ideas. Liberal economic consensus pervaded. And as it did, what began as a set of liberal economic prescriptions aimed at limiting the rightful role of government in the market morphed over time into a doctrinal unwillingness to accept economics as subject to geopolitical choices and influence. Thus, certain liberal economic policy prescriptions, such as trade liberalization, that found favor initially at least in part *because* they were seen as advantageous to U.S. foreign policy objectives came over time to be justified predominantly on the internal logic of laissez-faire liberalism, not on the basis of (perhaps even in spite of) U.S. geopolitical grounds. "A policy of free trade logically can—and should—be viewed as a technique of economic statecraft," David Baldwin, international relations theorist at Columbia University, once put it.[4] "This is not to say, however, that the economic doctrine of laissez faire liberalism [has been] conducive to viewing free trade in this way, at least not in the 20th century."[5]

But now, of course, the so-called end of history has itself come to an end.[6] The United States once again finds itself competing for global influence and ideas—and doing so alongside a set of states, many of them rising powers, that pledge no particular allegiance to these same liberal economic understandings, do not make any such disciplinary divides between geopolitics and economics in their own policy making, and are thoroughly comfortable with harnessing economic tools to work their strategic will in the world. The result is a set of challenges for which the current tools of U.S. statecraft, dominated by traditional political-military might, are uniquely unsuited. In short, the time has come for America's foreign policy and national security establishment to systematically rethink some of its most basic premises, including the composition of power itself. A new way of addressing U.S. national interests and power must aim for a foreign policy suited to a world in which economic concerns often—but obviously not always—trump traditional military ones.[7]

There is some inkling that policy makers may be beginning to appreciate the point. A growing chorus of U.S. foreign policy leaders has argued that America must reorient its foreign policy to succeed in an era importantly defined by the projection of economic power.[8] But it will not be easy. This shift will require a reprogramming of certain aspects of America's foreign policy DNA—not just its policy objectives and priorities, but also the strategies and tactics it deploys in pursuing these aims.

As former Secretary of State Hillary Clinton noted in one of her final speeches as secretary, "Delivering on the Promise of Economic Statecraft," in many ways the current era calls for the introduction of a new discipline, endowed with its own set of questions, assumptions, and organizing principles, to help guide U.S. administrations through specific cases.[9]

But high-level calls and some positive steps notwithstanding, too little about the logic and conduct of U.S. foreign policy has so far changed. One reason is that what has been written on the often fuzzy intersection of economics and geopolitics has had little relevance to the making of U.S. foreign policy.[10] Certainly plenty of observers have taken up aspects of economic power projection in piecemeal, typically with sanctions as the favored focus, and several have asserted economic considerations to be newly salient to national power projection. These arguments tend to come, though, as part of larger calls for foreign policy to be preoccupied in the first instance with restoring domestic economic growth (this is especially true in the American context).[11] Others have noted that, going forward, state-to-state struggles will be largely about economic aims, not military ones (in recent times this view was put forth most notably by Mandelbaum, a professor at Johns Hopkins).[12] Although a basic intuition about the role of economic power projection in driving foreign policy outcomes seems to be slowly growing throughout the operational and intellectual ranks of U.S. foreign policy makers, conceptual accounts of economic and financial techniques of statecraft still remain little studied or developed, especially compared to the vast literature on the mechanics of political-military power projection.[13]

This book aims to advance an understanding of how states are currently applying economic instruments to advance geopolitical ends—that is, geoeconomics—and what today's geoeconomic practices imply for how America in particular should think about and conduct its foreign affairs. We do so by considering four broad sets of questions. First, what is geoeconomics, why is it growing in importance, and how, if at all, is its present use changing the international system? Second, what are the modern instruments of geoeconomics, and what determines their efficacy? Third, how is China using geoeconomic tools; how has the United States historically integrated geoeconomics within its foreign policy; and how is the United States using geoeconomic instruments presently? Finally, what might a more developed and effective U.S. geoeconomic strategy to defend and promote American national interests look like, and what would it require?

Chapter 1 begins by staking out parameters for inquiry. Over the decades, scholars have given the term *geoeconomics* a variety of definitions. We are less interested in joining these definitional debates than in simply focusing on a set of international activities that, as a plain empirical matter, seems to account for a growing share of foreign policy headlines. Thus, we define the phenomenon as follows: the use of economic instruments to promote and defend national interests and to produce beneficial geopolitical results; and the effects of other nations' economic actions on a country's geopolitical goals.

We explore the relationship between geoeconomics, so defined, and geopolitics. We then consider the many forms that geoeconomic policies can take. Next we distinguish our claim that geoeconomics is on the rise from the argument that national interests are themselves changing. Finally, we explain the relationship between geoeconomics and the concepts of mercantilism, economic liberalism, and international economic policy.

If geoeconomics indeed now drives foreign policy for many nations, Chapter 2 asks why—what accounts for this return of geoeconomics? For starters, some of the world's most powerful countries, especially many of the so-called rising powers, seem to like it. Taking a largely inductive approach, we offer examples attesting to how countries such as Russia, China, and the Gulf states are increasingly using economic instruments as a preferred means of conducting geopolitical combat. This is not to suggest that military power will become passé, as military buildups in China, Russia, the Gulf, and elsewhere underscore. Especially for today's most sophisticated geoeconomic actors, geoeconomic and political-military dimensions of statecraft tend to be mutually reinforcing, as has been demonstrated through Russia's actions in Ukraine and China's in the South China Sea. A second factor accounting for the modern revival of geoeconomics is that states today have vastly more economic resources at their direct disposal than in previous eras. This is largely a story of the modern return of state capitalism. Like geoeconomics, state capitalism is not new, but it is witnessing a distinct resurgence. Another factor in the return of geoeconomics has more to do with changes to global markets themselves, notably, today's markets—deeper, faster, more leveraged, and more integrated than ever before—tend to exert more influence over a nation's geopolitical choices and outcomes. To take one example, the fate of the European Union—a preeminent Western geoeconomic foreign policy triumph of the twentieth century and the closest U.S. international partner—has for the past several years been at least as much in the hands of bond markets as in those of European political capitals.

Chapter 2 then moves to consider how the modern rise of geoeconomics, practiced on a globally significant scale, is changing the logic and operation of foreign policy. At times these tools endow leaders with a wider set of policy choices—Venezuela, thanks to its recent support from Beijing, has been far better able to buck U.S. prerogatives in the region. On other occasions, today's form of geoeconomics comes with not only new options but also new diplomatic tools—globally competitive state-owned enterprises and deep-pocketed sovereign wealth funds, to name a few. Some of these instruments are, for a variety of reasons we will examine at length, largely unavailable to U.S. and Western leaders.

Chapter 3 surveys seven leading instruments of today's brand of geoeconomics: trade policy, investment policy, economic sanctions, the cybersphere, aid, monetary policy, and energy and commodity policies—again aiming only to take the geopolitical (as opposed to purely economic) measure of each. Compared to previous golden eras of geoeconomics—many point to the initial postwar years, as typified by the Marshall Plan and the early stages of the Cold War, as one such golden era—some of today's favored geoeconomic tools are altogether new (those in the cybersphere, for example).[14] Others, while not novel as such, are operating on such a vastly different landscape as to render them as good as new. For example, the American-orchestrated run on the British pound amid the U.S.-U.K. standoff over the Suez Canal crisis in 1956 stands as a canonical example of mid-twentieth-century geoeconomics. But the rise of new financial centers, combined with the complexity and leverage seen in today's financial markets, would make any repeat of Suez vastly more difficult for Washington to pull off, not to mention far more damaging to U.S. national interests. Still other geoeconomic instruments continue to function more or less as they did in earlier eras; development assistance is one example. Even these, though, have attracted important new players and dimensions.

To be sure, a number of previous efforts have studied each of these in isolation—asking, for example, "Do sanctions work?" or "Are China's holdings of U.S. debt more a strategic asset or a liability for Beijing?" This approach is understandable: each geopolitical instrument has been adopted by different countries and institutions, each is subject to distinct levers of state control, there are specific variables that determine whether each can be used effectively, and each raises specific concerns for U.S. national interests. But different as these geoeconomic instruments may be, there is also value in considering them comprehensively. By examining how countries integrate and use these instruments together to achieve particular geopolitical objectives, we can better illuminate how geoeconomics works in the real world. And including all seven of these tools within the scope of our inquiry also helps to bring to the surface important and often overlooked interactions—and tensions—between and among them.

If these are the leading instruments doing so much of the work of foreign policy today, what determines their effectiveness? What are the underlying capabilities and attributes that dictate whether these tools work to greater or lesser effect? In the third chapter's second half, we consider certain structural features—geoeconomic endowments, as we call them—that influence a nation's ability to put domestic capital to strategic use: a given state's decisions regarding commodity flows, a nation's centrality to the global financial system, and domestic market features such as overall size, degree of control over inbound and outbound investment, and expectations of future growth. While far from perfect predictors, these factors play a clear role in determining how effective a given state is likely to be in its use of geoeconomic tools.

Chapter 4 takes up the specific case of China. Beijing is often correctly described as the world's leading practitioner of geoeconomics, but it has also been perhaps the major factor in returning regional or global power projection back to an importantly economic (as opposed to political-military) exercise. "Beijing has been playing the new economic game at a maestro level," as Leslie Gelb, longtime foreign policy expert and former *New York Times* commentator, aptly put it, "staying out of wars and political confrontations and zeroing in on business—its global influence far exceeds its existing economic strength."[15] We explore China's use of geoeconomics through six case studies: Taiwan, North Korea, Japan, Southeast Asia, Pakistan, and India.

We then turn in Chapter 5 to two overarching questions that emerge from these case studies. First, how can we recognize geoeconomic pressure at work when we see it? When it comes to sizing up a country's use of geoeconomics, it helps to have clear examples. Such cases, at least by recent historical standards, seem to be on the rise—shutting off gas pipelines in the dead of winter, tabling bailout offers to sway the foreign policies of embattled neighbors, attaching openly geopolitical stipulations onto either potential investment decisions or aid agreements. Often, though, evidence of geoeconomic behavior is more circumstantial in nature—especially where it is coercive. Take, for example, China's decision to quarantine bananas from the Philippines amid escalations of tensions over competing island claims in the South China Sea, or Moscow's ban on Moldovan wine in the run-up to Moldova's deadline for signing a cooperation agreement with the EU. Compared to open political demands, such geoeconomic coercion is sometimes more difficult to measure. But like military power, geoeconomic sway can carry a long shadow of influence—it need not be explicitly brandished or attempted in order to register a desired coercive effect.

A second fundamental question these case studies raise regarding geoeconomic pressure is "Does it work?" The answer, on balance, is yes. At least in the case of China, Beijing flexes geoeconomic muscle—both positive and negative—and often succeeds in advancing its geopolitical aims.

On the back of economic pressure, China has managed to deter arms sales to Taipei and to steadily reduce the number of countries that recognize Taiwan; it has curtailed the activities of the Dalai Lama; it has restrained countries from offering political support for human rights issues; it has registered noticeable impacts on votes in the United Nations and frustrated various Western efforts to pressure Iran and North Korea; and it has raised the costs of challenging China's territorial ambitions along its borders and in the South and East China Seas.

At the same time, China's geoeconomic savvy is also sometimes exaggerated. There are natural limits and internal tensions running through many of Beijing's attempts at using geoeconomics to advance geopolitical objectives. China's heavy hand has produced a collective desire on the part of Southeast Asian states to draw closer to the United States. Japan is increasing its military capabilities. Both Japan and Vietnam overcame stiff domestic opposition to join the U.S.-led Trans-Pacific Partnership talks. The Philippines has granted the United States access to five military bases for rotating aircraft, ships, equipment, and troops. In China's case, geoeconomic power, like most other forms of power, may well be most effective when implied rather than exercised outright. The same seems true for Russia and other leading practitioners of geoeconomics.

Simply because countries have a mixed record when it comes to geoeconomics, however, does not mean they will abandon even the most counterproductive of attempts. This in turn raises a larger point: even where states try to wield geoeconomic power and either partially or fully fail to achieve their aim, the results and collateral damage can carry real, destabilizing consequences. Consider again the Cyprus bailout—an ordeal that was both largely (if mostly unintentionally) brought about by, and then further complicated by, geoeconomic factors from Russia, even as the EU's package ultimately won out.[16] Thus, even for those who remain skeptical that geoeconomics will ultimately secure the geopolitical outcomes these countries seek, there are reasons to take the phenomenon seriously.

Next we turn, in Chapter 6, to the United States, surveying the country's historical use of geoeconomics. The picture that emerges is, above all, a cautionary tale about the fallibility of historical memory. Period accounts show how U.S. policy makers have regularly (although not always successfully) employed geoeconomic means to achieve U.S. strategic interests since the country's founding—and how clear-eyed these policy makers were about this fact. But somewhere along the way, America began to tell itself a different story about geoeconomics, its role in statecraft generally, and even its historical place in American foreign policy. Roughly around the time of the Vietnam War, and continuing through to later stages of the Cold

War, U.S. administrations began to see economics as a realm with an authority and logic all its own, usually no longer subjugated to traditional state power realities—and something to be kept free of unseemly geopolitical incursions in any case. As this shift occurred, international economic policy making, except for economic sanctions, began to emerge as the near-exclusive province of economists and like-minded policy makers, no longer readily available to U.S. foreign policy strategists as a means of working America's geopolitical will in the world.

So began a structural divide, and a corresponding departure from geoeconomics, that remains largely the case today. For a time, this bifurcation was not a pressing problem for U.S. foreign policy: during roughly the first two decades following the Cold War, the United States faced no serious international challenge that required considering whether this alignment between liberal economic ideas and the country's foreign policy requirements still existed. But with this period of convergence now giving way to something else—arguably closer to the historical trend—the United States must come to grips with the reality that the geopolitical landscape is populated by a set of countries content to use the modern tools of economics and finance without regard for the liberal and neoliberal economic handling instructions and understandings that have traditionally accompanied their use. To recognize this new reality is not necessarily to advocate that the United States respond in kind. But Washington at least needs to recognize the degree to which markets and economics are indeed embedded in larger realities of state power. Policy makers' capacity to understand this embeddedness and the historical arc of geoeconomics in U.S. foreign policy will prove critical to the shape American foreign policy ultimately takes (and in turn, how well it succeeds) in the coming decades.

We move in Chapter 7 to assess how the United States presently uses geoeconomics. It is clear that the United States, with the largest economy in the world, possesses a great deal to work with geoeconomically, if it so chooses. Moving toward a more self-consciously geoeconomic brand of foreign policy, however, would first require Washington to confront a series of questions about its basic level of comfort with restoring geoeconomics as a more considered part of American foreign policy.

These questions are not easy ones. Many geoeconomic approaches carry real trade-offs. But this is true for every foreign policy option. Too often, unlike debates around political-military statecraft, which tend to be argued and considered against a logic of best known alternatives—geoeconomic approaches are debated in isolation. Criticisms attacking a given sanctions program because "the costs outweigh the benefits," for example, are silent on the more operative question of whether these costs and benefits would have been a desirable alternative to other available political or military options.[17] Not only do policy makers fail to consider geoeconomic approaches against the best alternative, but they also tend to measure them using the wrong standards—judging them by their economic rather than geopolitical impacts. For Russia, waging pipeline politics might not amount to a sound economic strategy, but whether it represents an acceptable (or, more to the point, the best available) means of venting displeasure with the foreign policy choices of the European Union or the United States stands as an entirely separate matter. Dismissing potential geoeconomic approaches as unwise or unlikely simply because they do not fit within the confines of economic rationality is a bit like discounting the risk that a jilted paramour would exact his revenge with a gun on the grounds that the bullets would cost him money. After all, most wars, especially the most destructive ones, would fall into this category of "not particularly economically rational." When it comes to considering the various foreign policy alternatives available to countries in a given situation, there is no reason to create a separate logical standard of review for options that aim at the same result by relying on other (in this case economic) means.

Still, even with a clearer understanding of how various geoeconomic approaches stack up compared to non-geoeconomic alternatives, it may be that the geoeconomic options available to Washington simply look much different from those available to other states. This is partly a function of America's unique domestic political and legal makeup, and partly a result of its unique role and responsibility in the world. In simple terms, America is proudly a nation of laws, begun as an experiment in deliberately curtailing state power. These constraints mean that Washington will probably never be capable of using trade and investment tools to advance its foreign policy interests in many of the short-term transactional or coercive ways that suit other countries (with vastly different political and economic traditions) just fine. Moreover, the United States, as the leading supplier of global public goods, may well have a greater geopolitical interest than other states in keeping the geopolitically motivated uses (especially coercive uses) of certain economic instruments to a minimum.

At present, however, it is far from clear that Washington's present relative discomfort with geoeconomics reflects either inevitable domestic constraints or any considered strategy, rather than the residual workings of a set of assumptions and habits honed during the post–Cold War era. It may or may not be the case that if U.S. policy makers begin using geoeconomic tools more or differently, the result could undermine larger, more important U.S. interests. Such games of line-drawing are inevitably fact-bound; answers will vary from case to case, and from policy maker to policy maker.

Our point is not to argue for a certain outcome. What matters far more, we argue, is how policy makers construct these debates, and in particular the kinds of reasons that are allowed to count as valid arguments for or against a geoeconomic move by the United States. Too often, those opposing a given U.S. geoeconomic action do not couch their reasoning in terms of a concern for maximizing U.S. foreign policy interests; too often, their concerns lie elsewhere.

Consider it this way: The most common of these objections tends to cite some vague, unspecified threat to the "rules-based order" as a reason against undertaking a given geoeconomic action. But if indeed this rules-based order were understood to be such a valuable geopolitical asset for the United States (and if indeed it were the reason the United States has not pursued a more conspicuously geoeconomic foreign policy in recent years), then one would expect to see U.S. foreign policy engaged in a more all-hands undertaking—stretching across U.S. military, diplomatic, and economic lines—to shore it up. Not only is there no evidence of this sort of undertaking, but there is plenty of evidence of the converse: the United States remains the international laggard in its contributions to the IMF, and Washington seems unwilling to put even a fraction of the diplomatic muscle it routinely expends on political and security crises in the Middle East toward curbing China's plans for a multilateral alternative to the World Bank.

But gaps between stated beliefs and demonstrated priorities are hardly new to U.S. foreign policy. For many policy makers it may well be that, so long as upholding the rules-based system is still seen as geopolitically advantageous for the United States, most forms of geoeconomic power will need to be at least neutral in their impacts on this rules-based system for them to pass muster. Adhering to this standard will constrain the United States far more than many other states, especially in more coercive, shorter-term cases. But even working within this exacting standard, there remains much room for geoeconomics to play a larger role in U.S. foreign policy.

Unsurprisingly, for U.S. policy makers these normative questions outlining the boundaries of acceptable use are more easily confronted for some geoeconomic tools than for others. American use of sanctions has seen a profound revolution in thinking and approach in the years since 9/11, for example, while trade and investment remain regarded as an almost exclusively economic exercise. Often U.S. trade officials take pains to downplay the strategic stakes for the United States, fearing an encroachment of geopolitics onto trade. For instance, when the Obama administration decided to go ahead with the Trans-Pacific Partnership (plans that were incubated during the final months of the Bush administration), the agreement's name was changed, with the term *strategic* dropped from what was initially the Trans-Pacific Strategic Economic Partnership, concluded in 2005 between Brunei, New Zealand, Chile, and Singapore.

For all of the difficult questions of line-drawing and acceptable use where geoeconomics is concerned, one of the most promising areas of U.S. geoeconomic potential is in the energy realm. The North American shale revolution is remaking geopolitical realities around the world, with dominating economic and strategic benefits for the United States. We examine this in detail in Chapter 8. Beyond economic gains, the shift toward more diversified and oftentimes more localized energy sources will diminish the geopolitical leverage that certain energy suppliers have for decades sought to use to their advantage. No longer as dependent on Gulf energy supplies as it has been in the past, the United States will be freer to influence the terms of its engagement with the Middle East. All the great powers will ultimately be touched by these developments. One of the most important, if overlooked, features of the U.S. energy revolution is the way in which it reinforces several other geoeconomic assets available to Washington: sanctions targeting Iran's (and potentially other countries') oil sectors are made easier by the growing abundance of North American energy supplies, trade pacts with the United States are made more attractive by the prospect of accessing these supplies, and the dollar's continued status as the world's reserve currency is made more certain by the prospect of the United States coming online as a net energy exporter.

There are signs that the United States may be waking up to its geoeconomic potential, even if the process is too slow and often not yet fully conscious. Chapter 9 begins by reviewing the evolution of this realization. Much of the progress seen to date has been primarily in diagnosing the challenge and developing an initial conceptual framework—amounting to little more than a down payment on what is needed.

Coming up with a specific geoeconomic vision for U.S. foreign policy and translating it into initial lines of action is obviously a complex task. It clearly requires specific policy solutions; we outline our own recommendations at the end of Chapter 9. But because reasonable minds can and no doubt will differ on the specifics, it is worth ensuring they derive from the right framework. We therefore preface our specific recommendations with four stylized lessons drawn from the previous chapters. Lastly, beyond the specifics of any affirmative policy agenda, and beyond the more universal assumptions that ought to underpin these specifics, any meaningful effort by U.S. administrations to reengage with geoeconomics ought to start with a certain educational diplomacy regarding geoeconomics as such. At a minimum, these leaders need to explain in detail to the American citizenry and to the country's allies and friends what today's brand of geoeconomics consists of, publicly call out geoeconomic coercion when it takes place, develop responses together with like-minded partners, and more generally discuss with these countries the rightful role of geoeconomics in Western grand strategy.

Chapter 10 concludes on precisely this question of where geoeconomics fits within the broader context of U.S. grand strategy and American national interests. Beginning with the "Germany first, then Japan" approach to World War II, continuing on to containment and deterrence during the Cold War, and moving into the decade of "global war on terror" following 9/11, U.S. grand strategies were developed to guide America's most important foreign policy decisions and to help policy makers avoid the temptation, as former Secretary of State Warren Christopher once put it, merely "to careen from crisis to crisis." Far from the singular, strategic clarity of any of these eras, the United States presently faces a blizzard of international problems: the rise of Chinese power, what now seems to be the return of Russian systematic destabilizing policies in Eurasia and beyond, chaos in the Middle East, and the continuing danger of terrorism involving weapons of mass destruction. We return in this final chapter to a discussion of using American national interests as a compelling compass for U.S. external behavior and grand strategy, and we examine briefly again how geoeconomic instruments, as informed by history and illuminated in these pages, might promote these interests.[18]

The research and writing of this book necessarily entailed an inductive process. The relative lack of any widely accepted conceptual framework to guide questions of how states use economic tools to pursue geopolitical aims required building a picture from the ground up. Generalizations and counterfactuals are a necessary element of any such attempt. Considering what would have happened absent various geoeconomic displays may amount to little more than educated guesses, "but this is preferable to ignoring the problem," as David Baldwin pointed out.[19]

Second, as with any inductive approach, questions of relative scale and importance can be difficult to pinpoint. It is obviously the case that some of the geoeconomic examples presented here matter more than others. Even those cases that may not rise to systemic global importance—Russian swipes at Moldovan wine as part of the Kremlin's larger campaign to shore up its regional dominance, for example—may nevertheless hold unknown precedential importance, boosting the odds that similar tactics may be replicated in the future by other states in ways that carry greater systemic stakes.

Likewise, just as not all shows of geoeconomic power are created equal, some practitioners carry greater global significance than others. As both the

largest and most consequential practitioner of today's brand of geoeconomics, China serves as the book's central example (apart from our focus, in
the book's second half, on the United States). For the same reasons, Russia
and the Gulf states also warrant particular focus. Regrettably, this approach
means that some other avid if systemically less significant practitioners of
geoeconomics—Norway and Singapore, for example—go only peripherally
highlighted.

To suggest that geoeconomics is reemerging as a favored form of geopolitical combat for some of the world's most powerful states and is shaping
outcomes across some of the world's most important strategic challenges is,
of course, not to suggest that the modern return of geoeconomics is a universal phenomenon. There are plenty of states that are not evincing a particularly new or robust role for geoeconomics, and many challenges that
will be decided primarily on non-geoeconomic variables. Nor does this
book attempt to predict whether today's brand of geoeconomics can be
expected to spread further—only that it has already risen to a level of systemic importance that foreign policy practitioners, especially those in the
United States, minimize at America's peril.

Lastly, and perhaps most important, this book seeks to explain how, not
what, to think about geoeconomics.[20] Each case and crisis is different, and
it is impossible to say ex ante whether geoeconomic approaches should be
adopted in any given scenario. But geoeconomics should at least be given
more regular, rigorous, and sophisticated consideration by U.S. policy
makers, especially since so many of today's greatest strategic challenges
cannot be fully understood, let alone addressed, without appreciating the
considerable geoeconomic forces driving them—a subject we begin to address in Chapter 1.

CHAPTER ONE

What Is Geoeconomics?

War and commerce are but two different means of arriving at the
same aim, which is to possess what is desired.

—BENJAMIN CONSTANT, FRANCO-SWISS POLITICIAN

THE TERM *geoeconomics* is in much use today, but almost always
without a specific working definition.[1] Some authors tend to focus on
the use of geopolitical or military power for economic ends.[2] Others tend
to define geoeconomics more broadly, as "the entanglement of international
economics, geopolitics, and strategy," a kind of catch-all definition that
obscures more than it clarifies.[3] Still others primarily stress trade and the
protection of industries.[4]

In the particular context of U.S. foreign policy, those who use the concept have likewise primarily confined themselves to traditional examina-
tions of international trade and sanctions.[5] Typically, these inquiries depart
from a narrow understanding of U.S. trade policy—trade, done well,
strengthens America's economic standing, and thus, at least in theory, enhances its power projection accordingly—but have no specific geopolitical
dimension, apart, perhaps, from a widely held belief, rooted in the early
twentieth-century liberalism of Norman Angell and others, that expanded
trade promotes peace.[6] It is essentially trade for trade's sake. Others apply
the term to almost all American economic activity, domestic and foreign.[7]
These analysts sometimes begin by connecting U.S. power projection in a
general way to the strength or weakness of the U.S. economy or even American society.[8]

Indeed, these calls are finding purchase, as the two most recent U.S. national security strategies attest.[9] A strong domestic economy over the long

term will of course remain a general requirement for any country's power projection, the United States included. History has not looked kindly on any country that has allowed its geopolitical responsibilities to outstrip its economic wherewithal for long. It is as good a universal law as one could hope to find in politics. And just as with physical laws of nature, there are no exceptions for size: great powers have found their economic constraints no more pliant in the face of geopolitical burdens than any other country.

These and other earlier interpretations of geoeconomics are useful, but they are also incomplete. Strikingly, none of the existing written understandings of geoeconomics succeeds in comprehensively capturing the phenomenon that, as a plain empirical matter, seems most responsible for the term's recent resurrection: the use of economic instruments to produce beneficial geopolitical results. Despite the considerable attention paid to the global financial crisis and its geopolitical aftereffects, as well as to the growing need to place U.S. foreign policy more firmly in the service of the country's domestic economic interests, matters of where, how, and how well states today wield economic instruments as tools of statecraft remain sorely underexplored analytic and policy territory.[10]

With this in mind, we urge the following definition of geoeconomics:

GEOECONOMICS: The use of economic instruments to promote and defend national interests, and to produce beneficial geopolitical results; and the effects of other nations' economic actions on a country's geopolitical goals.

On this understanding, geoeconomics stands as both a method of analysis and a form of statecraft.[11] The first dimension of this three-part definition ("the use of economic instruments to promote and defend national interests") applies in a general way to traditional understandings of how domestic economic strength promotes U.S. power projection, at least in theory. This dimension is important and well understood.[12]

Similarly, the final element of this definition of geoeconomics ("the effects of other nations' economic actions on a country's geopolitical goals"), while historically underattended compared to other aspects of international relations, has attracted growing interest in recent years. The revival of international political economy certainly deserves some of the credit for this renewed interest.[13] But across much of that literature, the predominant focus remains at the level of the system, rather than the nation-state, in attempts to explain how broad economic phenomena—globalization, for instance—might impact multilateral institutions. With some important exceptions, contemporary debates in the field of international political economy still show little interest in more applied matters of power projection and managing relations between nation-states. These positive steps notwithstanding, Alan Dobson is quite right that "economic affairs still often sit uneasily beside political and diplomatic matters."[14]

Maybe it should come as no surprise, then, that the role of economic phenomena in shaping geopolitical outcomes also tends to go underreported in much of the press commentary on the foreign policy dilemmas of the day. For all of the discussion surrounding the causes and accelerants of the 2014 Ukraine crisis, for example, it was rare for anyone to highlight the role of international monetary policy in exacerbating the country's long-running economic woes into full-scale crisis. "Ukraine's financial problems had been mounting over many years," explained Benn Steil, director of international economics at the Council on Foreign Relations.[15] "But it was the mere prospect of the [United States] Fed pumping fewer new dollars into the market each month that pushed the cost of rolling over its debt . . . beyond Kiev's capacity to pay. . . . The rest is history."[16] That history, Steil correctly notes, has largely "overlooked the role that the Fed's taper talk played in the toppling of Yanukovych and the chaos that followed."[17]

But things may be changing. Thanks in large part to two particular economic headlines bearing undeniable geopolitical consequences, there are reasons to think that a revival of interest in this particular strand of geoeconomics could prove widespread and enduring. The first is the 2008–2009 financial crisis (and the attending eurozone crisis), which now, six years on, continues to prompt a flurry of popular and academic commentary trained on the geopolitical meaning of the ordeal.[18] The second is the rise of China, thus far largely an economic story, but one that is widely understood to carry some of the most profound geopolitical effects since the United States emerged from World War II as the world's leading power. Given their magnitude and long tails, both of these stories have helped bring economic phenomena and their geopolitical impacts into foreign policy reporting and commentary.

Our focus is instead the middle element of our definition of geoeconomics: "the use of economic instruments . . . to produce beneficial geopolitical results." For it is these economic techniques of statecraft that, while aptly describing much of foreign policy practice today, puzzlingly remain underexplored territory, especially in any conceptual way and especially in the United States.

British international relations theorist Susan Strange spotted this oversight as far back as 1970, arguing that "what is noticeably missing from the picture are more general studies of international economic relations—whether of problems or issue areas—treated analytically, with the political analysis predominating over the economic analysis."[19] This conceptual gap is not for lack of topical interest; the last several years have seen considerable, sustained attention to individual geoeconomic instruments, as well as around specific countries.[20] Among the most compelling of these country-specific portrayals is Edward Luttwak's most recent book on China. In it, Luttwak argues that because the "logic of strategy . . . mandates growing resistance to growing power," and because "any significant warfare between nuclears [is now] largely inhibited," opposition to Chinese ascendance will manifest geoeconomically.[21] For Luttwak, because "China's continuing rise ultimately threatens the very independence of its neighbors, and even of its present peers, it will inevitably be resisted by geoeconomic means—that is, by strategically motivated as opposed to merely protectionist trade barriers, investment prohibitions, more extensive technology denials, and even restrictions on raw material exports to China if its misconduct can provide a sufficient excuse for that almost warlike act."[22]

Others have looked at the role that economic techniques of statecraft have played historically—a slight but important difference from those historians, such as Gavin and Sargent, who tend to focus more on explaining how various economic considerations have shaped foreign policy outcomes. Impressively researched over ten years, Dobson's 2002 *US Economic Statecraft for Survival* amounts to a revisionist Cold War history, one that accounts for the neglected role of economic statecraft in explaining U.S. policy between 1933 and 1991. And, although not his apparent motivation in writing, the particular question that Dobson asks—how the United States moved from assiduously defending its neutral trading rights in wartime (prior to entering World War I) to prosecuting a kind of economic warfare against the Soviet Union in peacetime (immediately post–World War II)—is itself a testament to the sort of schizophrenic, often contradictory relationship the United States has had with geoeconomic techniques over its history.

Despite ample attention to historical, topical, and country-specific issues, there has been far less in the way of conceptual thinking about economic and financial instruments as tools of statecraft. Noting Susan Strange's original call to this effect, David Baldwin's 1985 *Economic Statecraft* remains among the few works that have sought to answer it. Baldwin's primary task is "to think about thinking about economic statecraft," and he does so by taking explicit aim at the double standards and intellectual hindrances that impede clear policy reflection about geoeconomic techniques. His insights, now thirty years on, remain more evergreen than not.[23]

Baldwin's purpose, however, was less to understand how states deployed these techniques and more to vindicate these practices "as more useful than the [prevailing] conventional wisdom would have one believe"—a feat he attempts through a series of historical case studies on sanctions, as well as important looks at trade and aid.[24] He does not address whether these techniques were in regular or effective use by foreign policy practitioners of his day, and he does not attempt to apply his framework to gain insight into the challenges foreign policy makers faced.

Nor has there been much progress on these fronts since Baldwin, as several observers—Dobson, Walter Russell Mead, Juan Zarate, Robert Zoellick, and others—have lamented in more recent years.[25] While for a time this relative neglect may have been regrettable but not concerning, the situation seems different today. With economic instruments of statecraft now in such widespread use, promulgated by some of the world's most powerful countries, it seems worth a clearer acknowledgment and understanding of the phenomenon. Ultimately, however, definitions count for only so much. Much of understanding what geoeconomics is comes in acquiring the capacity to think about it. It is worth elaborating our definition with a few additional clarifying points:

POINT 1

Geoeconomics is different from geopolitics.

Rather than focusing on economics as the means to advance geopolitical aims, some definitions of geoeconomics have reversed this means-ends relationship, emphasizing instead how countries might apply military or geopolitical muscle (what some call "hard power") to bring about beneficial economic results.[26] It is undoubtedly an important topic, but one more for a book on geopolitics than for a volume on geoeconomics. For when it comes to classifying various forms of statecraft, it is the means, not the ends, that should dictate. After all, as David Baldwin explained, "bombing a library is not called cultural warfare; bombing homes is not called residential warfare; bombing nuclear reactors is not called nuclear warfare; and bombing factories should not be labeled economic warfare."[27]

Indeed, there has been a tendency to treat geopolitics and geoeconomics as interchangeable. While the two are doubtless related, they should be distinguished.[28] Part of the difficulty is that, much like geoeconomics, there is no single agreed-upon definition for *geopolitics;* if anything, that term is invoked even more loosely than *geoeconomics.* According to one of the most widely cited definitions, geopolitics is a method of foreign policy analysis that seeks to understand, explain, and predict international political behavior primarily in terms of geographical variables.[29] Other, more general definitions tend to focus on the relationship between politics and territory—that is, the art and practice of using political power over a given territory.[30]

Put otherwise, geopolitics is really a set of assumptions about how a state exercises power over territory—what constitutes this power, and how it is increased and spent down. The same is true of geoeconomics as we define it here. But most geopolitical accounts traditionally explain and predict state power by reference to a host of geographic factors (territory, population, economic performance, natural resources, military capabilities, etc.).[31] Geoeconomics, in our view, is about providing a parallel account of how a state builds and exercises power by reference to economic factors rather than geographic ones.

On this understanding, then, the use of military power in service of economic goals fits more comfortably as a facet of geopolitics than of geoeconomics. Even so, the two are obviously closely linked, and the relationship between them begs for study and further thought. In particular, it is worth questioning whether the growing use of geoeconomic tools as instruments of statecraft is changing patterns of when and how countries engage in the use of military power.[32] While not directly within the scope of this book, it is an important question and one we touch on intermittently throughout the coming chapters.

Critically, understanding geoeconomics requires appreciating deeply embedded differences in the operating assumptions of geopolitics and economics. The logic of geopolitics is traditionally zero-sum, while the logic of economics is traditionally positive-sum. As Michael Mandelbaum put this point in his latest book, "The heart of politics is power; the aim of economics is wealth. Power is inherently limited. The quest for power is therefore competitive. It is a 'zero-sum game.' Wealth by contrast, is limitless, which makes economics a positive-sum game."[33] Geoeconomics essentially combines the logic of geopolitics with the tools of economics, viewing the economic actions and options of a given state as embedded within larger realities of state power. This fact often puts geoeconomic approaches in tension with the assumptions of economics.

Consider it this way: returning to the idea that, as Mandelbaum puts it, in "economics, unlike in war, everyone can be a winner," the point about geoeconomics is that this distinction holds up only as long as economic actions are being pursued for the sake of economic ends.[34] It turns out, however, that when put to geopolitical use, economic instruments can produce outcomes that are every bit as powerful and as zero-sum as those resulting from traditional military showings of state power.

Symptoms of these disciplinary tensions between economics and foreign policy surface in the U.S. context all the time. Most of the calls to reorient U.S. foreign policy to account for the expanding role of economic power—to do geoeconomics better—also tend to speak plaintively about the U.S. government's *institutional* inability to integrate foreign policy and economic strategy. Former secretary of state Hillary Clinton did so in her confirmation hearing.[35] Clinton is joined by a chorus of outside observers that spans former U.S. military leaders, economists, and foreign policy strategists, Republicans and Democrats alike.[36] Shortly after her economic statecraft agenda debuted, David Rothkopf, CEO and editor of *Foreign Policy*, penned a piece on Hillary Clinton "ingesting" the Commerce Department, deeming "the Clinton speech a sign of a successful Secretary of State continuing to work to reinvent the department she leads—to 'think different' in the words of Steve Jobs . . . [and] the sign of an administration maturing and developing better priorities and vital competencies where they are needed."[37] Others, such as former State Department official Nicholas Burns, began to ask whether Secretary Clinton's new agenda would enable the Obama administration to change the way Washington has traditionally worked by placing economic issues on par with military and diplomatic ones in calculating the national interest.[38]

Why has any exchange across the realms of foreign policy making and economics proven so difficult? The most commonly held view is that it was not always so; that in fact, the United States historically has been quite adroit at economics-centered foreign policy. As Robert Zoellick, former U.S. trade representative and World Bank president, recently put it, this "separation of economics from U.S. foreign policy and security policy reflects a shift from earlier American experience. For its first 150 years, the American foreign-policy tradition was deeply infused with economic logic. Unfortunately, thinking about international political economy has become a lost art in the United States."[39]

Zoellick details this view with a powerful historical account—what amounts to a far better reading of U.S. history.[40] But this account raises a crucial question: if the United States was once so adept at this brand of economics-centered statecraft, why are we not anymore? This important question we take up later, in Chapter 6.

POINT 2

To focus on the use of economic instruments to advance geopolitical ends is to say nothing about the nature of the ends
themselves; whether the ends of foreign policy are also changing
stands as a separate question.

If some understandings of geoeconomics employ a reverse means-ends con-
figuration (again, military power in service of economic aims), others focus
only on the ends. Indeed, many a foreign policy commentary has invoked
the term *geoeconomics* as a way of arguing that the priorities of foreign
policy either would or should shift toward economic goals and away from
military-oriented ones.

Most would agree that this understanding of geoeconomics entered the
modern lexicon of international affairs with a 1990 article by Edward
Luttwak, wherein Luttwak argued that "the waning of the Cold War is
steadily reducing the importance of military power in world affairs." "World
politics," he believed, was giving way to geoeconomics, "the admixture of
the logic of conflict with the methods of commerce." "As the relevance of
military threats and military alliances wanes," Luttwak observed, "geoeconomic priorities and modalities are becoming dominant in state action." He
expounded on the topic of his article in a 1993 book, this time in a more
alarmist tone. Geoeconomics, he explained,

> is not more and not less than the continuation of the ancient rivalry of the
> nations by new industrial means. Just as in the past when young men were
> put in uniform to be marched off in pursuit of schemes of territorial conquest,
> today taxpayers are persuaded to subsidize schemes of industrial conquest.
> Instead of fighting each other, France, Germany and Britain now collaborate
> to fund Airbus Industrie's offensive against Boeing and McDonnell-Douglas.
> Instead of measuring progress by how far the fighting front has advanced on
> the map, it is worldwide market shares for the targeted products that are the
> goal.

Similarly, while they do not explicitly use the term *geoeconomics*, scholars
like Mandelbaum and Francis Gavin make a case that the nature of states'
geopolitical aims would shift away from military issues and hard security
dilemmas toward economic preoccupations. This may well be true, but it is
largely outside the scope of this book.[41] By contrast, geoeconomic approaches, as defined here, are concerned only with how states are exercising
economic and financial tools to achieve their desired geopolitical aims.
However, as a state comes to perceive the geopolitical climate as increasingly
about economic power projection and hones its own geoeconomic reflexes

accordingly, it may—indeed, should—be the case that this realization and re-tooling process leads to changes in its foreign policy strategies.

Next, to suggest that a state is marshaling an economic tool in furtherance of some geopolitical objective is not necessarily to imply that there are *only* geopolitical objectives at stake. States can and often do design geoeconomic policies that simultaneously advance multiple interests—geopolitical, economic, and otherwise. China's strategic investments in Africa stand as perhaps the strongest example. But in this respect, geoeconomics is no different from any other brand of statecraft (think, for example, of the economic spoils that war can produce). It is the presence (and not the solitary presence) of an important geopolitical interest that is controlling, in other words. And while countries typically do not offer much insight into the rank-ordering of relative motivations, design choice is often telling. As we argue in Chapter 7, there are plenty of economic policies that could ostensibly simultaneously advance economic and geopolitical goals; often, though, a trade agreement conceived as a serious means of pursuing some foreign policy objective would be a different sort of agreement from one that was aimed narrowly at economic goals.

POINT 3

Geoeconomic attempts at power projection can take many forms. And just as not all states are created equal in their capacity to project geopolitical power, there are certain structural features—or geoeconomic endowments—that dictate how effective a country is likely to be in the use of geoeconomic tools.

Not only do states deploy geoeconomic tools against a broad range of non-economic ends, they also use these tools in a variety of ways. The most obvious distinction here is between positive and coercive forms of geoeconomic leverage. But geoeconomic attempts differ across a range of other scores: objectives can be shorter-term or longer-term; some measures are more transactional (where objectives are narrowly construed and anticipated benefits are fairly well identified), while others are more general (where objectives are broader and benefits are less understood); and the range of geoeconomic techniques during wartime will differ from those in peacetime or in the absence of active military conflict.

The decision by President Carter to impose a grain embargo against the Soviets in response to the USSR's 1979 invasion of Afghanistan and the

Truman administration's offer of concessionary loans to U.S. allies to purchase war materials in World War II were both targeted measures, enacted in response to particular events and intended to elicit a specific set of responses. The push in the late 1970s by the Federal Republic of Germany to adopt a single European currency (which it saw as necessary to preempt Western fears over Germany's increasing strength at the time) and the advent of the European Union itself were both longer strategic plays, where the goals were broad, involving multiple targets, and where the benefits, while understood to be powerful, went mostly unforeseen among the chief proponents of these policies at the time. The $8 billion Qatar invested in Egypt between President Mubarak's fall in early 2011 and President Morsi's ouster in mid-2013 probably falls somewhere in the middle, bearing some reciprocal, shorter-term, specific assurances, if still coming with a fairly broad set of objectives and some expectation of benefits over an extended time horizon.

Second, geoeconomic power, like geopolitical power, is a function of certain structural factors and policy choices. Much as states differ in their capacity to project geopolitical power, there are certain structural features— or geoeconomic endowments—that shape how successful a country is likely to be in the use of geoeconomic tools. Indeed, compared to the vast literature on the inputs and workings of geopolitical power, no similar analytic framework exists for geoeconomics; there is no consensus as to the range of geoeconomic tools that presently exist or to the set of factors that make states more or less suited to wield them effectively.[42] Are nondemocracies better suited to apply geoeconomic tools? Are small countries just as disadvantaged when it comes to geoeconomics as with geopolitics? Absent any sort of conceptual blueprint or predictive logic for these instruments, it should hardly be surprising that foreign policy makers seem far more reluctant to analyze their choices in geoeconomic rather than geopolitical terms. We take this up in more detail in Chapter 3.

POINT 4

There are some fuzzy, borderline cases.

When it comes to applying this conception of geoeconomics to real-world cases, no matter how carefully constructed the parameters, inevitably certain fuzzy, borderline examples will arise. Most analysts—although not all—would share David Baldwin's intuition that bombing a factory should be excluded from any conception of geoeconomics, seeing this as belonging more to the realm of traditional military application.[43] But what about using elements of force—a naval blockade, perhaps—to impose an economic embargo, which itself comes as part of larger war-fighting? What of state-sponsored cyberattacks targeting banks or critical infrastructure as a means of venting disagreement over another country's foreign policy decision?

There are no bright-line answers. Broadly speaking, the actions and policies of interest here are economic *techniques* of statecraft; sometimes these techniques will involve tools that are straightforwardly economic in nature (for example, coercive trade measures, economic aid, or sovereign investment), and on other occasions they will involve mechanisms that are not purely economic in nature (such as state-sponsored cyberattacks) but where the means by which states are trying to influence the behavior of other states are economic. By this logic, certain cyberattacks—say, those targeting the critical economic or financial infrastructure of another country—would be considered geoeconomic, whereas other types of cyberattacks (against military and other government targets) would not.

Like anything, the liminal cases are the hardest. Some might argue, for example, that this logic could be stretched to include bombing a factory as a geoeconomic technique of statecraft. After all, basic market mechanisms of supply and demand are being manipulated—dampening a country's productive output, or causing supply shortages—to produce geopolitical results. What accounts for the widely shared instinct to exclude bombing a factory from the realm of geoeconomics, however, is not the fact that bombing is a noneconomic tool; it is rather that questions of military targets belong to a whole different set of social and normative practices around the conduct of war. That is not to say that geoeconomic techniques of statecraft cannot exist in conditions of warfare; of course they can. But the choice to counterfeit an enemy's currency during wartime, for instance— a clear form of geoeconomic statecraft—stands as an enterprise substantially separate from questions of military targets and war-fighting strategy.

By this reasoning, economic blockades that rely on aspects of military power arguably pose something of a hybrid case, but they are worth including within the realm of geoeconomics for at least two reasons: such economic blockades can exist in conditions short of a hot military conflict, and, more important, the variable doing the work in this case is the policy of economic denial, not the fact that it is achieved in part through relying on military power.[44] Finally, many would place military and humanitarian aid outside the scope of geoeconomics. Certainly both are well-developed fields, populated with experts who do not seem to regard themselves as engaged in a particularly economic technique of statecraft. But it is also the case that, especially where states and governments are concerned, money is fungible—meaning cost savings in one area can help offset expenses in another. This fact argues for including all forms of aid—including military and humanitarian aid—as part of a conceptual understanding of geoeconomics, even while admitting that military and humanitarian aid are among the most well understood, least interesting aspects of geoeconomic instruments; as such, we touch on them only intermittently in the coming chapters.

Whether a given case falls just inside or outside of geoeconomics, the larger point is that certain cases are fuzzy. They demand greater attention as a result. But the lack of bright-line answers in some instances speaks to a muddle of circumstances, not definition or practice.

POINT 5

Geoeconomics is distinct from foreign (or international) economic policy, mercantilism, and liberal economic thought.

Finally, it is worth distinguishing geoeconomics from foreign economic policy (or international economic policy), mercantilism, and liberal economic thought.[45] Benjamin Cohen and Robert Pastor define foreign economic policy as governmental actions intended to influence the international economic environment (as opposed to the geopolitical environment). And while many use the terms interchangeably, Stephen Cohen sees "international economic policy" as distinct from and preferable to "foreign economic policy," precisely because the former can and should remain beyond the reach of foreign policy makers. By Cohen's telling, "international economic policy must be viewed as being a separate phenomenon, not a tool for use by either foreign policy or domestic economic policy officials."[46]

Many of the most common and insidious misperceptions about geoeconomics actually stem from a separate set of misunderstandings involving two other economic concepts—namely, a tendency to view mercantilism and liberal economic thought as direct opposites and a corresponding tendency to view geoeconomics as some repurposed form of mercantilism and therefore as somehow inherently in tension with or opposed to liberal economic thought. The tendency to contrast the liberal emphasis on limited state involvement in private markets against the mercantilist emphasis on heavy state intervention in economic life, as if the two occupied opposing ends of some spectrum, "easily leads to portrayal of liberalism as postulating economics and politics as separate, distinct, and autonomous spheres of social life."[47]

History tends to credit Adam Smith with severing the mercantilist link between politics and economics.[48] But this amounts to a massive misreading.[49] Smith knew well the limits of economic logic, always clear that what was mutually beneficial in economic terms might not be so in political terms. According to him, "the wealth of a neighboring country" might be "dangerous in war and politics" even though "certainly advantageous in trade."[50] Smith saw no contradiction between his views on free trade and his belief that "the great object of the political economy of every country, is to increase the riches and power of that country."[51]

Indeed, Smith's writings offer little support for a portrait of economic liberals as bent on separating politics and economics and intent on seeing economic rationality as determining political relations. For Smith, "the first duty of the sovereign . . . [is] that of protecting the society from the violence and invasion of other independent societies." "Defence is more important than opulence," he wrote, and "the capricious ambition of kings and ministers has not . . . been more fatal" than "the impertinent jealousy of merchants and manufacturers."[52]

Of the many mistaken distinctions between mercantilism and liberalism, however, the one that most hinders clear thinking about geoeconomics surfaces around the question of whether "subservience of the economy to the state and its interests" differentiates the two doctrines.[53] As Baldwin rightly cautions, that mercantilists viewed extensive state intervention in the economy to be in the national interest and liberals did not does not mean that liberals were unconcerned with state interests. On the contrary, most liberals saw laissez-faire as merely a better means of advancing the interests of the state.[54] Even their critics recognized how motivated economic liberals were by matters of war, peace, and state interests. "What did the nineteenth-century free traders . . . believe that they were accomplishing?" Keynes once remarked.[55] "They believed that they were serving not merely the survival of the economically fittest, but the great cause of liberty . . . and . . . they believed, finally, that they were the friends and assurers of peace and international concord and economic justice between nations."[56] For economic liberals such as Adam Smith and Norman Angell, laissez-faire was but a form of geoeconomics; they differed from the mercantilists only on the tactics. For both camps, the question was how, not whether, to shape economic policies to serve state interests.[57]

Like anything, though, the practical boundaries of geoeconomics tend to be shaped through disagreements—that is, in cases where a state's economic and geopolitical interests diverge. For early liberal economists such as Jacob Viner, a tendency to assume congruence across economic and political interests meant they seldom found themselves forced to choose between them. For these early liberals—as for many policy makers today— free trade was the surest route to achieving both economic welfare and national security.[58] Gilpin's characterization of mercantilism as "the striving after security by economic means" hardly differentiates it from liberal beliefs that regarded free trade as the surest route to national and international security.[59]

Not only did early economic liberals actively take up geopolitical questions, but where liberals did confront divergent economic and political goals, they usually reconciled the conflict by privileging politics over economics. Depression-era historian Edward Mead Earle, a founding father of the field of security studies, spent considerable energy on this question of how economic liberals reconciled their theories with national security interests of the state. For Earle, the "critical question in determining [Smith's] relationship to the mercantilist school is not whether its fiscal and trade theories were sound or unsound but whether, when necessary, the economic power of the nation should be cultivated and used as an instrument of statecraft. The answer of Adam Smith to this question would clearly be 'Yes'—that economic power should be so used."[60]

The same is true of Richard Cobden, once hailed as "the towering figure among the free traders and internationalists in the first half of the nineteenth century."[61] But Cobden was also quite comfortable subjugating economics to politics where necessary. He opposed free trade in cases where it threatened to undermine peace, as with loans to foreign governments to purchase arms.[62] As World War II British intelligence officer turned Cambridge historian Harry Hinsley once summarized Cobden, "He worked for free trade because he wanted peace, not for peace because he wanted free trade."[63]

In sum, the real divides between mercantilism and liberalism concern how best (not whether) to pursue geoeconomics. "Its fundamental characteristic is simply that economic policy be deliberately formulated so as to promote the foreign policy goals of the state—whatever those may be," wrote Baldwin.[64] Mercantilism thus stands as only one of many forms of geoeconomics. By the same token, to the extent that leaders pursue prescriptions of economic liberalism (minimal state intervention, free trade, etc.) in the belief that these policies serve geopolitical interests, liberalism, too, falls comfortably among the many shades of geoeconomics.[65]

CHAPTER TWO

Geoeconomics and
the International System

Power turns out to depend less on common displays of charisma
and strength, and more on unseen manipulations of markets and
money.

—JEREMI SURI, AMERICAN HISTORIAN

IN 1991, a full two decades before writing his influential essay "GDP
Now Matters More than Force," Leslie Gelb urged the United States to
"replace the historic anti-Soviet focus of U.S. Asian policy with a new emphasis on geoeconomics, to forge new economic bonds and use them to
resolve political problems and prevent economic disputes from exploding
into political confrontations."[1] Reginald Dale, a specialist in European affairs, noted that "with the end of the Cold War and the advent of the global
economy, geopolitics and geoeconomics are becoming ever more closely
intertwined."[2] Appealing to those who waxed nostalgic for the clarity of
the Cold War—mutual assured destruction focused U.S. and Soviet policy
makers' minds—historian Thomas Stewart called upon the United States
to "create the geoeconomic equivalent of deterrence: that is, a way to
project economic power so as to prevent quarrels, win those the U.S. cannot
avoid, and encourage nations to seek prosperity together rather than beggar
their neighbors."[3]

Yet even as geoeconomics is perceived as newly important, there remains no common consensus or even discussion as to the motivating factors that might explain it. If geoeconomics has indeed returned to occupy
a decisive place in the foreign policies of many states, *why?*

Geoeconomics owes its modern resurgence primarily to three factors.
The first is that today's rising powers are increasingly drawn to economic
instruments as their primary means of projecting influence and conducting

geopolitical combat in the twenty-first century. Compare, for instance, present debates about the rise of Chinese power, dominated as it is by calculations of economic strength, to analogous Cold War debates regarding the Soviet Union. For American policy makers who dealt over the decades with the Soviet challenge, the notion of according great-power status to China, a country lacking a credible blue-water navy and decisively outmatched militarily by the United States, would have seemed baffling.

Central as China's rise is to this reemergence of geoeconomics, focusing too narrowly on China risks obscuring what is a larger, more complex phenomenon. Emerging powers of all kinds look to geoeconomic tools as foreign policy instruments of first resort across nearly every conceivable type of aim—from the transactional and immediate (for Qatar, a country with only 250,000 citizens, paying the salaries of rebel fighters in Syria and Libya was the surest way to achieve its desired outcomes) to the longer-term and nonspecific (for Mexico and Colombia, curbing the influence of regional heavyweights Brazil and Argentina is best achieved through a new trade grouping, known as the Alliance of the Pacific, which presently excludes Brasilia and Buenos Aires). These countries use geoeconomics in ways that run from positive inducements meant to charm, such as major purchasing decisions or investments timed to coincide with certain diplomatic campaigns, to punitive measures meant to coerce, such as a cyberattack on a hostile state's banking sector.

At least among nondemocratic rising powers, tendencies toward certain, often more coercive geoeconomic behaviors may arise out of an inability to achieve other, more preferable geoeconomic alternatives. The fact that these regimes do not have the luxury of convincing their neighbors, almost always wary, of any sort of economic integration premised on mutually advantageous agreement means they must fall back on other strategies. While Moscow or Beijing might ideally prefer to replicate the success of the European Union as a means of coalition building, "relations between authoritarian governments are based on oppression and subordination, not compromise," as one press report put it.[4] President Vladimir Putin's Eurasian Union project would not have come this far had it not been underwritten by the coercive financial might of the Russian state. By some estimates, support for the Lukashenko regime in Belarus costs Russia between $7 billion and $12 billion annually, while Lukashenko's periodic threats to withdraw from the Eurasian project are typically met with further Russian economic assistance. President Almazbek Atambayev of Kyrgyzstan has proven a particularly quick study in adapting to Moscow's geoeconomic methods, demanding a $200 million loan from Moscow in addition to trade and economic preferences; when he did not get all he wanted, Atambayev delayed his country's entry into the Eurasian Union.[5]

If the return of geoeconomics is driven at least partly by its popularity among rising powers, what explains their attraction? It may be a lack of promising alternatives. The logic of challenging the United States in a large-scale war is growing more remote (especially for state actors and especially in any land-war scenario). One need only observe the way that other countries are looking at their respective military equations—none is even attempting to challenge American military primacy in a comprehensive way. At most, they seek to blunt the ability of the United States to exercise unilateral dominance in a given regional context (as with China's ongoing military buildup). The theater of contest has shifted in important ways.

Even if countries were challenging the United States militarily, there remain separate questions about whether today's security challenges are best suited to military tools. Even as U.S. military and security investments have climbed over the past decade, military intervention buys less and less: America spent as much on Iraq as on Vietnam, and a decade after the U.S. invasion of Iraq, that country's future remains highly cloudy or worse. Despite this, extremist Islamic militants in Iraq have staged an impressive comeback since 2009. Harvard researcher Linda Bilmes estimates that the wars in Iraq and Afghanistan will eventually cost American taxpayers $4 trillion to $6 trillion.[6] In Afghanistan, meanwhile, the Taliban could well mount a nationwide return to power.[7] While the United States has significantly degraded al-Qa'ida's core operational capacity, al-Qa'ida's affiliates—along with jihadist organizations that are operationally independent but sympathize with its mission—have proven resilient.[8]

Some skeptics of geoeconomics will invariably point to the military crisis of the day to argue that military muscle remains very much in fashion. Many looked at Russia's invasion of Georgia in 2008, for example, as proof that the hoped-for transition from geopolitics to geoeconomics was illusory. As Robert Kagan explained at the time, "Many in the West still want to believe this is the era of geoeconomics. But as one Swedish analyst has noted, 'We're in a new era of geopolitics. You can't pretend otherwise.'"[9]

Kagan's binary construction—conceiving of geoeconomic muscle as somehow zero-sum in combination with military power—misses the point. The same is true for those who would read similar lessons into today's military contests, both those that are realized (in Crimea, for example) and those that are merely implied (as with China's naval buildup). To argue that states are looking more and more toward economic methods of advancing their geopolitical aims is not to suggest that the potential use of military force does not also remain an important ingredient in how many states pursue geopolitical aims.

But it is no longer a sufficient ingredient, or usually even the leading one. Today, economic factors can enable states to pursue more traditional

geopolitical aims or constrain them from doing so. Consider the U.S. and
EU response to Putin's encroachment upon Ukraine, where the Kremlin "is
gambling that old alliances like the EU and NATO mean less in the 21st
century than the new commercial ties it has established with nominally
'Western' companies, such as BP, Exxon, Mercedes, and BASF."[10] China's
increasing assertiveness suggests that it may be making a similar wager
around U.S. treaty commitments in Asia.[11]

Understanding when and how modern geoeconomics works requires appreciating it as inextricably intertwined with traditional military and diplomatic strands of foreign policy. In fact, many of the topical criticisms of
certain geoeconomic tools—especially sanctions—conclude that they are
ineffective precisely on account of misunderstanding these linkages. This is
not a new problem. Contemporary debates in the United States and Europe
on whether and how aggressively to sanction Russia over its recent territorial
aggressions, for instance, share striking parallels to similar debates in the run-
up to World War II. When Mussolini's Italy annexed Abyssinia (what is now
Ethiopia) in 1935, the United States and United Kingdom agonized over how
to respond. "Prime Minister Baldwin [of Britain] was to say somewhat wist-
fully that any sanctions that were likely to have worked would also have
been likely to lead to war," Henry Kissinger once recalled. "So much, at any
rate, for the notion that economic sanctions provide an alternative to force in
resisting aggression."[12] But as historian Alan Dobson explained, "Italy could
not have prevailed against France and Britain, or either of them separately,
but the danger of retribution had to be conveyed effectively. If economic
sanctions had been imposed in a different way . . . and had been made to appear as a clear preliminary to the use of force by France and Britain, then
the story might have been very different."[13] In other words, more aggressive sanctions might have worked, but they would not have worked as a
geoeconomic instrument unrelated to other aspects of statecraft.[14]

A second factor in the reemergence of geoeconomics is that, compared
to previous eras, those states most prone to economic displays of power
today have vastly more resources at their direct disposal. This is largely a
story of the modern return of state capitalism.[15] Like geoeconomics, state
capitalism is not new, but it is witnessing a resurgence. Governments, not
private shareholders, now own the world's thirteen largest oil and gas firms
and 75 percent of the world's energy reserves.[16] Between 2004 and 2009,
120 state-owned companies joined the ranks of Forbes's list of the world's
biggest 2000 companies, while 250 private firms dropped off.[17] According
to reports from 2013, state-backed companies account for 80 percent of
China's stock market, 62 percent of Russia's, and 38 percent of Brazil's—and
since 2005 have claimed more than half the world's fifteen largest initial
public offerings (IPOs).[18] One-third of the emerging world's foreign direct

investment (FDI) from 2003 through 2010 came from state-owned firms.[19] Governments are now the largest players in some of the globe's most important bond markets. In the early 2000s, the world held around $2 trillion in reserves; as of mid-2015, that total now exceeds $11 trillion, with sovereign wealth funds—a term only coined in 2005—holding another estimated $3 trillion to $5.9 trillion in assets. (By some projections, this amount could rise to $10 trillion by the end of the decade.)[20] The reserves of emerging nations have likewise increased, from just over $700 billion in 2000 to around $7.5 trillion in 2015, vastly exceeding reserve levels needed for import purchases.[21]

Across a number of measures, from major industries to equity and bond markets, from capital flows to foreign direct investment, the state's hand is visible and growing. Moreover, the continued pattern of larger structural forces—for example, Asian trade surpluses and high commodity prices—suggests that state coffers will remain considerable (notwithstanding bouts of oil price volatility as seen in 2014–2015).[22] The financial crisis that began in 2008 has done little to undermine these structural forces or to alter the political status quo in such centers of state capitalism as China, Russia, and the Gulf Cooperation Council (GCC) countries. If anything, it has reinforced the views of leaders already skeptical of core U.S. economic, diplomatic, and strategic capacities.

The emergence of this new generation of state capitalists—significantly larger, wealthier, more global, less democratic, and more sophisticated than their predecessors—raises important questions for U.S. foreign policy. For example, the only democracy represented among the world's ten largest sovereign wealth funds is Norway.[23] The concentration of such wealth and large levers of economic influence in state hands offers these governments new sources of power and foreign policy instruments. Today's state capitalists are entering markets directly, at times "shaping these markets not just for profit," as former U.S. secretary of state Hillary Clinton explained, "but to build and exercise power on behalf of the state."[24] One would have to search for a better or more telling U.S. government identification of geoeconomic applications.

A third factor explaining the resurgence of geoeconomics has less to do with evolving patterns of state behavior and more with changes to global markets themselves. Notably, today's markets—deeper, faster, more leveraged, and more integrated than ever before—exert more influence over a nation's foreign policy choices and outcomes, compelling more attention to economic forces along the way. Apart from how states are turning more to economic instruments to produce beneficial geopolitical results, market forces and economic trend lines are themselves dictating strategic outcomes across the most important of U.S. national interests. The fate of the European

Union—perhaps the West's greatest foreign policy achievement of the
twentieth century and the closest U.S. foreign policy partner—for several
years rested at least as much in the hands of bond markets as in European
political capitals.[25] The ability of Egypt (and, by extension, the region) to
navigate its way from transition to stability hangs largely on its economic
performance. Indeed, the very terms of U.S. engagement in the Middle
East may perhaps be significantly rewritten in the next decade, thanks to
a shale energy revolution now under way in North America.[26]

To dwell on this final North American example just a bit more: according
to the U.S. Geological Survey, recoverable gas resources have increased by
more than 680 percent since 2006, and production of light tight oil (LTO)
soared eighteen-fold between 2007 and 2012.[27] As America's LTO production increases and its oil imports decline, countries in West Africa, North
Africa, and the Middle East will increasingly send their exports to China.
And as trade routes redraw themselves, so too will the foreign policies of
these energy producing countries. If U.S. production eventually hits the
upper end of projections, 14–15 million barrels of oil per day, the global
oil market could undergo a fundamental transformation. The longtime
ability of the Organization of the Petroleum Exporting Countries (OPEC)
to set the price of a barrel between $90 and $110 would be undercut if not
ended. Good as this sounds, the convergence between the market price and
production cost of a barrel of oil would not be uniformly advantageous
to U.S. geopolitical interests. While some countries that depend upon oil
revenues as a major source of public financing are traditionally unfriendly
to U.S. interests, such as Iran, Russia, and Venezuela, others are friends, including Saudi Arabia, Mexico, Norway, and increasingly Vietnam.

As the energy revolution brings jobs, industries, and capital investments
back to the United States, will America leverage its growing economic
strength to reassert its leadership abroad, or will it decide to withdraw?
Will the United States protect the global commons—sea-lanes in particular—
as vigorously when it is no longer the principal energy beneficiary? Will it
be inclined to use its status as an energy superpower as a tool of geopolitics? An America that is awash in shale gas and LTO could use energy as a
geoeconomic instrument to strengthen its relationships around the world
(as Chapter 8 argues in more detail), but will it?

How Is Geoeconomics Changing
the International System?

The modern resurgence of geoeconomics, now practiced on a globally significant scale, brings with it a set of deeper, structural changes to the very

logic and operation of foreign policy. At times it is a straightforward account of flexing economic muscle to advance geopolitical ends—the $12 billion that funneled into Egypt from the Gulf countries in the weeks after former President Morsi was removed from office is one example.[28] As often, though, these shifts come less from the deliberate workings of a given geoeconomic policy and are far more the stuff of collateral consequence. We identify six ways in which geoeconomic tools and approaches are changing the current geopolitical landscape and, often, the practice of foreign policy itself.

CHANGE 1

Geoeconomic statecraft enables new policy choices.

The Russia of 2014, even with the extended slide in the value of the ruble, bears little resemblance to the Russia of ten or fifteen years ago. In 1998, Moscow, with less than $15 million in official reserves, was itself a customer of the IMF.[29] But by 2008 Russia had amassed over $600 billion in reserves (more than forty times its 1998 reserve levels), enabling the Kremlin to bully its neighbors in Georgia and Ukraine and, at least at this writing, more or less weather any market fallout.[30] Now roles have fully reversed and Russia is the one offering bailouts. Understandably, Moscow's bailout to the ailing Yanukovych regime in late 2013 may be the most iconic example. But increasingly, Kremlin bailouts are targeting the EU's own ranks—especially its weakest links (Cyprus, Greece, and Hungary, for example)—with packages and terms unequivocally aimed at fracturing the EU and undermining its alliance with the United States.[31]

What is more, Moscow now has recourse to deep-pocketed friends, which—even if they are of the purely tactical sort—might well see fit to cushion Moscow from any economic fallout for their own geopolitical reasons. Whereas the Beijing of 1998 or even 2004 may not have seen itself as having the financial resources or the foreign policy inclination to help Moscow flout the United States and EU, the Beijing of 2016 seems to have plenty of both. There emerged a flurry of energy, financing, and military deals from Moscow and Beijing in the wake of U.S.-EU sanctions against Russia. Asked about the string of deals and whether it signaled a new form of Sino-Russian alliance, Russia's ambassador to the United States summed it up thusly: "You are pivoting to Asia," he said, "but we're already there."[32]

In other words, newly deep coffers and the willingness to use them for the sake of geopolitics widens a state's options and can lend new room for maneuver to governments not traditionally friendly to the United States—Angola, Ecuador, Guinea, Venezuela, and Zimbabwe are all recent examples—enabling them to make decisions at odds with U.S. national interests without nearly the same negative consequences.[33] For Ecuador and Guinea, Chinese lending has acted as a buffer against market fallout from bad behavior. Lending from China (at interest rates roughly 3 percent below market) meant that Ecuador could afford to forgo tapping international credit markets in 2012, President Rafael Correa said in February 2012—thus rendering political decisions such as granting asylum to Wikileaks founder Julian Assange easier.[34] In Guinea in 2010, just fifteen days after soldiers shot down 157 pro-democracy demonstrators, the Guinean government signed a $7 billion mining contract with a Chinese state-owned enterprise.[35]

Then there was Qatar's autumn 2011 takeover of Iran's national airline, Iran Air, which was strapped by UN sanctions and unable to procure necessary parts. State-owned Qatari Airways, widely described as one of the country's most effective diplomatic tools, quickly offered itself to Tehran as a means to circumvent the sanctions.[36] "Allowing Qatar or any other foreign country to operate some of our domestic flight is aimed at diminishing the pressure of the sanctions, and it is a suitable policy under the current conditions," Iranian lawmaker Ali Akbar Moghanjoughi explained after Iran and Qatar reached a deal.[37] But, as with so many of Qatar's investments, the deal came with strategic influence over its sometime friend in Tehran, also one of the region's most crucial geopolitical states. "A very small country will be in charge of Iran's domestic flights," Kamran Dadkhah, a U.S.-based professor of Middle Eastern economies, said of the deal. "As a result of the deal the services provided by Iranians and their jobs will practically be under the control of another country."[38]

CHANGE 2

Geoeconomics enables states to use new foreign policy tools, some of which are unavailable to U.S. and other Western leaders.

Beyond enjoying a wider set of policy options, at least some states also find they have new geoeconomic tools available to them that the United States and other Western countries cannot exercise. When Chinese president Xi Jinping visited Russia in March 2013, he called for closer cooperation between the two nations. As a goodwill gesture, he outlined a $2 billion loan by China to the Russian oil company Rosneft, which will repay China in oil over a period of twenty-five years. And when Brazilian president Dilma Rousseff arrived in Beijing on her first state visit to China in April 2011,

Chinese president Hu Jintao, aiming to strengthen diplomatic ties with Brazil, greeted her with an order for thirty Brazilian Embraer planes plus five options, executed via three different Chinese state-owned airlines.[39] As one observer noted, "That is not the sort of gift that the U.S. government, or Japan's could or would give—All Nippon or United would not obediently line up to buy diplomatically preferred aircraft, and announce their purchase exactly on the diplomatically preferred date."[40]

Moreover, especially when applied coercively, today's brand of geoeconomics seems to confound Western governments, straining their ability to respond. Europe and Japan, America's closest security partners, are facing some of the most brazen shows of coercive geoeconomics anywhere. Yet in both cases these U.S. allies have struggled to mount any effective and united rejoinder to Russia's economic intimidation of Ukraine and to China's coercive economic tactics vis-à-vis its own region, including Japan. Tensions between the United States and the EU over their seeming inability to mount a fitting and collective geoeconomic response, meanwhile, seemed to wear heavily on the relationship, exposing tensions and existential doubts about what sort of EU foreign policy is realistic for Washington to expect.[41]

CHANGE 3

As certain states come to employ geoeconomic tools, it can change not only the nature of diplomacy but that of markets as well.

In 2008, South Africa–based Standard Bank sold a 20 percent stake to the state-owned Industrial and Commercial Bank of China (ICBC), expecting to streamline global operations and refocus on Africa through increased cooperation.[42] But the deal did not turn out as hoped. By 2010 losses had climbed to $114.3 million.[43] Asked a few years later why the agreement failed to yield the returns expected, Martyn Davies of Frontier Advisory, a Johannesburg-based research firm suggested that Standard's 20 percent stake to ICBC was not enough to allow it to compete with fully state-owned entities—explaining that for regions (like Africa) awash in state-backed deals, counterparties without diplomatic credentials may be at a disadvantage.[44] As states adopt a more direct footprint in markets, discussions once reserved for corporate boardrooms are removed to diplomatic negotiating tables, and as this occurs, private (often Western) firms stand to lose out.

Major deals are no longer decided strictly on the business merits. Returning to China's purchase of Embraers, for instance, it is unlikely that any offer by Boeing or Airbus could have swayed the choice of Chinese

leaders looking to mark the visit of the Brazilian president with a strengthening of the links between two of the BRICS countries. To take one more
example, Argentina and China became engaged in a tit-for-tat dispute a
few years ago that began with a move by Argentina to level new tariffs on
low-value-added goods—a move widely seen as directed squarely toward
China—and quickly escalated, as Beijing countered with spurious safety
bans on Argentine beef. Eventually Argentina blinked first, repealing the
tariffs. But it was not until Argentina mollified Beijing by awarding several
contracts to Chinese state-owned enterprises, including one for a major
rail project, that China ended its "public safety" embargo on Argentine
beef.[45] Insofar as the goal for Argentine officials in awarding these contracts was assuaging China, not necessarily finding the best bid, the result
is a class of deals decided more for coercive reasons than on market logic,
and as such, only really open to a few select firms.

And finally, as dealmakers, states have shown a willingness to bargain
with tools that are uniquely sovereign—spurious tax charges, forced joint
ventures, police raids, state secrets, and even incarceration of business rivals. In 2007, Hermitage Capital (Russia's largest private equity fund at
the time, with a sizeable global presence) paid more than $230 million in
fraudulent tax charges.[46] Less than twelve months later, the British oil
multinational BP lost more than $1 billion when TNK-BP, a joint venture
in which BP was a partner, was threatened with the loss of its license for
the giant Kovykta oilfields in East Siberia, and BP was forced to sell a majority stake in the fields—roughly 63 percent—to the state-owned Russian
company Gazprom.[47] Another state-controlled company, Rosneft, announced in October 2012 that it had acquired all of TNK-BP for $61 bil-
lion, billable to the Russian state; analysts described that deal as having no
economic logic. As economist Anders Aslund put it, "The gravest concern
is that TNK-BP, a well-managed and successful oil company, may be na-
tionalized for no other reason than Kremlin intrigue."[48]

Where business dealings occur on terms that go well beyond purely
market means or profit logic, it imposes a class of international commerce
fundamentally out of reach for private firms; it also creates a new front for
diplomacy that, for better or worse, will exclude many countries, including
the United States.

In more extreme cases, such geoeconomically minded deals can change
how entire markets operate, especially in strategically important sectors.
Take energy, for example. That Chinese energy insecurity poses national security risks—risks that Beijing has sought to mitigate through its international energy investments—is by now a widely agreed fact. Where such geo-

economic logic is present, it can compel a different sort of deal structure. Some states, led by Beijing, have chosen not to look to open markets to provide the best price, opting instead to tie-up long term supplies through state-led contracts with other governments—and typically marshaling all aspects of national power to secure the best terms.[49] The fact that China may find itself unable to satisfy domestic demand in a wartime scenario, says Rosemary Kelanic, an energy expert at George Washington University, "casts a new light on China's 'going out' initiatives to secure petroleum through equity oil arrangements and closer ties with exporters like Saudi Arabia."[50]

In some instances, this preference for state-led dealmaking may have a self-propagating quality, spurring other countries to nationalize defensively or at least supplying pretext for preexisting nationalization agendas. Ukraine's reassertion in the energy sector was, according to some, necessary "to protect the country's independence from the powerful and predatory energy producer next door."[51] Likewise, in mid-2012, the government of Argentina moved to nationalize Spanish energy firm Repsol's Argentine assets on rumors that Repsol was in talks with Chinese state oil major Sinopec.[52] This trend represents a fundamental challenge to prevailing assumptions about how global commodity markets operate, with vastly more geopolitical dimensions than has been the case for the last several decades.[53]

CHANGE 4

These geopolitically motivated deals can become important factors in a given state's foreign policy calculus.

The series of strategic investments China has made across Africa are instructive. Premier Li Keqiang announced during his May 2014 African trip that Beijing would expand its existing line of credit to several African states by $10 billion, to a total of $30 billion.[54] Behind many of these investments lay important development objectives.[55] Often the amounts actually delivered fall well short of those promised, but they are still substantial. And especially when funneled into weak and nondemocratic states, these sums can themselves come to influence the foreign policy orientations and perceived national interests of the governments committing them. In other words, means can quickly blur into ends. Despite its stated policy of nonintervention, in recent years Beijing has waded directly into the domestic political processes of several countries on the receiving end of significant Chinese investment, including Sudan, Zimbabwe, and Venezuela.[56] Whether these investments are indeed a direct factor motivating China's military modernization or simply strengthen the argument for those inside the Chinese Communist Party who have long called for such a spending priority, China's military buildup is couched in terms of backstopping its resource investments overseas.[57]

Sudan provides the strongest current example. Sudan, an oil importer before Chinese investment spurred development of its oil industry, now earns some $2 billion per year in oil revenues, half of which comes from China. Before South Sudan gained formal recognition as independent in 2011, nearly 80 percent of Sudan's oil revenue went to the purchase of weapons for use in subduing separatist fighters in the South.[58]

With Chinese assistance, the Sudanese government built three weapons factories near Khartoum. China has deployed about 4,000 troops to Southern Sudan to guard an oil pipeline, and it has reaffirmed its intention to strengthen military collaboration and exchanges with Ethiopia, Liberia, Nigeria, and Sudan. Beijing has thus far stymied UN Security Council efforts to intervene in eastern Sudan's ongoing violence. At the same time, China has rapidly expanded its role in UN peacekeeping efforts, with more than 2,000 Chinese participating in ten peacekeeping missions as of 2014 (and a pledge to permanently contribute 8,000 troops to UN peacekeeping). This makes China not only Africa's largest trading partner but also the largest provider of peacekeepers to Africa of any of the five permanent members of the UN Security Council.[59]

Apart from exerting pull momentum for China's military buildup, these resource investments in less than creditworthy regimes beg the question of how China would respond should any of these investments fail. Given the poor credit record of many of these countries, it is not clear why China would be any more immune from risks of expropriation or default than other sovereign creditors. Nor is it obvious that Beijing has always weighed its risks appropriately.[60]

According to one study, released in fall 2013 by the RAND Corporation, Beijing has tended to ask "financially-pressed borrowers . . . for concessions or accommodations such as according favorable access to Chinese investors, or granting wider scope for the number and activities of China's Confucian Institutes that expand awareness and understanding of China's culture and language. Other concessions linked to debt-forgiveness or extended or refinanced loans may involve the granting of geopolitical port-of-call and refueling rights for People's Liberation Army naval vessels, or landing rights for PLA air units."[61]

One of the biggest such tests for China came in January 2012, when an oil-sharing dispute between Sudan and South Sudan prompted South Sudan's government to halt oil production and expel the head of a major Chinese state-led oil company from the country for "noncooperation." With significant oil supplies and investment at stake—China accounts for 82 percent of South Sudan's oil exports—China could not avoid getting "uncomfortably drawn into the high-stakes conflict between north and south."[62] Beijing's envoy for African affairs, Liu Guijin, was dispatched to break the deadlock, warning that if the two sides failed to resolve the problem, the "whole region would be affected; the repercussions would be very serious."[63]

Such adventurous dealmaking may prove a good thing, pulling Beijing toward more constructive, hands-on diplomacy in brokering crises. What is clear is that Beijing will face an increasingly difficult task in clinging to nonintervention as an ordering principle for its foreign policy.

CHANGE 5

Many of these contracts, often negotiated autocrat to autocrat, seem designed to bolster the respective regimes in question, often proving effective.

Deals, especially bad ones, can be easier to negotiate autocrat to autocrat, unencumbered by the same levels of transparency or scrutiny that democratic publics tend to demand. In these cases, the terms might well come with financing for an important political goal. Early in 2012, as former Venezuelan president Hugo Chavez was gearing up for presidential elections, the Venezuelan state oil company PDVSA accepted an oil-backed loan of $1.5 billion from Chinese state-run bank ICBC for new housing construction projects (to be built by CITIC, China's largest state-owned investment company). The projects were seen in Caracas as an important part of Chavez's campaign strategy. Worse, PDVSA was forced to sell a 10 percent stake in one of its most promising joint ventures (with Chevron) to CITIC as part of the deal.[64]

The same basic plot lines are found in states where China and Russia have embraced various autocratic regimes hostile to the West, such as Belarus, Uzbekistan, North Korea, Zimbabwe, Sudan, Angola, and, until recently, Myanmar. These deals and other forms of support are clearly motivated by material interests, whether China's need for oil or Russia's reliance on the sale of conventional weapons and nuclear reactors as important revenue sources. Some analysts see Russian and Chinese support for nondemocracies as motivated more or less exclusively by material factors (a fact that hardly makes China or Russia unique, some note, pointing out that Ethiopia, for instance, has for years been among the top recipients of U.S. assistance dollars, even though it is not a democracy). Others see more to it. "Defending these governments against the pressures of the liberal West," Robert Kagan explained a decade ago, "reflects their fundamental interests as autocracies."[65]

Parsing motivations misses the larger point. Regardless of what, if anything, can be said for the origins of these deals, the fact is that some of today's leading practitioners of geoeconomics, notably (but not only) Russia and China, also rank as the most important business partners and financing sources for some of the world's most brutal autocrats, typically in ways that strengthen the domestic political strength of these regimes. China, concerned about preserving access to oil in the event of a confrontation with the United States, seeks improved relations with the governments of Venezuela, Sudan, and Angola, all out of favor with the West, and prioritizes ties with the former military dictators of Myanmar in exchange for access to port facilities.[66] And with the People's Republic of China (PRC) in a constant struggle for votes at the United Nations to promote its positions relative to Taiwan and Japan, it makes sense that Beijing courts leaders such as Zimbabwe's Robert Mugabe, another autocrat who stands in pointed opposition to the West.[67] To be sure, few if any of these countries make for natural allies. But as nondemocracies, China and Russia have important interests in common, both with each other and with other autocracies—interests that, returning to Kagan, "are under siege in an era when liberalism does seem to be expanding. No one should be surprised if, in response, an informal league of dictators has emerged, sustained and protected by Moscow and Beijing as best they can."[68]

CHANGE 6

Once-distinct security and economic tensions tend to reinforce each other to a greater degree than in previous eras.

As argued above, states are now more often opting to flex geopolitical muscle in economic terms—in short, adopting geoeconomic approaches. This is not to slight recent shows of military force—Russia's invasions of Georgia in 2008 and Crimea in 2014, for example, or Chinese aggressive naval behavior in the South and East China Seas, not to mention the American-led wars in Iraq and Afghanistan. But increasingly states are airing disagreements with foreign policies in economic terms, from export bans on key commodities to cyberattacks on a country's banking sector. As this occurs, it means that economic and security tensions risk reinforcing each other. Cases of economic drivers motivating security tensions—access to critical resources as a leading example—are not new. Increasingly, though, security challenges that themselves bear no great economic content are nevertheless managing to provoke economic disruptions.

This is especially true in East Asia. One possible explanation for the region's growing security tensions lies with China's perception of its own economic strength—namely, a belief that the United States, Japan, and Korea are now too economically dependent on China to resolutely stand behind existing security commitments, a doubt often raised in the Western media. This in turn emboldens more aggressive behavior. In this light, some see the fact that China's initial challenges to the Asian security status quo came in 2009—amid the world's largest financial crisis in seventy years—as more than coincidence.[69]

It is impossible to know where these trends are headed. Much will depend on how the United States, as the world's reigning superpower, comes to understand and respond to them. This recognition is likely to be impacted by the fact that while many states are repurposing economic tools for geopolitical use, the United States is moving in the reverse direction. It is true that Washington is taking a more active foreign policy interest in the international economic arena, but for reasons that have far more to do with the economic welfare of the United States than with geopolitical outcomes. There is a growing (and, in our view, accurate) recognition in the United States that, more than ever, U.S. foreign policy must be a force for economic renewal at home. In fact, some speculate that in the decades to come, America's economic performance will grow more important to its geopolitical fortunes than its possession of nuclear weapons or its seat on the UN Security Council.[70] This is partly a story of how financial crises and their resulting economic insecurity can come to preoccupy foreign policy debates.[71] And it is in part a cautionary tale of how two prolonged and expensive wars have affected the United States in recent decades and how, as a result, cost considerations of major American military engagement now preoccupy U.S. policy makers.

Shoring up U.S. competitiveness will require a thoroughly reformed manifestation of U.S. diplomacy. Though America's growing interest in foreign policy as an engine of domestic economic revival is well founded, it is no substitute for coming to terms with the widespread reemergence of geoeconomic statecraft. Washington must still reckon with the rest of the world's move in the inverse direction—toward putting economic and financial instruments in the service of geopolitical goals. There will be trade-offs. But as with most things, understanding the nature of the exercise in which one is engaged tends to boost the odds of success. In Chapter 3, we look at the leading instruments of geoeconomics and the underlying variables that determine their effectiveness.

CHAPTER THREE

Today's Leading Geoeconomic Instruments

> In one brief sentence . . . monetary policy is foreign policy . . . and that is still my view today, very much more than previously. . . . [I]t is not only domestic policy, but also definitely foreign policy.
>
> —HELMUT SCHMIDT, FORMER GERMAN CHANCELLOR

THIS IS not the first time geoeconomics has enjoyed ascendancy in global geopolitics, but it might as well be. Compared to previous eras of geoeconomic salience—many point to the early postwar years as typified by the Marshall Plan and the initial stages of the Cold War—the world looks much different.[1] Some of today's favored geoeconomic tools, such as cyber, did not exist in Marshall's day. Others, such as energy politics, while not new, are operating in such a vastly different landscape as to render them as good as new. Still others of these instruments, with development assistance as one example, function more or less as they did in earlier eras. Even these, though, have attracted important new players and dimensions.

Today, seven economic tools are, at least in theory, suited to geopolitical application: trade policy, investment policy, economic and financial sanctions, cyber, aid, financial and monetary policy, and energy and commodities. We survey each instrument below, again aiming to take only the geopolitical as opposed to the purely economic measure of each.

Different as these instruments may be, it is worth examining them jointly and severally. Each carries its own leading cast of countries and institutions, its own levers of state control and determinants of success, and its own set of externalities and implications for U.S. national interests.

Trade Policy

Trade as a geoeconomic tool has traditionally been utilized through positive inducement. Consider, for example, the Qualifying Industrial Zones (QIZs) in Jordan and Egypt. Created in association with the Camp David peace accord, an iconic example of American geopolitical accomplishment, the QIZs were designed to lure Jordan—unsuccessfully, as it turned out—into publicly supporting the Camp David agreement and subsequent peace process.[2]

But trade as a geoeconomic tool can just as easily assume a more coercive form. Take a closer look, for example, at some of Russia's most notable trade measures since it joined the World Trade Organization (WTO) in 2012. As the *Economist* put it, "Product bans are a tried and tested form of political pressure in Russia."[3] In the recent past, Georgian wines, Ukrainian chocolates, Tajik nuts, Lithuanian and even American dairy products, and McDonald's have all fallen afoul of sudden injunctions.

In the years before the 2008 Georgian war, Russia's chief sanitary inspector closed the Russian market to all Georgian agricultural products, including imported Georgian wines and mineral water.[4] The trade blockade only worsened when Moscow halted air, sea, road, and rail transport to Tbilisi, along with postal communication.[5] Russia's wine embargo was only lifted in the summer of 2013, a step that paved the way for a meeting in Prague between the two countries. Georgia's president, Giorgi Margvelashvili, has expressed his country's wish to pursue closer ties with Europe.[6] But it is unlikely that the country will manage to orient too far westward so long as Moscow remains unilaterally capable of cutting off trade and crippling the Georgian economy.

Russia has since visited similar tactics on Moldova and Ukraine in an effort to coerce both countries away from signing association agreements with the European Union.[7] In July 2012, Russia stopped imports from Ukraine's main confectionary producer—due to the alleged presence of carcinogens in its products—and intensified customs checks on Ukrainian goods at the border, which reportedly led to some $500 million in losses for Ukraine.[8] Throughout the spring and summer of 2014, the Russian government closed the border to most trucks coming from Ukraine, forcing some Ukrainian factories in Russia to shut down. And, as was expected, it increased the price of natural gas in an attempt to curb pro-Western enthusiasm as Kiev eyeballed the EU.[9] Moreover, Russian officials have publicly stressed that signing the EU pacts would debar Ukraine from further integration with the Eurasian Customs Union and lead Russia to increase trade restrictions.[10]

In addition to targeting Ukraine with aggressive geoeconomic actions, the conflict has also led Russia to throw around its economic weight with EU countries that do not sympathize with its narrative of the Ukrainian issue. A year after Russia's August 2014 ban on EU dairy products, European producers are seeing a 25 percent reduction in dairy prices resulting from the decrease in demand for their products.[11] In a similar vein, the Dutch investigation into the downing of Malaysia Airlines Flight 17 over Ukraine found Russia at least partially culpable. Moscow retaliated by destroying huge quantities of Dutch flowers and cheese at the behest of the Kremlin in August 2015. The Russian government made little attempt to conceal the political motivations behind its economic reprimand. "The tit for tat has been so obvious," explains Andrew Kramer, a Moscow-based correspondent for the *New York Times,* "that even pro-Kremlin commentators have dropped the pretense, saying the flower burning is intended as a warning to the Netherlands over risks to trade if the investigation proceeds unfavorably for Russia."[12]

While dealing a significant blow to the Ukrainian economy, Moscow's geoeconomic moves served, first, to remind Ukraine—and others in the region—of the consequences of decreasing ties to Russia in favor of the European Union; second, to reinforce Russia's role as an economic regional hegemon; and third, to prevent the continued expansion of the North Atlantic Treaty Organization to Russia's borders.[13] Facing Russian threats on countless levels, Ukraine halted its plans to sign deals with the EU at the November 2013 Eastern Partnership summit in Vilnius.[14]

The U-turn, the Yanukovych government said, was for the "benefit of Ukraine's national security."[15] Greeted overwhelmingly by Ukrainian popular opinion as a "disappointment . . . for the EU and the people of Ukraine," the decision came as a clear if temporary victory for President Putin.[16] The lesson Moscow learned was that skillful economic maneuvering can produce substantial geopolitical returns. And even where those returns fall short of their desired aim—the reintegration of Ukraine into President Putin's revamped Russian sphere of influence—the consequences can be destabilizing and costly for the United States, for Europe, and for the world.

There are reasons to think that Moscow will find the task of coercion easier elsewhere in the region than with Ukraine; Kiev may still exercise the option of warming ties with the EU (Ukranian president Poroshenko told his country that it should prepare to join the EU by 2020).[17] The president of Kyrgyzstan, widely seen to be next on President Putin's list of potential members for the Eurasian economic partnership, expressed his predicament clearly in December 2013: "Ukraine has a choice, but unfortunately we don't have much of an alternative."[18]

Russia's 2013 ban on Moldovan wine marked the second time Moscow has clamped down on Moldovan vineyards, doing little to hide the fact that the bans are cudgels meant to dissuade Moldova from signing EU agreements.[19] In the run-up to the 2013 Vilnius summit, the Kremlin also made threatening noises about cutting off Moldova's gas supply and subjected Moldovans working in Russia to extra checks on their legal status.[20]

Moscow's tactics ultimately did not work on Moldova either; Moldova did sign important agreements to deepen its ties with the EU at the Vilnius summit in 2013. But notwithstanding Moldova's immediate decision at Vilnius, the big question is whether Ukraine, its giant neighbor, stays the course on its own ambitions to integrate with the EU. If not, Moldovans admit that it will be difficult to resist Russian pressure to abandon their country's path to European integration. Though pro-Western political parties won 55 out of 101 parliamentary seats in Moldova's November 2014 election, they lost the popular vote.[21] Even as the country remains divided on European integration, Moldovan prime minister Iurie Leanca has made it clear that "we do not want to be a Ukrainian hostage."[22]

That Russia would so brazenly resort to coercive trade measures, so close on the heels of its own 2012 accession to the WTO, bespeaks a certain exaggeration by the West of the power of its institutions; at the very least it reflects an underestimation of the growing presence and effectiveness of geoeconomic pressure, even in the face of Western alternatives and institutional constraints. "Hard power trumped soft power at the Vilnius Summit," as one commentator quipped, referring to the way in which Moscow's aggressive tactics proved the limits of the EU's gravitational pull.[23] The Eastern Partnership reflects a general allergy in Brussels to issues of hard security and geopolitics and a preference for economic integration as an instrument for enhancing stability and peace.[24] During the chaotic months that followed the Vilnius summit, there was a pervasive sense that the Eastern Partnership, a key program of the EU, had lost out in the contest of "geopolitics versus economic modernization."[25] On the one hand, this interpretation misunderstands that the episode was really a struggle between two forms of geoeconomics—the magnetic power of the EU and the coercive pull of Moscow. The fact that the EU's brand of pallid geoeconomics could be lost on so many, however, and could be widely seen as stripped of any geopolitical dimension offers a revealing indictment of the EU's current geoeconomic performance, at least with respect to its Eastern neighbors.

Returning to a question posed in Chapter 1—how might the rise of geoeconomics alter the way states exercise military power?—the way Russia and the EU handle the EU's Eastern Partnership going forward may offer one important data point.

Investment Policy

Forty years ago, 90 percent of all cross-border flows were trade-based; in 2014, 90 percent were financial.[26] A large part of the current flows comes as some form of investment—whether shorter-term, more liquid "portfolio" investment or longer-term "direct" investment. From a geoeconomic perspective, then, investment matters more than in previous eras because there is simply a great deal more of it passing between states today, in both relative and absolute terms.

Beyond issues of scale, the patterns of investment—the "capitals of capital," so to speak—are different. Twenty years ago, the United States enjoyed a dominant position (what some have called "uniquely dominant") in terms of where capital originated, how it was intermediated, and where it ended up.[27] But this dominance has eroded on all three scores. According to the Global Financial Centres Index, Middle East financial centers, with Qatar leading, continue to rise; Tokyo, Seoul, and Shenzhen are doing significantly better than neighboring Asian finance hubs.[28] Gross capital transfers to emerging markets have quintupled since the early 2000s, according to the IMF, with portfolio flows becoming a more important, and volatile, part of the mix.[29] South-South flows of capital are also rising sharply, with approximately $1.9 trillion in foreign investments between emerging economies.[30]

In addition, compared to the past, states directly own or control a far greater share of this cross-border investment. Obviously for commodity producing states such as Russia, Brazil, and many Gulf countries, these assets have long represented sources of revenue and power too attractive to leave in private hands. But it is only with sharp rises in commodity prices over the last decade that these resource flows have generated the sort of profit margins—and swelling state coffers—seen today.

The concentration of outbound foreign direct investment, in particular, into state hands now extends well beyond the energy sector. State-owned companies and state-owned investment vehicles of all kinds are venturing abroad, in some cases as a result of coordinated, state-financed campaigns.[31] And it is not just the suppliers but now too the consumers of these flows that are state-owned. One clear example is China's increasing appetite for energy supplies. The vast majority of China's energy deals are with other governments. The result is a growing set of transactions that involve sovereign counterparties on both sides, such as the Gazprom-China National Petroleum Corporation $400 billion deal or the 2013 Rosneft-Sinopec oil deal.[32] It would be difficult to imagine that geopolitics would not enter into these agreements.

Finally, along with new sums, new players, and new investment patterns, today's investment tools are also relatively novel—in kind, by order of magnitude, or both. As of mid-2015, foreign exchange reserve levels exceeded $11 trillion globally, up from $2 trillion fifteen years ago.[33] Emerging nations in particular have increased their reserves from just over $700 billion in 2000 to $7.5 trillion in 2015. Levels like these—many times beyond what is needed to provide import cover—mean that the states sitting atop these reserve stockpiles enjoy greater flexibility to invest them in a broader range of asset classes.[34] If China maintains $4 trillion in reserves and roughly $125 billion in monthly imports, for instance, these stockpiles yield over two years of import cushion for Beijing. (For those who argue that these stockpiles are less about import cushion than insurance against fickle capital markets—in effect, learning the lessons of the 1997–1998 Asian financial crisis—it is worth remembering that Chinese swap lines amounted to $30 billion during that crisis, far less than what China is currently holding.)[35] With such investment flexibility comes greater diplomatic sway and, at least for certain types of asset classes, the possibility of geopolitical leverage during crises.

Twenty years ago, state-owned enterprises (SOEs) were little more than domestic employment vehicles. Ten years ago, there was widespread skepticism about whether these firms, saddled with bad debt and inexperienced leadership, could succeed beyond their home markets. Today they include some of the world's biggest companies, backed by some of the globe's largest pools of capital, and can claim over half of the world's top ten IPOs over the last six years. Bearing little resemblance to yesterday's SOEs, today's state-backed companies supply a growing share of outbound FDI globally (over a third of all outbound FDI from emerging markets) as well as the majority of listings on some of the world's leading stock markets.[36] That is not to say that today's SOEs do not come with problems of their own—most are notoriously less efficient than their private counterparts.[37] But economic efficiency is not the point. What matters is that SOEs are far more politically pliant than most private firms.[38]

Likewise, global sovereign wealth funds (SWFs) have ballooned rapidly. By the time the term *sovereign wealth fund* was coined in 2005, these funds had already begun to challenge dominant Western private capital flows. Estimates from mid-2013 state that SWFs hold between $3 trillion and

$5.9 trillion of assets under management (estimates vary depending on whether calculations include domestic invested funds as well as foreign invested funds, and on whether certain reserve asset management entities are included).[39] By way of comparison, the total value of all hedge fund assets under management globally reached a record $2.4 trillion as of mid-2013.[40] There are roughly thirty-seven SWFs with holdings that exceed $1 billion.[41] As a class, SWFs remain highly concentrated—the top ten SWFs account for roughly 85 percent of total SWF assets, or $3.5 trillion. As noted earlier, Norway is the only democracy represented among these ten.[42]

Added to these sources of direct financing for states are large state-owned banks. China's biggest four banks have a combined balance sheet of over $9 trillion, as well as "an ongoing responsibility to balance commercial decisions with the government's broader economic and social objectives," as a recent Standard & Poor's assessment put it, "[where] the government maintains heavy influence over banks' decision-making through its major shareholder status."[43]

In taking the strategic measure of these various instruments of state wealth, SWFs offer a good benchmark, since they are often described as the most professionally managed and least worrisome form of state wealth from a geopolitical perspective.[44] That is not to say that concerns do not exist. Much of what has been written on SWFs in the past decade speaks of market participants and governments alike harboring mounting anxiety.[45] Nor are these worries necessarily hypothetical, as Russia proved by channeling fully one-sixth of its SWF—which, up until that point, was avowedly apolitical—into the December 2013 bailout package Moscow offered to Kiev as part of its bid to keep Ukraine tethered to Russia.

Even beyond the Russia-Ukraine case, there is research suggesting geopolitical motivations influencing SWF investment patterns. Studies have found political relations between the SWF's country of origin and the country of its target investment to be a factor in SWF investment, with geopolitical motives able to explain variance in SWF investment patterns in some cases.[46] The irreducibly sovereign nature of SWFs, some argue, endows them with unique geopolitical levers—many of which need not be exercised to achieve their desired effects. SWFs are part of what Georgetown University law professor Anna Gelpern describes as "a new generation in state commerce where diverse economic, political, and legal systems come in continuous, intimate contact."[47] The legal and regulatory systems of most Western countries poorly anticipated this new generation of investment, and as Gelpern explains, the task of retrofitting long-standing goals of openness to accommodate SWFs may not be easy:

SWFs are public and private at the same time; as such, they do not fit into neat legal and regulatory boxes. Even when they act commercially, SWFs are sovereign—profit will drive them, until it does not. States may not respond to regulatory incentives as private actors do; yet they are often subject to the same laws. SWFs have separate information and communication channels to regulators, raising the possibility of both insider trading and regulatory capture. Their decision-making may be insulated from politics and markets alike, or exposed to both. More daunting yet, each state is different: Brazil, China, Norway, Qatar, and the United States mix public and private in different ways. When their hybrids go global, they expose distinct tensions in the law and structure of global finance.[48]

In terms of what sort of clout such investment buys, at times there are fairly explicit geopolitical conditions. Norway banned its $810 billion sovereign wealth fund—the biggest in the world—from investing in Israeli firms with ties to settlements in the disputed West Bank territories.[49] Prior to his ouster, Libyan leader Muammar Qaddafi offered to use funds from Libya's SWF to dampen the impact of the Greek debt crisis and to help rid African countries of Western influence.[50] China's leading asset manager has openly predicated investment on disavowal of Taiwan, most notably succeeding in persuading Costa Rica into severing relations with Taiwan through the purchase of $300 million in bonds.[51] Chinese FDI in Africa likewise comes only on recognition of Beijing's one-China policy.[52] It has proven effective. Within five years of China's first investments in Africa, the number of African states to recognize Taiwan fell from thirteen (roughly half of all states to recognize Taipei globally) to only four.[53]

Apart from whatever terms might characterize a deal initially, these sovereign investments may yield influence in the breach. Consider voting patterns within the African Union regarding support for coalition air strikes against Qaddafi and how well they map to investments by the Libyan Investment Authority across the continent.[54] As the Libya case suggests, there is also a risk that geopolitically motivated investments gone awry can backfire, creating a separate, if equally real, set of foreign policy challenges. Prior to his ouster, many Libyans thought Qaddafi was wasting Libyan money on Africa, which in turn fueled what at least one analyst called "very strong anti-African sentiments in rebel-held areas."[55]

There is a tendency, especially among market watchers, to treat the fact that a SWF has a given economic return benchmark as somehow prima facie evidence of purely commercial motivations. (As one former IMF economist wrote, investments by Gulf-based SWFs are "based on pure economic criteria and are not politically motivated. For instance, ADIA, one of the world's largest SWFs, sets a benchmark annual rate of return of 8%

for its portfolio, and has met or beat this portfolio for several years."[56]) But of course there is nothing to preclude the possibility of attractive geo-economic investments that also happen to offer an 8 percent or better return. GeoEconomica, a SWF watchdog firm, recently singled out Qatar's SWF for its failure to comply with the Santiago Principles, a compact meant to increase transparency and guard against political investments by SWFs. "Qatar's foreign policy interests have strongly informed Qatari sovereign wealth management," GeoEconomica said.[57] Apparently whatever geopolitical adventures the Qatari SWF was getting into also made for good business, as the fund's annual returns are reported to be close to 17 percent.[58]

And even where states are investing purely on the basis of economic considerations, it stands as a separate question whether these investments nonetheless alter the strategic landscape in some way. As Ashley Thomas Lenihan, a fellow at the London School of Economics, writes, SWFs "may be employed as a means to increase a state's relative economic power, even when their individual investments are generally made on the basis of economic, market-driven, logic."[59] Because states, as sovereign actors, also have the advantage of advance knowledge of geopolitical events, and thus the unique ability to move their funds accordingly, other concerns center on a form of insider trading—the idea that sovereigns could tilt a policy environment, domestically or abroad, to place their investments on preferential market footing—and the notion that compared to private investors, SWFs are far less constrained by shareholder accountability, a fact that itself can give SWFs significant market advantages.[60]

Finally, where the pull of a country's domestic market is strong enough, its handling of *inbound* investment can be as powerful a geoeconomic instrument as its outbound investment flows.[61] While some countries place entire civilian sectors off-limits, others screen all forms of inbound foreign investment, rending approvals on a case-by-case basis in ways that invite geopolitics into the decision making. The U.S. investment screening process, carried out by the Committee on Foreign Investment in the United States (CFIUS), has come in for its share of criticism in recent years, but for all its infirmities, it is far more limited in scope than similar bodies in other countries, conducting only 193 investigations of inbound investment between 2009 and 2013 (or roughly 40 percent of "covered investments" potentially subject to investigation during those years).[62]

Again, even granting that much of today's state-led investment is not geopolitically motivated, it can nevertheless carry real geopolitical consequences. The resulting impacts can be subtle, perhaps seen only in aggregate, and sometimes not even necessarily intended. As Chapter 4 illustrates,

Chinese investment flows have begun to wear away at long-held assumptions about how certain markets operate. These flows have altered the foreign policy calculus for certain nations, widening the options of some and narrowing those of others. And in some cases they have also lent new arguments to supporters of China's own military buildup.

Economic Sanctions

Sanctions, like trade and investment, have traditionally been a story about the perks of size. While most countries have practiced some form of sanctions, their effectiveness turns on two basic variables: domestic market size (the loss of America as a potential market for one's exports versus, say, Lichtenstein) and global market share (some countries have a near monopoly on the production of certain goods).

But there are exceptions, especially where niche entities have adopted systemic importance. Virtually all electronic banking payments are executed via the Society for Worldwide Interbank Financial Telecommunication (SWIFT) network, and the fact that SWIFT is domiciled in Belgium—as opposed to a country less sympathetic to U.S. and European geopolitical interests—made it considerably easier to leverage this network in the context of the Iran sanctions. Likewise, the fact that the United Kingdom remains such a dominating player in the shipping insurance industry has conferred considerable geoeconomic leverage for Western countries seeking to deter Iran's nuclear ambitions. Maritime insurer Lloyd's announced in July 2010 that it would stop underwriting gasoline imports to Iran, a move of compliance with the U.S.-led sanctions regime, and one that further exacerbated the plunge in the value of the Iranian rial and loss in foreign reserves.[63] Just six months later, in January 2011, Lloyd's issued a market bulletin providing guidance for subsequent compliance with U.S. and EU-led sanctions against Iran: no new contracts, renewals, or extensions for insurance to Iran or its government, Iranian citizens or entities, or those acting on behalf of Iran would be permitted.[64] With no insurance for oil tankers, Iranian oil buyers were compelled to act in accordance with the sanctions regimes; India was forced to cancel an Iranian shipment, for instance, and Japanese oil refiners asked for clauses to be added to purchase contracts so they could back out if the requisite shipping insurance could not be obtained.[65]

As Chapter 6 explores in more detail, the strongest such systemic choke point remains the ubiquity of the U.S. dollar. Thanks to the dollar's continued universality and America's central role in financial markets, the U.S. Treasury Department is able to deliver a credible ultimatum to international banks: either do business in the U.S. dollar or do business with the target country or bank.[66]

Such choke points notwithstanding, sanctions regimes since the 1970s have had a decidedly mixed record when it comes to altering state geopolitical and domestic behavior. When one sizes up these cases, some lessons become clear. First, the use of sanctions between adversaries is more frequent (and more costly to the sanctioner) than sanctions applied between friendly states, and extract fewer geopolitical concessions, as adversaries tend to prefer near-term economic costs over longer-term geopolitical ones.[67] This fact has accounted for the general failure of U.S. economic coercion to achieve its goals against Iraq, Cuba, China, and North Korea.[68]

Next, sanctions work best when the objectives are modest and the targets well-defined. This leads some experts to counsel restraint, arguing for example that "modern sanctions should be targeted at specific objectionable activities . . . or at the Swiss bank accounts of elites such as Iran's Revolutionary Guard."[69] Certainly, changing specific behavior is of course easier than bringing down a regime, though foreign policymakers do not always have such luxury of choice, and in any case, modern sanctions have demonstrated an ability to help accomplish both.

And, of course, sanctions also need friends and allies. Washington learned this the hard way in early 1980 when it imposed a grain embargo on the Soviet Union to punish it for invading Afghanistan. The embargo failed to gain international support, even from strong allies such as Canada and Australia.[70]

Finally, sanctions also underscore the dependencies and tensions that can exist across various geoeconomic instruments. For example, certain financial sanctions—such as those on Iran's central bank—are effective only because these entities deal in U.S. dollars. As such, each time the United States uses these sanctions, Washington may be hastening other countries' search for alternatives to the dollar, which in turn would undercut the future effectiveness of sanctions. For example, Russia's state-owned energy company Gazprom has started to accept payment in rubles and yuan, rather than euros and dollars, amid escalated sanctions toward Moscow over Ukraine.[71]

Cyber

While much about the precise nature and magnitude of cyberattacks remains fuzzy, there is good reason to view cyber as among the newest, most powerful geoeconomic instruments.[72] Some aspects of the problem are clear: the overwhelming share of attacks can be traced back to IP addresses inside Russia and China.[73] According to one private study, cyberattacks account for roughly 15 percent of global Internet traffic on any given day. This figure "plummeted to about 6.5%" around October 1, 2011, China's National Day, "when many workers take leave."[74]

Certainly not all cyberattacks are geoeconomic. One example is Russia's July 2008 cyberattacks against Georgia's Internet infrastructure in the run-up to hostilities between the two over South Ossetia; another is the 2009 Stuxnet attack against Iranian nuclear facilities, thought to have been launched by Israel and the United States in a bid to disrupt Iran's nuclear weapons program; a third is Iran's 2013 attacks on U.S. Navy computers, seen by some as possible retaliation over escalations in sanctions weeks earlier. All of these would be considered non-geoeconomic, as they all sought primarily to alter a given military equation between states. The same is true of the persistent attacks by Chinese hackers targeting private firms, typically government contractors, searching for information around U.S. military systems. According to press reports, these hacking attempts against the U.S. military and defense contractors have succeeded in stealing information from more than two dozen weapons programs, including the Patriot missile system, the F-35 joint strike fighter, and the navy's new littoral combat ship; concerning as this is, it is not geoeconomic by our definition.[75]

To be considered geoeconomic, a cyberattack should meet two basic criteria. Because geoeconomics is necessarily concerned with state behavior, a geoeconomic cyberattack must be state sponsored (or at minimum, materially encouraged by government actors). It must also involve an attempt at economic influence. A cyberattack on a major Internet service provider for the sole purpose of reading emails would not be geoeconomic in nature, but attacking the same provider in a way that aimed to weaken the company itself or wreak economic havoc in the target country by causing widespread internet disruptions would be geoeconomic.

Generally speaking, geoeconomic cyberattacks are those making use of economic or financial market mechanisms and seeking to impose economic costs as part of a larger geopolitical agenda. In practice, this will entail cyberattacks meant to degrade or compromise another country's critical economic or financial infrastructure or its major economic or commercial entities (whether such infrastructure or entities are privately or publicly owned)—again, in a way that produces actual or potential geopolitical benefits for the attacking country. In addition to massive theft of commercial intellectual property, geoeconomically directed cyber capabilities provide governments the means to bring down individual companies, undermine entire national economic sectors, and compromise basic infrastructure from electrical grids to banking systems. All this over time can produce weaker nation states more susceptible to external geopolitical manipulation, including in times of crisis.[76]

Of course, as a practical matter, distinctions are hard to come by. Some cyberattacks manifestly involve both geoeconomic and non-geoeconomic elements. In 2007, in what were the first known state-sponsored cyberattacks leveled against another country, Russia unleashed a three-week wave of massive distributed denial-of-service (DDoS) cyberattacks on Estonia. The attacks came amid a heated row between the two states over the Estonian government's removal of a Soviet war monument from the city center in Tallinn to a military cemetery. Websites were suddenly swamped by tens of thousands of visits, thus disabling them. According to reports, the main victims of these attacks were a mix of geopolitical and geoeconomic targets: the websites of the Estonian presidency and parliament, Estonian government ministries, political parties, three of the six major news organizations, two national banks, and one communications firm.[77]

In the days and weeks following the ordeal, most of the headlines focused on the attacks against government targets; the private targets got relatively little notice. But Estonian officials saw in the latter far greater reason for concern. "All major commercial banks, telcos, media outlets, and name servers—the phone books of the Internet—felt the impact," Estonian defense minister Jaak Aaviksoo explained at the time.[78] Aaviksoo was quick to stress that while the medium of influence may have been economic, the scope and effects of the ordeal were unambiguously geopolitical: "This was the first time that a botnet threatened the national security of an entire nation."[79] Much in the way the Russian government has employed other geoeconomic tools, Moscow's cyber intimidation was about reminding Estonia (and other Baltic states) of Russia's continued status as the region's dominant actor and geopolitical arbiter.

As with most geoeconomic instruments, cyber is a tool better suited to some countries than others.[80] Not only do countries such as Russia, Iran, North Korea, and China face fewer legal and popular constraints in committing cyberattacks against private firms, but they also tend to be adroit at translating the stolen data into national security gains without ever leaving the remit of state-controlled channels.

One oft-cited example is China's Project 863, thought to be at least twenty-five years old, which reportedly provides central government funding and guidance for clandestine efforts to acquire U.S. technology and sensitive economic information.[81] It is clear that these attacks have yielded details with vital national security consequences for the United States, including the 2015 theft of the confidential personnel records of millions of U.S. government employees. Leading news outlets as well as private security firms such as Mandiant conclude that the Chinese military may have "obtain[ed] the ability to manipulate American critical infrastructure: power grids and other utilities."[82] And, say outside experts, still other attacks may yield similarly detailed blueprints, although for designs too sophisticated for Chinese targeting entities to translate into immediate operational use.[83]

Also like most other geoeconomic forms of statecraft, the motives and nature of geoeconomic cyberattacks can vary. While many are about industrial espionage in sensitive or strategic sectors and tend toward stealing data, others are more straightforwardly retaliatory.[84] Most analysts took the 2010 attacks on Google and the 2013 attacks against the *New York Times* (following David Barboza's exposé on Chinese premier Wen Jiabao's personal wealth) as primarily acts of intimidation.[85] In September 2012, Telvent, a firm that monitors more than half of North America's oil and gas pipelines, learned that Chinese hackers had penetrated its computer systems. Concerned that the Chinese military was attempting to plant bugs that would cut off energy supplies and shut down the power grid during a future U.S.-China crisis, Telvent was forced to immediately stop remote access to its clients' systems.[86] The Telvent case, say some experts, may be a deterrent signal—a sign that, to quote one Asia expert, "the U.S. shouldn't think that a regional conflict [in the South China Sea or Taiwan Strait] won't touch the U.S. homeland."[87]

Attacks can persist undetected for years, in some cases reportedly draining terabytes of data. Even once attacks are discovered, attribution is extremely difficult (especially when attacks are state sponsored, as states tend to be particularly adroit at covering their tracks). And even when attribution is possible, it remains politically fraught. In the spring of 2013, U.S. officials began openly accusing the Chinese government of persistent cyberattacks against private U.S. firms and critical infrastructure—but this was only after investigative work by private entities produced a strong body of open-source evidence linking the overwhelming share of Chinese-origin cyberattacks to the Chinese army.[88] In its 2014 indictment of five Chinese military members, the U.S. Department of Justice alleges that the Chinese military targeted a number of America's top manufacturers over an eight-year period, from 2006 through early 2014, including nuclear power plant maker Westinghouse Electric, a U.S.-based subsidiary of SolarWorld AG, United States Steel, Allegheny Technologies, and Alcoa. According to press reporting, sources suggest the U.S. government had been readying the case for years, with much of the wait simply over convincing the affected firms to go public.[89]

The sectors most often targeted—finance, energy, IT, aerospace, automotive—are by and large also those sectors that Chinese officials have designated as priority, or "strategic emerging industries."[90] DuPont, Johnson & Johnson, General Electric, RSA, Epsilon, NASDAQ, hundreds more—attacks linked to the Chinese government have grown so pervasive in recent years that most mid- and large-scale U.S. and Western firms now accept that when they express interest in entering the Chinese market (or find themselves bidding against a Chinese firm), cyberattacks will follow.[91]

In one 2009 episode, soon after Chinese state mining giant Chinalco launched its bid to gain a controlling share of Australian mining firm Rio Tinto, Rio Tinto along with two other leading Australian mining companies were hit by crippling cyberattacks. Australian authorities noted more than two hundred attempts to hack into Rio Tinto's networks. The attacks—which continued for the duration of Rio Tinto's negotiations with Chinalco—succeeded in gaining confidential information related to major contract negotiations. Ultimately the talks collapsed. More interesting than the outcome is how the cyberattacks against Rio Tinto figured alongside other, uniquely sovereign bargaining tools Chinese officials openly wielded in pursuit of a deal in a sector Beijing considered "strategic." As Australian press covering the cyberattacks reminded readers, "Rio Tinto Group faced cyber-attacks from China at about the time of the arrest of four executives in the country, while BHP Billiton Ltd. and Fortescue Metals Group Ltd. have also been hit . . . by hackers during a takeover bid for Rio."

And even with sectors that are not particularly strategic, sheer deal size can be threatening to the Chinese government, especially when it comes in the form of foreign direct investment seeking entry into China's domestic market. Coca-Cola was penetrated by Chinese hackers in 2009, amid a failed $2.4 billion bid to acquire the China Huiyuan Juice Group.[92] Had it been concluded, that agreement would have been the largest foreign acquisition of a Chinese company; as such, it would have weakened the Chinese government's own hold on the market, theoretically opening up new avenues of political influence inside China by non-Chinese firms. For the Chinese Communist Party, whose political survival is linked to the degree of economic control the Party holds over the country's domestic markets and factors of production, deals of a certain size necessarily stimulate security concerns. Unsurprisingly, such cases provoke geoeconomic hacking attempts that are, at least in the view of the sponsoring government, meant to protect against national security threats.

Still, whether the hacking is offensive or defensive in nature, the degree of the problem is breathtaking. The overall scope and costs—which

concentrate overwhelmingly on U.S. and European firms—are so great
that even where motives of a given attack are either difficult to define or
more straightforwardly commercial than geopolitical, such attacks nevertheless come with substantial geoeconomic consequences and co-benefits.
The FBI in 2013 alone privately notified 3,000 U.S. companies that they
had been hacked, according to James Lewis, a noted cybersecurity expert
with a Washington-based think tank.[93] Problems of underreporting by firms
notwithstanding, more than 20 percent of the Fortune 500 and roughly one-
third of the Fortune 501–1000 reported exposure to business interruption
as a result of a cyber event (over 20 percent of Fortune 500 firms also reported perceived exposure to cyber penetration).

The costs are difficult to know. Problems with systematic underreporting
by firms and with pinpointing state sponsorship make the job of tabulating
these costs more impressionism than accounting. One British company reported that it lost $1.3 billion from a single state-sponsored attack.[94] An-
other attack, believed to have been launched by North Korea (North
Korea's cyber army receives training and tacit support from China), shut
down tens of thousands of computers and wreaked havoc on major banks,
media, and government agencies in South Korea, where officials estimated
damages at $800 million.[95] All told, estimates by private security researchers
place the annual cost to the global economy from cyber crime (including
both state-sponsored and ordinary criminal activity) at more than $400 bil-
lion, with U.S. losses accounting for one-quarter of this figure.[96] If correct,
these estimates suggest that cyber crime extracts between 15 and 20 percent
of the value created by the Internet.[97] It also serves to shift employment
away from many of the most economically-productive jobs. In the United
States alone, studies estimate that losses from cyber crime could cost as
many as 200,000 American jobs, tantamount to roughly a 0.3 percent decrease in employment for the United States (in other words, in fall 2014,
with U.S. unemployment around 6 percent, correcting for cyber losses
would have reduced unemployment to 5.7 percent).[98]

Energy is among the most attractive targets. The energy sector, including
oil and gas producers and infrastructure operators, suffered more targeted
malware attacks over a six-month period in 2012 than any other industry,
according to one study.[99] Energy companies were targeted in 41 percent of
the malicious software attacks reported to the U.S. Department of Homeland Security in 2012.[100] These attacks have successfully penetrated several of the world's major oil and gas producers, including Saudi Aramco
(officially the Saudi Arabian Oil Company) and Qatar's RasGas.[101]

Arguably the most damaging known attack against American energy targets was "Night Dragon." The cybersecurity firm McAfee, which first un-

covered the attack, described Night Dragon as a "coordinated, covert, and targeted" campaign by China-based hackers to obtain proprietary data from five major Western energy firms, "beginning around 2008 and extending into early 2011."[102] Night Dragon exfiltrated gigabytes of highly sensitive material—everything from financial transactions and bidding data, to information about oil and gas field operations.[103] One U.S. oil executive acknowledged that on at least one occasion a rival national oil company appeared to know his firm's bidding strategy in advance of an auction, which resulted in his firm losing the bid.[104]

In 2012, Iranian hackers attacked Saudi Aramco, the Saudi Arabian national oil company (also the world's largest oil company). Malware linked to Iran struck Aramco's networks, destroying data on and ultimately disabling approximately 30,000 computers and knocking out part of the company's system for as long as two weeks, according to intelligence officials.[105] Leon Panetta, then U.S. secretary of defense, called the attack "probably the most destructive . . . that the private sector has seen to date."[106] According to Saudi officials, the attack aimed to disrupt oil production and although, fortunately, Aramco's physical operations were unharmed by the attack, some security experts believe it could have eventually succeeded in damaging production had it penetrated further into the network.[107]

Some months later, Iran's cyber army turned its sights toward U.S. energy firms. Energy economist Blake Clayton and cyber expert Adam Segal chronicle an episode that began in February 2013 when "malware unintentionally downloaded by workers incapacitated networks on some rigs and platforms. Two months later, U.S. officials revealed that a wave of attacks on U.S. companies, particularly energy companies, had been under way for several months. The attacks, which were unsuccessful in compromising their intended targets, appeared to have originated in Iran."[108] The attacks seemingly aimed not simply to destroy data but to take control of critical internal control systems.[109]

Concerning as Iran's attacks were to U.S. security officials, things would soon get worse. Later in 2013, security researchers at several American cybersecurity companies uncovered a Russian cyber espionage campaign, in which Russian hackers were systematically hacking more than one thousand Western oil and gas computers and energy investment firms. Given Russian dependence on its oil and gas industry, the motive was at least partly industrial espionage. But the hackers were choosing their targets in a way that also seemed intended to seize remote control of industrial control systems, a clear geoeconomic objective.[110]

The asymmetric nature of geoeconomic cyberattacks—a state actor targeting a private firm—can confound the ability of U.S. and other Western government officials to respond. In the spring of 2012, the computer networks of some of the largest banks in the United States came under attack. Sites were brought down for hours at a time. Customers had trouble accessing their accounts. The assaults, believed to have been launched by Iran, marked the first major digital assault of its kind undertaken against U.S. banks by a foreign adversary. Launched shortly after the expansion of U.S. sanctions against Iran, the attacks showed impressive skill and went on for months. By September, Wells Fargo, Bank of America, JPMorgan Chase, and other U.S. financial institutions were besieged with waves of electronic traffic that had swelled from normal levels of 20 gigabits per second to 40, 80, and ultimately 120 gigabits per second—more than three times the volume of traffic that most large banks' websites were equipped to handle. Banks were spending tens of millions of dollars to mitigate the problem.

Meanwhile, in Washington, experts from different agencies debated their options. There were few good ones, given the risks of confrontation and the desire for effectiveness.[111] Later that fall, as the assault continued, the White House decided on a sort of middle course. In a move that was part diplomatic, part technical, officials appealed for help to 120 countries, asking them to target the traffic locally and to remove the malicious code from those servers serving as springboards for the attacks.[112] It was largely though not entirely effective. Attacks slowed, but did not stop entirely for several more weeks; when they finally did cease, it was more on account of the opening of a diplomatic process for easing the sanctions against Iran. Apart from effectiveness in halting the attacks, many saw no real deterrent value. "What was the sanction?" intoned one former defense official who favored a more aggressive response. "The effort didn't hinder the adversary's objectives in the least."[113]

Comparing the episode to the U.S. government's far swifter response to the 2008 attacks on Pentagon computer systems demonstrates how confounding it can be for U.S. legal and policy regimes when states target private commercial actors to make a geopolitical point. Washington faced a similar challenge in December 2014 as policy makers struggled to determine the appropriate retaliatory measures toward North Korea following an attack on the American company Sony Pictures, a subsidiary of the Japanese multinational.[114]

Similar plotlines had emerged earlier in 2014 as U.S. financial firms again fell victim to a wave of sophisticated cyberattacks, once more on the heels of a decision by the Obama administration to ratchet up sanctions against a major country. This time the attacks traced back to Russia, and investigators have said they believed there was at least a "loose connection" between the hackers and the Russian government (at this writing, investigations are ongoing). Certainly there is circumstantial evidence surrounding the timing of the attacks. In April, the Kremlin singled out JPMorgan for criticism when, complying with U.S. sanctions against Russia, the bank blocked a payment from a Russian embassy to the affiliate of a U.S.-sanctioned bank. Russia's foreign ministry called the move by JPMorgan "illegal and absurd."[115]

Attacks on the electronic systems of JPMorgan and nine other major U.S. firms followed within days of the Kremlin's criticism. By the time they were uncovered in August, they constituted the largest such attack against any American company—the breach at JPMorgan alone touched between 76 million American households and 7 million small businesses.[116] The hackers penetrated 90 of JPMorgan's servers, stealing sensitive information on company executives and a list of every application and program deployed on standard JPMorgan computers.[117]

As the scale and gravity of the breach became more clear to U.S. officials, there were few answers to the one question the White House thought most important: what was the motive for the attack? "The question kept coming back, 'Is this plain old theft, or is Putin retaliating?'" one senior U.S. official said, referring to sanctions on Russia. "And the answer was: 'We don't know for sure.'"[118]

Many months after the first attacks were discovered, the source remains unclear, and there is no evidence any money was taken from any institution (casting further doubt on the notion that the hacks were mere criminal activity). Those searching for a motive believe the attack may have been intended to give U.S. leaders pause as they make foreign policy decisions. "If you can steal the data—if you can reach in that far and steal it—you can do anything else you want," former NSA director Keith Alexander explained. "You collapse one bank and our financial structure collapses. . . . If you wanted to send a message, do you think that was significant enough for the U.S. government to say one of the best banks that we have from a cybersecurity perspective was infiltrated by somebody?"[119]

All of this raises the question of what, precisely, is to be done about the problem. Analysts believe countries will tolerate cyber crime as long as it stays at "acceptable levels"—thought to be less than 2 percent of GDP (current estimates suggest cyber crime in the United States is between 0.64 and 1 percent of GDP).[120] Government tolerance levels for state-sponsored cyberattacks, geoeconomic or otherwise, are even less well understood.

Most analysts interpret the United States as drawing a red line at loss of life or major economic damage. But U.S. officials have remained intentionally vague as to what "major" might mean, so as to avoid specifying a clear standard and thereby giving attacking countries a threshold they could remain just shy of in their attacks.

To date, U.S. officials have attempted to maintain a distinction between the type of spying that the United States does, which they claim is done for national security purposes, and spying for commercial purposes, which they accuse China of doing. As *New York Times* reporter David Sanger explained, the United States "does not go in and steal trade secrets the way they accuse the Chinese of doing, so that they can then give those trade secrets to American companies."[121] But in countries like China, where economic and regime security are so closely linked, and where geoeconomic tools are so often the instruments of first resort, the attempted distinction tends to be lost on its target audience. Thus, when the Chinese President pledged during a visit to the U.S. in September 2015 that, "the Chinese government will not in whatever form engage in commercial theft," many in Washington were skeptical.[122] Indeed, just three weeks after President Xi's pledge, the cybersecurity firm Crowdstrike reported that it had detected continued efforts by Chinese attackers "affiliated with the Chinese government" to "penetrate U.S. corporate networks—just the kind of behavior that Mr. Xi promised to stop."[123]

"It's a very American way of thinking about this," says Sanger. "It somewhat puzzles the Chinese and many other countries for whom their state-owned industries are part of their national security structure. They sort of look, and don't really understand what it is the United States is trying to accomplish by making this distinction."[124]

Economic Assistance

The practice of deploying aid—whether military aid, bilateral development assistance, or humanitarian assistance—to buy strategic influence is one of the most straightforward examples of geoeconomic tools and has been around as long as diplomacy itself. To be sure, most military and humanitarian aid is geoeconomic only in the broadest sense, because money is fungible (meaning that any military or humanitarian assistance dollars a government receives can enable it to redirect or save funds that it would have otherwise spent). This alone makes military and humanitarian aid worth at least including—although perhaps not prioritizing—in any conceptual framework of geoeconomics. But there are other reasons for including them. First, there are exceptions to this general rule—instances where military or humanitarian assistance comes with geoeconomic underpinnings that go beyond the mere fungibility of official assistance. Second, even when there is nothing especially geoeconomic about cases of military and humanitarian aid beyond their fungibility, they can nevertheless interact with other, more clearly geoeconomic aspects of statecraft in important ways.

Some of the largest and longest-running examples come from the United States, which spends upward of $5.5 billion in foreign military financing every year. Amounts are often written into diplomatic agreements, as with Israel and Egypt within the terms of the Camp David accords.[125]

But beyond the "how much," there are also important questions in the "how" of military financing and the motivations underlying it. In particular, as both Russia and Saudi Arabia have recently proven, military aid, when done well, can register powerful geopolitical impacts on parties other than the beneficiary.

Certainly Saudi Arabia's December 2013 $3 billion aid package to Lebanon furthered Riyadh's desire to help the Lebanese government counter the Shi'a militant group Hezbollah. "If a wealthy patron were all the Lebanese Army needed to counter the Shiite militant group Hezbollah as the dominant force in the country," press reports explained at the time, "the recent $3 billion grant from Saudi Arabia might make a decisive difference in the country's complex political landscape."[126] But, curiously, the package—nearly twice Lebanon's $1.7 billion annual defense budget—came earmarked to buy French (rather than U.S.) arms and, as such, would be "unlikely to give the army what it needs most," according to both supporters and opponents of Hezbollah in Lebanon.[127] And even if it does, it will likely take years to make an impact.[128]

Why would the Saudis accept less than maximum strategic return on their investment? Because weakening Hezbollah was not Riyadh's only geopolitical aim. Though the Saudis are "clearly alarmed at Hezbollah's staying power and its intervention in Syria's civil war," the December aid package to Lebanon "was intended as much to send a message to the United States as to shift the military balance."[129] The Saudis were declaring what some called a "tactical divorce" from Washington over their frustrations with U.S. policies on Syria and Iran.[130]

Armenia was among several countries from the former Soviet Union that, on considering enhanced links with the European Union, found itself subject to intense pressure from Moscow beginning in 2013. Intent on seeing Armenia remain within Russia's orbit and having exhausted other powers of persuasion, Russia stepped up military aid to Azerbaijan, delivering nearly $1 billion worth of tanks, artillery systems, and infantry fighting vehicles in 2013—thereby exaggerating tensions lingering from the Nagorno-Karabakh War of 1988 to 1991.[131] Shortly thereafter, Armenia announced that it would not sign an association agreement with the European Union and would join instead the Eurasian Customs Union, which to that point included only Russia, Belarus, and Kazakhstan.[132] From Azerbaijan's perspective, the episode itself seems a fairly straightforward case of military assistance. Other than the fact that this military assistance potentially allowed Azerbaijan to redirect at least some of its planned military spending to other uses, it evinces little geoeconomic logic. But from Moscow's perspective, $1 billion in military spending was a cost-effective means of signaling that Armenia could expect disastrous geopolitical consequences for any refusal to join Russia's customs union. As such, the episode attests not just to how traditional politico-military and geoeconomic tactics can work in tandem but also to how some states are putting military activities firmly in the service of geoeconomic aims.

Humanitarian aid, while arguably an even less interesting form of geoeconomics than military assistance, can yield outsized geopolitical dividends. Humanitarian aid tends to come with a crisis discount of sorts: for countries on the receiving end, reeling from disaster, vulnerability tends to magnify the geopolitical significance of aid (or the lack of it, in some cases). This seems straightforward enough. But a survey of some of the most geoeconomically resonant cases of humanitarian aid demonstrates that it is not so much that geopolitical sensitivities are magnified *because of* crisis or disaster; rather, these are cases where geopolitical stakes were heightened well prior to humanitarian assistance. As a result, states are not shy about treating humanitarian aid as a geoeconomic exercise. In the wake of 2013's Typhoon Haiyan, for example, the outpouring of foreign assistance to the hundreds of thousands of homeless Filipinos quickly proved to be a testing ground for geoeconomic tools.[133] The United States and its allies worked intensely to get the Philippines—an important actor in the U.S. pivot to Asia—back on its feet through aid and other support. China, on the other hand, kept its attention on its maritime disputes with Manila around the Scarborough Shoal, choosing to keep its aid at what many described as "paltry" levels.[134] The Obama administration's prompt response was geopolitically advantageous, cementing the Aquino government's shift toward the United States.

If military and humanitarian aid can be sometimes borderline in their geoeconomic dimension, bilateral economic (development) assistance has no such ambiguities. Not only is it often squarely geoeconomic, but—courtesy of a newly emergent set of development donors, replete with their own rules—it is also the most interesting class of aid as a geoeconomic tool. Official development assistance (ODA) reached a record high in 2013, helped along by spending increases topping 20–30 percent in countries such as Russia and Japan.[135] With the rise of new donors, the profile of recipient states is shifting as well. Even as overall assistance levels touched record highs in 2013, combined assistance to Africa fell by 5.6 percent over the same period.[136] Aid flows to certain middle-income states, meanwhile, are on the rise—some of the largest aid increases have gone to states such as Pakistan, Egypt, and India, which also tend to carry greater geopolitical weight. This at least raises the question of whether bilateral assistance flows are, on the whole, growing more oriented toward strategic goals than pure development ones.

No set of countries better epitomizes this new donor class than the Gulf Cooperation Council countries, nor is there any better demonstration of the geoeconomics motivating the GCC's aid than in Egypt, where pledged GCC assistance has totaled roughly $22 billion between 2011 and 2013 alone. Between President Mubarak's downfall in February 2011 and President Morsi's ouster in July 2013, Qatar provided $8 billion to Egypt, including $4 billion in central bank deposits and $1 billion in grants.[137] Qatar pledged a further $18 billion in 2012, intended to support tourism and industry projects along Egypt's Mediterranean coast over five years, but the Egyptian military intervened to remove President Morsi before Doha managed to deliver on it. Other GCC states took an equal and opposite bet on Egypt's political future. Kuwait, United Arab Emirates (UAE), and Saudi Arabia responded to Doha's $8 billion during Morsi's rule by raising the ante, pledging some $12 billion in Egypt immediately upon Morsi's removal. (Kuwait, UAE, and Saudi Arabia have since given even more money to Egypt, reportedly totaling more than $20 billion as of fall 2014.) For UAE, development assistance increased 375 percent in 2013.[138]

At least for some Gulf countries, this strategy of propping up Morsi's successors appears to be paying geopolitical dividends. After two years of helping the current el-Sissi regime weather economic and security woes, Saudi Arabia and Egypt marked the anniversary by signing the July 2015 Cairo Declaration, which calls for the establishment of a joint Arab military force and the expansion of economic ties between the two countries. Egypt's first contribution to the partnership came soon after, when, in September 2015, it sent 800 troops to Yemen to join the Saudi-led fight against Houthi rebels there, lending the campaign an air of multilateralism.[139]

With neighbors so openly vying for influence through assistance, it is little surprise that 10 percent of Egypt's GDP now comes from foreign assistance. A similar if scaled-down version of these events has played out in Lebanon, where the $12 billion the Lebanese government has received in GCC assistance over the past decade has so embedded itself in the country's fiscal picture that "Lebanon cannot survive without the Gulf countries," admits Mohammad Choucair, Lebanon's head of commerce, industry, and agriculture.[140] Gulf official donors distinguish themselves on sheer magnitude—the $8 billion in assistance Qatar spent on the Morsi government in Egypt alone in 2012 and 2013 amounts to roughly 40 percent of the entire bilateral economic assistance request presented to the U.S. Congress for 2013.

GCC donor states are also uninhibited about their geoeconomic motives. Such was Qatar's support (economic, military, and humanitarian) for Libyan rebels that, on taking Qaddafi's Bab al-Aziziya palace complex in August 2012, the rebels raised the Qatari flag in appreciation.[141] Or take the $1.5 billion Saudi Arabia loaned to Pakistan in March 2014 "to help Islamabad shore up its foreign exchange reserves, meet debt-service obligations and undertake large energy and infrastructure projects, Pakistani officials [explained to] Reuters."[142] According to press reports, "the offer [came] in exchange for Pakistani assistance with internal security needs in Saudi Arabia."[143] However, Pakistani opposition officials claim the Saudi aid has "come at the cost of Pakistan's independent stand on Syria."[144]

It is true that virtually all of the billions in bilateral assistance dollars spent by Gulf countries remain confined to the Middle East and North Africa. But it hardly follows that Gulf leaders do not have countries outside their region in mind as primary targets of this spending. In fact, Gulf states, all too aware they are locked in a neighborhood spending race, regularly compete and spend regionally in ways designed to win the favor of the United States, or at least to shift policy in Washington.[145] "Qatar is a secure little kernel with huge resources that has chosen to use those resources in foreign policy," Middle East expert Paul Salem told the *New York Times* after Qatar announced new financial support for Hamas in late 2012. "They have no constraints. They can take any position anytime anywhere."[146] And the value of this dexterity goes both ways: Washington shows little pause in calling on Doha's connections when necessary. Qatar led the negotiations with the al-Qa'ida affiliate in Syria that freed American writer Peter Theo Curtis in August 2014, and it engineered the prisoner swap that freed U.S. soldier Bowe Bergdahl in exchange for five Taliban prisoners in Guantánamo Bay.

Beyond the GCC states, this geoeconomic donor set includes new donors such as South Korea, "re-emerging donors" such as Russia, and long-standing donors such as Japan that are overhauling their traditionally large assistance portfolios to bring greater strategic returns.[147] The only member of the OECD's development assistance committee that was itself once a recipient of aid, South Korea views its overseas assistance as a centerpiece of its self-described ascent into a "global middle power."[148] Roughly two-thirds of Korea's assistance remains in Asia, especially in Southeast Asia, where regional press commentators are quick to note that "South Korea's official development assistance (ODA) will be a major and useful instrument for fostering a new constructive relationship with other ASEAN states."[149]

Japan's national security strategy, released in December 2013, directs Japan to step up its official development assistance and make a greater contribution to regional peace, in part through the "strategic utilization of ODA."[150] In June 2014, an expert panel under Japanese foreign minister Fumio Kishida finalized a report that recommended transforming Japan's foreign aid policy into a strategic diplomatic tool; swiftly embracing the panel's conclusions, Prime Minister Shinzo Abe ordered the reforms to be enacted within six months. The move marked the final about-face for Japan's long-standing aversion to aid as a geopolitical tool.[151]

In its sharper varieties, however, these more geoeconomic-minded assistance sums can come with implicit noncompete clauses, as Belarus found out the hard way when it caught Moscow's ire for seeking aid from China.[152] It can also be used to supplement negative pressure, as Moscow's December 2013 aid package to Kiev proved.[153] The aid packages, promulgated as they were in conjunction with punishing trade sanctions, were Moscow's way of making crystal clear its ability to reward and punish Kiev's foreign policy choices with equal force.[154]

Among the newest, most powerful conduits for converting development-minded investment dollars into geopolitical influence are the cohort of state-owned development banks, which are extending financing to the developing world at less than market rates and in record volumes. As of April 2014, Brazil's BNDES had amassed four times more lending capacity than the World Bank, while the China Development Bank CDB, with total assets in excess of $980 billion, offers a loan book bigger than that of JPMorgan Chase.[155] These state owned banks have far, far deeper coffers than most organs of government policy; in some cases, as with China's CDB, these banks are also under orders to build a customer base outside their domestic borders. Thus far this has included not just private clients but other foreign government entities, often drawn in by substantial financing at below-market terms (the $40 billion Venezuela has received from the CDB—about $1,400 for every Venezuelan man, woman, and child—being a leading example).[156]

The emergence of the BRICS Bank—billed somewhat openly as a BRICS-led alternative to the World Bank—is one of the clearest signals yet that assistance will no longer always be dictated on Western terms. Capitalized initially at $100 billion and almost sure to focus on Africa, the bank will provide China with additional means of financing its expansion on that continent. But there may be more to it. Given the plethora of existing tools to finance resource investment in the developing world, the move to set up a multilateral development bank of which no Western nation is a member signals not only confidence in an alternative model but also a desire to instill it with a knowledge base and, say some, to rethink basic organizing principles of the international financial system.[157] The bank is still a long way from completion, but BRICS leaders have begun to outline certain structural features—for example, the new bank will come with an agreement meant to safeguard a role for the many state-owned enterprises of its member countries (similarly, analysts expect that projects stemming from the new Chinese-led Asian Infrastructure Investment Bank will be dominated by Chinese firms).[158] The idea was initiated by Beijing and met with strong interest from the remaining BRICS participants—all reportedly eager to ensure that their state champions were not cut from BRICS bank-funded projects.[159]

Financial and Monetary Policy

From the Maidan in Ukraine to the vegetable vendor in Tunisia, the tendency to cast popular uprisings and individual figureheads as the leading protagonists in revolution or the rise of empire seems as strong today as in Bismarck or Napoleon's day. But several historians have tended to argue that "quiet transformations in management of finance have a much greater effect on national power and its global expressions."[160] Jeremi Suri surveys some of the world's most dominating empires—the United Kingdom, Qing China, and the Soviet Union—to demonstrate how "ambitious ideological projects and impressive territorial conquests have less enduring influence on the leverage of states than the mobilization and management of capital. . . . National power is fundamentally financial."[161]

Suri's view recalls similar arguments by Paul Kennedy, Charles Tilly, Michael Mazarr, and David Landes, among others, each pointing to the availability of cheap capital for investment and spending as forming "the necessary foundation for all manifestations of state power."[162] Consider the British Empire. The single largest reason British imperialism prevailed against improbable odds and hostile powers was the late seventeenth-century creation of a new system for the management of revenue and credit. In return for favorable borrowing terms, the British crown under William III provided legal sanction for London credit markets and judicial enforcement of contract obligations, even obligations against the crown. By binding the crown as subject to credit obligations, British rulers succeeded in opening up new, vastly more affordable financing streams and flexibility that "in turn greatly strengthened its options in war and other forms of international competition," Suri explains.[163]

The chief lessons learned by William III and his successors are at least as relevant today. And while again there is no shortage of casual observation linking a country's financial and fiscal health to its power projection in general terms, strikingly few have attempted to pinpoint the precise transmission channels between the two, or to revisit how, if at all, these channels have evolved in light of the sweeping changes that have redrawn the global financial and monetary landscape over the past decade or so.[164]

The reasons for this may be largely structural. These fields are not well incentivized to interact, especially in Western policy-making circles. Probably more than any other dimension of geoeconomics, financial and monetary policy tends to lie beyond reach for U.S. officials primarily preoccupied with geopolitics—just as finance and monetary officials downplay the geopolitical dimensions of their work, perhaps more so than any other brand of U.S. international economic policy maker. Both sides have their reasons. And this strict bifurcation worked well enough for the more than six decades of Pax Americana.

But there are several reasons to think that over the coming years the geopolitics of monetary and financial policy might resurface in sharpened form: a rising renminbi (RMB), a set of countries agitating for a smaller role for the dollar, a euro that despite current troubles may continue to mature, and global debates about quantitative easing. If a sharpened brand of financial and monetary geopolitics does resurface, it is doubtful that the current norms—unwritten rules that keep the work of Western foreign ministries comfortably distant from that of finance ministries and central banks—will serve either side well.

Beyond the general ties linking sound monetary policy to a healthy economy and then to geopolitical influence, there are three basic transmission channels through which states can translate monetary policy tools into geopolitical influence: the global footprint of a country's currency, the ability to raise funds at low cost, and the ability to impact another country's borrowing costs. And while these channels themselves are not new, they operate on such a vastly altered landscape as to bear little resemblance to their former shape.

Beginning with the first of these, how does the global footprint of a country's currency allow it to project power?

As Charles Kindleberger once put it, "a country's exchange rate is more than a number. It is an emblem of its importance in the world, and a sort of international status symbol."[165] Consider the introduction of the euro. When the European Union launched its common currency in 2001, the euro was widely hailed as the largest development in global currency markets since the Bretton Woods conference of 1944.[166] But whether or not the euro's introduction indeed marked "the start of a new era for Europe," a period in which European economies are knitted into a "single, more efficient, and productive whole," these benefits were of secondary importance to the euro's early architects.[167] A clearer account begins in 1970s Germany—in particular with German chancellor Helmut Schmidt's visit to the German Bundesbank in 1978, on the eve of the European Council gathering that initiated the European Monetary System. In a transcript that merits quoting at length, Schmidt exhorted German central bankers to support a European monetary (and currency) union—making clear that this was, above all, an issue of geopolitics:

> What now concerns German policy, I will say in all simplicity, yet all urgency, without an efficiently functioning Common Market, without an economically and politically influential European Community, German foreign policy is not to be conducted successfully. German foreign policy rests on two great pillars: the European Community and the North Atlantic alliance. . . . The whole game that we have played in the last ten years towards the Soviet Union, towards the eastern European countries, that we have played over Berlin, in order to steady this fateful city in its position, all this would not have been possible without these two pillars behind it. . . .
>
> By holding firmly to our duties we have grown ever stronger relative to our own Western allies. And we have also attained very great political weight in their eyes. It is all the more necessary for us to clothe ourselves in this European mantle. We need this mantle not only to cover our foreign policy nakednesses, like Berlin or Auschwitz, but we need it also to cover these ever-increasing relative strengths, economic, political, military, of the German Federal Republic within the West. The more they come into view, the harder it becomes to secure our room for manoeuvre. The more desirable it is that we are able to lean on these two pillars, which are simultaneously here a mantle for us, in which we can conceal our strength a bit. . . .

On the other hand, I said the European Monetary System involves risks. I repeat: it involves essential chances too, especially if it is successful, the chance for us that the European Community will not decay. It is really a vital precondition for German foreign policy and its autonomy. It offers chances of the economic sort too, which I have not placed in the foreground of this presentation, but which I do not wish to hide. . . .

Here there are limits even for us, ladies and gentlemen. We cannot intervene *ad libitum* in favour of a dollar that is treated like a football by its own government, by its own treasury, by its own Federal Reserve Bank. We cannot do that. But if we then sometime have to say: this is the end of the line, we will then need allies here in Europe. For that is not so easy to do to the chief military member of the North Atlantic alliance. Then we will need comrades who will stand by us and say: yes, indeed, the Germans are right and it's not in our French interest that European currencies constantly be sacrificed in market intervention in favour of a dollar badly treated by its own country . . . [F]or me the whole thing has been embedded from the start and remains embedded [in] foreign policy considerations.[168]

Nearly four decades on, several EU member states continue to regard the euro as mostly a geopolitical project. In January 2014, even as the euro crisis remained far from resolved, Latvia became the eighteenth EU member to adopt the currency. Headlines greeted the move in straightforwardly geoeconomic terms: "Latvia Sees Joining Euro as Extra Protection against Russia." Latvian finance minister Andris Vilks pointed to the crisis in Ukraine as underscoring the importance of Latvia's move toward the euro. "Russia isn't going to change," Vilks explained to the media.[169] "We know our neighbor. There was before, and there will be, a lot of unpredictable conditions. It is very important for the countries to stick together, with the EU." Lithuania joined in early 2015, with ministers in Vilnius couching their decision in similar terms. "It has a symbolic connotation: we see ourselves being as integrated as possible into Europe," explained Rolandas Krisciunas, Lithuanian vice-minister for foreign affairs.[170]

When it comes to understanding how having a large global footprint for a country's currency can bring geopolitical benefits, beyond the euro there is only really one other present case, only one other truly global currency, from which to draw. To be sure, the United States enjoys a number of strategic benefits arising from the dollar's global role.[171] It serves as "disaster insurance"—in times of international financial or geopolitical turmoil, money flees to dollars, boosting U.S. buying power and hence the nation's capacity to respond effectively.[172] It affords the United States the unique ability to run sizeable fiscal and current account deficits while borrowing in its own currency.[173] And it enables the sort of financial sanctions that—whether leveled against particular banks or companies or meant to isolate entire countries, as with Iran—now seem a fixture of U.S. foreign policy. After more than sixty years, these geoeconomic "privileges" have so permeated American thinking as to become implicitly assumed.

Yet doubts are growing about how long the dollar's unrivaled status will last.[174] Reserve holders have been diversifying—the share of minor monies in global reserves has tripled over the last six years.[175] Calls to replace the dollar's global role, stoked by the 2008–2009 financial crisis and more recently by the string of fiscal and debt ceiling domestic political stand-offs in Washington, are now standard refrains in the yearly BRICS summitry—and can also be heard in friendlier capitals, including Paris and Brussels.[176] "Among Chinese officials and scholars," explains *Financial Times* journalist Geoff Dyer, "there is a widely held view that the U.S. has been abusing its position as controller of the main reserve currency by pursuing irresponsible economic policies. Nor do they hide the underlying geopolitical objective of the currency push—to place limits on the role of the dollar in the international monetary system."[177] In its commentary amid the October 2013 U.S. debt ceiling debates, the official Chinese press agency, Xinhua, strengthened its call for a new reserve currency with "a scathing indictment of the United States' broader role in the world," calling for a "de-Americanized world" and criticizing the United States on a series of political and security issues well beyond the realm of monetary or economic policy.[178]

If present trends continue, the next decade may see the largest changes to the world's monetary architecture since 1945 and (equally important to China) since the reforms of Deng Xiaoping.[179] Chapter 4 outlines China's long-term strategy for the renminbi in more detail; at this stage, just two points are worth noting. One, an internationalizing RMB comes with several economic and geopolitical implications, some of which are in tension with one another, at least in terms of U.S. interests. Sanctions are made harder, even as certain U.S. economic interests (a market-determined exchange rate for the RMB, for example) are helped. Because reconciling these tensions would require trade-offs across U.S. national interests, these issues tend to defy Washington's ability to consider them in any comprehensive way.

Second, little is known about the ability of the global monetary system to accommodate an additional reserve currency.[180] The world already has two reserve currencies, the dollar and the euro, and beyond general assumptions, the effects of accommodating a third are largely unknown and untested.[181] History provides little precedent for the world's ability to operate with multiple "fiat" reserve currencies (previous such eras of floating exchange rates among major currencies all ultimately linked back to gold), and it remains an open question as to whether the United States can retain enough of the economic advantages of reserve currency status while accommodating the emergence of the RMB as a reserve currency.[182] Further, the world has no modern precedent for a global reserve currency that is not administered by a democratic country.[183]

Even if the United States can retain enough of these economic advantages, there are geopolitical considerations to weigh, including dampened effectiveness for U.S. economic sanctions and diminished regional influence in Asia and beyond. In today's financial world, it is difficult to know whether these American "privileges" reside on a spectrum or are more binary in nature. What is clear is that losing these advantages would force the United States to confront new trade-offs between foreign policy objectives and the higher domestic economic costs required to support those objectives.

Such uncertainty comes at an interesting time. Questions of reserve currency status matter more today than in previous eras because reserves are now at far greater levels than in previous eras (ten times what they were fifteen years ago), with much of this reserve buildup in developing Asia.[184] Some argue that Asia's acquisition of reserves is a function of its security environment.[185] Further, these reserve stockpiles tend to be far more opaque than in decades past, creating more uncertainty and potential for reverberations into geopolitics. In March 2014, for example, the U.S. Federal Reserve saw the sharpest-ever weekly drop in U.S. government debt held on behalf of official foreign institutions—$105 billion in a single week. While it was officially unclear which country was responsible for the drop, all sides were virtually certain that it was Russia, withdrawing its U.S. holdings in response to tensions and threats of sanctions over Ukraine.[186]

These concerns pale against those posed by the size and opacity of Beijing's holdings. Because China uses intermediaries, typically based in Europe, to mask large portions of its holdings, neither global markets nor U.S. officials have a clear understanding of exactly how much U.S. debt China holds.[187] By February 2014, for example, Belgium had vaulted past countries known for their financial centers, as well as major oil-exporting nations, to become the third-largest foreign holder of U.S. government debt behind China and Japan, with $341.2 billion (up from $166.8 billion just six months earlier, in August 2013)—this in a country of 11 million people with an annual gross domestic product of $484 billion.[188]

The curious climb in Belgium's U.S. Treasury holdings merely reflects the secret buying of top-rated sovereign debt by other countries using intermediaries to mask their purchases. "We know it's not Belgium buying, it's way too much. We need to look at that country's custody services," said Marc

Chandler, chief currency strategist at Brown Brothers Harriman.[189] Others in the financial blogosphere were more direct: "In summary: someone, *unclear who,* operating through Belgium and most likely the Euroclear service (possible but unconfirmed), has added a record $141 billion in Treasury holdings since December, or the month in which Bernanke announced the start of the Taper, bringing the host's total to an unprecedented $341 billion!"[190] Others eventually traced the mysterious Belgian purchases back to Beijing.[191]

Beyond the size of a currency's footprint in global markets, a second channel through which monetary policy can translate into geoeconomic influence is the extent to which a country can raise funds at low cost. This is mostly a story of how a nation's domestic economic housekeeping can determine its ability to mobilize and sustain financing for wars and other less extreme security contests. Certainly this channel can be related to the first, insofar as the ability to borrow cheaply in one's own currency, especially at times of political or economic uncertainty, undoubtedly constitutes one of the biggest perks of reserve currency status. But the point is also broader. For example, countries where debt is primarily domestically held tend to be somewhat better insulated in times of crisis—as with Japan after the 2011 earthquake and Fukushima nuclear disaster.[192]

There are plenty of examples attesting to how one state's ability to impact another's borrowing costs can confer geopolitical leverage—often when states are at their most vulnerable. "Weak currencies make for timid states," as Cornell's Jonathan Kirshner has put it, referring to the geopolitical headaches that precarious borrowing positions can create for countries.[193] Here the 1956 Suez Canal crisis again enters as the paradigmatic case. The U.S. use of loan guarantees to force Israel to the negotiating table with the Palestinians in 1991 is equally instructive.[194] When Israel requested $10 billion in loan guarantees from Washington to finance the resettlement of Soviet Jews in late 1990, President George H. W. Bush asked Congress to delay action on the loan guarantee while he worked to arrange an Arab-Israeli peace conference. Only after Israeli prime minister Yitzhak Rabin announced a settlement freeze was the loan guarantee program approved.[195]

More recently, in response to the EU's April 2013 proposed bailout for Cyprus (which would have entailed losses for Russian investors), the Kremlin threatened to review the euro's share in Russia's €537 billion of foreign exchange reserves, while the Russian finance minister issued unspecified warnings of retaliation. Few took the Kremlin's threats seriously. But, coming as they did amid a flaring of the eurozone crisis, portents of this sort did not necessarily need to stand up to individual scrutiny in order to register effect. Investors' nerves were frayed, and threats, even seemingly minor ones, had a way of compounding in self-reinforcing and unpredictable ways.

Alongside cases like this, where a state brandishes but does not act on threats to manipulate another state's borrowing costs, there are also opposite cases: states that actually follow through on what are almost certainly geoeconomic gestures involving another state's borrowing costs, all without any official acknowledgment of what is afoot. Qatar tripled its holdings of Egyptian treasury bills in the third quarter of 2013—immediately after President Morsi was ousted, and right as Egypt's new military rulers were in the process of giving back billions in Qatari assistance that Doha had lavished on President Morsi's administration. Given Doha's newly limited options for leverage in a post-Morsi Egypt now hostile to its attempts at influence, Egyptian treasuries were not merely a cost-effective alternative but were arguably among Doha's only options.

And not least, some geoeconomic attempts to capitalize on a state's borrowing costs in moments of crisis are just that: neither threats nor denials, merely attempts. Take Russia's November 2013 bailout package to Ukraine. In its initial proffering, the package stood out as an example of how Russia, by meeting Ukraine's pressing financing needs at rates Ukraine could afford (well below what the market would have commanded and without any of the difficult reforms the IMF would have demanded), managed to bend the course of Ukraine's foreign policy toward Moscow's preferences at a critical juncture. But within months, the package, or at least the $3 billion in euro-denominated bonds that Moscow actually delivered before halting the remaining portions, came to stand for the leverage that a sovereign creditor can have over a sovereign debtor.[196] "Ukraine has two debt problems," as Anna Gelpern put it. "First, it faces shrinking revenues, rising costs, and a spike in foreign debt payments over the next two years. This is a common problem, easily managed with familiar market tools and international institutions. Ukraine's other debt problem is neither common nor manageable: its leading bond holder is annexing parts of its territory and stoking militant separatists from within."[197]

Together Ukraine's two debt problems expose an awkward oversight in the world's financial architecture. "The system is set up as if market finance and political patronage were distinct," adds Gelpern. "When governments participate as debtors or creditors in the global capital markets, they are expected to use private deal technology, and abide by the rules and incentives of these markets. When governments put on their power-political hats, they are expected to retreat to political fora, removed from the markets. Being sovereign, they do not have to."[198]

Russia can be counted on to act crudely in its geoeconomics more often than not. But in many respects, the more powerful examples here are the more subtle ones. China's decision not to devalue its currency during the 1997–1998 Asian financial crisis earned Beijing gratitude across the region that lingers today and provided Beijing an opportunity to buoy up its neighbors, especially newly repatriated Hong Kong.[199] The U.S. handling of the 1994 Mexican peso crisis also reaped significant geopolitical returns. After President Bill Clinton failed to pass a stabilization act in Congress, he went to a fallback option, authorizing U.S. financial assistance through the Treasury's Exchange Stabilization Fund (ESF). The ESF allowed the provision of funds to Mexico without legislative approval; unilaterally drawing upon $20 billion to stabilize America's southern neighbor was, in the words of Treasury secretary Robert Rubin, the "largest nonmilitary international commitment by the U.S. government since the Marshall plan."[200] Largely thanks to U.S. assistance, the Mexican economy averted disaster.[201] And, of course, a stable Mexico is essential to U.S. power projection in the world.

The most powerful present-day example is that of Germany and its handling of the eurozone.[202] Harnessing the power of bond markets, as Helmut Schmidt anticipated in 1978, Germany has done more to remake Europe in its likeness in the past four years than it had accomplished in the past century.[203] Through forging the eurozone, German has also realized its century-long quest for a pliant European market for German manufacturing.[204] Both of these were things it had previously tried (and failed) to accomplish by force. Further underscoring the growing extent to which market realities are shaping geopolitical outcomes, Germany is effectively dictating the terms on which foreign capital into the eurozone is solicited.[205] Often this occurs in ways that impinge on U.S. leverage.[206]

Obviously, the degree to which a state depends on external creditors for financing determines the degree of vulnerability. Japan has for more than a decade managed with debt that was predicted to hit 230 percent of GDP by late 2014—a level that for most other countries would be considered as risking saturation among bondholders.[207] But, again, a far greater share of Japan's debt is domestically held. For other nations, a much higher percentage of debt is externally held. In particular, this is true of the United States, where one creditor, China, possesses more than half of all outstanding debts at certain maturities.[208] Reserving the specifics of this China-U.S. case for Chapter 4, there are, generally speaking, three points worth keeping in mind when it comes to sizing up the potential geopolitical leverage that might come from the ability to influence another country's sovereign borrowing costs.

The first point is that, from a geopolitical standpoint, it matters whether a country's external debt is in mostly private or sovereign hands. Returning to the British Empire, one lesson that William III's successors failed to appreciate is how the Bank of England's investors would also become supporters of the revolutionary settlements, their financial fates intertwined. But if King George misjudged just how easily creditors' investment portfolios can come to dictate their foreign policy preferences, America's early founders made no such mistake. This, after all, is exactly what Alexander Hamilton had in mind with the Bank of the United States and the assumption of state debts. The bank's creation meant that creditors of the United States, wealthy elites in all thirteen colonies, now had a vested interest in the success of the Union.

The second point is that there is still a good deal of domestic bias in most sovereign debt markets, meaning that a sizeable portion of a country's sovereign debt is still domestically held; the United States and Europe are no exception. But with this sharp rise in official reserves and the corresponding preference for "safe" assets, reserve managers can and do account for a large share of some markets (in recent years foreign official investors have held around 55 percent of the one-to-five year segment of the U.S. Treasury curve, with China likely accounting for more than 20 percent of the outstanding $10 trillion stock of marketable U.S. government debt).[209] This in turn creates the risk of large and destabilizing portfolio shifts. The prospect of such a sudden shift is remote—to be sure, the U.S. Federal Reserve has proven its ability as a purchaser of resort—but it is not zero.

The third general point is that there is at least the potential—again, albeit remote—that foreign official purchasers could marshal these assets to make a geopolitical statement. Evidence to this effect is scant and generally not well supported. After leaving public office, former Treasury secretary Hank Paulson claimed that Moscow had approached China in 2008, urging that their governments execute a coordinated shorting of U.S. government-sponsored enterprises (GSEs), including Fannie Mae and Freddie Mac, in an apparent effort to put financial pressure on the U.S. government.[210] As noted earlier, Moscow more recently signaled its displeasure with the EU's handling of the Cyprus bailout by threatening to review the euro's share in Russia's €537 billion of foreign exchange reserves (the outsized Cypriot banking sector serves as an offshore hub for substantial Russian savings).[211] Similarly, during tensions between the West and Russia over Ukraine, Moscow threatened to dump its holdings of U.S. sovereign debt (a feat that would go well beyond simply moving these holdings so as to remove them from any risk of sanctions) and not so subtly withdrew more than $100 billion in custodial holdings from the U.S. Federal Reserve.[212]

Still, most of today's large external creditor states have so far largely shied away from overt attempts to exercise the geoeconomic power implied by their respective official savings—Costa Rican bond purchases for repudiating recognition of Taiwan are the exception, not the rule. Nor, in the case of China, is there any evidence that observed portfolio shifts in Chinese official holdings have been driven by anything other than loss aversion; at worst, certain shifts have been accompanied by official statements meant to help punctuate policy positions and messages to Washington that Chinese officials had long sought to underscore.

The reason most often cited for why any large-scale sell-off is unlikely is that it is economically irrational, as it would affect the value of the seller's holdings. This, though, assumes an economic lens on a question that may well be motivated by geopolitical interests. Most people think nothing of it when countries spend billions of dollars developing and deploying military weapons systems. If, say, Russian president Vladimir Putin is looking to invest $100 billion in blunting the power projection capacity of NATO and the EU, why is it seen as so forthrightly rational to spend this sum on weapons that are unlikely to alter the balance of military power in the region, but somehow irrational to spend the same $100 billion to undermine the ability of Ukraine's new government to borrow at reasonable rates and thus its capacity to resist Russian demands? For many states, if the aim is geopolitical rather than economic return on one's investment, it is far from clear that investment in military hardware is the wiser of the two choices.

There may be reason to hope that as China internationalizes the RMB and finds itself in the position of having sovereign creditors for its sovereign debt, the prospect of direct reciprocity may further raise the costs of geopolitically motivated buying or selling of debt. A notable step in this direction unfolded in March 2012, when Japan became the first major developed country to receive Beijing's blessing to invest in Chinese sovereign debt (a handful of other countries have since followed suit). More recently, the IMF announced in November 2015 that it would include the RMB in its basket of currencies which comprise the IMF's Special Drawing Right, or SDR.

But rising stockpiles and purchases of reserves still means expanding geopolitical influence. Consider announcements by Chinese officials in the first half of 2015 outlining plans to recycle the country's reserves into several of Beijing's signature foreign policy projects, including its "New Silk Road" initiative and its Asian Infrastructure Investment Bank.[213] And the concentration of U.S. (and to a lesser extent eurozone) liabilities in the hands of a few sovereigns carries certain risks and vulnerabilities, which necessarily come with geopolitical consequences. Even though any wholesale sell-off of U.S. Treasuries has drawn analogies to mutual assured nuclear destruction (and the possibility is therefore extremely remote), when any single creditor holds a substantial enough potion of the total marketable pool of a given U.S. security, it may be able to cause undesired shifts in these markets without harming its economic interests—or without even necessarily bearing any malign intent.

National Policies Governing Energy and Commodities

In 2006 and again in 2008, Russia suspended gas supplies to parts of Europe amid a political dispute. In all, Russia has brandished or acted upon this threat more than fifty times since the dissolution of the Soviet Union according to analysis.[214] Part of the Kremlin's strategy in building Novorossiya, or New Russia, has been to match its diplomatic embrace with deals and investments in key commodity sectors. In January 2014, Gazprom took control of Armenia's state gas company, even renaming it Gazprom Armenia. In April of that year, it paid $1 for Kyrgyzstan's gas company, now called Gazprom Kyrgyzstan. Analysts say the push is geopolitical. "What's the economic purpose of Gazprom acquiring the Kyrgyz gas network? It's clear that the goal there was strategic," explains Columbia University's Alexander Cooley.[215] The gas deals are matched by similar Russian state investments in nuclear, hydroelectric, and oil sectors across Russia's "near-abroad"— leading one former Kyrgyz member of Parliament to complain that these sales have turned Kyrgyzstan into a "client state of the Kremlin."[216]

Increasingly, Moscow is extending this reach beyond its "near-abroad." Russia is fast "becoming the nuclear Wal-Mart of the Middle East," as one expert put it, positioning itself as the main supplier of no-strings-attached nuclear power technology in the Middle East.[217] After landing a flurry of nuclear cooperation agreements with Egypt, Jordan, Algeria, and Saudi Arabia, Russia broke ground on its first nuclear power plant in Turkey in April 2015. For Russia, at least some of these deals seem to defy commercial logic.[218] But for states on the receiving end of this Russian nuclear technology, it is cheaper and faster than Western alternatives, and, unlike the United States and other Western partners, it comes unencumbered by certain conditions on nonproliferation.[219]

The tendency to put energy and commodities to geopolitical use is not uniquely Russian. In fact, many of these same central Asian countries are balancing Russia's tightening embrace through energy deals with China. A week before signing the Eurasian Economic Union into existence in May 2014, Kazakh president Nursultan Nazarbayev announced a string of energy deals with China. Nazarbayev used the joint press conference with Chinese president Xi to reiterate that "both Kazakhstan and China have much common ground on major issues" and, in an unsubtle message to Moscow, that "both sides stick to the principle that countries have the right to choose their own development path."[220]

Thus far, China has not evinced any real desire to use its economic weight to challenge Russia geopolitically in Central Asia.[221] However, in conversations with leaders in the region, it is clear that this possibility weighs heavily on their minds.[222] Certainly, Beijing has not shied away from energy and commodities as instruments of geopolitics in other parts of the world. China in 2010 enacted export bans on rare earth elements as a means of registering dissatisfaction with the policies of neighboring countries around the South and East China Seas. In 2012, again amid tensions in the South China Sea, China National Offshore Oil Corporation chairman Wang Yilin characterized China's deepwater rigs as "mobile national territory and a strategic weapon."[223]

But leverage can be fickle, and healthy appetite is the next best thing to market share. China's energy and resource scarcity is a crucial driver of global politics in the post–Cold War era.[224] And it is no doubt a strategic vulnerability. At the same time, though, and perhaps counterintuitively, the sheer size of China's resource appetite also functions as a form of geopolitical leverage. To understand why, consider America's oil dependence. A major reason the United States has influence in the Middle East—the reason oil is pegged in dollars—is that America is among the largest consumers of the region's oil exports.[225] But a more limited U.S. appetite for Middle Eastern oil, either because the United States is using less oil or because it is securing oil domestically, may mean diminished geopolitical sway in the area and perhaps an eventual decision in the distant future by some of the countries to price oil in RMB rather than U.S. dollars.

States enlist energy or commodities to help with all sorts of geopolitical needs. The totemic case tends to be fairly overt coercion—an image initially formed by the Gulf petropolitics that played out in the 1970s Arab oil embargo and then reshaped by Russia's pipeline politics in more recent years (though there are other examples, including China's periodic threats to cut off fuel supplies to North Korea amid geopolitical spats).[226] In April 2014, with tensions over Ukraine still mounting, in place of a customary letter from the head of Gazprom to counterparts at European gas firms came instead a letter from President Putin addressed not to these firms but to eighteen European heads of state. In it, Putin openly suggested that European gas supplies were at risk of a shutoff.[227] As often is the case, though, this geoeconomic coercion need not be threatened explicitly to be effective. In fact, the mere prospect that Russia might use gas supplies to Europe as a weapon in its standoff over Ukraine was enough to temper EU policy.

But energy and commodities need not be coercive at all to make for effective geoeconomic tools. For some, they can be an insurance policy of sorts. Qatar, long obsessed with maintaining its autonomy and survival in a tough neighborhood, now supplies 85 percent of the United Kingdom's natural gas needs—a fact that would surely weigh in Doha's favor should the United States, the United Kingdom, or NATO ever find itself in the position of needing to prove its security commitments regarding the tiny country.[228] For others, pipeline politics are neighborly shows of enlightened self-interest. In a bid to shore up friendly Sunni monarchies in its neighborhood, Saudi Arabia has allowed the Bahraini government—traditionally more popular with Bahrain's Sunni population—to produce oil from a Saudi field "on loan" to Bahrain.[229] Finally, in still other cases, the geoeconomics of energy can be more about collateral consequences. In its quest for oil China sold twelve oil tankers to Iran, even with sanctions against Iran in place. With each tanker capable of carrying 2 million barrels of oil in the years ahead, Iran will presumably continue oil exports to China, among other countries—thereby better insulating itself from the United States.[230]

Leading Geoeconomic Endowments

If a central question is how states work their geopolitical will in the world through the application of economic leverage, then at least as important as the tools and tactics—aid dollars, sanctions, trade policies, and the like—are the underlying geoeconomic capabilities and attributes that help explain whether these instruments work. In other words, just as not all states are created equal in terms of their capacity to project military power, there are certain structural features—or geoeconomic endowments, as we call them—that dictate how effective a country is likely to be in the use of geoeconomics.

ENDOWMENT 1

Ability to control outbound investment.

First is a state's willingness and ability to put domestic capital to geopolitical use—be it outbound portfolio investment or outbound FDI, debt or equity. Across several of today's rising powers, governments control not just vast sums but a growing array of mechanisms for channeling this investment: state-owned investment vehicles for deploying reserve assets, sovereign wealth funds, state-owned banks, and state-owned enterprises, to name a few. These mechanisms also tend to be mutually reinforcing.[231]

Many of the cases involving the use of investment as a geoeconomic tool are distinctly ill-suited to several countries, including the United States. A mix of legal, political, economic, and cultural factors renders it highly unlikely that the United States would create a sovereign wealth fund at the national level, for instance. And compared to the more traditional investment tools that are more universally available to states (for example, free trade agreements, or FTAs, and bilateral investment treaties, or BITs), many of today's geoeconomic tools differ in two key respects. One, they are often direct rather than indirect conduits for the state—that is, FTAs and BITs channel investment only insofar as they shape the choices of private sector actors. And on balance, private sector actors are far less likely to pull out their investment over foreign policy disputes. But today's SWFs, state development banks, and SOEs are taking orders from their government owners, whose motivations may not always be primarily commercial. The fact that nearly all top executives of Chinese SOEs have red "Party phones" (and Russian SOEs have similar "white phones") on their desks, or that many of these SOEs would be loss-generating if stripped of their subsidies, would seem to support the idea that SOE decisions are made within the province of Party officials, whose motivations go beyond revenue and profit.[232]

This key difference in turn helps to account for a second: direct economic channels tend to retain their geopolitical value far better than indirect channels. The fact that, for example, Moscow, Riyadh, or Beijing can reroute substantial sums in investments if a country makes a choice at odds with the major power's national security interests can confer leverage long after the investment is made. As alluded to earlier, the patterns of Gulf financing to Egypt across the various stages of Egypt's revolution and counterrevolution punctuate the point, as Saudi and UAE financing abruptly halted following the ouster of President Mubarak, never to return during the year that the Muslim Brotherhood drove the country's political process. Within days of the Egyptian military's ouster of President Morsi, however, Saudi and UAE pledges of state-led investments (apart from pure assistance dollars) reappeared, reaching into the tens of billions.

By contrast, in the case of FTAs or BITs, it is highly unlikely that a country could "turn off" an FTA or otherwise reroute trade or investment flows it enables, once such agreements become a matter of domestic and international law. While the WTO does have a national security exemption that member states could invoke, as a practical matter the fact that no state has ever done so does not inspire confidence as to its relevance.

Domestic market features (overall size; degree of control over one's domestic market, both in dictating terms of entry and in controlling import levels from a given sector or country; asymmetries in economic relationships with other states; perceptions of future growth).

As Chapter 4 highlights, China's geoeconomic performance is in part a story about the advantages of size and speed. The fact that, as former foreign minister and current state counselor Yang Jiechi put it, "China is a big country and other countries are small countries" may work to its advantage in using economic instruments in pursuit of the country's geopolitical objectives.[233]

Size may still matter, but this is less true in geoeconomics than in traditional geopolitical and military realms. Singapore and Qatar are two of the strongest examples.[234] Singapore punches far above its weight with its two primary SWFs, Temasek and the Government of Singapore Investment Corporation (GIC), accounting for 60 percent of the $23 billion in cross-border deals by global SWFs in early 2014. Along with the country's central bank, the Monetary Authority of Singapore, the two SWFs generate the financial returns necessary to sustain the tiny city-state's nearly $10 billion defense budget.[235] Qatar—a country smaller in size than the state of Connecticut and with a population (of 260,000 citizens) on par with JPMorgan's workforce—emerged as a pivotal player in nearly every violent revolution to unfold in the Middle East since 2011.[236]

Beyond sheer size, sums, and growth rates, four more variables help explain a country's ability to translate its domestic market into geopolitical leverage: ability to exercise uniquely tight rein over access to domestic markets, capacity to redirect domestic import appetites to make a geopolitical point, actual or perceived consensus that a country's domestic market is too large to ignore (this, of course, especially applies to China and is merely a regional dynamic in the case of Russia), and a growth trajectory that makes other countries see rising future costs to opposing its foreign policy interests today. Of the various geoeconomic instruments currently in use, these domestic market features are probably most relevant in determining how fruitful particular trade and investment policy and sanctions efforts will be in producing geopolitical benefits.

Influence over commodity and energy flows.

There are three basic variables that determine how successfully a country can, through its energy policies, influence its geopolitical standing: monopoly power (market ownership, as with OPEC members), monopsony power (purchasing power, as with the United States and China), and centrality as a transit point between major buyers and sellers (e.g., the Suez Canal, as a major international oil route, enhances Egypt's strategic relevance). All three are undergoing serious shifts. The shale revolution generally, and the ascendance of the United States as a net energy exporter in particular, places new pressures on an already strained OPEC that could ultimately dissolve the cartel.[237] As growing energy appetites in China, India, and elsewhere come to absorb sizeable shares of a given country's exports—and as these deals take the form of multiyear bilateral contracts between states—this purchasing power can come with new sources of geopolitical leverage for the importing country. Consider the 2014 deal between Russia and China finalizing the terms of a thirty-year gas supply contract: it was Beijing's purchasing power and geopolitical importance to Russia that ultimately gave China the upper hand, finally steering the agreement to completion after a decade of negotiations. Finally, long-standing transit arteries—the Panama Canal, the Strait of Malacca, the Strait of Hormuz, gas thoroughfares in central Asia—may become more or less strategically important as new sources of supply begin to redraw existing trade and demand patterns.

Centrality to the global financial system (e.g., reserve currency status, some forms of financial sanctions).

The reason that the dollar's global footprint carries greater geopolitical benefits for Washington than, say, the Peruvian nuevo sol does for Lima is the same reason that U.S. sanctions carry greater bite than would similar sanctions from Peru: a vast share of global transactions directly touch, or at least rely upon, the U.S. financial system in some way. But this is changing.[238] Countries that have large, systemically vital financial sectors also tend to have a relatively easier time raising and mobilizing capital at low borrowing costs, and relatively greater ability to impact another country's borrowing costs.[239] At the same time, the link is easily exaggerated, as policy choices (e.g., fiscal health) and asymmetric dependencies (e.g., banking exposure) can of course also weigh heavily on a given geopolitical landscape. And again at the opposite end of this spectrum, North Korea has proven how a *lack* of financial market integration can be advantageous, at least for countries on the receiving end of geoeconomic coercion. In early 2015, after President Obama leveled new sanctions on North Korea following the cyberattack on Sony Pictures, U.S. Treasury officials privately admitted that their newfound power to implement sanctions would amount to little; their problem was not a lack of power but a dearth of targets. North Korea has shown itself highly resilient and creative in the face of sanctions, ironically aided by its own self-imposed isolation from global markets.[240]

WHILE THESE systemic endowments might help offer some predictive insight into a country's effectiveness in wielding various geoeconomic instruments, they, like any structural features, can only predict so much. Countries are hardly operating in a vacuum. Beyond these endowments, other variables will matter greatly in deciding the effectiveness of geoeconomic tools. Many of these variables will be case-specific: targets matter, for instance, and it is important to keep in mind that the targets may be multiple. As Baldwin aptly points out, identifying primary, secondary, and tertiary goals and targets of geoeconomic tools is advantageous, for while "not all goals or targets are equally important . . . none is intrinsically unimportant."[241] And certainly there is the question of aims, as some geopolitical goals lend themselves more readily to geoeconomic instruments than do others.[242]

But the issue here is also broader. Where, for example, a country's goal is regime change rather than something more targeted, how well do geoeconomic instruments *as a whole* perform in that regard? How well do certain geoeconomic tools perform compared to others?

These are but a few of the questions and possible variables that could meaningfully influence the success of a country in any particular instance of geoeconomic power projection. Assessing how suited a given country is to using a given economic tool in a given situation will inevitably depend on the circumstances at hand and invariably be a highly fact-bound exercise. It is important to recognize, first, the basic logic and operation of these as specifically geoeconomic tools, as well as their various interactions and tensions, and, second, the structural features likely to count most in determining a state's overall ability to project geoeconomic power. And perhaps most important, when weighing the relative utility of these tools, it is crucial to do so not only through a cost-benefit calculus or even a stacking up of relative costs ("does it cost country X more than country Y?"). Rather, efforts to size up the relative utility of a geoeconomic approach should be judged by the same measure used to weigh any other form of statecraft: against the next best alternative. With this basic taxonomy in place, the remaining chapters turn to the specific cases of China and the United States.

CHAPTER FOUR

Geoeconomics in Chinese Foreign Policy

China is using economic statecraft more frequently, more assertively, and in more diverse fashion than ever before.

—Dr. James Reilly, East Asia specialist at the Lowy Institute

NEVER IN history has one government controlled so much wealth.[1] As China's economic might has grown, so too has its ability and temptation to use this power to advance geopolitical ends. China is often correctly described as the world's leading practitioner of geoeconomics. It is also the major reason regional and global power projection has become such an economic (as opposed to military) exercise. "Beijing has been playing the new economic game at a maestro level," as one observer aptly put it, "staying out of wars and political confrontations and zeroing in on business—its global influence far exceeds its existing economic strength. Nations do not fear China's military might; they fear its ability to give or withhold trade and investments."[2]

Taking China as the best available lens to understand how geoeconomic tools operate in practice—and, crucially, how they can be combined—we now turn to explore China's use of geoeconomics through six case studies. We begin in Taiwan, which has been a flash point for Chinese Communist Party leaders since their earliest days in power. Beijing well understands how the threat of force is far more useful for defending the status quo than it is for forging any progress toward reunification. For that, Beijing has instead taken to a two-prong economic encirclement strategy, steadily picking off Taiwan's remaining international allies through a mix of geoeconomic measures while also aiming plenty of geoeconomic pressure directly at Taipei. Next we move to North Korea, where Beijing's close and complicated alliance with Pyongyang has been as much a constant as its tensions with Taipei. Unlike Taiwan, though, Beijing has no credible threat of force at its disposal, and as Pyongyang has grown more difficult to control, China has moved beyond its long-standing reliance on economic aid and toward a fuller battery of energy, trade and investment, and monetary tools to keep North Korea in line.

We then move eastward to Japan—for Beijing, also a case plenty fraught with historical tension, but one that more directly involves the United States, as Japan's only defense treaty ally. Looking to assert Chinese territorial claims while undermining the U.S.-Japan alliance, Chinese leaders once again realize that military strength alone will not suffice; hence their decision to vent geopolitical frustrations with Tokyo through a variety of geoeconomic measures, nearly all of them purpose-built to exploit Japanese economic dependence on China's manufacturing and consumer base. Likewise, many of these same geoeconomic tactics are well represented in China's foreign policy throughout Southeast Asia. But things in this region are more complicated, the region itself more up for grabs, and so China's geoeconomic posture is just as often one of positive inducement.

We conclude in South Asia, on China's dealings with both India and Pakistan. Even as the familiar story of triangular relations between these countries remains largely intact, the tactics have evolved. After decades of military dynamics largely dictating the mood between Islamabad, Beijing, and New Delhi—nuclear rivalry between Pakistan and India, border skirmishes between India and China, and Chinese military aid to Pakistan—China has come to rely more on geoeconomics in its dealings with both countries. These measures range from the straightforward and transactional (unabashed budget support and pipeline politics directed at Pakistan, for instance, or blocking multilateral aid to India amid tensions over territorial disputes) to the longer-term and more strategic (solidifying Pakistan's place in China's New Silk Road, or making India the newly appointed Chinese premier's first official stop outside of China, with forty-one Chinese companies in tow). Among the most striking features of this case, however, are early signs that under Prime Minister Narendra Modi, Delhi is also migrating toward a similarly geoeconomic posture, appearing to be at least partly in answer to Beijing's geoeconomic turn.

Divergent and unique as these six cases are, common patterns and similarities emerge between them. That China's leadership opts for many of the same tactics across such wide-ranging circumstances and objectives raises the possibility that its foreign policy apparatus has forged some basic operational consensus as to the when, how, and why of its geoeconomics. The evident refinement and revision to these tactics suggest that China's brand of geoeconomics comes with a capacity and eagerness for learning. At the same time, it is a learning curve with plenty of room left, as the several geo-economic attempts that were either botched or have somehow backfired make clear. This in turn raises larger questions of just how effective and significant these geoeconomic measures are. While the six cases themselves certainly offer some initial clues, we turn to these questions more fully in Chapter 5.

Taiwan: Beijing's Geoeconomic Endeavors on a Path Aimed at Reunification

From Beijing's perspective, all historical facts and laws prove that "Taiwan is an inalienable part of China."[3] Taiwan, meanwhile, insists on the rights it has retained as a self-governed entity since 1949, when Chiang Kai-shek's forces escaped to the small island after suffering defeat by Mao Zedong's Communist army. Even beyond these highly sensitive sovereignty issues, there are other, broader geopolitical stakes. Beijing understands that in peacetime, Taiwan could constrain China's ability to develop and project naval power and maritime security; in times of high tension, Taiwan could serve as a base for foreign military operations.[4] Chinese leaders hope that strict adherence to the one-China principle will yield peaceful reunification and the emergence of "one country, two systems" across the Taiwan Strait. Beijing will not rule out the use of force, however, and some 1,600 missiles still pointed at Taiwan help punctuate the point.[5] This threat of force has been a fixture of cross-strait relations for decades, though, and cannot alone explain Beijing's progress in tilting regional and global perceptions of the Taiwan issue in its favor in recent years.

Backstopped by this threat of force, Beijing has supported its desire for reunification by pressuring Taipei with a full range of geoeconomic instruments. China now increasingly relies on a strategy of economic encirclement and penetration to push Taiwan in the direction of eventual reunification. It has two parts: the first is multilateral, reflected in how China uses geoeconomics in its relationships around the world to advance a one-China policy on its terms; the second mirrors this, but on a bilateral level, seen in how Beijing makes use of geoeconomics in its direct dealings with Taiwan.

Internationally, China has long-conditioned aspects of its diplomacy on disavowal of Taiwan. For example, in 1992, France sold Mirage fighter jets to Taiwan, and the Chinese government responded by shutting down the French consulate in Guangzhou, thereby denying French companies the

chance to construct a subway there.[6] The one-China policy, which pro-
claims that Taiwan is an inalienable part of China and countries cannot
have relations with both China and Taiwan simultaneously, also served as
the first step in "normalizing" South Africa's economic relationship with
China.[7] China has worked to extend these same diplomatic conditions
to the Western Hemisphere and Africa as well.[8]

The strategy has worked. Because support for China's position on
Taiwan is a prerequisite, in some cases an explicit one, for Chinese invest-
ment or economic ties of any consequence, Gambia in late 2013 became
the most recent nation to accede to Beijing's one-China policy, leaving
Taiwan with just twenty-two allies, mostly small nations in Latin America,
Africa, and the Pacific such as Nicaragua and Tuvalu.[9]

And in what marks a major ideological shift for China, Beijing has also
begun hinting at a willingness to use sanctions against countries it views as
engaging in measures that reinforce Taiwan's de facto independent status.
In 2010, following the U.S. announcement of a $6.4 billion arms sale to
Taiwan, Chinese vice foreign minister He Yafei threatened Ambassador Jon
Huntsman that China would "impose sanctions against [U.S.] companies
that . . . engage in arms deliveries to Taiwan."[10]

The open declaration that it would employ economic sanctions has since
allowed the Chinese to clear what James Reilly, a China expert at the University of Sydney, calls a huge "ideological hurdle—they [have] opened the
path for more explicit use of sanctions in the future."[11] Possible future scenarios could include export, import, financial, or investment sanctions,
and—if past precedents hold—the deliberate slowing or withholding of
business.[12] China could dramatically reduce its interaction with Taiwan's
economy, creating an asymmetric vulnerability that leaves Taiwan far more
exposed than China.[13]

Taipei has long been aware of the geoeconomic pressure Beijing can
exert upon the island—in fact, some of the most powerful reminders have
come even without Beijing needing to exercise that pressure in explicit
fashion. In 1995, after President Lee Teng-hui delivered a speech asserting
the de facto status of the Republic of China on Taiwan, Beijing responded
with threats and conducted military exercises and missile tests off the
coast of Taiwan.[14] The episode, which has since been termed the Third
Taiwan Strait Crisis, caused the Taiwanese stock exchange (TAIEX) to
lose approximately 30 percent of its total value. The magnitude of the
decline set off speculation that China had perhaps had a more direct
hand; Beijing denied any concerted manipulation, while acknowledging
that political relations at the time were strained.[15] Taiwan was again reminded of the economic costs of political rupture with Beijing when, later

in Lee's years as president, comments on a "special kind of state-to-state relationship" with China caused TAIEX to drop 13.25 percent in one week.[16] It is impossible to know whether the drop was anything more than purely market-driven. Regardless, Taiwan learned an important lesson with Lee's suggestion of Taiwanese independence: political ruptures have economic consequences.

But the story of China's growing use of geoeconomics in its direct dealings with Taiwan really begins in 2000, when the president of Taiwan at the time, Chen Shui-bian, lifted a fifty-year ban on direct trade and investment with mainland China. Taipei was not blind to the geopolitical risks that economic opening could entail—government reports openly cited worries that Beijing would "use economic interaction to force political concessions."[17] But Taiwan's domestic challenges—record unemployment, a worn-out economy, and the specter of municipal and presidential elections—left President Chen little choice.[18]

And so it was that Taiwan embarked on a historic shift away from its well-established "no haste, be patient" stance to one of "aggressive opening, effective management," scrapping a long-standing $50 million ceiling on individual investments in China and allowing offshore units of Taiwanese banks to remit money to and from China.[19] Under President Ma Ying-jeou, who succeeded President Chen in 2008, the two sides followed these initial steps with a series of specialized agreements that furthered economic ties. Formal restoration of the "three direct links"—direct postal services, trade, and transportation across the strait—in 2008 eliminated the need for transit cities and dramatically reduced travel time in both trade and tourism.[20] In June 2010, the Economic Cooperation Framework Agreement (ECFA) was signed with the aim of establishing a "systematic mechanism for enhancing cross-strait economic cooperation." In a departure from the hard-bargaining negotiating posture China is known to take in many trade deals, the ECFA strongly favors agricultural interests in Taiwan's "green South"—a traditional stronghold of anti-mainland sentiment.[21] Beginning with preferential duty cuts and protection for bilateral investments, the ECFA aspires to the full elimination of nearly all cross-strait trade restrictions, opening each side's markets to the other in "unprecedented ways."[22] To date, Taiwan has made available more than 400 sectors to Chinese investment, including manufacturing, services, public construction, and finance.[23]

These economic policies were aimed at more than economic outcomes. They arose as part of a largely unspoken mutual consensus on both sides of the strait to address more pressing economic issues first rather than tackling more difficult political questions.[24] That is, Taiwan may have had little alternative given its dire economic situation, but improving economic ties stood as a geoeconomic project for both sides. Defending his record in a late 2013 interview with the *Washington Post,* Ma explained that these economic gestures both marked a necessary point of departure in a broader strategy aimed at improving the whole of cross-strait relations and increased what Ma called Taiwan's "international room for maneuver."[25] Ma described how these economic gestures have changed cross-strait relations from a "vicious cycle" into a "virtuous cycle," citing a long list of economic benefits, as well as elevated international standing for Taiwan—all made possible by this economic détente.

Still, these newfound ties have also left Taiwan in a position of asymmetric dependence on China. In part, these vulnerabilities were inevitable— merely the ordinary market physics one could expect from liberalization, and no one ever promised that market physics would be neutral in its geoeconomic consequences. But the magnitude and pace of these consequences do help explain Beijing's reasoning in leading with an economic détente. By 2003, only three years after lifting the ban, China replaced the United States as Taiwan's largest trading partner, and by 2020, Taiwan expects to send some 62 percent of its exports to the mainland, bolstering its substantial trade surplus with China.[26] Already, Taiwan is moving in that direction, with China consuming 40 percent of the island's exports in 2015.[27]

This cross-strait economic liberalization has also proven to be a source of indirect leverage for Beijing over Taiwan. Describing this newfound "international room for maneuver," for example, Ma was fairly explicit that Taiwan's ability to sign economic deals with other countries hinges on improvements in cross-strait relations. "After we signed with mainland China the ECFA in June 2010, two months later, in August, Singapore expressed willingness to begin talks about signing an economic cooperation agreement," Ma explained. "Since we have signed the ECFA agreement with mainland China, many countries have shown interest in holding talks with us."[28] Ironically, Ma's statements came as an attempt to fend off criticisms over precisely the issue of Taiwan's vulnerability to Chinese geoeconomic pressure. But in citing these recent economic deals (Ma signed twenty-one trade agreements with China during his first six years in office), as well as other recent achievements in joining several international institutions, Ma made it clear that all paths to economic and political progress run through Beijing.[29]

And as Taiwan's economic dependence on China has grown, Beijing has gradually toughened its stance on political and military negotiations. In October 2013, at a meeting with envoys from Taiwan, Chinese president Xi said a final resolution on Taiwan's status must be reached and that the island's political estrangement from the mainland "cannot be passed on from generation to generation."

During the Chen Shui-bian years (2000–2008), Beijing voiced staunch opposition to what was perceived as Taipei's gradual steps toward independence. In reality, Chen, sensing that progress toward both political and economic independence was not an option, chose political independence. He pushed to rewrite the Taiwanese constitution with an emphasis on the island's independence while allowing greater economic interdependence. He continued large weapons purchases from the United States, even as he christened offices and industries bearing the name "China," steps aimed at solidifying Taiwan's identity as the one independent China.[30] In retrospect, it is doubtful that political and economic dependence could be separated for purposes of strategy, and in any case, Chen's steps toward political independence wreaked economic consequences. Beginning with President Chen's inauguration, Taiwanese investments took a hit. Upon his election, TAIEX fell by 2.7 percent on concerns that Chen would inflame relations between China and Taiwan, causing the Taiwanese government to intervene.[31] And on his first day in office, the stock market fell by nearly 3.5 percent.[32]

Investors had good reason to be nervous, it turned out, as Beijing officials subsequently announced (twice) that China would no longer welcome investments by pro-Taiwanese-independence businessmen.[33] Beijing also reportedly delayed the granting of visas to some Taiwanese trying to visit the mainland, and boycotted the Computex 2004 conference in Taipei.[34] Some PRC actions went further, targeting specific companies seen as having ties to Taiwan's Democratic Progressive Party. A Taiwanese plastics company, Chi Mei, saw its stock price drop 5 percent overnight, while its plans to open a factory in China were postponed indefinitely.[35] Officials in Beijing were uncharacteristically forthright about it all, explaining that "Beijing has been actively encouraging Taiwan investment in the mainland despite lingering political tension. . . . [T]he policy stems from a strong belief that closer economic ties will benefit and help accelerate eventual reunification of the mainland and Taiwan . . . [B]ut a small number of Taiwan investors have abused the policy . . . they have funded pro-independence politicians with profits earned on the mainland."[36] Zhang Mingqing, a former spokesman with the PRC's Taiwan Affairs Office, noted that Beijing "does not welcome people who make money on the mainland and return to Taiwan to support independence."[37]

When President Chen was reelected in 2004, Beijing embarked on what became known as the "fruit offensive" of 2004–2005, aiming to "woo farmers in rural southern Taiwan by offering economic carrots to those who might have an interest in gaining access to the Chinese market."[38] Beijing allowed the importation of eighteen types of Taiwanese fruits (up from five) and promised to give duty-free status to fruit exports as well as ensure that customs clearance, inspection, and quarantine procedures were expedited.[39]

When the Kuomintang's candidate, Ma Ying-jeou, was elected president of Taiwan in 2008, TAIEX stock prices soared, a not-so-subtle sign that Beijing's approval still weighed heavily on investor approval for the country.[40] Just as Beijing has been quick with geoeconomic ways to punish earlier proindependence administrations, it showed equal zeal in using geoeconomics to reward Taipei for its choice of leadership in President Ma. The Taishang (Taiwanese business leaders who view economic interdependence as a catalyst for common visions of shared national identity, and who perhaps not coincidentally have hefty business deals and investments inside mainland China), always welcomed on the mainland, found even more favor.[41] From Beijing's perspective, the more economic interdependence there is between the two sides, the less likely Taiwan's bid for independence becomes.

President Ma proved to be a reliable supporter of Beijing's efforts to deepen economic interdependence. A cross-strait currency swap agreement signed in August 2012 has cleared a path for China to use monetary policy as a means for further influencing Taiwanese behavior at the global level.[42] Renminbi-denominated bonds, or "Formosa bonds," were issued by four Chinese state-owned banks in late 2013, a move that further boosts Taiwan's bond market and sets a precedent for other mainland Chinese issuers. With combined values of RMB 4 billion, the first issuance of these bonds helps give mainland China broader access to offshore renminbi funds as the market for Formosa bonds continues to develop.[43]

China's currency efforts—these Formosa bonds as well as a currency swap agreement that will reduce exchange rate risks between the two countries in both the trade and financial sectors—may well be as purely economic in motive as anything ever can be when it involves Taiwan.[44] But from Taiwan's perspective, even if the reasons are purely economic, when dealing with China it is the contingencies that matter. "With Taiwan hoarding hundreds of billions of yuan, especially now average citizens are also including renminbi as part of their assets, any significant fluctuation in the yuan's exchange rate may undermine Taiwan's financial stability," explains Kenneth Lin, an economist at National Taiwan University. "With the renminbi's exchange rate controlled by the government rather than decided by the free market, Beijing could wield it as a weapon."[45]

Keenly aware that reliable friends across the strait can be difficult to find, China worked to influence Ma's reelection. Recalling its fruit offensive nearly a decade earlier, China embarked on another agricultural buying spree—this time of Taiwanese milkfish—as the 2012 presidential elections approached. In a bid to help President Ma win reelection, a company based in Wuhan signed a letter of intent to buy 200 tons of milkfish and milkfish products within two years—targeting Tainan milkfish farmers, concentrated in a part of the island that traditionally favors Taiwanese independence and is more closely aligned with Ma's rival party, the Democratic Progressive Party.[46]

Even better, when Beijing's milkfish farming tactics did not translate into voter support, China's ranking official regarding Taiwan visited the province to learn why.[47] Perhaps, as one commentator wrote in Taiwan's leading newspaper shortly after Beijing's listening tour, "the big fanfare China made about how much money it was spending to buy milkfish from Taiwan offended Taiwanese people's sense of dignity."[48] At the same time, he cautioned against dismissing China's geoeconomic tactics, heavy-handed as they were. Arguably most striking about the episode was not so much that China attempted to buy geoeconomic influence in such an open fashion or that the effort seemingly failed but rather that Chinese leaders later came to Taiwan to understand why. For Du Yu, deputy chairman of the Taiwan Affairs Office, and others, Zheng Lizhong's visit came as evidence that Beijing is always learning, always seeking out ways to hone its geoeconomic techniques.

Learning and adaptation aside, there may be limits to how far Beijing's geoeconomic reward strategy can reach. Taiwanese citizens are becoming acutely aware of their deepening vulnerability to Chinese geoeconomic pressure, and public opposition to continued economic liberalization with China has caused Taiwan to partially hit the brakes.[49] Nowhere were these anxieties more in evidence, however, than in the mass demonstrations that erupted in Taipei and across the country in March 2014, with crowds of 100,000 or more rallying against an acceleration of the Cross-Strait Services Trade Agreement.[50] Polls suggest that roughly 90 percent of Taiwanese were against the agreement even though it favored Taiwan on paper, opening up eighty mainland services sectors to Taiwanese investment, compared with sixty-four Taiwanese sectors opened to mainland investors.[51]

Nor has Beijing restricted itself to just incentives. Beijing's patriotic army of hackers has actively used cyber warfare to target the Taiwanese government and infrastructure networks. For over a decade, Chinese hackers have launched countless cyberattacks intended to harass, disrupt, or paralyze Taiwan's financial, transportation, shipping, military, and other networks.[52] The external websites of at least one government agency were attacked by hackers 3.34 million times in 2012.[53] The attacks have been enough to convince Taipei that a targeted, coordinated cyberattack could alter the strategic calculus, possibly "[determining] the tactical landscape before a kinetic [Chinese] military operation" aimed at reunification.[54] Beijing insists it is falsely blamed for hacking in Taiwan, all the while conceding the utility of cyber warfare in shaping economies and infrastructure.[55]

Beijing's use of geoeconomic instruments to influence cross-strait dynamics in its favor has clearly been most effective when least aggressive. High-profile, high-pressure geoeconomic tactics used during the Lee and Chen presidencies backfired more often than not.[56] But the far-reaching use of trade, investment, monetary policy, cyber warfare, aid, and the threat of sanctions has helped prevent Taiwanese independence and supported regime behavior favorable to Beijing. Given the economic interdependence linking the two sides, Beijing will inevitably continue to use geoeconomic tools to influence Taipei, thereby guiding the island's geopolitical trajectory toward gradual reunification.[57]

Finally, so much of the effectiveness of China's economic interdependence strategy stems from the fact that it not only raises the costs of conflict for Taiwan but—because of the financial center that Taiwan represents to the world—also raises the costs of conflict for the rest of the world.[58] China is quite aware that for Washington, Tokyo, or others who might look to deter China from military action to take Taiwan, there are reasons to think the economic costs for outsiders could be far higher than for virtually any other territorial dispute in the world. In this way, Taiwan's systemic importance to global markets is likely more of a geoeconomic vulnerability than an asset for Taipei.

North Korea: Preserving Chinese Influence over Pyongyang through Assistance Flows

Absent Chinese assistance flows to North Korea, which are almost entirely geopolitical in design and objective, the Korean Peninsula would look vastly different today. The China–North Korea bilateral relationship, once deemed by Mao Zedong to be as close as "lips and teeth," continues to be dominated by North Korea's heavy reliance on China.[59] Since the end of the Cold War, China, through its bilateral assistance to Pyongyang, has dictated the terms of North Korea's domestic stability and its economic relations with the outside world. China has fashioned these terms along a series of core Chinese national interests, defined by Samuel Kim, a senior researcher at Columbia University, as the "five no's": no instability, no collapse, no nuclear weapons, no refugees or defectors, and no conflict escalation.[60] Ensuring the continuation of the status quo on the Korean

Peninsula, promoting stability along its borders, and expanding Chinese influence in the region has been the modus operandi for China's assistance to North Korea.[61] Chinese geoeconomic policy toward North Korea, in short, supports an overarching geopolitical strategy of buffering against any intensified foreign presence in the region.

Despite ideological preaching of self-reliance (or *juche*), North Korea has been anything but self-sustaining since the end of the Korean War. While assistance from Beijing to Pyongyang has steadily increased since the 1950s, reaching new highs during the severe famine of 1994–1998, it was not until the late 1990s that China began to utilize its economic ties with North Korea in support of China's geopolitical relationships within and beyond northeast Asia.[62] Beijing's leverage is considerable. China accounts for between 65 and 85 percent of North Korea's total trade volume.[63] It also serves as North Korea's chief food supplier; while exact numbers remain unknown, fertilizer aid totals are thought to average 200,000 tons per year, while annual food aid from Beijing exceeds 2 million tons.[64]

China has on three occasions also purchased gold from Pyongyang, cash-only transactions that point to the feeble state of the North Korean economy—and China's desire to keep the hermit kingdom afloat.[65] The last thing Beijing wants is a collapse of the Kim regime, a political transition thought to be rife with opportunity for U.S. intervention along China's periphery.[66]

But by far the most significant component of China's geoeconomic leverage over Pyongyang is the export of approximately 500,000 tons of oil per year, which accounts for roughly 90 percent of North Korea's energy imports (these export levels are all the more striking considering China's own energy insecurity).[67] Without this oil, the North Korean military would be seriously weakened and the already faltering industrial sector would come to a standstill. Beijing demonstrated its awareness of this dependence, using it to send a message to the Kim regime by shutting off the Liaoning–North Korea pipeline for three days after Pyongyang conducted missile tests in 2003.[68] In April 2014, reports surfaced that monthly shipments of crude oil from China to North Korea had been halted in the first quarter of the year, suggesting Beijing's displeasure at indications that Pyongyang sought to escalate tensions on the peninsula.[69]

China has also shown itself unwilling to be supplanted by other oil suppliers. In October 2013, light oil heading to North Korea from Iran was held at port in China under a penalty of $2 million in storage expenses. Terms of a North Korea–Iran oil export contract dictate that Pyongyang pays Tehran for light oil but must route its purchase through China's state-run petroleum companies for refining.[70]

No one really knows the full sums of Chinese aid and investment to North Korea each year. In the words of one expert, "The aid that Beijing gives Pyongyang is kept and treated in China as a national top secret."[71] What is clear is that there is a gap between what North Korea expects to receive and where China actually directs its aid. Pyongyang may request support in niche sectors, but the majority of Chinese aid is funneled into sectors where China's own needs lie (e.g., resource extraction, infrastructure development).[72] The special economic zone (SEZ) currently under development in the North Korean city of Rason is one such example. Rason was already a warm-water port for both China and Russia, but China won fifty years of control over the port after promising an airport, new boat piers, a coal-fired power plant, a railway line connecting Rason with China's Jilin province, and an additional $3 billion in investments. Chinese development of the SEZ creates trading opportunities for landlocked Jilin province, the potential for an Arctic shipping route to Europe, and a strategic port city for the Chinese navy.[73]

Similar selection patterns are seen in China's infrastructure development assistance to North Korea—essentially, the bigger the strategic benefit to China, the more likely it is that Beijing will support development. For instance, three high-speed rail tracks are currently planned to link Chinese and North Korean cities.[74] Sources suggest that North Korea offered China development rights in seven major mines in exchange for railroad development.[75] Thus, the Chinese have turned to building new bridges and wider roads at key border crossings—namely, Dandong and Rajin—to better transport coal and iron ore back into China.[76] All infrastructure projects also serve the overarching geopolitical purpose of bringing North Korea more tightly into China's web of geopolitical influence.

China's largest investments in North Korea are probably in commodities and natural resources. While the terms of these deals tend to reflect a "strategic discount" for Beijing, from China's perspective a reduction in price does not always translate into commercial success.[77] In 2012, for example, a $40 million investment by one of China's largest mining companies, Xiyang, flopped when the North Koreans again seized the iron ore mines and evicted the Chinese.[78] Apart from a few high-profile failures, China undoubtedly has access to these resources with little to no competition and at low prices.[79] Price discounts of this sort aside, it seems safe to conclude that China's commodities investments in North Korea, whether in iron ore or gold, also serve its broad geopolitical interests in promoting Pyongyang's stability (and consequently its ability to act as a buffer against U.S. and South Korean encroachment).

Beijing seems to be evolving its sense of what this stability requires, however; increasingly, Chinese direct investment in North Korea, in addition to supporting Chinese geopolitical objectives and keeping Pyongyang

afloat, is also now targeted at encouraging economic reform. After Pyongyang's nuclear test in 2009, as the West sought to further economically
isolate North Korea, China has taken the opposite approach, seeing it as
an opportunity to engage with and invest in North Korea in hopes of
nudging its political and economic trajectory toward reform.[80] More than
150 Chinese enterprises have invested in North Korea, primarily in mineral resources, manufacturing, construction, food, medicine, transportation, and light industry, since at least 2003.[81] To further encourage private
sector investment, in August 2012 China established a $490 million fund
for investment in North Korea under the auspices of the central government's China Overseas Investment Company.[82] The renminbi is also slated
to become legal tender in special economic zones at Rason, Hwanggeum-
pyong, and Wihway Island.[83]

Beyond these nudges toward political and economic reform, China has
also used its investments in North Korea to encourage forthrightly
helpful geopolitical behavior from Pyongyang. Using infrastructure development as an incentive, Beijing hoped to encourage Pyongyang
toward participation in the six-party talks aimed at dismantling North
Korea's nuclear program, for instance, with the donation of a $24 mil-
lion glass factory in 2004.[84] In fact, by virtue of its geoeconomic handling
of North Korea, China holds virtually all of the external influence over
the country.

China's considerable trade and assistance statistics with North Korea
would actually be far higher were they to account for black market trade
or to include Chinese assistance in building and exporting weapons from
North Korea to other rogue states.[85] In late 2009, a company named Union
Top Management was created in Hong Kong just days before an Il-
yushin IL-76 aircraft transported arms from Pyongyang to Iran.[86] North
Korean tank parts and other military equipment bound for the Republic
of Congo were discovered behind sacks of rice on a boat that had been
loaded in China while it was refueling in Durban in early 2010.[87] A shipment of missile parts from North Korea thought to be headed for Syria
on a Chinese-flagged ship was intercepted in 2012 outside Pusan, South
Korea. North Korea's illicit trafficking networks allow Beijing a backdoor
means of evading its stated nonproliferation commitments.[88]

UN- and U.S.-led sanctions regimes have done little to curb Chinese economic assistance to North Korea. Since 2006, China has supported all UN
Security Council resolutions against North Korea, but only after it first di-
luted the proposed measures. Despite issuing a 236-page list of goods
banned for export to North Korea and shutting down ties to North Korea's
Kwangson (Foreign Trade) Bank, Beijing circumvents its own sanctions.

Money can be readily transferred into North Korea from the Bank of Dandong, a state-owned Chinese bank.[89] Although Chinese exports to North Korea may have shrunk to $1.59 billion in the first half of 2013, even embargoed goods are finding their way back into the North via Dandong's thriving black market.[90] Ultimately, China's plans to expand trade, investment, and infrastructure around its North Korean border are at the core of a geopolitical strategy aimed at buffering against the U.S. pivot to Asia and bolstering China's regional influence—strategic objectives that China's UN obligations are unlikely to change.[91]

The Xi Jinping government may be realizing that North Korea's value as a geopolitical ally is eroding and that North Korea will not reform and open up to the world as hoped, despite Beijing's seemingly endless economic incentives intended to coerce Pyongyang to the contrary. North Korea may well in some ways be growing as a liability to Beijing at this stage. But that is hardly the point. Simply because the geopolitical risks North Korea poses for Beijing have increased is not to suggest that China can or will abandon Pyongyang. And while it may be a bad hand all around, China still holds all of the cards, largely thanks to its geoeconomic policies over the last fifteen years. In evaluating a given country's geoeconomic options, just as with its geopolitical options, the operative calculus is not a cost-benefit analysis but rather an assessment of next-best alternatives. In this case, in Beijing's view, the next-best alternative—more geoeconomic pressure on Pyongyang—would risk North Korea's collapse.

Japan: Abating Territorial Sovereignty Concerns and Keeping U.S. Influence in Check

Relations between China and Japan, typically characterized as "warm economic ties, cold political relations," have become "politically cold and economically cool."[92] Chinese and Japanese ambassadors have accused each other of provocations and flagrant disregard for their neighbors, even summoning images of famed *Harry Potter* villain Voldemort.[93] Charged rhetoric aside, Beijing has employed geoeconomic statecraft readily, and punitively, in getting its message to Tokyo (and its ally, the United States).

Behind Beijing's use of geoeconomic tools toward Tokyo lie two fundamental geopolitical objectives. First is protecting Chinese claims to territorial sovereignty. Once driven by the desire to develop oil and gas reserves around the islands, China's claims to the disputed Diaoyu/Senkaku island chain now carry as well notions of national honor and regional strength.[94]

Second, China's efforts to pressure Japan geoeconomically are often meant to weaken the strength of Tokyo's alliance with Washington.

Over the course of the past decade, China has repeatedly cut trade flows to Japan amid political disputes. In 2001, following testimonies in a Tokyo court about World War II–era germ warfare research conducted on Chinese nationals and a visit by Prime Minister Junichiro Koizumi to the Yasukuni shrine memorializing Japan's war dead (including convicted war criminals), Beijing announced plans to cut the annual quota for Japanese automobile imports by 40 to 60 percent.[95] Five years later, when Tokyo approved new history textbooks that glossed over Japan's wartime atrocities in China, Beijing engineered huge anti-Japanese demonstrations and consumer boycotts, dealing a further geoeconomic blow.[96] The boycotts strengthened quickly over a short period of time, bolstered implicitly by the support of various Chinese ministries (what one Commerce Ministry spokesman called "rational patriotic activities").[97] Economic retaliation manifested in other mediums, too, as inspections of seaborne imports from Japan grew stricter, approvals of work visas for Japanese were significantly delayed, Japanese firms were requested to withdraw from an international trade fair in Chengdu, and outbound Chinese tourists were discouraged from putting Japan on their itineraries.[98] As James Reilly of Australia's Lowy Institute points out, even more noteworthy was the decision by Chinese banking and financial officials to withdraw from the annual World Bank–IMF meeting, held in October 2012 in Tokyo.[99] As in 2001, declines in Japanese car sales and investments in China led JPMorgan to downgrade its projections for Japan's economy for the final quarter of 2012.[100]

Beijing has used regulation of commodity trade flows to influence actions surrounding the Diaoyu/Senkaku territorial disputes. In 2010, a Chinese fishing trawler collided with two Japanese coast guard vessels near the contested island chain. The Chinese captain was arrested by Japanese officials; China retaliated by halting shipments of rare earth oxides, rare earth salts, and pure rare earth metals to Japan.[101] These materials are crucial components in Japanese industries and manufacturing. Without them, Japan cannot produce electrical components required by U.S. and European companies. China's geoeconomic move, one with significant implications for the global supply chain, ultimately contributed to Tokyo's decision to release the fishing captain.[102]

A second instance of China's leverage of rare earth exports was seen just a year later in attempts by Beijing to incentivize foreign companies reliant upon rare earths to move their production centers and technology to China in exchange for a low-cost supply of rare earths. Both Hitachi Metals and

Toyota ultimately relocated plants in China, decisions that fold into Beijing's strategic objective of growing its domestic rare earths industry.[103]

China's intermittent use of rare earth bans toward Japan is striking for its brazenness. Beijing's initial resolve to curtail Japan's access to economically important materials seemed to mark a geoeconomic coming-out moment for China. Earlier instances of geoeconomic bullying toward Taiwan or North Korea seem feeble in comparison, as the rare earth bans highlight the first time China so boldly coerced a U.S. treaty ally. It is particularly telling that Beijing chose to strike out at Japan through geoeconomics rather than military actions. Some analysis of the rare earth bans miss this point: coercion, quite clearly, need not be explicitly stated to be effective. In fact, the arbitrariness of China's regulatory system is part of what makes Beijing so effective in its use of geoeconomic instruments.[104]

In the case of these rare earth bans, China achieved far more through smartly adapting tools of geoeconomic coercion than it could have obtained through other means. Beijing successfully sent a signal of strong protest against Japan's territorial claims (but not to the point of Tokyo invoking the U.S.-Japan treaty alliance); secured the release of a Chinese fishing captain (ended one of the causes of the 2010 crisis); and consolidated its market share (by forcing Japanese rare earth firms to relocate to China), thereby enhancing its ability to translate supply chain power into geopolitical leverage.[105] Perhaps most important, these geoeconomic moves signaled to the world that Beijing was no longer afraid to take on a U.S. treaty ally. In fact, some analysts have suggested that the rare earth export bans were aimed not at Japan but rather at the United States. "The evidence has shown that Japan was prepared and resilient regarding the possible risks of a rare earth shortage," notes Yun Zhang, an associate professor of international relations at National Niigata University in Japan.[106] "On the contrary, the U.S., and its defense sector, in particular, was much less prepared as it had lost capability throughout practically the entire rare earth supply chain."[107]

Two years later, after the Japanese government purchased part of the disputed Senkaku/Diaoyu island group (a step Japanese leaders claim was intended to prevent Tokyo's conservative governor from buying the islands), riots forced the shutdowns of Japanese manufacturers located in China, costing Japanese carmakers alone upward of $250 million in losses.[108] In the context of relentless anti-Japan media coverage, nearly two-thirds of Chinese citizens voluntarily boycotted Japanese products, a trend that increased Japanese concerns about an economic recession.[109] Here China is uniquely positioned, able to exercise certain kinds of geoeconomic leverage in ways that other countries are not. Following the escalations over the Senkaku/Diaoyu islands, Japanese exports to China fell 14 percent in September 2012 from the previous year. As a result, the bilateral trade deficit reached around $7 billion, while Japan's overall exports sank 10.3 percent year-on-year.[110] Japanese automobile manufacturers again took the brunt of the damage, with Toyota posting the largest drop, 48.9 percent on year in September 2012.[111] As tempers flared, Chinese authorities began other economic recriminations, including cutting commodity flows to Japan (decreasing the number of permits to mine rare earths by 41 percent).[112]

These continued territorial disputes and Japanese prime minister Shinzo Abe's December 2013 visit to the Yasukuni shrine have only continued the geoeconomic fallout from Beijing. Incensed Chinese consumers produced a substantial decline in bilateral trade levels in the first half of 2013, the first such in four years. And in the last few years Chinese producers have shifted en masse to new components suppliers, replacing Japanese parts with those manufactured in South Korea—clarifying the costs that Tokyo could expect for future assertive geopolitical behavior.[113]

Chinese monetary policy toward Japan has remained relatively unchanged amid territorial disputes and other geopolitical disagreements. But there are signs of at least rhetorical bluster. In 2012, again surrounding the Japanese purchase of the Diaoyu/Senkaku islands, an op-ed in the *China Daily* by prominent trade expert Jin Baisong urged China to use its power as Japan's biggest creditor, with $230 billion in bonds, to "impose sanctions on Japan in the most effective manner" and bring Tokyo's fiscal crisis to a tipping point.[114]

Jin further threatened that China should do what no other country ever has—invoke the WTO's security exemptions clause to impose economic sanctions upon Japan.[115] While sanctions ultimately did not materialize, Japan-related stocks fell sharply in both Hong Kong and Shanghai, impacting Japanese automobile and appliance manufacturers in particular.[116] Chinese investors blamed "barriers" for an overall drop of 9.1 percent year-on-year.[117] It is not just Japan that suffers from these tactics. China also pays a price, borne primarily by Chinese consumers and manufacturers. That boycotting Japanese goods and suppressing Japanese investment in China hurts Chinese workers, however, only underscores Beijing's tolerance of pain when it comes to accepting domestic costs for its geoeconomic policies.[118]

China also actively uses cyber tools in hopes of weakening Tokyo's resolve for staking Japanese territorial claims. Shortly after cyberattacks on the Japanese parliament in the summer of 2011, Chinese hackers attacked Japanese commercial firms, stealing information pertaining to Japanese defense equipment (fighter jets, helicopters, submarines, and destroyers) as well as nuclear power plant design and safety from Japan's

Mitsubishi Heavy Industries.[119] Despite Japan finding Chinese-language script in both instances of hacking, Beijing denied having any hand in the attacks.

China's geoeconomic pressure against Japan has not gone entirely unchecked. Some experts believe that "economic coercion has proven counterproductive in China's maritime disputes."[120] In response to economic pressure and the consumer boycotts of 2013, Japan has refused to back down over the island claims, instead strengthening its cooperation with other Asian neighbors. The Japanese have realized their vulnerability to Chinese geoeconomic influence and have slowly begun to look elsewhere in the region for support, including India and Vietnam.[121]

Japan has also initiated a geoeconomic blitz with the Pacific Islands, several of which are connected to the so-called second island chain, a term often used by military strategists to describe the likeliest path that attempts at expanded Chinese maritime influence may take beyond the South China Sea. At the seventh Pacific Islanders Leaders Meeting (PALM), held in Fukushima in May 2015, Japan pledged $440 million in aid to Pacific Rim countries, bringing its total aid commitment to $1 billion from 2013 to 2019. In addition to outspending China in the region, Japan is also far more proactive in humanitarian and disaster relief efforts—all of which appear to be paying off. At Japan's urging, the thirteen Forum Island Countries (Fiji, Kiribati, Marshall Islands, Nauru, Niue, Palau, Papua New Guinea, Samoa, Solomon Islands, Tonga, Tuvalu, Cook Islands, and the Federated States of Micronesia), together with Australia and New Zealand, ended the recent PALM gathering with as forceful a message—clearly intended for Beijing—as Tokyo could have hoped to send, resolving that "maritime order should be maintained in accordance with the universally recognized principles of international law," and reiterating the significance of "exercising self-restraint and peacefully resolving international disputes without resorting to the threat or use of force."[122]

Seen in its dealings both with Japan and (as the coming section discusses) across Southeast Asia, China's larger goal is a test of the U.S. alliance system in Asia. Thus far, the United States and Japan appear to be responding with political-military measures, which is helpful but hardly sufficient. This is a geoeconomic contest—China's entire strategy is predicated on the belief that exercising a military option in the next decade would simply prove too costly for the United States and Japan, and for that matter China itself. Thus Beijing builds and exercises its power projection not primarily through the deployment of military assets (except in the South and East China Seas) but rather through coercive and incentivizing geoeconomic policies toward its neighbors.

Southeast Asia: Expanding China's
Sphere of Influence

In December 2009, under heavy pressure from China and despite UN objections, Cambodia agreed to deport twenty ethnic Uighurs seeking asylum back to China to face prosecution in connection with the violent antigovernment protests that had occurred in Xinjiang months earlier.[123] Shortly after, China's vice president, Xi Jinping, arrived in Phnom Penh bearing gifts: $1.2 billion in grants and loans.[124] The U.S. State Department responded to Cambodia's decision to deport the Uighurs by scuttling a shipment of 200 military trucks to Cambodia.[125] Three weeks later, Beijing sent 257 trucks.[126]

In China's neighborhood, a fast-changing and heavily contested test case for Beijing's use of geoeconomics is Southeast Asia. The many projects demonstrating China's geoeconomic influence in Southeast Asia are all cross-subsidized by China's considerable non-geoeconomic strengths—namely, that it is a proximate power, and a big one at that.[127] China directs its geoeconomics in the region primarily at three deeply interrelated objectives: imposing costs on countries that cross China on territorial disputes, disrupting the U.S. system of alliances in Asia, and keeping old friends (including Cambodia, Laos, and Myanmar) close.

Beijing has staked its claims in no fewer than eight territorial disputes in the South China Sea. Broadly speaking, China's "nine-dash line" (the shorthand reference to China's self-drawn maritime map) claims the bulk of these waters, overlapping with claims of Brunei, Malaysia, the Philippines, and Vietnam, and stretching over roughly 90 percent of the South China Sea.[128] The Chinese have staked claims to island reefs there, including the Paracel and Spratly Islands as well as the Scarborough and James Shoals. Chinese claims to these territories, however small, suggest an interest both in developing untapped energy reserves and in building strategic military outposts.[129] China also disputes a series of maritime boundaries along the Vietnamese coast, off Borneo, in the waters north of Indonesia's Natuna Islands, and near the Philippine islands of Palawan and Luzon.

Beyond simply recovering territory China perceives as its own, prevailing in these claims would enable China to maintain close control of trade routes and, more important, expand its military umbrella to much of Southeast Asia—eventually resulting in a "string of pearls" that could counter the rebalancing of the U.S. military to Asia and the rise of Indian power projection in the region.[130]

For Beijing, however, realizing this vision requires weakening the current U.S. alliance system. China's territorial strategy is designed to push the U.S. Navy beyond the "first island chain," usually understood to include the Greater Sunda Islands, Japan, the Philippines, and Taiwan. Should it succeed, China would be able to seal off the East China Sea, the South China Sea, and the Yellow Sea, rendering it nearly impossible for the U.S. Navy to reach Korea in the event of war.[131] Some in China talk about going further, eventually pushing the U.S. Navy beyond the "second island chain," which runs along the eastern coast of Japan to Guam and then down to the Maluku Islands.[132] This would mean Japan and the Philippines could be cut off from American naval support.[133]

Beginning roughly in 2010, Beijing has grown increasingly aggressive in these claims, exerting administrative prerogative and tightening fishing regulations in the contested areas, moving a large oil rig inside waters within Vietnam's exclusive economic zone, instigating near-collisions between Chinese and U.S. naval vessels and aircraft, and declaring an East China Sea air defense identification zone (generating speculation that China will soon declare a similar zone for the South China Sea).[134] China has paired these more conventional military escalations with a full spectrum of geoeconomic pressure—positive to coercive to forthrightly punitive. As described earlier, Japan found itself on the receiving end of Chinese geoeconomic fallout, beginning with the 2010 rare earth ban and still continuing intermittently in various forms.

In 2012, the Philippines came in for similar geoeconomic treatment amid territorial disputes with Beijing. After a Philippine naval ship attempted to arrest Chinese fishermen working off the disputed Scarborough Shoal in 2012, China refused to allow 150 containers of bananas to enter its markets, claiming that the bananas were "crawling with insects." This was a symbolic move with the suggestion of more to come; it hit the core of the Philippine agricultural sector and cost farmers some $760,000. Subsequently, the Chinese also slowed inspections of papayas, mangoes, coconuts, and pineapples from the Philippines. These targeted geoeconomic steps dealt a substantial blow to Philippine exports, as more than 30 percent of local fruits go to China.[135] Around the same time, the Chinese government announced that it would begin an annual ten-week fishing ban on waters around the Scarborough Shoal, allegedly to replenish the fishing stock.[136] Additionally, China sent out a directive to travel agencies that tours to the Philippines were highly discouraged.[137]

To help Manila absorb some of the economic shock, the United States accepted more fruits from the Philippines. But while this marked progress in Washington's geoeconomic acumen, it was far from enough to help Manila withstand the pressure. Within several weeks the Aquino government relented. As soon as the Philippines pulled its ships from around the Scarborough Shoal, Beijing dropped the banana ban and abandoned the economic coercion. At least in this case, Beijing's heavy-handed use of geoeconomics was unambiguously effective in getting Manila to stand down over its claims to the shoal.

More often than not, however, China's geoeconomic coercion in Southeast Asia happens in a far more subtle fashion. Foreign firms routinely feel the pressure of doing business in an environment marked by Chinese intimidation: any ratcheting up of tension that impedes the flow of supplies and products between China and Southeast Asian nations—especially Vietnam or the Philippines—will ripple across the global economy.[138]

China's leverage in the region is helped by strong bilateral trade levels. Trade between China and the Association of Southeast Asian Nations (ASEAN) reached $350 billion in 2013; in that year bilateral trade reached $36.4 billion with the Philippines, $40 billion with Vietnam, and $60 billion with Indonesia.[139] China's emergence as the most important trade and investment partner for virtually all of Southeast Asia lends a preemptive, foreshadowing quality to any geoeconomically coercive threats Beijing may issue. Vietnam, for instance, has softened its approach to territorial claims with China as a result of watching what happened to the Philippines.[140] China's economic hold over Vietnam is such that Hanoi remains more vulnerable than Manila to Chinese coercion: Vietnam is highly dependent upon the PRC for rubber, and major Chinese imports are used in the goods Vietnam ultimately exports.[141] Unlike the Philippines, Vietnam does not enjoy a mutual defense treaty with the United States. Perhaps not coincidentally, China's claims in the South China Sea are particularly aggressive toward Vietnam, threatening 70 percent of Vietnam's exclusive economic zone—not particularly auspicious for a country so reliant on fishing as a food source.[142] Nor are the trend lines comforting. The Vietnamese government has set a "very bold" target for the maritime economy to account for 60 percent of the country's GDP by 2025.

Vietnamese leaders have developed contingency plans of sorts to diversify away from the Chinese in the case of economic sanctions, but current dependency levels make the prospects for diversification limited.[143] And, perhaps telling of the preemptive power of China's geoeconomic coercion, Hanoi has not asserted its claims in a way that has tested those contingency plans.

In a region where "nothing is as charming as money," China's geoeconomic efforts in Southeast Asia, in addition to policing territorial disputes, have been equally pinned on the broader goal of disrupting and supplanting U.S. influence.[144] Xi Jinping and the rest of China's current leadership seem to have a renewed appreciation for the power of institutions, particularly given how many of China's geopolitical objectives in the region are dependent upon preserving legitimacy. For Beijing, this realization process began with the 2010 ASEAN summit, hosted by Vietnam, where, country by country, ASEAN succeeded in advancing a largely united front against China's more exotic maritime claims, resulting in a joint statement that was sharply, if implicitly, critical of China.

China's learning curve proved quick. During its tenure as ASEAN chair the following year, Indonesia mainly reiterated the statements of the previous year, neither conceding nor gaining progress on the issue. By the time Cambodia took its turn as ASEAN chair in 2012, Beijing had amply learned its lesson. China pledged $2.7 billion worth of loans and grants to Cambodia that year (a sharp uptick over the $1.9 billion it had invested in Cambodia in 2011); it was more than double the investment by all ASEAN countries combined and ten times that provided by the United States.[145] Beijing's benevolence paid off. Cambodia used its power as chair of the ASEAN summit to block a joint statement criticizing China's approach to territorial disputes in the South China Sea—marking the first time in forty-five years that the ASEAN countries failed to reach consensus on a joint communiqué.[146] The fact that the summit was hosted at the Peace Palace, completed in October 2010 with Chinese funding, lent a fitting irony to the whole affair. In 2013, China blocked Philippine president Benigno Aquino III from attending a China-ASEAN trade expo, insisting that he withdraw the Philippines' UN arbitration case on the disputed South China Sea islands as a condition of attending. Rather than caving in to Beijing's demands, President Aquino decided not to go to China, sacrificing potential trade opportunities both with China and throughout the region.[147]

As ASEAN chairs in 2013 and 2014, respectively, Brunei and Myanmar both succeeded in maintaining a more middling course, keeping the maritime disputes on the agenda but without prioritizing them or explicitly referencing China. In comparing the Brunei and Cambodia summits, many attribute Brunei's lesser vulnerability to Chinese pressure to the fact that, thanks largely to its oil wealth, it is less economically dependent on China.[148] For its part, Myanmar fell under what some ASEAN officials described as enormous pressure from China, but thanks to the priority that Burmese officials have assigned to the country's efforts to reduce economic dependence on China, and the fraught relations between Naypyidaw and Beijing since Myanmar's 2011 opening, China did not overreach and Myanmar "acquitted itself quite well as ASEAN chair," according to press commentary.[149]

China has also sought to create altogether new institutions. Under the leadership of Xi Jinping, China is launching a new Asian Infrastructure Investment Bank (AIIB). Notably absent from AIIB discussions, however, have been the PRC's regional rivals Japan, India, and the United States.[150] Notwithstanding U.S. opposition, China ultimately lured some 57 countries to join its new bank, including fourteen advanced economies of the G20 and every major treaty ally of the United States save one (Japan). Left alone in its opposition, the United States was forced to soften its position.[151] Management and operational details have also been conspicuously lacking, but China would likely be the institution's largest shareholder, with a stake of up to 50 percent of the registered capital of around $50 billion.[152] The bank will offer quick financing for transportation, telecommunications, and energy projects in underdeveloped countries across the region, rivaling the reach and responsibilities of the World Bank. U.S. officials have been uncharacteristically blunt in their assessment, warning that the bank is a deliberate attempt to undercut the international financial institutions established after World War II (and dominated since by the United States, Europe, and Japan). Beyond attempting to weaken the U.S. alliance fabric of the region, the AIIB could allow China to pull its neighbors closer into its orbit, into relationships that promise increased geoeconomic benefits including decreased tension over territorial claims.[153]

China has focused intensely on deepening trade and investment with Southeast Asia. While driving a hard bargain in trade talks with large, wealthy nations, Beijing has been munificent toward smaller if strategically important partners.[154] China included a generous Early Harvest Program in the 2002 China-ASEAN Free Trade Agreement (CAFTA), opening China's markets to ASEAN agricultural imports. Rather than extracting the best possible deal for China, Beijing instead structured CAFTA to reassure China's Southeast Asian neighbors and give them a stake in China's economic success, striving, as one analyst put it, to present itself as a "benevolent regional hegemonic power."[155] CAFTA also bolstered Beijing's pursuit of WTO recognition as a market economy—a status ASEAN accorded China in September 2004.[156]

This strategy offers Beijing what China expert James Reilly calls "a classic 'win-win' opportunity: drawing nearby countries into China's economic orbit while bolstering its diplomatic leverage and creating commercial opportunities for Chinese firms."[157] China's steady push for regional infrastructure lies at the heart of this effort. Beijing has financed an increasingly dense network of cross-border railways, roads, water projects, and oil and gas pipelines across mainland Asia in recent years. These projects enhance China's access to strategic natural resources and, by addressing severe infrastructure shortfalls in the region, curry political favor for Beijing—all while bringing these countries more tightly within Beijing's influence. Crucially, these infrastructure projects also help to lessen China's heavy dependence on maritime trade routes that are secured by the U.S. Navy. Currently, 90 percent of China's trade travels by sea, and to reach ports on China's eastern coast, seaborne trade from the west must pass through maritime choke points such as the Strait of Malacca (through which 82 percent of China's crude oil imports passed in 2013).[158]

As *New York Times* China bureau correspondent Jane Perlez wrote in August 2014, "A favorite export from China to its neighbors these days are high-speed rail lines designed to make trade routes in the vast stretches of Asia more accessible and fortify Chinese dreams of turning its southern reaches into the capital of mainland Southeast Asia."[159] Referring to one rail project proposed by China that would pass through the mountains of northeast Myanmar to the coastal plains on the Indian Ocean, giving China a shortcut to the Middle East and Europe, Perlez explains how "for China, the strategic importance of the proposed line can barely be overstated: The route would provide an alternate to the longer and increasingly contentious trip through the South China Sea."[160] China has pitched similar plans for a high-speed railway in Laos, to be built by the Chinese. Minerals will be used as collateral, allowing Laos to borrow $7.5 billion from Beijing to pay for the railway.[161] But the railway would connect Laos and Thailand with China, allowing for Chinese goods to move south and important resources to come into China.[162] In all, China wants to build thousands of miles of track that will loop through Laos, Cambodia, Thailand, and Malaysia, heading south to Singapore as part of a grand trans-Asian rail accord signed by nearly twenty Asian countries in 2006. When the people of the mainland countries soon find that through the convenience of high-speed rail the Chinese province of Yunnan is their closest neighbor merely a few hours away, Yunnan and its capital city, Kunming, may well eventually become the effective capital of mainland Southeast Asia.[163]

Beyond high-speed rail are water, agriculture, commodities, and energy. China's state-owned China International Water and Electric Corporation (CIWEC) has fifteen infrastructure projects across the Philippines to date, one of which is the water improvement project at Angat Dam, Manila's primary source of water supplies. In 2007, China's biggest state power company won a $3.95 billion bid for a twenty-five-year contract to manage the Philippines' entire electricity grid.[164] As of 2014, the State Grid Corporation of China owned as much as 40 percent of the Philippines' National Grid Corporation (NGCP), and four senior officials of the State Grid of China sat on the board of NGCP. A senior Philippine government official told the *South China Morning Post* that the government was "quite concerned" that a Chinese state-owned company controlled the technical aspects of the national grid.[165]

Two states among the most central to China's success are Malaysia and Indonesia. Neither is among Beijing's outspoken skeptics in the region, nor its reliable supporters. And both are sizeable in their own right. Two new Malaysia-China industrial parks were launched in 2013, Kuantan Industrial Park and Qinzhou Industrial Park, to further boost bilateral trade and investment. Similar to the Singapore-Suzhou Industrial Park, these areas will offer attractive land prices, tax incentives, and financial support for Malaysian and Chinese investors. These deals also help solidify Kuala Lumpur's place in China's "maritime silk road" (the term, first coined by Xi Jinping in October 2013, appears to be little more than a euphemism for what more-skeptical observers call China's "string of pearls" strategy), allowing Beijing to stake a claim to the Malacca Strait, challenging the United States' geopolitical advantage in those waters.[166] Indeed, China is expected to insert $62 billion into state-owned "policy banks" to support this strategy to build infrastructure and increase influence in Southeast Asia.[167]

In Indonesia, China's geoeconomic influence is partly aimed at checking Jakarta's desire to play a leading role in Southeast Asia.[168] Often, it comes down to timing and vigilant opportunism. China timed investment deals to coincide with the October 2013 Asia-Pacific Economic Cooperation summit in Bali, and the two sides signed $28 billion worth of investment agreements, including province-specific initiatives, with bilateral trade exceeding $50 billion annually.[169] In the words of one Chinese saying, "sending coal in the midst of a snowstorm" maximizes political benefits.[170] For Beijing's geoeconomic aspirations in Southeast Asia, the 2008–2009 global financial crisis, just like the Asian financial crisis a decade before, marked a proverbial blizzard—an opportunity for Beijing to purchase political capital at a discount.[171] Often the investment deals themselves are designed in such a way as to register maximum geopolitical returns for Beijing. Southeast Asian diplomats describe how "Chinese aid is often carefully targeted, so that money to Malaysia, for example, is directed specifically to the state of Pahang, the political base of the prime minister."[172] "In Myanmar and Thailand, [the Chinese] make sure the generals get their share of the contracts," one diplomat from the region explained.[173]

As China's economic strength grows, so too does its urge to take care of old friends. Atop this list are Cambodia and Laos, countries linked to China through historical legacies of Chinese support. In the case of Laos, Beijing has a particular interest in propping up one of the few remaining Marxist-Leninist single-party socialist states. Included in China's 2009 crisis support package to fund ASEAN regional infrastructure was a $15 billion line of credit for poorer ASEAN nations, and $40 million in "special aid" for Cambodia, Laos, and Myanmar. In the aftermath of the 1997 coup in Phnom Penh, China extended a $10 million loan to Cambodia to replace aid suspended by traditional donors; two years later, Chinese premier Zhu Rongji visited Phnom Penh and announced the cancellation of all Cambodian debts. China is the largest outside investor in Cambodia, and the Chinese are pouring ten times more money into Cambodia than the United States, simply to keep the country functioning.[174] According to the Cambodia Investment Board, Chinese investment pledged in Cambodia has totaled $9.1 billion since 1994, including almost $1.2 billion in 2011—nearly 10 percent of Cambodia's GDP that year.[175]

Myanmar used to be on Beijing's list of reliable clients. But things are now more complicated. For China's part, it wants to avoid a burgeoning democracy on its back porch, particularly one that looks to assistance from the United States to supplant Chinese influence. Myanmar figures as a key part of China's plans for a New Silk Road, which, as noted above, aims to link China's western Yunnan province to Myanmar and on to Bangladesh, India, and westward. Beijing also sees Myanmar as vital to diversifying its energy routes, allowing for shorter transit to Middle Eastern oil. Even more important, geopolitical connections with Myanmar enable the Chinese navy to access the Pacific and Indian Oceans more quickly, shortening the distance for military ships—as well as energy tankers—by forgoing the need to pass through the Strait of Malacca to the Bay of Bengal.

In 2011, shortly after Myanmar's historic opening, the country was hit with a devastating earthquake. China responded with more than $500,000 in humanitarian aid—a rather feeble offer compared to India's $1 million, but greater than the $100,000 or $200,000 offered by Thailand and South Korea, respectively.[176] The two sides have since signed more than fifty economic and technical aid agreements through mid-2014.[177] The Economic and Technical Cooperation Agreement of 2012 allowed China the chance to provide "350 sets of integrated housing with 30 million RMB and $1 million in cash [for] the resettlement of [earthquake] victims."[178] The domestic energy sector in Myanmar has seen an influx of Chinese investments and development efforts since opening up to external investment.

In particular, China has succeeded in laying two oil and gas pipelines traversing Myanmar. Owned and operated by China National Petroleum Corporation (CNPC), more than 2,500 kilometers of pipeline became operational in 2013, and at full capacity, the pipeline is expected to send as much as 12 billion cubic meters of natural gas across Myanmar and into southwestern China annually (the pipeline continues on from Yunnan into China's northwest and eastern provinces).[179] An additional $2 billion oil pipeline became operational in 2014, allowing China to import oil from the Middle East and Africa. The pipeline is expected to move up to 200,000 barrels of oil per day, 40,000 of which will go to Myanmar along with an additional $7 million in transit payments per year from Beijing. Such are the benefits of serving as a transit country.[180]

At the same time, the oil and gas pipelines built through Myanmar stand as a lesson in how things do not always go as intended. China's Wanbao Mining—an offshoot of weapons manufacturer China North Industries Corporation—agreed in 2013 to invest just under $1 billion in the Latpadaung copper mine project.[181] The deal sparked violent local protests, prompting renegotiations on the contract. The new contract allocates 51 percent of profits to the Myanmar government, 19 percent to the Union of Myanmar Economic Holdings Ltd. (owned by Myanmar's military), and 30 percent to Wanbao.[182] And in August 2014, Burmese officials allowed a memorandum of understanding regarding China's proposed high-speed rail line through the country to lapse.

The scuttled rail line comes as the second major Chinese project to be suspended in Myanmar since a civilian government took over in 2011. Construction of another Chinese-financed hydroelectric dam at the source of Myanmar's Irrawaddy River was suspended after protests by locals and ongoing violence between the military and the Kachin Independence Army.[183] Local concerns center on the fact that if the dam is completed, China will likely generate 90 percent of the electricity needed in Myanmar.[184] "China has not been the flavor of the month for some time," said Thant Myint-U, a Burmese historian.[185] According to Vietnamese officials, "It can be seen, although not very clear, that Myanmar has been trying to reduce the influence of China in its country, economically and politically."[186]

But as wary of further dependence on Beijing as Myanmar's new leaders are, they are also mindful that they may be too late in arriving at such concern, given how much of Myanmar's viability already depends on China's trade, aid, and investment in the country. Certainly Myanmar is not independent enough for Naypyidaw to behave in ways that risk angering Beijing over sensitive issues such as the South China Sea.[187] China's trade with the once-closed country has risen sharply, with Myanmar's exports to China surpassing $8 billion in 2013, up from $1.2 billion in 2004 (a substantial sum considering that Myanmar's overall GDP in 2013 was just $60 billion). China's success in capitalizing on Myanmar's opening is partly thanks to a twenty-five-year head start over other countries.[188] Even amid U.S.-led sanctions on Myanmar in the 1990s following the military's nullification of election results, China rebuffed pressure from the West, maintained economic relations with Myanmar, and criticized Washington and others for intruding upon the internal affairs of a sovereign nation.[189] In a sign of just how confident Chinese leaders are that Myanmar will eventually sign up for its high-speed rail project, Beijing is moving ahead with plans to gouge an eighteen-mile rail tunnel out of the rugged Gaoligong Mountains that straddle China's border with Myanmar and serve as the entry point to Yunnan province.[190]

Finally, at perhaps the subtlest end of China's geoeconomic spectrum lies the expanding role of the renminbi as a regional reserve currency across Southest Asia. As the RMB's footprint in the region grows, Beijing will inherit many of the same perks that have heretofore translated the dollar's reserve status into strategic influence for the United States. Vietnam, for instance, has expressed a willingness to work with China in expanding the current scale of currency swap and settlement agreements in order to "help advance liberalization and facilitation of trade and investment"—in other words, to further the renminbi's continued globalization.[191] Direct trading between the Singapore dollar and renminbi was introduced in 2013, reinforcing Singapore's role as an offshore trading center and further internationalizing the Chinese yuan. Beijing also granted Singapore-based investors an $8.2 billion investment quota to allow those holding renminbi to invest in Chinese stocks, bonds, and money market instruments.[192]

In many instances, Chinese geoeconomic coercion has proven costly but effective—the Philippines is one clear example. In other cases, China has merely signaled to its neighbors the costs of risking geopolitical daylight between it and them, making those governments less inclined to act in ways that would run counter to China's strategic objectives; Cambodia, Vietnam, Myanmar, and Malaysia are prime cases of this. However, in some instances, even where it has achieved short-term objectives, China's economic pressure has reinforced the longer-term resolve of governments, such as those in Manila and Hanoi, to act in ways far less conducive to Beijing's underlying strategic objectives. At bottom, though, China does not perceive self-defeating costs to this geoeconomic coercion, and until this changes, China is likely to persist.

Pakistan and India: China-Pakistan-India Triangular Relations and the Growing Role of Geoeconomics

When it comes to China's current relationship with Pakistan and India, the old story is still the dominant one—China-Pakistan relations can only be understood within the context of each's relationship with India.[193] In 1950,

Pakistan became one of the first countries to end official diplomatic relations with Taiwan, initiating the start of an enduring "all-weather friendship" between China and Pakistan. By contrast, the "pendulum" of China's relations with India has "swung from friendship in the 1950s to confrontation that escalated in the border war of 1962 to various forms of conflict and cooperation in the 1990s" that continue today.[194]

While the familiar refrain of triangular relations between India, Pakistan, and China has endured across the last half century, it has evolved in substantial ways. In part it has grown deeper, with more complex interactions and interests. China and Pakistan have long valued each other as a strategic hedge against India.[195] On rare occasions, each has looked to New Delhi as a means of gaining tactical leverage vis-à-vis the other. But as India has graduated into the ranks of an aspiring global power, New Delhi has evolved from an occasional hedge or foil in this triangle into a full and direct participant in its own right.[196]

As this triangle has grown deeper and more complex, it has also come to rely more on geoeconomic strategies. Pinpointing exactly why geoeconomics has become a preferred medium of influence among these three countries is difficult, but three factors stand out. For starters, Chinese leaders well appreciate that if China is to expand its influence vis-à-vis India or Pakistan without escalating military tensions or regional rivalries between them (inevitably drawing in the United States), much of what they have at their disposal to accomplish this task is geoeconomic in nature.[197] Historically, Beijing has relied on military influence in its relations with Pakistan and, dating back to the U.S. embargo on weapons to Pakistan in 1965, China has played a major role in building up Pakistan's defense capabilities by supplying arms factories and weapons systems.[198] But Beijing has come to understand that, unlike supplying fifty JF-17 fighter jets to Pakistan, initiating a currency swap agreement between the People's Bank of China and the State Bank of Pakistan is less likely to provoke a security response from the United States or India.[199]

Another reason behind China's relatively greater focus on geoeconomic ties with both countries is that after more than a decade of strong growth averages and global ambitions, India has become too economically and politically valuable to China to risk intensifying tensions. Indeed, many experts expect that India will outpace China in real growth sometime in 2016.[200] Given the massive (and growing) economic footprints of both countries, cooperation between China and India also offers both sides a potentially potent means of challenging U.S. prerogatives. The point is not lost on either New Delhi or Beijing, surfacing, for example, in each side's commitment to the BRICS process, a largely geoeconomic project for all involved.[201]

A third reason China is turning to geoeconomics in its relationship with Pakistan may have to do with limitations to its more traditional military means. Put plainly, the United States has cornered the military relationship with Pakistan in the past fifteen years.[202] Notwithstanding China's history of supplying military technology and expertise to Pakistan, China's military contribution is overshadowed by that of the United States since 9/11. "The immediate aftermath of 9/11 saw US-Pakistan relations grow dramatically as they collaborated in the war on terror," explains Rajshree Jetly, of the Institute of South Asian Studies.[203] Washington designated Pakistan as a major non-NATO ally and sent it massive economic and military aid as a front-line state in the war on terror. Though China is Pakistan's primary supplier of sophisticated military technology from missiles, to combat aircraft and radar equipment, to submarines, it cannot match U.S. military aid levels, which totaled $15.8 billion from 2002 to 2012.[204] Even if the diplomatic returns to these investments have not been what the United States and NATO have hoped, these military ties between Washington and Islamabad have been such that China is likely to gain more strategic influence in Islamabad through geoeconomic means.

There is a more fundamental motivation in China's geopolitical calculus with both countries. Beijing's dealings with Pakistan and India seem increasingly motivated by a silent fourth party in this strategic triangle: the United States. Beijing's foreign policy choices regarding Pakistan draw substantially from the fact that Pakistan is an enduring serious problem for U.S. foreign policy. For China, having strong ties with one of the Americans' greatest geopolitical headaches is itself a considerable source of leverage over the United States. To be sure, China and the United States have substantial convergence in their interests in Pakistan, and at least over the past decade China has been urging Pakistan to be more restrained in its relationship with India.[205] But the point here goes deeper. However aligned China's interests and constructive its actions in Pakistan from the standpoint of the United States, the fact remains that Pakistan needs China far more than the reverse, and so long as Pakistan remains one of the world's most skilled countries at causing problems for the United States, China's significant leverage over Islamabad marks an important if indirect source of leverage for Beijing vis-à-vis the United States.[206]

There are recent examples of Beijing's long-standing readiness to supply a wide array of strategic options to Pakistan, especially when Pakistan is acting contrary to U.S. and Indian interests. In 2011, when Osama bin Laden was captured and killed, Chinese officials responded by expediting a deal to sell Pakistan fifty more J-10 advanced fighter jets; the United States, in contrast, "repeatedly delayed delivery of F-16s to Pakistan, and insisted that they not be used against India."[207] Not long after this expedited weapons deal with China, reports surfaced that the Pakistani military allowed the Chinese access to the U.S. stealth helicopter that crashed and was abandoned during the raid on bin Laden's compound in Abbottabad.[208]

China's interest in Pakistan as an indirect hedge against the United States, while far from new, is heightened by the fact that India and the United States have been steadily transforming their relationship since 2001. On his 2014 visit to New Delhi, U.S. secretary of defense Chuck Hagel quantified the expanding U.S.-Indian partnership, noting, "Since 2008, over $9 billion in defense contracts have been signed between the United States and India, compared with less than $500 million for all the years prior."[209] In the last decade, the United States has dispensed with its long-standing policy of parity in its dealings with India and Pakistan, seen most clearly in Washington's 2010 decision to formally back India's bid for a permanent seat on the UN Security Council. The unqualified U.S. support for India's emergence as a powerful democracy—one that could help to limit the negative consequences of the rise of Chinese power—now adds new stakes and complexities to triangular relations among neighbors India, China, and Pakistan.[210]

Chinese anxieties at the warming ties between India and Washington surfaced acutely in May 2013 when Chinese premier Li, shortly after taking office, made a visit to India his first trip outside of China. In press coverage of the Li trip, China did little to hide its concerns. "We would not like to see India become a tool of other major countries, especially the U.S., to counterbalance or check or contain China," Hu Shisheng, an India specialist at CICIR, a Chinese-government-backed think tank in Beijing explained at the time. "We want, through closer relations, to support New Delhi's policy that maintains equal distance. It's not realistic to expect India to be closer to one country than the other." Premier Li's trip was itself a display of Chinese geoeconomic power. Li, traveling with executives from forty-one Chinese companies, called on the two countries to do more business together instead of relying on others for development. "With a long border and extensive common interests, China and India should not seek cooperation from afar while neglecting the partner close by," he said.[211]

Finally, leading with geoeconomics in its approach to India and Pakistan may be intuitive for China not simply because it is the best available medium for influence in present circumstances but because, once again, it is an area where Beijing has plenty to work with. China's asymmetric trade relations (China is the largest trading partner for both India and Pakistan), heavy assistance levels in the case of Pakistan, and sporadic investments in the region suggest that China has the potential to exercise geoeconomic leverage in its dealings with both countries.

As for how China actually exercises this leverage, some of its geoeconomic attempts are straightforward (and indeed often constructive, from the standpoint of U.S. interests). In March 2012, for instance, the Party chairman of China's Xinjiang province decried that extremist groups in the province have a "thousand and one links" with Taliban forces in Pakistan.[212] Despite Pakistan's best efforts to convince Beijing that it would not allow extremism to be exported across its borders, a few weeks later China withdrew promised financing for a gas pipeline from Iran to Pakistan, signaling Beijing's displeasure.[213]

More often, though, China prefers incentives in its dealings with Islamabad. The China-Pakistan Economic Corridor marks one of Beijing's most ambitious efforts to keep Pakistan within China's sphere of influence. With a total investment of $46 billion, it is a centerpiece of China's New Silk Road initiative (also known in China as the "Belt and Road" initiative) and what Pakistani prime minister Nawaz Sharif calls "an example of the very close friendship between the two countries."[214] Other Pakistani officials have gone further, hailing the initiative as "the game changer for the entire region."[215] As part of the agreement, Beijing has promised to enhance transportation and trade by constructing an airport at the Chinese-managed port of Gwadar, as well as renovating roads between Lahore and Karachi and upgrading the region's rail system. Other longer-term projects include building a new nuclear power plant near Karachi and developing Gwadar as a major international oil port between the Middle East and East Asia, as well as specialized economic zones modeled after China's Shanghai free trade zone. The planned corridor will originate at Gwadar and pass through to the Karakoram Highway in Pakistan before going to the Pakistan-China border and on to Urumqi and western China.[216] The Chinese government estimates that, upon completion, more than one-quarter of China's foreign trade will travel through the corridor.[217]

It is an example of how Chinese geoeconomic leverage, even used constructively, is leverage all the same. Built by China, the Gwadar port, intended to be "a nexus between Pakistan, Iran, China and Central Asian States," will be under the control of the China Overseas Ports Holding Company, ensuring that the economic corridor's expansive blueprint will remain firmly within China's sphere of influence.[218] Indian security officials, for their part, view the plan with suspicion, "fearing China wants to increase its economic influence in South Asia and use Gwadar as one of a string of Chinese-financed ports in the region, where [China's] navy could seek shelter and supplies as it expands operations in the Indian Ocean."[219]

And just as with much of China's infrastructure investment in Southeast Asia, another aim of China's New Silk Road initiative is to mitigate China's dependence on maritime trade routes that remain under the control of the U.S. Navy. In fact, part of Beijing's diversification strategy is to find new ways to link land and maritime routes, bypassing the South China Sea choke points and minimizing the distance of any single maritime leg of Chinese shipping.[220] The China-Pakistan Economic Corridor could prove helpful, allowing some Chinese goods to travel overland to Pakistan before embarking for Europe at the Chinese-constructed port at Gwadar.

Other large-scale energy projects by China in Pakistan tell a similar story. In 2013, China agreed to build two 1,100-megawatt nuclear power plants for Pakistan in Karachi under a $9 billion deal, financed largely through a concessional loan from China. In October 2015, following a summer heat wave that claimed around 2,000 Pakistani lives, China announced that it would construct a 2,000 km power line from Xinjiang province to Lahore by 2020 to support Pakistan's overburdened power grid.[221] Pakistani government officials have committed to improve security in areas where it is seeking Chinese investment—a diplomatic win for Chinese leaders increasingly unnerved by restive provinces along the China-Pakistan border. "We've always cooperated with them on security," one official said. "The success of the Economic Corridor depends on stability."[222]

But the U.S. government sees it differently. As Pakistan expert Daniel Markey summarized the reaction in Washington, "The Chinese have announced plans to finance two new nuclear reactors in Pakistan. The move has rankled U.S. policy makers who consider it a violation of China's obligations to the Nuclear Suppliers Group."[223] Especially given Pakistan's history of proliferation, the United States has, what journalist Pir Zubair Shah described as, "serious concerns over this cooperation."[224]

Beyond the sort of strategic investments seen in China's New Silk Road vision, China's geoeconomic sway with Pakistan also tends to show itself in the breach—in how China responds to not-infrequent crisis moments in Pakistan. Compare Beijing's financial backing for Pakistan in 1996 to that it provided in 2008. In 1996, China offered $500 million in balance-of-payments support, pulling Pakistan back from the brink of default. Javed Burki, Pakistan's then finance minister, recalled how simple the fix was back then: he simply flew to Beijing to ask for the money. But that time has passed, for "China is no longer inclined to grant cash outright without structural reforms from the receiving government," he said.[225] By 2008, Pakistan again found itself verging on default. With the United States and other nations preoccupied by the global financial crisis, and Saudi Arabia, another traditional ally for Islamabad, refusing to offer oil concessions, China was again seen as the last port of call before the IMF. Despite press accounts noting how "accepting a rescue package from the fund would be seen as humiliating for Mr. Zardari's government," which had been in office less than a year at that point, Chinese officials this time largely did not oblige, giving Pakistan only $500 million and sending Islamabad instead to the IMF for the remaining $7.5 billion it needed.

A third variant of China's geoeconomic displays vis-à-vis these two countries tends to aim more at India than Pakistan and is simply about undermining Indian political will when it comes to territorial disputes still simmering along the Sino-Indian border. In 2009, China blocked approximately $3 billion in multilateral aid to India amid tensions surrounding Arunachal Pradesh, a region currently governed by India but claimed by China.[226] The episode does not bode well for what the United States and others can expect as China gains the influence it is seeking in multilateral organizations such as the IMF and the China-led Asian Infrastructure Investment Bank: should future initiatives in these institutions infringe on what Beijing sees as its core national interests, there will likely be geoeconomic consequences.[227]

Finally, there are signs that India, for its part, is beginning to turn more toward geoeconomics-led foreign policy. It is in part a function of the leadership style of Prime Minister Modi. Since taking office in May 2014, Modi has consistently cited strengthening India's underlying economic fundamentals as the country's surest route to projecting influence and power: "I believe a strong economy is the driver of an effective foreign policy," as Modi put it in an October 2013 speech.[228] Modi may intend a turn toward geoeconomics in the broadest sense (as shoring up domestic economic foundations necessary for enhanced power projection).

But there may be more to it. There are reasons to think that India's nascent geoeconomic instinct is partly a response to China's own geoeconomic statecraft.[229] New Delhi appreciates that India is in a contest for influence with China over its neighborhood. With the exception of Pakistan, India has enjoyed generally stable ties with its South Asian neighbors. But critics charge that Modi's predecessors, the previous center-left Congress Party, started to take things for granted, allowing China—which shares a border with four of India's neighbors—to step into the breach.[230]

That appears to be changing under the Modi government. Billed as an upgrade to India's long-standing "Look East" approach, the country's new "Act East" policy comes as an effort to remedy any regional vacuum left by the previous government; as local media explain the policy, it aims to strengthen "strategic and economic ties with Southeast Asian countries that would possibly act as a counterweight to the influence of China in the region."[231] Modi has signaled his aim to reset India's relationship with its neighborhood, evidenced by securing the participation of most South Asian Association for Regional Cooperation leaders, including Pakistani prime minister Nawaz Sharif, at his swearing-in ceremony and by choosing Bhutan, a country actively courted by China, as his first foreign destination after becoming prime minister.[232]

In their direct bilateral dealings, India and China may look to economics as a means of anchoring relations amid rising geopolitical struggles. "Modi is well aware that China needs the big Indian market, while India desperately seeks large Chinese investments to build transit and other infrastructure critical to its economic revival," India expert Niranjan Sarhoo explains. "Acrimony over borders and geopolitical rivalry in the region notwithstanding, trade will be the centerpiece of India's policy toward China."[233] At minimum, China's heavy-handed geoeconomic tactics seem to be coloring New Delhi's decision making. There had been expectations Modi would pick Tokyo for his first trip, "but such a choice could have upset China," according to Indian press reports.[234]

Finally, India's priority on improved economic ties with the United States and its allies in the region offers further circumstantial evidence of a more concerted geoeconomic tone from New Delhi, driven at least in part by concerns over China. "The prime minister is an unabashed pioneer of trade and economic diplomacy. As chief minister of Gujarat, he made several trips to China, Japan, and South Korea, cultivating a personal rapport with leaders like Japanese Prime Minister Shinzo Abe. Modi plans to expand his Gujarat template to all of India. He will seek trade routes to deepen relations with big powers that matter to India's economic revival and geopolitical rise."[235]

Indeed, the first-ever reference to the South China Sea in a joint Indian-U.S. statement came during Modi's September 2014 trip to Washington, a fact that "has riled Beijing, and revived the latter's fears about the world's two largest democracies acting in concert on a larger China containment strategy."[236] Modi's joint statement with President Obama pledged cooperation on plans to integrate the subcontinent with the markets of East Asia through an "Indo-Pacific Economic Corridor"—a proposal unmistakably similar to China's own plans for a maritime silk road linking the Pacific and Indian Oceans. For India, which appears wary of China's plans for the Indian Ocean, "the Indo-Pacific Economic Corridor could be the first step towards building its own maritime silk road."[237]

ENLISTING Pakistan in a grand hedge to slow India's rise as a regional rival, single-handedly propping up the Kim regime in North Korea, intensifying maritime disputes with six of ASEAN's ten member states—it seems clear that China employs geoeconomics as a tool of first resort in pursuing a broad range of foreign policy aims across Asia. But where China's brand of geoeconomics has proven effective, what do these cases tell us about why it has succeeded? What do other, less successful cases say about why those attempts fell short? In Chapter 5, we turn to exactly these questions.

CHAPTER FIVE

Geoeconomic Strength in Beijing and Beyond

We want the Chinese to leave and the old colonial rulers to return. They exploited our natural resources too, but at least they took good care of us. They built schools, taught us their language and brought us the British civilisation. . . . [A]t least Western capitalism has a human face; the Chinese are only out to exploit us.

—ZAMBIAN OPPOSITION LEADER MICHAEL SATA, 2007

I have come here to thank China for helping Zambia to develop. The Chinese have done tremendous things in Zambia.

—ZAMBIAN PRESIDENT MICHAEL SATA, 2013

THE CASES outlined in Chapter 4 focus only on China's use of geoeconomic tools in its region, but the phenomenon stretches beyond Asia. Since the Norwegian parliament awarded Chinese dissident Liu Xiaobo the Nobel Peace Prize in 2010, Beijing has frozen relations with Oslo, dealt a serious blow to Norway's share of the Chinese salmon market, and abandoned talks on a bilateral free trade agreement.[1] With relations still frosty nearly four years on, Norway began to look for ways to appease Beijing. The Norwegian prime minister refused to meet with the Dalai Lama when he visited Oslo in May 2014, a visit partly intended to celebrate the twenty-fifth anniversary of the latter's Nobel Peace Prize. "The Dalai Lama has visited Norway roughly a dozen times since receiving the prize in 1989—but things are different now. . . . We need to focus on our relationship with China," Norway's foreign minister, Borge Brende, told reporters on April 2014. Beijing's message had been received not only in Norway but apparently too in neighboring Denmark, where Prime Minister Helle Thorning-Schmidt similarly declined a meeting with the Dalai Lama the following spring—a stark about-face for a politician who, prior to becoming prime minister, spent years staking out highly public support for the Tibetan leader.[2]

High as the domestic political costs were for the Danish and Norwegian leaders in snubbing the Dalai Lama, the economic fallout from such a meeting would likely have been much worse. For those countries that are willing to host the Dalai Lama, one study shows that export levels to China drop by an average 8.1 percent after meetings between a prime minister or monarch and the exiled Tibetan leader, a decrease that takes roughly two years to return to normal.[3]

China's geoeconomic influence has also found its way—to a lesser degree—into multilateral institutions, from the UN General Assembly, to ASEAN, to the IMF. In August 2012, countries that were absent, abstained, or voted against a resolution on the violence in Syria were largely those under China's geoeconomic sway. (In opposing the measure, China remained true to its long-standing voting solidarity with Russia on the UN Security Council. Russia, a loyal ally of the Assad regime, staunchly opposed the measure; in return, China enjoys Russian support at the United Nations on issues related to North Korea and Taiwan.)[4]

Collectively, these cases raise two fundamental questions. First, does geoeconomic pressure work? Much depends, of course, on one's metric for success, but at least in the case of China, the body of evidence points toward yes: China openly flexes geoeconomic muscle—both positive and negative—and much of the time it succeeds in advancing Chinese geopolitical interests, at least to some degree, on issues of concern to it. This is not to suggest that China's geoeconomic tactics are always efficient, in either economic or geopolitical terms, or that there are not cases of overreach and backfire. But by exercising this pressure China has managed to deter arms sales to Taipei and to steadily reduce the number of countries to recognize Taiwan; it has curtailed the activities of the Dalai Lama; it has deterred countries from political showings of support for human rights issues; it has registered noticeable impacts on votes in the UN and frustrated various Western efforts to pressure North Korea; it has given tactical support to a newly emboldened Russian foreign policy; and, not least, it has challenged the balance of power in Southeast Asia, forcing some countries to alter course in pursuing territorial claims, and placing others on notice.

The ability to pass judgment on a country's level of geoeconomic savvy presupposes another, even more basic question: how does one recognize geoeconomic statecraft when it is occurring? There is no definitive means to inventory cases of geoeconomic pressure, or then to measure whether such cases are on the rise. But at least by recent historical standards, the incidence of such overt geoeconomic efforts by China and by others certainly seems to be growing—threats to shut off gas pipelines in the dead of winter, geopolitical aims candidly aired as factors in the production decisions of major oil producers, investment deals now openly predicated on disavowal of Taiwan, explicit stipulations in aid agreements requiring a leader to step down at the end of his or her term, or prohibitions on purchases from firms in a given third country.[5]

When it comes to evaluating a country's use of geoeconomics, it helps to have clear instances like these. More often, though, evidence of geoeconomic pressure is circumstantial—especially in cases that are coercive in nature. Take, as noted earlier, China's quarantine of bananas from the Philippines amid escalations of tensions over competing claims to the Scarborough Shoal, or Russia's ban of Moldovan wine in the run-up to Moldova's deadline for signing a cooperation agreement with the EU. Compared to open political demands, such coercion is sometimes more difficult to measure.

Fortunately, limiting this story strictly to these two categories—explicit or circumstantial uses of geoeconomic power—would be too narrow in any case. Like military power, geoeconomic sway can carry a long shadow of influence. It need not be exercised or even brandished to register a desired effect. According to press reports, some energy companies drilling in the disputed South China Sea have publicly admitted to the necessity of partnering with Chinese state-owned energy firms so as not to be harassed.[6] The fact that the China Development Bank and Brazil's BNDES have portfolios larger than the World Bank's means that these states can wage diplomacy with capital on a scale largely unmatched within the West.[7] This influence tends to be subtle—more often correlation patterns than clear causal arrows. But it is nonetheless real.

At the same time, geoeconomic success is sometimes exaggerated, including with respect to China. There are natural limits and internal tensions running through many of Beijing's attempts to use geoeconomics to advance geopolitical aims. It is possible that China's ability to employ such instruments will be increasingly hampered by domestic problems—housing and stock market bubbles, a weak social welfare system, reform of the *hukou* (household registration) system, government corruption.[8] Powerful, protectionist-leaning industries and agencies have added to their domestic political power in recent years, strengthened by absorbing the preponderance of China's post-financial-crisis stimulus. In China, just as anywhere else, the pursuit of geopolitical objectives and the importance of purely economic interests can clash, and these actors, newly emboldened, seem less willing to be trumped by geopolitical needs. There are regional challenges, too. China's heavy dealing has sparked a collective desire on the part of Southeast Asian states to achieve a measure of balance by drawing closer to the United States. In China's case, geoeconomic power, like most other forms of power, may well prove most effective when implied rather than exercised outright.

Unlike in other areas of statecraft, when sizing up the effectiveness of geoeconomic attempts, there is an odd tendency against assigning partial credit. To be sure, in its bid to escape U.S. and EU sanctions pressure, Russia's efforts to buy off certain cash-strapped EU countries—the so-called weak links in the U.S.-EU sanctions coalition—may not have succeeded in sinking the sanctions during 2015. But it was hardly as if Russian leaders were, to believe press reports at the time, simply "shoot[ing] themselves in the foot and wast[ing] this money."[9] The Kremlin's well-timed overtures and outright financial support (to Greece, Cyprus, and Hungary, as some examples) scored important geopolitical victories, raising the costs to U.S. and EU leaders of maintaining the sanctions, puncturing U.S. hopes of imposing even tougher sanctions on Moscow, and ultimately making the daunting task of keeping the eurozone together even tougher, ensuring that Europe's attention stayed focused inward.

In any event, simply because countries have a mixed record when it comes to geoeconomics does not necessarily mean they will abandon even the most misguided attempts. This in turn raises a larger point: even where states try to wield geoeconomic power and either partially or fully fail to achieve their aim, the results and collateral damage can carry real, destabilizing consequences in their own right.

Consider virtually all of Qatar's foreign policy in the years following the Arab Spring. As revolution spread around it, Qatar took to spending enormous sums—and accruing a large and curious mix of bedfellows—as its survival strategy. "They like to back winners," as one Middle Eastern official summarized.[10] Qatari officials are forthright about their actions. When asked how much Qatar spent in the Libyan revolution, Qatar's prime minister answered, "It's a lot. It cost us a lot."[11]

And yet a survey of Qatar's largest bets—billions of dollars in support to rebels in Libya and in Syria (often paying rebel salaries); roughly $8 billion in aid to the Morsi regime and Muslim Brotherhood in Egypt; $400 million to Hamas (coming at a crucial time when Hamas began to distance itself from Tehran and Damascus over the conflict in Syria)—reveals that Doha has little to show for its expenditures, at least in terms of its desired outcomes. There was, however, no shortage of unintended, and unhelpful, outcomes. In fact, in a region where consensus is rare, nearly all sides agree that Qatar has had an important hand in destabilizing nearly every trouble spot in the region and in hastening the rise of radical and jihadi factions.[12] "The results have ranged from bad to catastrophic in the countries that are the beneficiaries of Qatari aid," Gulf-based journalist Elizabeth Dickinson summarized.[13]

If there is a silver lining, it is that Qatar's meddling has become a minor rallying point among other GCC countries, which have begun pushing back in unison—pressing their case in Washington and threatening to dismiss Qatar from the GCC membership ranks if Doha does not moderate its spendthrift foreign policy adventurism. In August 2014, neighboring UAE took the matter of Qatari damage control into its own hands and, using U.S.-made jets and operating out of Egypt, began several rounds of airstrikes to roll back Qatari-funded Islamists in Libya.[14]

Probably the most damaging of these foibles was the early funding that Qatar, as well as Kuwait (and to a perhaps lesser degree Saudi Arabia), funneled to more extremist factions of Syrian rebels—factions that, after some mergers and acquisitions, would eventually incorporate as the Islamic State of Iraq and al-Sham, or ISIS. Press reports describe how, at the height of the violence in Syria, Qatari-based businessmen would moonlight as remote leaders of entire brigades of Syrian rebels. So constant were the streams of delegations shuttling through Doha to petition the Qatari government for financial support that one could guess at a delegation's odds of success based simply on which of Doha's five-star hotels it was staying at. As Elizabeth Dickinson recounts, "The Four Seasons and Ritz-Carlton are old favorites; Hamas leader Khaled Meshaal has stayed at the former, the Syrian opposition at the latter. The W Hotel is a posh newcomer, mostly housing eager European delegations seeking investment or natural gas."[15]

Alarmed by the swift ascent and brutality of ISIS, Qatar did begin to crack down in 2014, although only as a result of strong pressure from others in the Gulf and the West. But it was too late. "Armed with the loot of half the Iraqi military, [ISIS] doesn't need its Gulf patrons to buy it sniper rounds anymore," one commentary put it.[16] Counterfactuals are inherently difficult, but the extraordinarily swift rise that ISIS enjoyed and its ability to threaten the entire region and the West almost certainly would not have occurred—certainly not to the extent and in the manner it did—absent the early funding these extremist factions received from Qatar and Kuwait.[17]

The unfortunate records of Qatar and Kuwait are only among the most recent, most disastrous lessons in how geoeconomic adventures can sometimes not just fail, but backfire, creating new challenges. The 2013 Cyprus bailout was an episode partly brought about by, and then further complicated by, geoeconomic factors from Russia, even as the EU's package ultimately prevailed over Moscow's alleged offer. (Two years later, however, the Kremlin did win access to Cyprus's largest port for Russian military vessels—reportedly among the concessions Moscow had sought as part of its 2013 bailout overtures—as well as Nicosia's support against further U.S.-EU sanctions on Russia, in exchange for a $2.5 billion loan on generous financing terms.) Or take the tricky diplomacy facing several of

Libya's African neighbors after Qaddafi's ouster—compelled by economic coercion from his regime, many of these states had voted against UN or African Union action in the run-up to Qaddafi's removal, complicating relations with their new Libyan government counterparts later.[18]

China, too, has seen attempted shows of geoeconomic power go awry, especially where Beijing has coupled heavy-handed geoeconomics with aggressive naval behavior in the East and South China Seas. The China experience shows that geoeconomics is not a perfect tool (nor, for that matter, are conventional diplomatic or military instruments). But it does not need to be. Whether successful or not, whether tried or merely implied, China's brand of geoeconomic statecraft produces a substantial coercive overhang that will be an Asian reality for at least the next few decades, potentially causing a number of states to alter their geopolitical course under its weight.

What, then, is it about China's brand of geoeconomics that makes it so seemingly effective? In looking back across the cases detailed in Chapter 4 for patterns and clues, what emerges is clearer insight into the how, why, and when of China's geoeconomic prowess. Certainly it is in large part a structural story—China undoubtedly has more than its share of the geoeconomic endowments outlined earlier—but this oversimplifies. First, there are plenty of tensions and complications even within these structural endowments; it is not as if these endowments are unalloyed positives, nor, taken together, do they all row in the same direction for Chinese foreign policy makers. Second is the obvious and easily forgotten fact that any full account of China's geoeconomic clout must look beyond structural factors to the role of deliberate policy calculations by Chinese leaders. And, as with any policy calculations, geoeconomic calculations are malleable—subject to change as new factors (including actions by other states) serve to alter how China's geoeconomic options compare to various alternatives.

Trade and investment. Compelled by its export-led growth model, China has been assiduous in pressing to liberalize tariff barriers. For many countries, according such a vital role to exports might translate into a weak negotiating posture in bilateral or multilateral dealings, and potentially limit the extent to which trade questions might be decided on geopolitical over economic aims where the two differ. Not so with China. Because of the sheer size and perceived growth potential of its domestic market, China has proven effective at using access to its domestic market as a means of shaping other states' geopolitical behavior. As Singapore statesman Lee Kuan Yew once put it, "China is sucking the Southeast Asian countries into its economic system because of its vast market and growing purchasing power. Japan and South Korea will inevitably be sucked in as well. It just absorbs countries without having to use force."[19]

What distinguishes Chinese geoeconomics on trade and investment is not only a willingness to put its market-opening initiatives to geopolitical use (seen, for example, in the more concessionary terms China has offered up in its most strategically valuable trade deals).[20] It is also an ability to foster asymmetrical economic dependence on China among certain countries—and, once that is achieved, to shape their foreign policies in ways congenial to China's national interests.[21] Certainly, the threat of force can loom over the whole equation, as with Taiwan. But recognizing that a military campaign to prevent Taiwanese independence would undermine much of Taiwan's value to China (which, apart from principled arguments of territorial integrity, is largely economic), China has sought to answer this problem through this same giant sucking sound that Lee Kuan Yew describes. Taiwan's economic dependency upon China has effectively forestalled the prospect of Taiwanese independence.[22]

This is mostly a story of deterrence. And as with all such examples, for that deterrence to continue working, Beijing must succeed in maintaining sufficiently credible threats of economic reprisal. An unusual feature is that Beijing has the ability to shape its domestic economic appetite in ways most other countries do not. And Beijing has shown itself capable and willing to redirect the consuming habits of its domestic market to punctuate a political disagreement. This is seen, for example, in the way that Japanese exports to China plunged some 14 percent in a single month (October 2012) amid tensions over maritime claims, and, more than three years on, still have not fully recovered.[23] Reflecting on the slump in Sino-Japanese trade during the height of the East China Sea conflict in 2012, China's Ministry of Commerce spokesperson Shen Danyang hinted that at least some of the drop was due to factors beyond economics. While he explained "the drop in trade volume between China and Japan [as] *mainly* caused by economic factors," he did not stop there. "Bilateral relations have cast shadows on trade relations," he added. "Japan needs to properly handle issues between the two countries, and provide a proper environment for the development of China-Japan economic ties."[24]

China has subtler ways of depressing imports as a means of registering political grievances—ad hoc customs measures affecting imports, retaliatory tariffs on a politically sensitive good or set of goods, new and arbitrary regulations on foreign firms and importers. In one case, Chinese authorities announced a new licensing requirement for online payments systems. Two years after the licensing requirement was authorized, the approval process for foreign firms still had not been released. Curiously, however, one foreign firm was somehow able to procure a license, notwithstanding the fact that no foreign licensing measures yet existed.[25] Chinese leaders draw geopolitical leverage from this sort of ad hoc regulatory system and the arbitrariness it affords, venting displeasure with the foreign policy decisions of another country through punishing its companies (not unlike how Russia does it, as seen in Moscow's campaign to expel McDonald's, Apple, and other iconic U.S. brands from the country in the wake of U.S. sanctions over Ukraine).[26] Following the U.S. Justice Department's indictment of five Chinese military officers on charges of cyber espionage, China banned the use of Microsoft's Windows 8 on all government computers. Chinese state media at the time went as far as to brand Google, Facebook, Apple, and Yahoo as "pawns" for the U.S. government.[27]

In sum, China no doubt has an attractive domestic market, but it manages to translate this into geopolitical influence above and beyond what any reasonable appraisal of its market value suggests it should command. This is traceable in large part to the relatively tight control Beijing still exercises over access to its market. First, Beijing exercises relatively tight control over access to its domestic market. Whereas most Western countries screen would-be investment only on narrow national security grounds, China exerts a far higher degree of control, deciding each investment on a case-by-case basis, closing off entire sectors to foreign investment, and for other sectors attaching a price of entry—from forced joint ventures with state-owned enterprises to mandatory technology transfer. (For this reason, China's pledged commitments to depart from this sort of case-by-case adjudication in the course of U.S.-China negotiations on a bilateral investment treaty would mark a crucial breakthrough. But those negotiations, frequently stalled since their 2008 start, have once again begun to lose steam, leaving many observers expecting that it could be years before any agreement is reached).[28]

Meanwhile many see signs that conditions are growing more challenging for companies entering China. A new business in China, for instance, must navigate twice as many start-up and construction procedures as it would in another East Asian or OECD country.[29] According to Kerry Brown, a professor of Chinese politics at the University of Sydney, "Increasingly multinational companies will in all sorts of subtle and not subtle ways be made to adapt their behavior to meet the political and economic needs of the party."[30]

When it comes to outbound global investment, no government has more working capital at its disposal, or more tools to channel it, than the PRC.

Many of these tools are novel—either in kind, by order of magnitude, or both—and found exclusively or almost exclusively in China. To take a few leading examples, China has around $3.5 trillion in foreign exchange reserves, the majority of which is managed by the State Asset Foreign Exchange (SAFE) and the China Investment Corporation (CIC), its leading sovereign wealth fund.[31] China's largest SOEs—many of them global competitors and Fortune 500 companies—make their largest purchases and overseas investments at the direction of the Chinese government, often with geopolitical objectives and conditions. SAFE has openly predicated investment decisions on nations' disavowal of Taiwan.[32] Chinese FDI in Africa likewise comes only on recognition of Beijing's one-China policy. China has diplomatic ties.[33] (As the striking correlations between voting patterns in the African Union on Qaddafi's ouster and Libya's SWF investments on the continent suggest, such geoeconomic techniques are not confined to China.)

Returning to a point raised in Chapter 2, this influence is not just unidirectional. China's substantial strategic investments, often directed towards weak and authoritarian states, can in turn shape Beijing's foreign policy instincts, policies, and perceived national interests.[34] Some of these effects may be salutary, some not. Recall how years of Chinese involvement in Sudan enabled China to help facilitate a North-South peace deal (once China finally came to terms with the political reality of two Sudans[35]), but for years leading to the eventual peace talks, had also helped to undermine U.S. sanctions there.[36]

At times this can create a mutually reinforcing dynamic, compelling Beijing toward greater shows of geopolitical muscle to protect these investments. In the case of Zimbabwe, China has demonstrated resilience in protecting its investments through the use of its veto power on the UN Security Council. In 2008, a resolution calling for arms embargo and financial and travel restrictions on Zimbabwean president Mugabe and other leadership was backed by nine UN member states but vetoed by both Russia and China.[37] Leading up to Zimbabwe's presidential elections, in 2011 China paid just $3 billion for exclusive access to the African country's extensive platinum rights, a contract estimated to be worth $40 billion. One headline in the *Zimbabwe Mail* went so far as to say that China's geoeconomic influence over Harare rendered Zimbabwe a "full-fledged Chinese colony."[38] More recently, in the spring of 2014, the People's Liberation Army donated $4.2 million to fund various projects for the Zimbabwe Defence Forces, Mugabe's military, including development, training, and equipment acquisition.[39] With the Mugabe government's continued isolation from the West and a national debt of over $7 billion, the Chinese investment is a significant factor in keeping Mugabe in power.[40]

Sanctions. The Chinese government typically regards sanctions as an abuse of power by developed countries, notably the United States. Sanctions, from the Chinese perspective, are seen to compound crises rather than help defuse them.[41] China has tended to oppose sanctions particularly out of fear of losing out on imports of vital commodities that support economic growth at home.[42] (By comparison, the United States has been the principal country imposing sanctions in more than 120 instances over the past century.)[43] In the case of Iran's nuclear program, while China unsurprisingly opposed unilateral U.S. sanctions on Iran, Beijing did vote in favor of all UN Security Council sanctions against Iran. Beijing has hardly proven itself an enthusiastic participant, maintaining economic ties with Iran in circumvention of Security Council commitments.[44] In July 2013, the U.S. government moved to impose penalties on foreign entities that maintain commercial ties with Iran. Undeterred, China has continued to seek out ways around these sanctions to further bolster the Iranian government, be it through importing Iranian crude oil (rather than fuel oil) or, as at least one Iranian lawmaker has claimed, the promise of $20 billion in development projects in Iran using oil money.[45]

Aid. While China has looked much less to official assistance as a source of diplomatic leverage than one might expect—the official Chinese bilateral aid budget is a meager $5 billion per annum—there are important exceptions.[46] Image projects—presidential palaces in Zimbabwe, Togo, and Sudan and more than fifty-two sports stadiums in Africa—are obviously part of China's campaign for closer political ties.[47] According to estimates compiled by AidData, a development watchdog group, China paid out $80 billion in "pledged, initiated, and completed projects" in Africa from 2000 to 2012. But "most of that aid went to areas where national leaders were born, indicating a strong political bias," AidData found.[48] "As soon as [a region] becomes the birthplace of an African president, this region gets 270% more development assistance (from China) than it would get if it were not the birth region of the president," says Roland Hodler, professor of economics at the University of St. Gallen in Switzerland and one of AidData's leading researchers.[49]

These projects can backfire. China has come in for criticism over some of its development choices, such as its 2007 decision to finance a new presidential palace in Sudan. While the international community focused on providing aid and supplies to African peacekeeping forces working to suppress the Darfur genocide, China's leader Hu Jintao provided Sudan an interest-free loan to build a presidential palace and called for other nations to "respect the sovereignty of Sudan."[50] The move—coming as it did in the run-up to the 2008 Olympic Games in Beijing, when China was already under intense public scrutiny—attracted widespread criticism, not just for the fact of China's aiding a brutal regime but also for the way that development took a backseat to blatantly political motives.[51] "China is not financing a presidential palace by mistake," Sebastian Mallaby, then a columnist for the *Washington Post,* wrote of the deal's announcement, "it is doing so deliberately. It is not financing just any presidential palace; it has chosen a president so odious that his fellow African leaders hold their noses at him."[52]

But, such clumsier missteps aside, have these sorts of image projects paid off for China? Generally speaking, popular perceptions of China in Africa or Latin America remain roughly unmoved from 2007 levels (if anything, the two most recent Pew surveys on the question show more cases of declining opinions toward China than of warming views).[53] But then, it is hardly clear that improving public opinion in these regions was the goal that Chinese leaders had in mind. Among elites and leaders in these regions, China has fared much better. A 2014 study by the RAND Corporation put it this way: "Africans' reactions to Chinese involvement have been mixed: Government officials have been overwhelmingly positive, while other elements of African societies criticize China for what they see as an exploitative, neo-colonial approach."[54] In an article in the *Financial Times,* former Senegalese president Abdoulaye Wade wrote, "China's approach to our needs is simply better adapted than the slow and sometimes patronizing post-colonial approach of European investors, donor organizations and non-governmental organizations."[55] To the extent that China's moves are as much influence attempts as aid projects, evidence suggests that they are succeeding on at least the first of these scores—and indeed often both.

In addition, China, along with several other emerging powers, has looked to state-owned development banks, which are extending financing to the developing world at below-market rates—as in Venezuela, which again has approximately $40 billion in Chinese loans and counting—and record volumes. By some estimates, the China Development Bank, holding nearly $1 trillion in assets, outstrips the World Bank's lending capacity by a factor of thirty-two.[56] One can be reasonably confident that at least some of this $1 trillion will be deployed toward geopolitical purposes, or at minimum with geopolitical co-benefits. And of course, when dealing in sums in the trillions, even small percentages can make for impressive investment numbers. When China launched the China Africa Development Fund (CADF) in 2007, a $5 billion fund backed entirely by the CDB, it marked the first private equity venture by a Chinese state bank. Eight years on, the CADF has invested in more than 80 projects across 35 African countries.[57] It assumes only minority stakes in projects alongside other Chinese investors, and allows Chinese firms to supply local partners with Chinese capital, technology, and know-how. Still, the CADF appears subject to the same ultimate political direction that defines every other Chinese state bank. Martyn Davies, CEO of Frontier Securities in South Africa, was telling in his lukewarm endorsement of the CADF's independence, calling it "largely commercially driven."[58] A look at the CADF's steering committee, consisting of Chinese officials, suggests this may be a charitable assessment. As one newspaper explained, "If the projects interfere with sensitive or material or economic or diplomatic policy, then they have to listen to the steering committee."[59]

In the case of Chinese aid to Venezuela, Chinese financial support assists the Venezuelan government in acting counter to U.S. national interests. Venezuela continues to allow Iran to illegally launder billions of dollars and stash "hundreds of millions" of dollars in "virtually every Venezuelan bank today." It also permits Hezbollah to establish terrorist training facilities on Venezuela's Margarita Island, a move that has further strengthened the "marriage of convenience" between narcotics traffickers and drug gangs.[60]

One additional geopolitical benefit of Chinese overseas aid is the continued diplomatic isolation of Taiwan. Sixteen years after China broke off relations with the African island nation of São Tomé and Principe over its diplomatic recognition of Taiwan, China has planned to open a trade mission to promote aid and investment projects in the tiny country, located in the Gulf of Guinea. In a few years' time, this may well lead to a unilateral move by São Tomé and Principe to cut its formal diplomatic ties with Taiwan, as was likely the case in Gambia's unexpected decision to withdraw diplomatic recognition of Taiwan.[61] In the years since Malawi broke off diplomatic relations with Taiwan in exchange for recognizing the Beijing government in 2008, China has aided the southern African nation in the "construction of a new parliament building, the Lilongwe International Convention Center, the Karonga-Chitipa Road, and the Malawi University of Science and Technology."[62] It is no surprise that countries see China, with its much deeper wallet, as having a much better payoff—literally— than Taiwan. Aid thus serves as a tool for China to protect its own definition of "one China": namely, that Beijing is the legitimate representative of China, to which Taiwan belongs.[63]

Monetary policy. Underpinning China's economic ascendancy is its monetary policy. By keeping its currency cheap, China has managed to make its exports more competitive than those from other developing countries, from Bangladesh and Vietnam, to India and Mexico. While the real exchange rate of the RMB against the U.S. dollar has appreciated significantly in recent years, China has intervened steadily since roughly 2001, doing so at record levels in 2014 (orchestrating some of the largest single day devaluations in decades in 2015).[64] While in most countries domestic politics would balk at the economic disadvantages that such currency restraint inevitably generates, China has more or less managed to buy off the opposition.[65] Many states resent how the undervalued yuan undermines their competitiveness, but offers of Chinese financial assistances, trade opportunities, and simple fear of Chinese political influence are enough to mute criticism.[66]

Increasingly, Chinese currency policy is about much more than simply maintaining a competitive exchange rate. Great powers have great currencies, and great currencies in turn help to build power. China is undeniably the biggest challenger to the dollar-led system.[67] The PRC is becoming a great power, and the internationalization of the renminbi is an important part of a grand strategy to accomplish this rise.[68] Nevertheless, fears of the RMB "replacing" the dollar are overblown. As experts such as Sebastian Mallaby and Olin Wethington argue, the narrative about the rise of the renminbi is mostly wrong. As they see it, "the global rise of China's currency will be slower than commonly predicted, and the yuan is more likely to assume a place among secondary reserve currencies . . . than it is to displace the dollar as the dominant one. Nor is it even clear that China wants the yuan to replace the dollar. . . . China's uncertain effort to internationalize its currency has exposed the profound struggles that lie behind the country's larger push to transform its economic model."[69]

But given its growing footprint, the RMB hardly needs to replace the dollar to reap real geopolitical benefits for China. If historical precedents around the rise of the dollar, the deutsche mark, and the yen all serve, then the internationalization of the renminbi will likely occur steadily as China's economic size grows, as other countries have increasing confidence in the currency, and as China's own financial markets deepen.[70]

For some experts, these changes cannot come too soon. Today's world, say economists such as Fred Bergsten, is one where emerging markets are growing faster than the United States, deepening their financial markets in ways that demand central bank holdings far above what the United States can sustainably provide.[71] Were the RMB to become a reserve currency, China could serve as a provider of this insurance, not just a demander. Launching the RMB as a reserve currency would also require China to liberalize its financial sector and undergo a slew of reforms that are fundamentally in America's national interest.

But the geopolitical implications surrounding reserve currency status for the RMB are less straightforward. The rising status of the RMB indicates that China is gaining regional influence through financial channels, activity that is much less well studied and understood than China's impact through traditional economic means.[72] Were the RMB to become a global reserve currency, its dominance would be largely concentrated in Asia (though more than fifty central banks from around the world have indicated that they plan to invest part of their foreign currency reserves in the renminbi).[73] This would give China substantial leverage—from the perspective of monetary policy as well as foreign policy—over countries in Asia in particular, potentially counteracting efforts by Asian countries to reduce their economic dependence on China.[74] According to a 2014 report from the Bank of International Settlements, changes in RMB/USD rates have a significant impact on other Asian currency movements against the dollar.[75] Looking beyond the region, with an estimated 60 percent of China's foreign exchange reserves in U.S. dollars, China would no longer be nearly as susceptible to fluctuations in the value of the dollar and changes in U.S. economic policies.[76] An internationally recognized RMB also would create ample opportunity for China to play a larger role in influencing international financial institutions, such as the IMF and the World Bank. In what many heralded as the RMB's symbolic graduation into the ranks of the world's elite currencies, the IMF announced in December 2015 it would begin including the RMB in its market basket of currencies (which currently includes the dollar, yen, pound, and the euro) that together comprise an accounting unit known as the IMF's "special drawing right." The move required the IMF to certify that the RMB satisfied a two-pronged test for inclusion—that it was both "widely used" and "freely usable." While China had long met the first criterion—the RMB already widely used to settle trade between countries—the "freely usable" question was more fraught and the reason the IMF's move did not come much sooner (for some, the IMF's decision came without sufficient progress by Beijing, as nation-wide caps still limit the amount of RMB-denominated debt foreigners can hold).[77]

By removing itself from the dollar system and becoming less reliant on low-yield government bonds from developed markets, Beijing will gain greater pricing power over global commodities markets, where China is already often the largest consumer.[78] A reformed, rebalanced economy that rapidly expands its imports would also provide the Chinese government more leverage over other economies, especially as China pays for increasingly more of those imports in yuan.[79] Renminbi internationalization would also be accompanied by growing Chinese FDI, some Chinese scholars predict, which in turn implies a need for China to protect its overseas assets.[80] To adequately guard these new overseas assets, explains Chinese political economist Di Dongsheng, "Beijing will have to be capable of projecting power. Time and again in modern history hard power has followed where capital leads, flowing from advanced economies to developing nations regardless of the religion, culture, and ideology of the home country. Thus, China is likely to abandon its foreign policy orthodoxy of non-interference in order to protect its overseas investments."[81]

China's steady march toward internationalizing the RMB is already lending it new forms of influence, not just in Asia but more broadly as well.[82] Even Taiwan is tempted with the opportunity to sign a RMB currency swap agreement, a move that would create yet another irreversible cross-strait linkage.[83] A successful currency swap agreement will, in the words of the Central Bank of Taiwan's deputy governor, Yang Ching-long, "not only contribute to Taiwan's goal of becoming an offshore RMB market . . . but [it] will also facilitate China's bid to internationalize its currency."[84]

Even where these influences are more symbolic than real—many suggest that the world's acceptance of the RMB as a global reserve currency would give China greater symbolic sway within the region—these beliefs can come to influence China's foreign policy in ways that are difficult to predict. As Chinese analysts themselves describe the prospects, "China's traditional dependence on the dollar-based system will gradually give way to more balanced relations as use of the renminbi spreads. Consequently, competition between the great powers will rise, even leading to a bipolar—or tripolar, alongside the eurozone—global political economic system in the coming decades."[85]

Finally, a rising RMB may also come with costs for particular aspects of U.S. financial leverage, especially in the realm of sanctions. Certain financial sanctions—like those imposed on Iran's central bank—are effective only because these entities deal in U.S. dollars. But the stakes change if countries begin to settle transactions in RMB or other currencies. According to reports from the *Financial Times*, Iran and China began settling oil transactions in RMB—which, while not freely convertible, allowed Iran to evade sanctions and use the funds on Chinese imports.[86] Russian companies are hastening to switch contracts to renminbi and other currencies amid concerns that Western sanctions targeting Moscow for its incursion into Ukraine will freeze them out of the U.S. dollar market.[87]

If Beijing's ability to translate reserve currency status into geopolitical heft remains largely on the horizon, another powerful monetary tool that is already fully incorporated into Beijing's geoeconomic arsenal is the ability to impact another country's borrowing costs. There are several concrete

examples attesting to how the PRC's ability to do this can confer geopolitical leverage—often when states are at their most vulnerable. China's
decision not to devalue its currency during the 1997–1998 Asian financial
crisis earned Beijing gratitude across the region that lingers to this day.
Another example is China's desire for market economy status, a designation that served as a point of leverage during China's negotiations to join
the WTO prior to 2001.[88] Market economy status would give leverage to
Chinese companies that are accused of dumping—a term used when export products are priced below their real production cost. Over the last
decade, Chinese companies have been investigated for dumping products
from solar panels to bedroom furniture and televisions.[89] At various points
during the eurozone crisis, the Chinese have rather explicitly set the EU's
granting of market economy status to China as the condition for any capital injection.[90] It is a depreciating asset—Beijing argues the status should
expire in 2016 by the terms of its WTO entry—but if the Europeans unilaterally move to recognize China as a market economy without U.S. agreement, one could expect a serious transatlantic row that would weaken U.S.-
European geopolitical cooperation, at least in the short term.

But the most well-known example of Chinese leverage in this regard is
of course Chinese purchases of U.S. debt since 2001. The most often cited
contingency is that China could undertake a large and sudden sell-off of
its substantial holdings of U.S. Treasuries. Chinese officials have suggested
that its holdings of U.S. debt could be used in regard to economic and political disputes with the United States (most notably in 2010, when PLA
military officials took to Xinhua, China's leading news agency, to publicly
urge Beijing to "dump some U.S. bonds" to punish the United States for its
decision to follow through on an arms sale to Taiwan).[91]

Fortunately, Chinese PLA officers do not set the country's monetary
policy. And as many observers have noted, any significant sell-off of U.S.
debt would carry substantial costs for China, which would see the value of
its remaining Treasuries depreciate as a result. This self-inflicted deprecia-
tion, combined with the fact that U.S. bond markets are the world's
deepest, most liquid pool of marketable securities, together relieve Beijing's holdings of much of their coercive value (indeed, in a rare point of
agreement between economists and foreign policy strategists, most in
both groups seem persuaded that, far from a source of strength, China's
holdings are on balance a liability for Beijing).[92] As one Chinese banker explained less than a year after Lehman Brothers declared bankruptcy: "Except for U.S. Treasuries, what can you hold? U.S. Treasuries are the safe
haven. For everyone, including China, it is the only option. We hate you

guys. Once you start issuing $1 trillion to $2 trillion [of bonds], we know the dollar is going to depreciate, so we hate you guys, but there is nothing much we can do."[93]

This is probably true. At the same time, any balanced assessment should contend with at least four considerations. First, as Yale Law School professor David Singh Grewal put it in a 2009 essay on the subject, perhaps "the issue is not really about economics."[94] One could well imagine cases with stakes great enough for Beijing to accept the economic losses: almost certainly Taiwan would qualify, but rising tensions around territorial disputes, especially in the South and East China seas, suggest there may well be other flash points worth probing here in terms of the stakes they hold for some in Beijing. Most recently, there have been semi-official calls for the use of force to assert China's maritime claims against the Philippines, a U.S. ally, as well as Vietnam. One notable example was an unsigned fall 2011 editorial in *Global Times,* a voice of the Chinese government (known for its often nationalist editorial stance): "The South China Sea, as well as other sensitive sea areas, will have a higher risk of serious clashes. If these countries don't want to change their ways with China, they will need to prepare for the sounds of cannons. We need to be ready for that, as it may be the only way for the disputes in the sea to be resolved."[95]

Questions about Beijing's economic pain tolerance seem especially pertinent when considering that the "mutual assured destruction" argument outlined above rests on assumptions of economic rationality. Such assumptions should be considered carefully, though, as China's very accumulation of these reserves is not economically rational, at least not as economists define the term. Indeed, for all the international ire surrounding China's currency policies, no country loses from China's exchange rate policies more than China itself: according to estimates by the Bank of Canada, the cost to China from delayed adjustment of the RMB is around 12 percent of its GDP (these same estimates place the costs to the United States of China's currency policy at around 6 percent of U.S. GDP).[96]

At a minimum, the prospect of any significant reduction in China's Treasury holdings should be viewed against the cost of other relevant policy alternatives for Beijing, especially the use of force. And compared to risking military conflict with the United States or one of its allies, the cost to China of suddenly and substantially reducing its holdings of U.S. Treasuries may not seem all that irrational.

This touches on a related point: it is easy to underestimate the considerable domestic pressure Beijing faces in holding such substantial and growing sums of U.S. debt. China's reserve managers fell under strong public censure for their ownership of GSE debt during the financing crisis and still face continued criticism for underwriting U.S. consumption. In short, while the risk of any sudden reduction in Chinese holdings of U.S. debt is currently remote, it is also poorly understood. And Beijing, already having proven itself a price-insensitive buyer of Treasuries, could react as a price-insensitive seller if confronted with sufficiently profound geopolitical contingencies vis-à-vis the United States.

Moreover, any investor with sufficient market share could shift its holdings from one type of dollar-denominated instrument to another. A significant holder could choose to divest all agency mortgage-backed securities (e.g., Fannie Mae and Freddie Mac) it owns, for instance, or could sell longer-term Treasuries and reinvest the proceeds in short-term instruments, steepening the yield curve. Such shifts in portfolio holdings could further stunt the U.S. housing market or cause a sudden shift in the yield curve (thus tightening financial conditions and undermining much of what the Fed has done through its asset purchases)—all without affecting the overall value of the exchange rate, and thus the value of China's dollar holdings.

Further, for sovereigns with enough share of a given market, the simple prospect of such action, or indeed even a move simply to purchase fewer securities in the future, may be enough to disrupt markets. For example, "if Sino-American relations deteriorate over economic or international political issues," explains Cornell's Jonathan Kirshner, "it is likely that U.S. macroeconomic stability will be ruffled by China shuffling its dollar cards, even if it never folds them."[97] In May 2009, Beijing for the first time aired public concerns about the viability of U.S. debt, and followed this with a relative downsizing in its purchases of long-term U.S. Treasuries.[98] The result was a marked steepening of the yield curve as rates rose on longer-term U.S. bonds.[99] While China quickly resumed and even accelerated its purchases of longer-term Treasuries, Beijing's point seemed to register clearly on markets.

Finally, while central banks can and should offset these shifts—as the Fed did during 2008–2009 (structural limitations prevented the European Central Bank from doing the same)—any disruption, however temporary, could prove costly. Beyond a spike in U.S. borrowing costs, temporary disquiet in U.S. bond markets could deepen doubts about the dollar's continued ability to anchor the world's monetary system and, by extension, about the U.S. role as lead manager of the global economy. Further, the Fed's room for maneuver is neither infinite—some economists have suggested that foreign sovereign purchases of U.S. government debt, especially by countries with already huge reserve stockpiles constrained the Fed's ability to contain the bubble prior to 2007 (and Federal Reserve chairman Ben Bernanke has publicly offered similar sentiments)—nor politically easy.[100]

National policies governing energy and commodities. China's appetite for energy and resources is a powerful driver of geoeconomics in the post–Cold War era.[101] Much of this is structural. With nearly "1.4 billion mouths and a growing appetite for nationalism to feed," China has little choice but to pursue geoeconomic strategies that support its geopolitical objectives abroad and prioritize the legitimacy of the Communist Party at home.[102]

At the same time, though, perhaps counterintuitively, the sheer size of China's resource appetites also functions as a form of geoeconomic leverage.[103] China's negotiating clout is seen, for example, in Beijing's ability to win equity stakes in its gas contracts—not just in contracts with Central Asian suppliers (Turkmenistan is one example) but in those with Russia as well.[104] It is also seen in the way that a shrinking U.S. energy appetite in certain regions, West Africa for instance, can mean a wholesale shift in the foreign policies of countries such as Chad and Angola; as these producer countries reorient their energy sales eastward toward Asia, their capital flows and geopolitical relationships inevitably follow.[105]

Structural determinants aside, there are some cases where China has forthrightly pursued or hinted at pursuing energy and commodities policies on geopolitical motivations—examples noted earlier include export bans on rare earths as a means of registering dissatisfaction with policies around the South and East China Seas, or the 2012 comments by China National Offshore Oil Corporation chairman Wang Yilin characterizing China's deepwater rigs as "mobile national territory and a strategic weapon."[106] One such glimpse into the dual-use nature of these rigs came in May 2014 when, amid escalations in the South China Sea, China parked its first deepwater rig in what one press report described as "one of the most sensitive spots possible, about 17 miles off a speck of an island claimed by both China and Vietnam."[107] As press reports described the rig's arrival: "Few believe that energy discoveries were the primary reason for the arrival of rig HD-981, which is owned by China National Offshore Oil Corporation, or CNOOC, the state-run energy giant."[108] As Holly Morrow, a fellow in the Geopolitics of Energy program at Harvard's Kennedy School of Government, put it, "CNOOC is a business but also a political actor. . . . It's never about energy completely, it's about sovereignty."[109]

And there are still other cases that fall somewhere between the two, suggesting that if a state is big enough, a little coercion can cast a long, forward-looking shadow. This is in evidence in Southeast Asia, where energy companies drilling in disputed waters admit to preemptively partnering with Chinese SOEs so as to avoid harassment, such as the Philippine-British company Forum Energy partnering with CNOOC to drill off Reed Bank in the South China Sea.[110] It is an extension of the dynamic seen for years now with major private energy companies, which—seeing no alternative to mandatory joint ventures as the only means of entering the Chinese market—have effectively joined their interests to those of onetime Chinese competitors.

Nature or Nurture? China's Geoeconomic Endowments

Finally, it is worth revisiting the geoeconomic endowments outlined in Chapter 3 in the particular context of China. It reveals a country well suited to geoeconomics, though again, not without vulnerabilities and weaknesses.

Ability to control outbound investment. First is a state's willingness and ability to put domestic capital to geoeconomic use—be it outbound portfolio investment or outbound FDI, debt or equity. Between the state-owned investment vehicles for its reserve assets, sovereign wealth funds, state-owned banks, and its SOEs, Beijing controls not just vast sums but a number of mechanisms for channeling this investment.

Often these mechanisms are mutually reinforcing: its state banks and foreign exchange reserves are being spun into financing to support the "going out" of its SOEs, frequently in foreign mergers and deals involving strategic industries. In mid-2012, CNOOC swept into Canada with a $15.1 billion deal to buy one of Canada's largest energy producers, Nexen Inc., a venture intended to enable CNOOC to play a central role in technologies reshaping the North American energy landscape. The bid won approval from Ottawa and the Committee on Foreign Investment in the United States—since Nexen has U.S. interests—giving CNOOC control of Nexen's Long Lake oil sands project in Alberta as well as billions of barrels of reserves in the world's third-largest crude storehouse.[111] In January 2013, in another example, the management entity overseeing China's vast foreign exchange holdings (known as SAFE) announced plans to create a new Co-Financing Office charged with providing added liquidity to Chinese banks as they lend to domestic firms investing overseas. "In recent years, the central bank and SAFE have been creating new ways of using foreign exchange reserves to support the real economy and serve for the 'venturing abroad' strategy," as SAFE explained the move in a statement on its website.[112]

Six months later, in June 2013, Premier Li Keqiang hosted a cabinet meeting at which, according to Chinese state media, he said the government would support domestic enterprises to "go out" and make China's foreign reserves management more "innovative."[113] Weeks later, China's central bank followed SAFE's initial moves with a potentially larger initiative of its own, announcing in August 2013 that it was studying a plan to set up a new agency to invest the bulk of the nation's $3.5 trillion of foreign exchange reserves overseas for better returns.[114] The world got a hint of what this could entail when Chinese media reported in April 2015 that China would invest some $62 billion of its foreign exchange returns into its ambitious New Silk Road project, a project widely hailed as a geostrategic effort to expand Beijing's influence across Asia while also diversifying China's transport routes away from current choke points controlled by the U.S. military.[115]

Domestic market features. China's geoeconomic performance is in part a story about the strategic advantages of size and speed. According to one estimate, Chinese per-capita GDP rose from 6 percent of the U.S. level in 1980 to 22 percent in 2008,[116] and India's rose from 5 percent to 10 percent.[117] Studies by Robert Kuhn have linked domestic market features to Xi Jinping's much-vaunted "Chinese Dream," wherein China becomes a "moderately well-off society" by about 2020—specifically, by doubling China's per-capita GDP by 2020 and incorporating 70 percent of China's population into cities by 2030—and becoming "a fully developed nation" by the 100th anniversary of the establishment of the People's Republic of China.[118] China will eventually overtake the United States in absolute terms as the world's largest economy, a title that the United States has now held for approximately a century and a quarter. And so long as China continues its climb up the value ladder, supply chains will continue their relative shift away from the West, potentially dealing a hefty psychological and financially costly blow to the United States.

But from Nigeria to Indonesia to India, many countries are big and growing quickly, and yet they are without anything approaching China's geoeconomic throw weight. Even if China stands out as superlative in matters of size and speed, these attributes are too widespread to alone account for China's geoeconomic leverage. In fact, four more factors help explain China's ability to translate its domestic market into geoeconomic leverage. To review: first, Beijing exercises case-by-case discretion over access to its domestic market; second, China has the ability to redirect its domestic appetite to make a geopolitical point; third, either in fact or in perception, there is a consensus that its domestic market is too large for other nations to ignore; and finally, its growth trajectory is such that other countries see rising future costs to upsetting Beijing today. Taken together, these domestic market endowments are most readily felt in China's use of trade and investment as instruments of statecraft.

Influence over commodity and energy flows. Chapter 3 outlined the three basic variables that determine how successfully a country can, through its energy and commodity policies, influence its geoeconomic standing: monopoly power (market ownership), monopsony power (influence that comes from being the world's leading customer), and centrality as a transit point between major buyers and sellers. While China can only claim one of these—its title as the world's fastest-growing energy consumer—it has nonetheless managed to pull from other strengths in ways that amply compensate.

Probably the best recent example is China's thirty-year gas supply deal with Russia. Announced May 2014 after ten years of negotiations, the deal reflects a clear upper hand by Beijing.[119] The deal also demonstrates China's desire for energy supplies that do not need to travel via sea-lanes controlled by the U.S. Navy. The deal should mean greater gas supplies in the region (and, in turn, lower prices). While the Russia-China deal was greeted by robust press attention, just a year earlier China had concluded an agreement with Turkmenistan that was twice the size of its Moscow accord.[120] With anxieties over Russian neoimperialism rising across Central Asia, Turkmen officials were quick to hail the arrangement with China as the consummation of a "new strategic partnership" between the two.[121] But these supplies will still be transiting pipelines, and so they will potentially be subject to the same sort of pipeline politics that always make downstream customers vulnerable.

Centrality to the global financial system. Of all China's geoeconomic endowments, it is the country's centrality to the global financial system that remains the least utilized compared to potential. China has yet to liberalize its capital account, and its domestic financial sector remains underdeveloped in many respects, especially its equity and debt markets. Despite the considerable progress and maturation that still await, China's centrality to the global financial system is already a driving force behind its success in translating economic power into geopolitical clout. As an ever-larger share of China's trade is settled in RMB, and as new offshore financing hubs are added to those already in Hong Kong, Singapore, and the United Kingdom, China will assume new stature as an intermediary of capital, not just a supplier. As the country's financial maturation progresses, Beijing may also deepen its recent experimentation with sanctions, especially financial ones.

IN SUM, China's use of geoeconomic instruments has produced a robust diplomatic tool to shape other nation's policies. Heriberto Araújo and Juan Pablo Cardenal argue: "By buying companies, exploiting natural resources, building infrastructure and giving loans all over the world, China is pursuing a soft but unstoppable form of economic domination."[122] But, underscoring how collateral consequences can prove just as geopolitically potent as intended aims, these policies have also locked up significant quantities of global energy resources, grown the coffers of dictators unfriendly to the United States; lent new momentum to domestic proponents of China's own military buildup, and arguably have increased the odds of resource-based conflict.[123]

CHAPTER SIX

U.S. Foreign Policy and Geoeconomics in Historical Context

> For its first 150 years, the American foreign-policy tradition was deeply infused with economic logic. Unfortunately, thinking about international political economy has become a lost art in the United States.
>
> —ROBERT ZOELLICK, FORMER WORLD BANK PRESIDENT AND U.S. TRADE REPRESENTATIVE

THE PRESENT hesitancy in the United States toward geoeconomics stems from several factors—a lack of presidential leadership that has spanned both parties; the dominance of economic sanctions as the near-reflexive geoeconomic instrument of choice; and difficult bureaucratic politics, reflected in the steady migration of geoeconomic decision making away from the State Department and those responsible for placing U.S. foreign policy interests above all others.[1] These factors are all important contributing causes, and the United States is unlikely to improve its present understanding and use of geoeconomics without meaningfully addressing them.

But, taken alone, they do not adequately explain the ambivalence. After all, various U.S. presidents have waned in their enthusiasm for geoeconomic techniques of statecraft over the years—Woodrow Wilson's rejection of "dollar diplomacy," for instance—even as they and their coterie of advisors still recognized, debated, and utilized these techniques with far greater sophistication than seen today. Likewise, the United States has relied heavily on sanctions at several points in its history, but during these periods U.S. policy still evinced a level of comfort with geoeconomic instruments beyond sanctions that is not seen today. Finally, while bureaucratic politics have long plagued U.S. geoeconomic efforts—congressional reports on the issue trace as far back as the 1950s—recent bureaucratic impediments are indeed new in some ways, as Chapter 9 discusses.

There is yet another culprit contributing to the present ambivalence toward geoeconomics in the United States today: a faulty historical memory. In recent decades U.S. policy makers have plainly forgotten the traditional role that geoeconomics has played in this country's foreign policy.

Even to the casual witness of U.S. foreign policy debates in recent years, these historical blind spots are not hard to find. As one analyst stressed, "While . . . all governments step into economic matters in one way or another," China and Russia today "do so in ways unthinkable in the U.S."[2] Economics and politics, according to many mainstream accounts, are "relatively separable and autonomous spheres of activity," and to the extent one has bearing on the other, it is "economic rationality [that] ought to determine political relations," not the reverse.[3] U.S. officials and experts concede, for example, that a potential U.S.-EU trade deal, the Transatlantic Trade and Investment Partnership (TTIP), "could be seen as a 'second glue' to shore up the transatlantic relationship."[4] But "calling TTIP an 'economic NATO' would . . . be wrong."[5] These assertions reflect a widely held worldview that markets are somehow apolitical, to be kept free from geopolitical encroachments, and in any case not a proper arena for state power politics.[6]

It has not always been so. The United States declared war on Britain in 1812 only after years of embargoes failed to change the latter's behavior. William Howard Taft's "dollar diplomacy" proved to be a long-term failure, especially in Asia: it "encouraged Japan and Russia to increase cooperation in dividing Manchuria, alienated their British and French allies from the United States, weakened Chinese integrity, and show[ed] American diplomacy to be both naive and heavy-handed."[7] But whether such geoeconomic adventures have been successful or not, the United States has a long and extensive record of attempting them. For most of its history, the United States has regularly understood—and exercised—geoeconomic tools as part of its strategic battery.

In recent decades, however, America began to tell itself a different story about geoeconomics, both about its role in statecraft generally and about its historical role in American foreign policy specifically. U.S. policy makers began to see economics as its own distinctive realm, to be protected from the whims of statecraft. Writing to President Nixon in 1969, Richard Cooper—then a young staffer at the National Security Council who would go on to become a prominent Harvard economist and senior U.S. government official—acknowledged this growing separation between foreign policy and foreign economic policy, viewing it as something between necessary and desirable in promoting the U.S. aim of a liberal trading environment.[8] "Given general guidance for the achievement of a liberal trading environment," Cooper explained, "it was felt that foreign economic policy should be left alone, free from interference by shorter-term political considerations."[9]

As this bifurcation grew more ingrained over successive U.S. administrations, economics largely became the exclusive province of economists, all but unavailable to foreign policy makers, and except for sanctions, America's comfort level with geoeconomics began to wane. So began a structural separation that remains today. Bridging this divide begins with correcting the historical record on America's use of geoeconomics, and with isolating when things changed and why. A surer sense of history—and with it, perhaps a clearer national self-understanding—on these points will be crucial to deciding where and how geoeconomics ought to figure into American strategic calculus and the promotion of U.S. national interests today.

The American Revolution to 1914: The Geoeconomics of Survival

In the years following the American Revolutionary War, the Founding Fathers argued that the United States could not achieve true independence unless it was economically robust and self-sufficient. Thomas Jefferson put the point in a May 1797 letter to statesman and eventual vice president Elbridge Gerry. The British and French, Jefferson wrote,

> have wished a monopoly of commerce and influence with us; and they have in fact obtained it. When we take notice that theirs is the workshop to which we go for all we want . . . that to them belongs either openly or secretly the great mass of our navigation . . . that they are advancing fast to a monopoly of our banks and public funds, and thereby placing our public finances under their control . . . when they have shown that by all these bearings on the different branches of the government, they can force it to proceed in whatever direction they dictate, and bend the interests of this country entirely to the will of another; when all this, I say, is attended to, it is impossible for us to say we stand on independent ground.

It is difficult to find a clearer example of geoeconomic concern and intent.

Jefferson voiced the common understanding that America's greatest early threats were geoeconomic in nature. Others never lost enthusiasm for shows of geoeconomic opportunism. Keenly aware that Europe would be the most likely source for possible threats to American security, Benjamin Franklin suggested that America should consider offering its commerce in exchange for the friendship of European states.[10] Thomas Paine, in *Common Sense*, explained how "our plan is commerce, and that, well attended to, will secure us the peace and friendship of all Europe; because it is in the interest of all Europe to have America as a free port. Her trade will always be a protection." Paine was under no illusions that America's economic interests might somehow be separated from Europe's. Rather, geoeconomics was Paine's solution. It was through trade that the United States might play off European states against each other in international politics. "By providing European states with equal access to American ports," one source explained, "each will have an interest in preventing others from threatening America's independence."[11] And Alexander Hamilton, the father of American capitalism, saw commerce as a weapon in power politics, a proposition not likely to win a referendum among today's trade policy makers.[12]

In a rare point of agreement between them, Hamilton and Thomas Jefferson shared a basic enthusiasm for geoeconomic tools of foreign policy. Jefferson is rightly remembered for having scored one of America's greatest geoeconomic successes in its history: in April 1803, he oversaw the purchase of 828,000 square miles of land between the Mississippi River and the Rocky Mountains, doubling America's size for a mere four cents an acre ($15 million in total). The economic rationale was self-evident; Jefferson wanted to ensure that American farmers in the Ohio River Valley had access to the Gulf of Mexico via the Mississippi River—the river offered these farmers a crucial vent for their surplus grain and meat. The more fundamental motivation, however, was geopolitical. In May 1802, Jefferson confided to James Monroe that "we have great reason to fear that Spain is to cede Louisiana and the Floridas to France." He knew that the United States could not undertake a military confrontation with Napoleon Bonaparte's France; he also assessed, however, that if France secured the aforementioned territories, it would be emboldened to expand into and plant roots in the very areas on which Jefferson had trained his strategic sights. As Jefferson warned America's ambassador to France, Robert Livingston, "The day that France takes possession of [New] Orleans, fixes the sentence which is to restrain her forever within her low-water mark. It seals the union of two nations, who, in conjunction, can maintain exclusive possession of the ocean."[13]

As with recent U.S. administrations and Congress, America's early leaders also showed a clear appreciation for sanctions as a geopolitical instrument. Jefferson believed that economic sanctions could be used to bring peaceful pressure on other states, and he instituted an embargo to protect American seamen and avert war with Britain on his watch.

Presaging the prolonged Washington debate on U.S. policy toward Iran, in November 1808 Jefferson himself argued that there were only three policies for responding to English belligerence: "embargo," "war," or "submission and tribute." Not unlike the latter-day struggles of his successors, Jefferson too lacked a perfect blueprint for the use of the sanctions tool. The 1807 embargo against British goods was unsuccessful and was eventually repealed. The American economy suffered, American public opinion opposed the policy, and the embargo failed to have a consequential impact on British actions. In 1815, Jefferson, with geoeconomics on his mind, wrote to the French economist Jean-Baptiste Say, lamenting how during wartime "the interception of exchanges . . . becomes a powerful weapon in the hands of the enemy," and extolling protectionism as a means by which the country may be secured "against a relapse into foreign dependency."[14]

During the Civil War, the Union successfully threatened Great Britain with trade sanctions, vowing a complete cessation of trade, including an end to grain shipments, and the loss of billions of dollars invested in U.S. securities. This potential geoeconomic coercion was one of the factors, along with U.S. willingness to use military force, British suspicion of French motives, and British repugnance toward slavery, that led London to stop supporting the Confederacy.[15] A few years later, as the task turned from warfighting to reconstruction, U.S. leaders did not lose sight of geoeconomic opportunities that would not merely restore America but strengthen it beyond its antebellum position. Secretary of State William Seward negotiated the purchase of Alaska from Russia in March 1867, increasing the country's size by more than 586,000 square miles for roughly two cents an acre ($7.2 million in total). Going on to begin negotiations similar territorial sales in Panama and Hawaii, "Seward laid the foundation for the United States to become not merely a continental power but an international empire."[16]

In December 1898, the United States paid $20 million to purchase the Philippines as part of the peace deal that would end the Spanish-American War. Concerned, then as now, about the future of China and arguing for an early pivot to Asia, Arthur MacArthur Jr., appointed in 1900 as the military governor of the Philippines, was convinced that "the only open field that presents any attractions to the practical economist is in the Far East." He concluded that "peaceful possession of the Philippine Archipelago by the United States . . . is absolutely essential to the progressive development of American national interests." MacArthur saw it as "the stepping stone to commanding influence, if not political, commercial, and military supremacy, in the East" and "a base from which American interests can be effectively protected."[17]

Thus geoeconomics was in the bloodstream of American leaders from the early days of the Republic. Facing predatory European nations and possessing weak military power projection, the founders as a matter of expediency instinctively reached for economic instruments to protect the young and vulnerable United States. As the North American continent was explored and conquered, their successors used the same tools decade by decade to broaden the U.S. strategic horizon into Asia and Latin America. Even as several of the founding leaders, such as Benjamin Franklin, evolved their views on basic questions of market orientation, abandoning mercantilism in support of free trade, their embrace of geoeconomics remained constant. The nineteenth-century grand strategy was established: military force at home to keep the country together and subdue Native American tribes, and geoeconomics abroad to generate wealth and expand the American empire.

As Americans from Alexander Hamilton onward understood with great clarity, the American economy existed within an international trading and investment system that was centered on Great Britain's naval might and industrial ingenuity and capacity. For many generations, geoeconomics in the United States involved the question of how the connection between the American economy and the British system could be accomplished so as to maximize American prosperity and security. But beginning with World War I and accelerating through the 1940s, this U.K.-supported global commercial system began to weaken, and London gradually lost its strength and eventually its political will to defend it, leaving Washington with the profound question of how best to manage world order.

World Wars I and II:
The Geoeconomics of Total War

The outbreak of war in 1914 brought a profound shift in America's relationship with geoeconomics. By World War I, geoeconomic policies, especially ones of economic privation, had entered into the bloodstream of British strategic thought. As British foreign secretary Viscount Grey of Fallodon recounted in his memoirs, "The object of diplomacy . . . was to secure the maximum blockade that could be enforced without a rupture with the United States," which still clung zealously to its neutral trading rights with Germany.[18] The British very nearly pushed too hard. But fortunately for London, the Germans' aggressive U-boat campaign in the Atlantic soon "helped to put things into a clearer perspective in the USA," especially following the sinking of the *Lusitania* in May 1915.[19] But once Washington entered the war in 1917, the Americans introduced economic embargo measures even tougher than the British. Within a matter of months, the United States pivoted to full cooperation with the Allies' food blockade of

Germany and then embargoed all exports to the Scandinavian countries and the Netherlands, all of which had stayed neutral. America's exposure to the horrors of total war in 1917–1918 "appeared speedily to disabuse it of any fond belief that the principles of extensive trading rights for neutral nations could be upheld in time of war."[20]

It was around the same time that Woodrow Wilson became outspoken in his criticism of "dollar diplomacy." Speaking at Independence Hall on July 4, 1914, on the nature of liberty, Wilson staked his opposition thus: "There is no man who is more interested than I am in carrying the enterprise of American business to every quarter of the globe . . . [But] if American enterprise in foreign countries, particularly in those foreign countries which are not strong enough to resist us, takes the shape of imposing upon and exploiting the mass of the people of that country, it ought to be checked and not encouraged. I am willing to get anything for an American that money and enterprise can obtain except the suppression of the rights of other men."[21]

Wilson took issue with the ends of "dollar diplomacy," not the means, in other words. So long as geoeconomic instruments were put in the service of U.S. foreign policy aims that Wilson considered valid, he believed they had a legitimate, even vital, role to play. This was seen certainly in his zeal for economic embargo once the United States entered the war. But by 1919, as Washington was shifting its focus from winning the Great War to the less familiar task of advancing the peace, Woodrow Wilson came to believe that the League of Nations could prevent war by imposing an "absolute" boycott on aggressor countries. "A nation boycotted is a nation that is in sight of surrender," he explained. "Apply this economic, peaceful, silent, deadly remedy and there will be no need for force. It is a terrible remedy. It does not cost a life outside the nation boycotted, but it brings pressure upon the nation that, in my judgment, no modern nation could resist."[22]

Even as American isolationism returned in the period following World War I, U.S. geoeconomic policy was still at work in the world—if anything, deepening during the interwar period. "Disillusionment with the war, international commitments that could lead to war, and economic uncertainty discouraged ambitious U.S. involvement in global affairs during the interwar period," as the State Department historian summarized the national mood at that time. Even as the United States fatigued of Europe's military dilemmas, President Wilson and his foreign policy architects turned to facilitating U.S. private investment overseas; U.S. investment dollars would be their mechanism of choice for expanding America's influence abroad.[23]

The Dawes Plan, for instance, allowed U.S. banks to lend Germany enough money to enable it to meet its reparation payments to France and the United Kingdom. Those countries used the received payments to service their war debts to the United States. Economic policy making in Berlin was reorganized under foreign supervision just as the reichsmark was adopted as new currency. Foreign supervision of German finances only ceased—and the last occupying troops left German soil—under the Young Plan in 1929.[24]

In 1934, the Roosevelt administration established the Export-Import Bank with the narrow objective of facilitating trade with the Soviet Union. In the late 1930s, however, its focus expanded. "In June 1938," according to one assessment, "the Bank made its first Latin American commitment that seemed to be influenced by considerations of foreign policy: an agreement with the Haitian government to purchase up to $5 million of notes to be issued to an American construction company in connection with an extensive public works program in the country."[25]

The Roosevelt administration intervened to preempt German encroachment in the Western Hemisphere, and more generally used trade to keep Germany out of its backyard. "Between 1934 and 1945, twenty-nine Reciprocal Trade Agreement treaties were made between the United States and various Latin American countries."[26] The administration also attempted to use the Ex-Im Bank to blunt the rise of Japan: citing a "bare chance we may still keep a democratic form of government in the Pacific," Secretary of the Treasury Henry Morgenthau Jr. helped arrange a $25 million loan to China in December 1938.[27]

A year and a half after the outbreak of World War II in Europe, the Lend-Lease policy of 1941 (formally titled An Act to Further Promote the Defense of the United States) enabled the United States to supply Great Britain, France, the Republic of China, and later the USSR and other Allied nations with defense materials, effectively ending the American pretense of neutrality. In all, some $50.1 billion worth of supplies (with a cost of approximately $660 billion in today's dollars) were shipped, or 17 percent of the total war expenditures of the United States. Of this, $31.4 billion went to Britain, $11.3 billion to the Soviet Union, $3.2 billion to France, $1.6 billion to China, and the remaining $2.6 billion to other allies.[28]

Secretary of War Henry Stimson regarded Lend-Lease as "a declaration of economic war."[29] Many in London saw it as a form of economic warfare against Britain. Their belief was not entirely unfounded: Lend-Lease exercised control over British exports, sought unilateral decision over the level of British gold and dollar reserves, and sought to extract U.K. concessions about the character of postwar commitments to participate fully in the new economic order. As such, Lend-Lease policies also helped sweep away whatever lingering discomforts there might have been in Washington about the unabashed wielding of geoeconomic power, at least in times of existential threat.

Interestingly, had the U.S.-U.K. alliance been less resolute, the British might have obtained more favorable terms under Lend-Lease. Throughout the eight years of Lend-Lease, the Americans were far tougher on the British than on the French or the Soviets. Despite massive U.S. aid to Moscow, interdependence between the Soviet Union and the United States did not exactly foster in Stalin a vested interest in working with the United States to create a liberal capitalist postwar world order. Washington's decision to refrain from exercising economic leverage on the Soviets during the European war was driven partly by fears of a separately negotiated peace between the Soviets and Hitler (à la the Nazi-Soviet nonaggression pact of 1939) and partly by the desire to gain Soviet support for defeating the Japanese.[30]

With its entry into World War II, America would once again see its views toward both neutrality and neutral rights to trade powerfully reshaped. In a transformation led principally by FDR, U.S. Treasury Secretary Henry Morgenthau, his assistant Harry White, and Vice President Henry Wallace, the United States developed a renewed zeal for economic warfare, going well beyond anything the British had contemplated in their sanctions and embargo efforts. Washington widened its definition of contraband, and no longer insisted that a blockade be physically enforceable to be a blockade—innovations that U.S. leaders touted in far more moralistic terms than the more legal, pragmatic rationales favored by Whitehall. "Moralizing was not exorcised from U.S. decision-making," explains historian Alan Dobson. "It was simply given a new direction and content."[31]

Geoeconomics may have been more strongly represented in U.S. foreign policy during this period, but it was not necessarily any easier. Bureaucratic tensions within the U.S. government vexed implementation of embargoes during World War II. As two members of the Foreign Economic Administration (a short-lived office established to overcome these tensions) summarized the situation:

> Even after we entered the war . . . the definition of responsibilities among the [U.S. government] agencies interested in various aspects of these programs was far from perfect. For one thing, economic warfare was a fascinating subject to dabble in, and everyone had ideas about what should be done. . . . The Board of Economic Warfare . . . had been intended to provide coordination and guidance, but it met infrequently and was abolished after the Wallace-Jones feud broke into the newspapers. Only the President could finally decide the controversies, and he usually had other things to do.[32]

When it comes to formulating and implementing geoeconomic policies, destructive U.S. bureaucratic politics have a rich history, it seems; such sentiments could just as well have been written by frustrated American foreign policy strategists yesterday.

Nor was foreign policy back then necessarily more self-aware than it is today. In what would go down as one of America's most ironic displays of geoeconomic statecraft, after threatening Sweden with retaliation for not upholding its neutral rights in January 1943, U.S. Secretary of State Cordell Hull returned to the subject eighteen months later, this time warning Sweden of retaliation if it did not abrogate those very same rights (by Hull's account, "nothing short of embargo and radical change in Sweden's German policy would satisfy our [Allied] demands").[33] This serves as yet another reminder that consistency has not always been a hallmark of U.S. diplomacy, then or now.

But these geoeconomic efforts were better resourced, more ambitious, and more in the foreground of U.S. strategy than is true today. In 1943, the United States established the Office of Economic Warfare, dispatching more than 200 market analysts around the world and housing nearly 3,000 experts in Washington with orders to safeguard the dollar by bolstering the U.S. current account position and by securing vital imports at favorable terms.[34] In July 1944, delegates from the Allied countries signed the Bretton Woods Agreement, seeing strengthened international economic cooperation as their best hope for avoiding the horrors of another global war. Secretary of State Hull explained: "Unhampered trade dovetailed with peace; high tariffs, trade barriers, and unfair economic competition, with war . . . [I]f we could get a freer flow of trade—freer in the sense of fewer discriminations and obstructions . . . so that one country would not be deadly jealous of another and the living standards of all countries might rise, thereby eliminating the economic dissatisfaction that breeds war, we might have a reasonable chance of lasting peace."[35] The goal, of course, was lasting peace on America's terms. Baldwin notes, echoing a widely shared view, that "the American use of trade policy to construct an international economic order based on nondiscriminatory trade liberalization in the period after World War II was one of the most successful influence attempts using economic policy instruments ever undertaken."[36]

To be sure, other economic techniques, such as aid (especially the Marshall Plan), currency stabilization, and promotion of private investment, were also important components of American foreign policy. But American trade policy was the key to success. Even at the time of the Bretton Woods conference in 1944, this was well understood. As one attendee, writing in the *New York Times,* put it, "Commercial policy . . . is the key to the whole show, for there is practically no one here who has the slightest confidence in the efficacy of any of the machinery in the process of building in the absence of an American trade policy that lowers tariff barriers and makes it possible for the world's greatest creditor nation to perform her proper function of buyer."[37]

The Postwar Period and the Early Cold War:
A Golden Age of American Geoeconomics

America's geoeconomic reflexes remained in full flower after the war, abetted by U.S. economic dominance and the USSR's economic isolation. As early postwar consensus began to settle on economic factors as being among the leading causes of World War II, U.S. policy makers answered with a largely geoeconomic plan for achieving lasting peace, in Europe and beyond. Lend-Lease was rolled over to become one of the first forms of U.S. postwar assistance. A fierce debate erupted within the U.S. government over whether to include the Soviet Union among the eligible recipients of postwar Lend-Lease financing, with some favoring the move as liberalizing and others seeing the need to use economic leverage to bring the Soviets into line. But by 1946 Truman had lost patience with Moscow, declaring himself "tired of babying the Soviets," and by the following year the debate had shifted away from extending postwar financing to applying geoeconomic pressure.[38]

These various preoccupations finally came together in June 1947, when Secretary of State George Marshall, delivering commencement remarks at Harvard University, famously declared that "the United States should do whatever it is able to do to assist in the return of normal economic health in the world, without which there can be no political stability and no assured peace. Our policy is directed not against any country or doctrine but against hunger, poverty, desperation, and chaos. Its purpose should be the revival of a working economy in the world so as to permit the emergence of political and social conditions in which free institutions can exist."[39]

Even though countering the threat of Communism was the central impetus behind the European Recovery Program, Marshall mentioned neither Communism nor the Soviet Union in his remarks. In a secret memorandum prepared the previous month, George Kennan had advised him to counter a prevalent impression among Americans that "the effort to restore sound economic conditions is . . . not something we would be interested in doing if there were no Communist menace."[40] Kennan's careful efforts to hide the geoeconomic underpinnings of the new U.S. policy—even at a time that was essentially the high point of geoeconomic thinking in U.S. foreign policy—illuminates how rarely geoeconomic motives are plainly stated (and why, consequently, conceptual frameworks for geoeconomics cannot reasonably be expected to rely on states explicitly acknowledging when geoeconomic factors are indeed driving policy).

All the same, Truman administration officials—including Kennan—certainly understood the Marshall Plan's geoeconomic objectives. In his secret memo, Kennan argued that "American effort in aid to Europe" should attempt to redress "the economic maladjustment which makes European society vulnerable to exploitation by any and all totalitarian movements and which Russian communism is now exploiting."[41] That October, Undersecretary of State Robert Lovett warned that Western European countries "would go to the Soviet [Union]" if the Marshall Plan was not implemented.[42] On August 22, 1949, Truman observed that "the military assistance program and the European recovery program are part and parcel of the same policy. There is the closest relationship between economic recovery and military defense. . . . [E]conomic recovery will lag if the haunting fear of military aggression is widespread."[43] Kennan argued that U.S. policy should not aim to develop Western European satellites but rather to ensure that "elements of independent power are developed on the Eurasian land mass as rapidly as possible, in order to take off our shoulders some of the burden of 'bi-polarity.' To my mind, the chief beauty of the Marshall Plan is that it had outstandingly this effect."[44]

Around the same time, U.S. and European allies agreed on a joint embargo against the Soviet Union. Enacted through a coordinating committee known as COCOM, the embargo initially prohibited the export to the Soviet Union of about 130 items deemed strategic. But a constellation of factors—the Chinese Communist victory over Chiang Kai-shek, the successful test of the first Soviet atomic weapon in 1949, the shift in Washington toward a more assertive strategy of "containment" (building largely from Kennan's ideas), and the outbreak of war on the Korean Peninsula in June 1950—would combine to push COCOM to expand its embargo. Overcoming European reluctance, the United States succeeded in extending the COCOM embargo to China and in expanding its scope to include not only certain strategic items, but also those with significant economic potential ("selected items in key industrial areas contributing substantially to war potential"[45]).

Whatever assumptions concerning the Cold War had emerged by January 1953, many of them were gone by July. In January, President Eisenhower succeeded Truman, the first U.S. presidential transition since the onset of the Cold War; in March, Stalin died; and in July, the Korean War ended with the establishment of the demilitarized zone. Faced with a much different strategic landscape, U.S. foreign policy considerations—while still the sole driver of East-West trade policy—soon began to push things in the opposite direction. President Eisenhower came into office committed to the idea of achieving relative gains through East-West trade, a prospect that would require him to liberalize aspects of the embargo. Within eight months, Eisenhower established the Commission on Foreign Economic Policy on precisely these grounds: "The national interest in the field of foreign economic policy is clear. It is to obtain . . . the highest possible level of trade and the most efficient use of capital and resources. That this would also strengthen our military allies adds urgency. Their strength is of critical importance to the security of our country."[46]

Eisenhower prevailed. Between 1953 and 1954, COCOM reduced the number of items on its Soviet Union embargo list by 50 percent. But the China embargo remained unchanged—partly out of a desire to keep maximum pressure on China during the Korean armistice, and partly because of a compromise to assuage opponents of Eisenhower's push for expanded East-West trade.

European allies continued to agitate for further liberalization in the Soviet embargo. There was by that time widespread acknowledgment that the embargo was neither restricting growth in the Soviet Union nor hindering its war-fighting potential (a point punctuated by the successful launch of *Sputnik I* in October 1957). Strikingly, while European members of COCOM seized on this lack of economic impact in their arguments for further liberalization of the Soviet embargo, it did not seem to much enter U.S. discussions of whether to liberalize; if anything, rationales simply shifted to justify the embargo on moral and symbolic grounds.[47] In 1958, on the heels of significant Allied pressure, the COCOM Soviet embargo list was reduced further, bringing the total down from the 282 items agreed upon in 1954 to 155. One salient feature of the debates over liberalizing the COCOM embargoes was the singular focus on security and foreign policy considerations—disagreements turned only on how best to achieve these aims, not whether these geoeconomic aims ought to be considered against other concerns. There was, in particular, no debate over a lack of capitalist, free-market principles in U.S. policy toward China and the Soviet Union.

When President Kennedy assumed office in 1961, he brought his own geoeconomic reasons for supporting COCOM liberalizations. For Kennedy, further easing the embargoes made sense not because they were having no real economic impact but because he thought it a potential means of eliciting quid pro quos from the Soviets. The strategy, known as "flexible response," was coined by State Department policy planning director Walt Rostow (also, incidentally, a top-notch economist and one of the few economists to hold that post since).[48] "Flexible response" did take hold in NATO regarding the nuclear defense of Europe, although not to any effect on the economic front. Its emphasis on a quid pro quo presented a first-mover problem, making the plan reliant on some showing of good behavior from Moscow that never came (or, at least, was preempted by the Cuban missile crisis in 1962).

Around this time the importance of the rest of the world came into geo-economic focus for U.S. Cold War policy makers. In 1960, a task force commissioned by President-elect Kennedy argued for liberalization in East-West trade, and assistance to developing nations as a means of keeping up with the Soviet Union (the task force's recommendations became known as the Ball Report, named for committee chairman George Ball).[49] Compared to 1950, when trading capacity in the Soviet bloc countries was negligible, by 1960, Ball argued, these countries had developed "the ability to export surpluses, which they are now beginning to use in furthering their external commercial and political objectives."[50]

While strict economic logic might welcome a pickup in trade between the Soviet Union and the non-Communist world as a heartening trend, this was not how Washington saw matters at the time. Between its commitment to liberal economic principles and fears over expanding Soviet influence, the U.S. government viewed Communist trade penetration of these markets with real concern, though the feeling was more one of reluctant acknowledgment than outright alarm: "if it had to happen, then the U.S. would try to ensure that the USSR abided, as far as possible, by free market rules."[51] Here again, the Ball Report, like earlier discussions of East-West trade, is striking for its sole focus on U.S. foreign policy aims (fidelity to principles of capitalism and free markets does not enter as an animating concern) and for its matter-of-fact subordination of economic instruments firmly in the service of U.S. geopolitical objectives—in short, a geoeconomic approach.

America's geoeconomic reflexes continued in ample force under President Johnson. In 1964, for instance, the United States seized upon the split between Moscow and Bucharest by offering Gheorghe Gheorghiu-Dej, president of the Romanian State Council, a package of commercial incentives and normalizing trade relations.[52] On the matter of East-West trade, the State Department by 1964 advocated loosening the embargo on the forthrightly geoeconomic grounds that "the amount of the trade, whatever it is, be substantial enough to make it available as a tool of United States foreign policy in advancement of United States objectives towards the Communist countries."[53]

Sensing growing U.S. public support for expanded East-West trade, President Johnson pledged in his 1965 State of the Union address to "explore ways to expand peaceful trade with [Eastern European] countries and the Soviet Union," establishing a task force on the issue. The deliberations and conclusions of the task force (known as the Miller Committee, named for chairman J. Irwin Miller, of the Cummins Engine Company) further underscored a basic comfort with employing trade policy as an effective and appropriate tool to advance U.S. foreign policy; even more striking is that this subordination of economics to geopolitical aims was seen as perfectly in keeping with the committee's explicit embrace of free-market capitalism.[54] At least for the historical moment that encompassed the Miller Committee and its work, geoeconomics and liberal, free-market economic policies coexisted quite comfortably.

Finally, even as senior U.S. policy makers trained much of their attention toward Europe and the Soviet Union during these early post–World War II decades, Washington was also greatly preoccupied with the economic vitality and geopolitical stability of South Korea and Japan. After fighting a war to defend South Korea, the U.S. policy toward that country was guided by a strong interest in avoiding its political or economic collapse and the possibility of a Communist revolution. Thus the U.S. geoeconomic chose to pour aid into South Korea—aid shifted from grants to concessional loans to Ex-Im Bank loans.[55] Dynamics were different in Japan, however, as Tokyo resisted repeated U.S. efforts to get Japan to open its markets more to foreign goods and to change other economic practices seen as adverse to U.S. economic interests. But even here, U.S. geopolitical preoccupations, centered as they were on the Soviet Union, led Washington to restrain itself from a full-fledged trade war with Japan.

War in Vietnam, the Defeat of Communism, the Rise of Terrorism, and the Steady Decline of Geoeconomics

The earliest origins of America's current preoccupation with political military measures over geoeconomic instruments trace back to the Cold War. Even as U.S. geoeconomic statecraft was at its prime, some of the country's most important Cold War policies were unintentionally helping to cultivate a bias toward military and political military statecraft. Containment and détente offer two such examples. In his seminal 1946 "Long Telegram" from Moscow and the article he published under the pseudonym "X" in *Foreign Affairs* in 1947, George Kennan concluded that Soviet foreign policy would reflect "persistent pressure toward the disruption and weakening of all rival influence and rival power." As such, he advised the United States to adopt a "policy of firm containment, designed to confront the Russians with unalterable counterforce at every point where they show signs of encroaching upon the interest of a peaceful and stable world."[56]

During this period, it was far from clear that the doctrine of containment was to be construed primarily in terms of military force. To Kennan's dismay, it slowly became so, but this narrowing process was gradual—elaborated largely through various refinements to containment. It was, for example, another historic document, known as NSC-68 (often seen as a corollary to Kennan's earlier containment concept), in which State Department policy planning director Paul Nitze and his colleagues in 1950 assessed that the United States would have to "possess superior overall power in ourselves or in dependable combination with other likeminded nations" to confront the Soviet Union. Without "superior aggregate military strength, in being and readily mobilizable," they explained, "a policy of 'containment' . . . is no more than a policy of bluff." NSC-68 went on to warn that America's "military strength is becoming dangerously inadequate."[57] It was clear that containment was increasingly interpreted and prosecuted as an overwhelmingly military exercise, embodied in NATO. At the same time, the Soviet Union's minimalist international economic activity meant that although geoeconomic levers were routinely deployed throughout much of the Cold War, they were understood in Washington as having low overall impact on Moscow's policies or the cohesion of the Warsaw Pact nations.

But this is not to say that American geoeconomic efforts did not at times cause a stir in the Soviet Union. In the early 1960s, the supposedly contradictory behavior of the United States—its deviation from laissez-faire principles of capitalism in the name of national security—sparked an angry outburst from Soviet leader Nikita Khrushchev. At the time the Soviet Union was hyper focused on developing its oil industry, partly for strategic reasons but also in the hopes of exporting oil and gas to the West in exchange for hard currency, which Moscow needed in order to purchase Western technology. Unfortunately, one of the production pitfalls involved a certain kind of wide-diameter steel pipes (made only in the West) needed to move oil from the wellhead to refineries and on to the market.[58] Rather than obliging the Soviets and selling large quantities of piping, the United States orchestrated concerted opposition through COCOM, through NATO, and via bilateral avenues with countries such as Japan.[59] Exasperated, Khrushchev reportedly burst out to his advisors, "Who the hell do these capitalists think they are, to believe that they can go around and not act like capitalists?"[60]

Whatever precipitating role earlier Cold War policies such as containment and its refinements might have played in the U.S. prioritization of military and diplomatic approaches against the Soviets, it was not until the Johnson and Nixon years that geoeconomics noticeably began to wane. This is attributable in large part to Vietnam; in an era of nuclear weapons, it was perhaps inevitable that the outbreak of armed conflict and U.S. troops on the ground in Southeast Asia would shift policy makers' attention in the direction of military use of force.[61]

But there was more to it. During the mid-1960s, a domestic commercial constituency for East-West trade began to emerge. By the December 1969 passage of the East-West trade bill, it was clear that this was not the legislation that Johnson or the Miller Committee had hoped for and proposed back in 1965. Strikingly, the 1969 bill was framed in far more liberal terms than either Nixon or Kissinger wanted; for the first time in the Cold War, Congress led the administration in promoting liberalization of East-West trade. In its reporting on export controls for the new act, the Senate Banking Committee expressly noted that circumstances had changed since the Export Control Act had been enacted; trying to control Soviet economic growth was now untenable, and as a result, the existing Export Control Act served only to disadvantage U.S. companies.[62] (It is noteworthy that exactly the same argument has been reprised by those who oppose economic sanctions against Russia regarding its behavior in Ukraine). Mere economic significance to the Soviet Union would no longer serve as a justification for export control.

Nixon himself seemed to have little affection for geoeconomics. Like Eisenhower, Nixon was skeptical of trade as a tool to spur political liberalization in the Soviet Union (as he once explained the relationship, "I do not accept the philosophy that increased trade results in improved political relations. In fact, just the converse is true. Better political relations lead to improved trade").[63] At the same time, though, it was not as if Nixon had alternative geoeconomic-minded strategies, either on the issue of East-West trade specifically or as part of his Cold War efforts more broadly. On the contrary, Nixon and his advisors viewed détente as a largely geopolitical exercise, with very little geoeconomic content.[64] Economic issues took a decided backseat in Nixon's foreign policy. For earlier administrations more inclined toward geoeconomics—those of Truman, Kennedy, and Eisenhower—the steady disintegration of the Bretton Woods system of exchange rates anchored by the U.S. dollar would have marked a "primary threat to United States interests and the health of the anti-Soviet coalition in 1969—a threat far greater than anything Ho Chi Minh could ever assemble in the far-off jungles of Indochina."[65] For Nixon, though, worrying about monetary coordination was hardly the stuff of first-order foreign policy. "I don't give a shit about the value of the *lira!*" as Nixon once expostulated to his staff.[66]

Nixon was not alone. Slowly but unmistakably, the mood in Washington had begun to turn away from geoeconomics. As political scientist I. M. Destler summarized it, the change in temperament progressed steadily, showing itself in the early 1960s, when "congressional leaders complained that the State Department neither understood nor represented U.S. economic interests."[67] In 1962, Congress forced JFK to establish a trade coordination office in the White House (rather than the state department) as a precondition for launching a major new trade liberalization effort. But a more palpable shift came in 1971, when Nixon ended the dollar's convertibility into gold and pushed allies into difficult U.S. economic interests.[68] Indeed, with his decision on the gold window, Nixon demonstrated his unwillingness to subordinate economic interests to geopolitical aims. (Kissinger was absent from the room when Nixon made the decision and informed the European allies—a slight that Kissinger would later recount as among the most difficult of all his years in government.)[69]

Similarly, when U.S. farmers, eager to turn their crop into cash, won the hotly debated question of whether to hold grain sales to the Soviets hostage to political concessions, U.S. foreign policy makers were put on notice. For Kissinger, who argued that "the U.S. grain crop was a tremendous asset," "merely pouring out grain for gold" was "very painful" when it "could have bought a year or so of Soviet good behavior."[70] The episode, which became known as the "Great Grain Robbery of 1972," made clear that no longer could policy makers expect geoeconomic approaches to be as readily available to them. Gone were the days when economic instruments could be exercised purely for geopolitical advantage.[71]

If Nixon was disinclined toward geoeconomic approaches to begin with, the 1973–1974 oil crisis and the general onset of economic insecurity in the mid-1970s only further lessened his enthusiasm, especially when it came to trading economic concessions for geopolitical objectives. By the mid-1970s, the domestic commercial constituencies for East–West trade had fully awoken to the possibilities of more liberalized flows. These constituencies, Dobson recounts, "became more influential, and although they still backed détente, they were primarily concerned with sales and profits; exchanging economic advantages for foreign policy gains had little appeal."[72] Soon Congress mobilized to their cause, and there were concurrent reviews of the issue. The final report by the Committee on International Economic Policy, in marked contrast to the Miller Report four years earlier, recommended reductions in U.S. lists to COCOM levels and less onerous licensing—not so much on national security grounds but in order to make U.S. companies more competitive. In an indication of the deteriorating environment for geoeconomics, the new report not only suggested that the administration should seek most-favored-nation (MFN) status with the Soviets but also cautioned that "we should not seek to use MFN as a political tool."[73]

In addition, the bureaucratic reorganizations that followed Watergate, coming as they did at the height of U.S. economic insecurity, served to shift geoeconomic responsibility and capacity away from the State Department and administration foreign policy leaders. During this period, no fewer than three reports touched on the making of U.S. foreign policy and what Dobson calls "the issue of economic statecraft toward NMEs" (nonmarket economies).[74] The Economic Policy Board, created by President Ford in September 1974, was to be chaired by the secretary of the Treasury and was to "provide advice to the President concerning all aspects of national and international economic policy . . . oversee the formulation, coordination and implementation of all economic policy of the United States and serve as the focal point for economic policy decision-making."[75]

Another important plot point in the steady shift away from geoeconomics came in Ford's rejection of détente, which carried with it a certain hardening of views on the moral superiority of capitalism and a remilitarization of the Cold War. After being overruled in the Great Grain Robbery, Kissinger seemingly lost interest in seeking out geoeconomic approaches to the Cold War and mainly occupied himself with the SALT II limitations on nuclear weapons instead. Next came the crisis in Angola, when the Soviets airlifted Cuban troops to fight in Angola's civil war. Not only was the move seen as a serious escalation by the Soviets, spurring Kissinger to authorize CIA support for anti-Communist forces there, but it also further trained policy makers' attention on the military aspects of the East-West conflict rather than its geoeconomic dimensions.

President Carter came into office wary of his predecessor's remilitarized anti-Communist stance. But by late summer 1977, before the end of Carter's first year in office, outgoing CIA director George H. W. Bush painted a worrying picture of U.S. military decline. So began a major push toward military modernization. NATO embarked on a modernization drive in 1978; Carter and Brezhnev scheduled SALT II talks for 1979; in 1980, the Rapid Deployment Force was established. That July, a subsequent White House directive, known as PD-59, marked the culmination of the Carter administration's shift toward a more political military posture. It ordered "mobilization of defense command and control for a long conflict," complete "with flexible uses of air forces, strategic and general purpose, on behalf of war aims that we would select as we engaged in conflict."[76]

It was around this time that Samuel Huntington, then a young staffer at the National Security Council, tried to reassert a role for geoeconomics in the U.S. Cold War policies of the late 1970s (Huntington would go on to become one of the great international political theorists of the 20th century). His frustrations paint a striking picture of just how sharply things had changed in the fifteen years since the early 1960s.[77] Huntington rejected the notion that economic instruments should not be subordinated to U.S. foreign policy aims, urging instead that "economic capabilities and economic relations must serve the basic U.S. foreign policy objectives of encouraging East-West cooperation, containing Soviet expansion, and promoting American values."[78] For Huntington, the failure to take a more proactive stance to counter the planned aspects of the Soviet centralized economy had led to a situation where the Soviets "had clearly benefitted more . . . than has the United States . . . What is needed is a new approach of conditioned flexibility in which changes in the scope and character of US-Soviet economic relations are linked to and conditioned by progress in the achievement of US political and security objectives. . . . [D]étente must be comprehensive and reciprocal."[79]

But both Huntington and Carter had inherited a situation where few economic carrots and sticks were available. "Harnessing economic power to foreign policy goals," Huntington wrote, "presents formidable obstacles: bureaucratic pluralism and inertia; Congressional interest and group politics; the conflicting pulls of alliance diplomacy; and most important, in dramatic contrast to military power, a pervasive ideology that sanctifies the independence, rather than the subordination, of economic power to government."[80] He summed up his wish list thus: "I am saying that we should be prepared to engage in economic diplomacy."[81]

If Huntington ever did have a shot to reassert geoeconomics, events would intervene to make that impossible. The 1978–1981 Iranian hostage crisis, followed by the oil spikes and then the Soviet invasion of Afghanistan, concentrated the U.S. gaze in a decidedly political-military direction. Despite all of the troubles between the United States and the Soviet Union during the Carter years, the fact that East-West trade flourished throughout these crises and escalations is itself indicative that America had struck a new balance when it came to commercial and geopolitical interests.

There were intermittent shows of geoeconomics under President Carter. In the early days of the Iranian hostage crisis, the United States froze Iranian assets because, as President Carter put it, the Iranian leaders needed to be brought "to their senses . . . I thought depriving them of about twelve billion dollars in ready assets was a good way to get their attention."[82] But the most significant exception to the waning use of American geoeconomic power under Carter was the grain embargo leveled against the USSR in retaliation for the Soviet invasion of Afghanistan. Telling of the difficult climate for geoeconomic measures at the time, however, Stu Eizenstat, then a close advisor to Carter, argued against the grain embargo on the belief that if it were couched as a foreign policy imperative, Congress would veto. It would also put the United States in breach of contract, leaving it vulnerable to accusations of commercial unreliability. Carter was unpersuaded. The embargo was seen largely as a failure—feeding skeptical views of geoeconomic statecraft as often ineffectual—and Reagan repealed it. The United States negotiated a new grain agreement with the Soviets in August 1983, "which included the humiliating provision that the United States would not impose export controls for foreign policy reasons."[83]

By the end of Carter's presidency, ideological opposition to Communism (provoked by the USSR's abysmal human rights record) together with principled opposition to Soviet aggression in Afghanistan had combined to push the administration to return to moral anti-Communism as the guiding assumption of American foreign policy.[84] "Morality and economics were back as driving forces in American policy," Walter Russell Mead wrote of Carter's foreign policy evolution.[85] But this was still the Cold War. And like all things during the Cold War, this moral and economic bent to U.S. foreign policy still demanded a stark contrast from the Soviet Union. The American capitalist system thus became portrayed not just as different from or irreconcilable with Communism, as in Truman and Eisenhower's day, nor merely as in the self-interest of the United States, as in Kissinger's realism, but as morally superior. What is striking about this period is the way in which economics and geoeconomics still sat in tension—but the national understanding became less that the United States could simply no longer afford to engage in geoeconomics, even though domestic economic insecurity still exerted a pull away from geoeconomics, and more that, insofar as repurposing economic tools for geopolitical rather than economic goals became seen as an intrusion onto laissez-faire liberal capitalism, geoeconomics itself became morally suspect.[86]

This admixture of morality and economics continued into Reagan's term. As Henry Bienen and Robert Gilpin, writing in 1980, summarized the national mood concerning geoeconomics at that time, "While this separation of international economics and politics (that is, of diplomacy and the market) has frequently been violated by the United States itself, this ideal has correctly remained a goal of American foreign policy. . . . The American goal of depoliticized and non-discriminatory trade not only fostered an unprecedented era of world commerce but it greatly reinforced the harmony of interest among the United States and its allies."[87] Domestic economic insecurity continued to do its part to suppress any appetite for geoeconomics, and concern over U.S. export performance in particular came sharply into focus. Between 1989 and 1991, the United States effectively wound down its embargo; it would waste little time filling the void, pioneering new assistance ventures with Russia and former Eastern Bloc countries. In 1992, COCOM was repurposed into a vehicle to help Russia and the Eastern European countries develop economically.

After the Soviet Union collapsed, U.S. policy planners and preeminent intellectuals focused on sustaining what some called a "unipolar moment."[88] As the post-Soviet reality became more fully absorbed, this newfound American primacy did little to change Washington's thinking that the United States had prevailed in the Cold War not because of decades of savvy tactics—more of them geoeconomic than often appreciated—but because of the correctness of its political and economic ideas and the intrinsic superiority of its system of democratic capitalism. To hear Presidents Carter, Reagan, and George H. W. Bush tell it, it was as if the U.S. victory could not have been otherwise. President Bush's call for a "new world order" and President Bill Clinton's emphasis on the expansion of free markets and free governments made clear that economic liberalization and expansion of human freedom were now top Washington priorities.[89]

As U.S. diplomacy occupied itself with transitioning the former Soviet Union countries toward democratic capitalism, the economic components of this remained squarely focused on economic outcomes. It was trade for trade's sake; financial and investment reform for the sake of deeper, faster, more efficient, better-integrated markets. The so-called Washington Consensus emerged as shorthand for the mix of economic measures all good market economies would go by—earning the term "golden straitjacket" for its constraining effect on government choice to deviate from the prescription even for domestic economic reasons, let alone geopolitical ones. Certainly at the time there was a general belief that economic liberalization would, in fostering peace and stability, redound to the geostrategic benefit of the United States. Yet even when it appeared these economic reforms were too much, too fast—straining the politics of these countries beyond what they could handle—there was not much willingness in Washington to deviate from the economic prescriptions for the sake of geopolitical aims.

In the 1997 U.S. National Security Strategy, one can see just how much geoeconomics appears to take a backseat to more political-military methods for managing the post-Soviet order. Laying out five different areas in which the United States had a strategic interest—Europe, the Asia-Pacific, the global economy (especially in Asia and Latin America), the need for peace in areas ranging from the Middle East to Haiti, and countering "growing dangers to our security"—the Clinton administration asserted that the United States "must have the diplomatic and military tools to meet all these challenges. We must maintain a strong and ready military. We will achieve this by selectively increasing funding for weapons modernization and taking care of our men and women in uniform."[90]

And while, from the 1994 National Security Strategy onward, one of the goals of the administration was to "bolster America's economic revitalization," geoeconomic instruments—except for the familiar use of economic sanctions and an abstract belief in free trade as a vehicle for political liberalization—were not explicitly seen as part of any strategy to achieve overall U.S. foreign policy objectives.[91] Rather, political-military tools appeared to dominate U.S. understandings about how best to assert its power and leadership throughout the world.

This view stretched across partisan lines. In an influential 1996 essay that helped to bring neoconservative ideas into the foreground of U.S. foreign policy, William Kristol and Robert Kagan argued that the "first objective of U.S. foreign policy should be to preserve and enhance . . . the strategic and ideological preeminence" that it had inherited with the Soviet Union's collapse. The United States must "make clear that it is futile to compete with American power, either in size of forces or in technological capabilities." Noting that the United States spent more on defense than the next six major powers combined, they proposed that Americans "may even want to enshrine this disparity in U.S. defense strategy" so as to "preserve its military supremacy regardless of the near-term global threats."[92] And it was, of course, during this period that U.S. and European governments did very little economically to help shape the direction of Boris Yeltsin's Russia (although there was plenty of bad private "shock therapy" advice)—a profound omission that haunts the world today.[93]

The events of 9/11 arguably made the shift to an even more militarized national-security strategy inevitable. Now the United States needed to prioritize the accretion of military power not only to preempt threats from states but also to counter nonstate actors displaying homicidal intentions and capacities. Although this period saw the beginning of U.S. efforts to curtail terrorist financing, al-Qa'ida and its affiliates were hardly vulnerable to geoeconomic coercion; in the wake of 9/11, it was primarily ground forces, fixed-wing aircraft, and drones that would have to do the job.[94]

The ongoing U.S. preoccupation with countering the threat of Islamic terrorism, while understandable after 9/11, has had opportunity costs. In 2010, one U.S. foreign policy commentator recalled a meeting he had had years earlier with the deputy director of the policy planning staff of China's Foreign Ministry. The official said that China's grand strategy was to "figure out how to keep you Americans distracted in small Middle Eastern countries."[95] No wonder, then, that former U.S. defense secretary Robert Gates warned that "any future defense secretary who advises the president to again send a big American land army into Asia or into the Middle East or Africa should 'have his head examined.' "[96]

It is not as if there were no attempts or success stories for U.S. geoeconomic power since Vietnam. In the months after 9/11, President George W. Bush launched a new multilateral trade round, hosted in Doha, Qatar, as a means of showing to the world that the United States neither was retreating from the world nor intended to reduce its relationship with the Middle East to exclusively military and security issues, according to those involved.[97] The United States under President Bush also successfully negotiated new trade agreements with Jordan, Morocco, and Bahrain partly as a way of rewarding their cooperation in the U.S. fight against al-Qa'ida.

There were also important strides around energy security, even if these were geared mainly toward shoring up newly apparent geoeconomic vulnerabilities. Just six months before the October 1973 Arab oil embargo was imposed on the West, President Nixon announced a package of new geoeconomic energy policies designed to alleviate fuel shortages that had broken out around the country and reduce U.S. strategic dependence on imported oil.[98] On November 27, Nixon signed the Emergency Petroleum Allocation Act, authorizing price, production, allocation, and marketing controls. And in the context of an OPEC decision to use oil as a strategic weapon following the October 1973 Arab-Israeli war, a decision that resulted in a fourfold increase in oil prices, Henry Kissinger convened the Washington Energy Conference.[99] Lastly, with the launch of his Project Independence, Nixon became first in a line of U.S. presidents and hopefuls, extending to the present day, to establish a national goal of making the United States energy independent.[100]

To be sure, the evolving integration of China into the global arena—begun during this period and still a work in progress—marks one of the most extensive, protracted uses of American geoeconomic instruments. But claims that are quick to cite China's integration as a potent example of U.S. geoeconomics are also easily exaggerated. Certainly the historic 1972 opening to China contributed to Nixon's objective of bringing China in from the cold, and Nixon's original strategy involved geoeconomic incentives.[101] But to hear Nixon and Kissinger tell it, most of these economic incentives were of secondary importance.[102] And in any case, as the China opening and integration agenda was handed down to successive U.S. administrations, it largely became reduced to a general belief in free trade as a force for political liberalization. For much of Washington's now forty-plus-year effort to integrate China into the international system, the benefits and motivations have been more economic and commercial.[103]

What Changed?

As this cursory sweep of U.S. history attests, there is much in the historical record to support the idea that this latter-day "separation of economics from U.S. foreign policy and security policy reflects a shift from earlier American experience," as former U.S. trade representative and World Bank president Robert Zoellick has put it.[104]

Mr. Zoellick's and similar accounts certainly come as a welcome correction of the historical record.[105] But if, in fact, the United States was once so adept at this brand of geoeconomic statecraft, why has Washington largely forgotten the instrument except for sanctions? What is it about the current historical moment that now seems to prevent successive administrations from doing what the United States once did so well?

Certainly there was a palpable shift in the attention spans of those making foreign policy; with the Cuban missile crisis, Vietnam, conflict in the Middle East, and Soviet military adventures in Angola, Mozambique, Central America, and Afghanistan, America became hyperfocused on the military dimensions of the Cold War. And undoubtedly much of the answer lies in the material factors described earlier—the onset of economic insecurity in the United States for the first time in a generation, and the rise of an organized domestic political constituency for trade.

Bureaucratic and institutional factors also played an important role. U.S. political scientist I. M. Destler describes how, beginning with "Nixon's shutting of the Gold Window . . . onward, the connections grew between domestic and international economic policy."[106] The White House trade office evolved, transforming from a special trade representative with modest staff and limited jurisdiction to the much larger present-day Office of the U.S. Trade Representative, with a broad mandate to lead and coordinate all U.S. trade negotiations. It also grew steadily more responsive to Congress and domestic economic interests, and by 1992 the Office of the Trade Representative had a staff of 160 and cabinet status, with two deputies holding ambassadorial rank.

The primary bureaucratic loser in all of this was the Department of State. "As long as the cold war persisted, however, the influence of the economic complex was a function of whether economic issues could be insulated from security concerns," Destler explains. "With a strong Treasury Department, an increasingly assertive USTR, with assertive external constituencies, this was often possible. But national security concerns retained primacy—they engaged presidents the most. But the fall of the Berlin Wall in 1989 and the Soviet Union in 1991 led to a questioning of this primacy at its core."[107]

Yet the larger answer explaining why the United States shifted away from geoeconomics may have less to do with evolving foreign policy habits than evolving economic beliefs—and, maybe more to the point, changes in the willingness of economists to perceive themselves and their discipline as embedded in larger realities of state power. One of the most interesting and provocative claims on this subject comes from Yale law professor David Singh Grewal, who suggests that what today's U.S. policy makers experience as a relatively recent phenomenon—this perceived divide between the logic and objectives of economics and of statecraft—actually marks a reversion to trend. In fact, Grewal argues, when it comes to any happy alignment between economists and foreign policy makers in the United States, it was the post-1945 period, not today, that stands as the aberration. Beginning roughly with Adam Smith and his critique of mercantilism onward, the non-zero-sum logic of liberal (and now neoclassical) economics, which favors liberalization, has been in tension with the historically more zero-sum logic of interstate politics.[108] And it was only for a brief moment of U.S. history that this tension temporarily abated, owing to what Grewal calls the "enormous convenience (for the U.S.) of the ideological terms of the Cold War."[109] Allowing the propagation of this liberal economic doctrine, then—from the original ideas of Adam Smith through to the revisions of Milton Friedman—actually quite suited U.S. foreign policy objectives during that time. For, in that unique conflict, the Soviet Union was opposed to free trade, "which meant that any gain for free trade anywhere was a gain for the Western world in its bid to win the Cold War. Ah, how easy it must have been to do 'grand strategy' in those days!"[110]

In fact, it was during this allegedly brief moment of alignment that liberal economics saw its intellectual ascendance—a rise that, for several scholars including Grewal, Baldwin, and others, owes much to how well the prescriptions of liberal economic thought aligned with the aims of U.S. foreign policy at the time.[111] This is not to suggest that these disciplinary tensions between economics and foreign policy were not also present for much of the country's early history—again, a period of relatively astute geoeconomic performance for the United States—only that classical and neoclassical economic ideas were not at the intellectual helm of the discipline during this long period. Rather, the prevailing standard-bearers of economic thought during the nineteenth and early twentieth centuries were much more willing to view economics as an instrument of state power.[112]

As the Cold War came to an end, the orthodoxy of neoclassical economic thought persisted, as did the resulting divides between foreign policy thinkers and neoclassical economists (who continued to hold economics and markets as a realm to be kept free from geopolitical interference). Again, for a while, it was of no great consequence; in roughly the first two decades following the Cold War, the United States faced no serious strategic challenge that required revisiting whether this once-happy alignment between neoclassical ideas and the country's foreign policy needs still held up. However, disciplinary tensions between neoclassical economics and U.S. foreign policy, on hiatus during past decades, have now returned—evidenced, for example, by the surfeit of commentaries lamenting the present failure of the United States "to craft a [foreign] policy that connects our national security and our economic interests."[113] Accordingly, any meaningful attempt to return geoeconomics to a considered place within U.S. foreign policy must reexamine the most basic assumptions and "[think] outside the bounds of . . . deeply established disciplinary conventions."[114]

What the United States faces today is a set of states, many of them rising powers, that are entirely comfortable employing most of the tools of economics to advance state power (defined to include geoeconomic and geopolitical elements alike). Often the results sit uncomfortably with the tenets and assumptions of neoclassical economics. For U.S. policy makers, to recognize this is not to advocate a response in kind. But it is to argue that many of the largest strategic challenges America faces are cases where the *tools* of neoclassical economics are being applied quite apart from the *priors* that have traditionally guided their application.[115] And it is perhaps to recall the advice of Keynes and other early neoclassical economists who, in fashioning Bretton Woods, clearly saw themselves as situated within— indeed, guided by—prevailing realities of state power in all its aspects, and who saw dangers in illusions to the contrary.[116]

And as Chapter 7 details, these geoeconomic factors, even when present, are not driving Washington's decision making.

CHAPTER SEVEN

America's Geoeconomic Potential

Harnessing economic power to foreign policy goals presents formidable obstacles . . . Yet if war is too important to be left to the generals, surely commerce is, in this context, too salient to be left to bankers and businessmen.

—SAMUEL P. HUNTINGTON, AMERICAN POLITICAL SCIENTIST, 1978

THE RISE of China is arguably America's most important foreign policy challenge.[1] If so, then in its dealings with China the strategic tests facing the United States for the foreseeable future will be primarily geoeconomic. As China transitions to a more consumption-based growth model, takes slow but decisive steps to internationalize the renminbi, and continues diversifying away from the dollar, its economic dependence on the United States will diminish—and so, too, will its hesitation to mount a greater geoeconomic challenge to U.S. power and influence.

As Henry Kissinger explained about a year after Lehman Brothers filed for bankruptcy, "As Chinese exports to America decline and China shifts the emphasis of its economy to greater consumption and to increased infrastructure spending, a different economic order will emerge. China will depend less on the American market, while the growing dependence of neighboring countries on Chinese markets will increase China's political influence."[2] That is not to discount China's military buildup or to suggest that China will inevitably swear off the use of force; rather, it is only to argue that, whatever the danger of military conflict involving China, the PRC possesses global power today largely because of the dynamism of its economy. As Leslie Gelb puts this point, "Nations around the world already see China as the future No. 1 economic power, even though it still lags behind the U.S. substantially in most categories. It's the perception of

[China] going up and [the United States] going down. And upon such perceptions, power is based."[3]

But there is an even simpler reason any strategic test between the United States and China is more likely to be geoeconomic than military: geoeconomics tends to be easier and cheaper.[4] As Chapter 1 noted, geoeconomics is also a realm where China finds itself less outmatched by the United States.

If the next great strategic test regarding the rise of Chinese power is to be primarily geoeconomic, the outlook for the United States is mixed: America stands well equipped but ill-prepared. Thirty years of neglect have clouded the role that geoeconomics played historically in U.S. foreign policy and given rise to a different set of understandings about its rightful role today. Consequently, the United States is underperforming compared to its present geoeconomic potential. But it is worth remembering that this potential is formidable.

Before prognosis or prescription, however, comes the question of diagnosis. How might one characterize the present use of geoeconomics in U.S. foreign policy today? Is it that geoeconomics has disappeared altogether from American foreign policy in the past few decades? Or, rather, are those making foreign policy still wittingly and deliberately practicing geoeconomics, albeit not particularly well? Or is it perhaps that they are still practicing geoeconomics, just not in a way they are conscious of, or comfortable owning up to?

Good Geoeconomics or Just Good Marketing?

In many cases, the United States is clearly pursuing economic policies for which a geopolitical case can be made. Geopolitical considerations can be read into certain policy choices—strategic and foreign policy arguments can be offered for both the Trans-Pacific Partnership (TPP) and the Transatlantic Trade and Investment Partnership (TTIP), for instance. And, indeed, as endgames for both agreements drew closer, U.S. officials turned increasingly to national security and geopolitical explanations to gain congressional support.[5] Just as when General Colin Powell pushed the passage of the North American Free Trade Agreement (NAFTA) through Congress in 1993, this is largely after-the-fact marketing, brought in to sell these agreements to Congress and the American public.[6]

And just as with NAFTA twenty-five years ago, geopolitical considerations, while certainly there for the arguing, were not leading considerations shaping the substance of either TPP or TTIP. Instead, and in keeping with many recent U.S. policies that could be construed as having some geo-economic logic, it is economic considerations, not geoeconomic ones, that largely drive how these policies are designed and whether they come into effect.

Take TPP, for instance. It was conceived primarily not as a geoeconomic answer to growing Chinese geoeconomic power and coercion in Asia but rather as a shot in the arm for a dying Doha Round at the WTO.[7] By se-curing agreement on issues that were being hotly contested in Doha nego-tiations, policy makers hoped TPP would unlock a path forward for Doha.[8] A December 2013 report by the Congressional Research Service explains this logic: "Past FTAs, such as NAFTA, incorporated new policy ideas . . . that were concurrently being negotiated in the Uruguay Round. . . . [T]he approval of NAFTA among Canada, Mexico and the United States helped push the Uruguay Round to conclusion. Today, the approval of a compre-hensive, high-standard TPP agreement could signal to recalcitrant members of the WTO that trade liberalization can proceed without them and might spur action at the multilateral level."[9]

Of course, a trade agreement like TPP could be both things. The United States could devise policies that are both economically and geopolitically minded, in much the same way that other countries enact measures meant to simultaneously advance economic and geopolitical goals—China's "stra-tegic investments" in Africa, for instance. But if TPP had been conceived as a serious means of pursuing U.S. foreign policy objectives regarding China, the result would have been a different sort of agreement.

In fact, as if to telegraph the extent to which TPP was *not* a foreign policy exercise, when the Obama administration decided to go ahead with TPP (plans that were incubated during the final months of the Bush ad-ministration), the agreement's name was changed. The original agreement, called the Trans Pacific Strategic Economic Partnership, was concluded in 2005 between Brunei, New Zealand, Chile, and Singapore. The move to drop the word *strategic* proved telling of the administration's substantive approach to the negotiations, as geopolitical considerations never mean-ingfully came to influence the agreement's substance and design.

One area that helps illustrate the lack of foreign policy considerations in TPP is currency—namely, whether TPP would include provisions around currency management. Beijing has made clear that it regards global reserve status for the RMB as a first-order geoeconomic aim and an important contribution to China's overall power projection going forward.[10] Arvind Subramanian and Martin Kessler of the Peterson Institute of International Economics suggested that a renminbi bloc is already emerging in Asia, where seven out of the ten East Asian currencies already track the yuan more closely than they do the dollar.[11] On foreign policy grounds, then, the United States would seem to have an interest in advancing provisions in TPP that, at a minimum, seek to ensure that any expansion of the RMB's global role does not also serve to strengthen China's ability to use financial and monetary policy to project state power, or as a means of undermining U.S. strategic primacy in Asia. Indeed, a foreign policy maker wishing to check a feared rise in Chinese power might go further—one could imagine TPP provisions that, while almost certainly intolerable to most economists, would explicitly seek to discourage a global reserve currency role for any currencies managed by authoritarian, nonmarket economies.[12]

And, although the issue is outside the scope of this book, it is worth noting that the United States also has compelling economic reasons for including currency within the scope of TPP. Since China continues to artificially restrain the value of its currency to gain export advantage, a TPP agreement that managed to establish binding rules against such behavior would clearly help the U.S. effort to pressure China to adopt a market-based currency. On geopolitical and economic grounds alike, then, the United States would seem to have an interest in seeing currency provisions included in TPP. Indeed, the notion has attracted bipartisan support in U.S. policy-making circles, championed by international economic policy thinkers such as Fred Bergsten, Simon Johnson, and Robert Zoellick.[13]

Opposition to the idea tends to come from finance ministries, typically warning of unduly "politicizing" monetary policy by inserting a "monetary policy issue" such as currency values into a trade agreement.[14] These arguments assume that the issue is not already politicized to an important extent—a shaky assumption given how openly China has couched its monetary aspirations in geopolitical terms, not to mention the extent to which currency intervention has driven global imbalances in recent years (and the difficult domestic politics, especially the exporting of unemployment, these imbalances bring). Concerns over whether the United States risks unduly politicizing currency by introducing it into a trade context also fail to acknowledge that current U.S. law already treats currency as a trade issue. Indeed, the very reason the U.S. treasury secretary is obliged to release a semiannual report on the incidence of currency manipulation around the world is that Congress mandated it as part of the Omnibus Trade and Competitive Act of 1988.[15] It is precisely this sort of historical distortion that winds up with geoeconomics being portrayed as somehow "abnormal" in contemporary U.S. policy.

Beyond currency, a second measure of how U.S. foreign policy considerations have failed to influence the design of TPP is seen in the handling of provisions on state-owned enterprises. SOEs are among the leading geo-economic vehicles through which China projects geopolitical influence abroad. To return briefly to just one of the several examples cited earlier, when China sought to assert its claims in the South China Sea by rede-ploying an oil rig owned by one of its national oil companies to another state-owned oil company (which then positioned the rig within Vietnam's claimed exclusive economic zone), the move captured Western head-lines and policy makers' attention. Following the episode, Asian media out-lets reported that Chinese SOEs had been quietly ordered to temporarily freeze any plans for new business in Vietnam.[16] Chinese foreign policy experts interviewed by local Chinese media were not shy about acknowl-edging the geopolitical motivations at play.[17]

While TPP did opt to include a designated chapter on SOEs, there is no indication U.S. negotiators focused on anything beyond the level-playing-field concerns SOEs present, nor did U.S. trade representatives prove willing to prioritize these issues over other strictly commercial objectives. As a re-sult, the scope of ambition for the SOEs chapter of the agreement has narrowed substantially during the course of the negotiations, as Obama administration officials have themselves acknowledged.[18]

During TPP negotiations, U.S. officials did explicitly confront and de-bate questions around currency and SOEs. However, looking at what the negotiations have ignored altogether can give insight into the effective ab-sence of foreign policy considerations in TPP. For example, there is a lack of any explicit attention to the growing class of geopolitically motivated economic and trade abuses seen in East Asia. Further, TPP does not con-sider the levers of state control (in other words, aspects of state capitalism) that enable many of these geoeconomic moves to occur in the first place. The popular face of today's state capitalists may be state-owned firms and investment vehicles, but it is these countries' unique domestic banking sectors—the financial plumbing—that connect and enable state capital-ism's other dimensions. The nature and caliber of state control may vary, but today's most ardent state capitalists, with Beijing and Moscow fore-most among them, still manage to direct nearly all key decisions in their domestic banking sectors, including interbank rates, deposit rates and bond prices, spreads, major lending decisions, and the handling and dispo-sition of bad loans.

Before fully discounting the possibility that TPP was crafted as a piece of foreign policy, however, there is one additional prospect to consider. Whatever the geopolitical benefits of a more geoeconomic-minded TPP, these benefits could also carry costs—costs that, from a foreign policy perspective, could outweigh the benefits. Perhaps for the United States, all things considered, upholding the rules-based system still remains the best strategy for maximizing present U.S. geopolitical objectives, and perhaps policy makers have further determined that the United States would be better off with a strategy that did not make this insight manifest. After all, the United States still supplies far more global public goods than any other country, including policing of the global commons; the rules-based system is in many ways meant to ease the cost of those tasks, and so the United States has more to lose if that system collapses on itself.

To put the point another way, it might be the difference between what basketball fans call "big ball vs. small ball"—the difference between strategy and tactics. So while the United States does not transparently respond to the various geoeconomic displays by China or Qatar, it does so advisedly, in the belief that responding in kind would harm or jeopardize other, far larger geopolitical benefits accruing to the United States. And so just as John Maynard Keynes, Harry Dexter White, and other British and American officials deliberately came to a view that the formula they settled on at Bretton Woods in 1944 was in fact the blueprint most advantageous to U.S. national interests at the time, U.S. officials could well conclude the same still holds true, albeit for their own, contemporary reasons. However, arriving at this sort of conclusion after rigorously evaluating what sort of trade policy maximizes U.S. geopolitical goals is altogether different from coming to this same conclusion out of a reflexive belief that foreign policy considerations have no real standing in trade deliberations.

In the case of TPP, which was it? Did U.S. officials opt to exclude foreign policy interests as falling outside of TPP's scope after careful consideration, or were foreign policy objectives excluded out of neglect or on principle? Had the design choices in TPP been to any meaningful degree about geopolitics, one would have expected to see some concerted attempt to assess those relative foreign policy benefits against their costs. There is no evidence any such effort was made.

Of course, just because TPP has not to date been a geopolitical exercise for the United States does not mean that Washington policy makers have shied away from invoking all arguments, including foreign policy and national security arguments, in seeking public and congressional support for the agreement. In fact, some of the same White House officials who oversaw the U.S. push to drop the term "strategic" from TPP's official name have gone on to become the most vocal public champions for TPP on foreign policy grounds, calling TPP "the perfect example of how the economic and strategic logic of U.S. trade policy are mutually reinforcing."[19]

A strikingly similar story can be told for the Transatlantic Trade and Investment Partnership. Many in the White House and the Office of the U.S.

Trade Representative voiced private disgruntlement in the fall of 2012 when Secretary of State Hillary Clinton pressed for TTIP as a strategic project, presenting TTIP as an "economic counterpart to what NATO represents on the security side."[20] The complaint was that such a portrayal of TTIP unduly geopoliticized trade policy. Yet eighteen months later, when Russian aggression in Ukraine and coercion elsewhere in former Soviet space became a rallying point for U.S. and EU trade officials, some of these very same U.S. policy makers mounted arguments on TTIP's behalf before Congress and the public with calls for, of all things, an "economic NATO."[21]

Such a schizophrenic posture is not surprising. The U.S. government comprises a variety of institutions, each with its own mandate and bureaucratic culture, and when it comes to accounting for a given policy choice, the sorts of reasons that are allowed to count as valid differ across these institutions. So while the principal organizations and policy makers charged with crafting U.S. trade policy—those leading the design choices in TPP and TTIP, and those with a veto over whether or not to negotiate a free trade agreement with a certain country—generally do not regard geopolitical factors as valid considerations in their policy making, other institutions, notably Congress, have their own sets of considerations guiding their decisions. Foreign policy, while largely absent in the U.S. trade representative's calculus, generally is included in Congress's.[22] "From a standpoint of national security, this agreement is important," Senator Chris Murphy (D-Conn.) explained in a September 2013 public event on TTIP, adding that he had opposed previous trade deals when he was in the House of Representatives but supported TTIP.[23] "The geopolitical concerns are what really put this over the edge for many of us."[24] In sum, tailoring a pitch to one's audience is one thing; crafting trade agreements with geopolitical considerations at the forefront—that is, conducting geoeconomic statecraft—is quite another. The problem is not so much that U.S. policy makers did not see fit to fashion these two trade agreements into robust geoeconomic tools; it is that they did not even consider it. Worse, for many policy makers the thought never even crossed their minds.

In urging the United States to reinvigorate its brand of geoeconomics, the point is not to argue for a certain outcome but to shift the terms of debate. It may or may not be the case that were U.S. policy makers to use geoeconomic tools more or differently, other important U.S. interests would be undermined. Answers will vary from case to case and depend on facts. Before those judgments can even occur, however, policy makers need to specify ground rules for debating geoeconomic options—especially the kinds of reasons that are allowed to count as valid arguments. Currently, when U.S. policy makers oppose a potential geoeconomic move, their grounds for opposition often do not even reference maximizing U.S. foreign policy interests. These debates do not now begin with a shared acceptance of a common geopolitical purpose; it is not as if opponents of a given geoeconomic proposal simply prefer a different route to maximizing U.S. foreign policy interests. Instead, these critics often argue by reference to a set of inviolate economic principles and institutions. Whenever a given geoeconomic action is deemed to risk undermining these economic principles, or sometimes even just when it comes uncomfortably close to doing so, these principles are invoked as sacrosanct. Rarely is there any onus to prove that these economic principles are indeed at risk, let alone that privileging them over a given geoeconomic proposal best serves U.S. foreign policy objectives. The mere invocation of threats to the existing rules-based order are, for too many, sufficient to summarily end the debate.

The result is that certain geoeconomic alternatives are never fully considered—and over time they fail even to be seen as possibilities. This dangerously circumscribes the scope of debate, impedes clear thinking, and deprives policy makers of the fullest accounting of all relevant options. Ironically, stifling debate in this way also poses a risk to the very economic rules and institutions that the more reflexive opponents of geoeconomics seek to defend. Like all laws and institutions, the international economic order and the institutions charged with administering it must have some permeability to politics; that is how they evolve and adapt. In too closely insulating these institutions from the tactical impulses and demands of U.S. geopolitical interests, in couching objections to certain geoeconomic options purely as threats to the institutional health of these organizations, the defenders of these institutions risk relegating them to irrelevance. To ask the United States (or any other country) to defend the institutional health of, say, the WTO or IMF for the sake of these institutions alone serves neither U.S. interests nor the interests of the institutions themselves.

Of course, there is still plenty of room to argue, without standing atop sacrosanct economic principles, that the rules-based system remains America's strongest geopolitical asset.[25] In practice, however, this argument suffers from two problems. The first is that it tends to imagine that the system's early benefits have continued unchanged and undiminished down to the present. This is not the case. However well this system performed as a U.S. geopolitical asset in the decades following World War II, it is delivering less and less in the way of strategic returns as rising powers (often through geoeconomic attempts of their own) undercut it.[26] China has already set up more than a dozen parallel structures that analysts say are designed to systematically realign the international order away from the United States and toward Beijing.[27] "This has been a power struggle," one senior European official explained after the United States failed to dissuade some forty-six countries—including all but one of America's treaty allies—to join China's new Asian Infrastructure Investment Bank.[28] "And we have moved from the world of 1945."[29] The second problem is that if indeed U.S. policy makers were rejecting various geoeconomic options out of deliberate concern for the rules-based system and the geopolitical value it holds, then one would expect to see U.S. foreign policy expending equally significant political weight and energy trying to shore up that system.

Shortly after leaving office as chairman of the Joint Chiefs of Staff, Admiral Mike Mullen gave an account of what this might look like. Asked for his feedback on an early-stage draft of Secretary Clinton's Economic Statecraft vision, Mullen answered that it "successfully paints the mountain." The next major task is "translating this into a new vision to organize our foreign and economic policy." Mullen went on to liken this task in scope and ambition to America's foreign policy after World War II. Just as in the immediate postwar years, when *all* U.S. officials understood that *all* of their efforts—military, economic, or diplomatic—were to advance a liberal economic order, Admiral Mullen argued that the United States now needs a new organizing vision to succeed the frayed post–Bretton Woods consensus. It needs to articulate why and in what ways our values and interests have changed as a result of the past ten years.[30]

If U.S. policy makers were in fact convinced that the "rules based order" represented one of America's greatest geopolitical assets, the task that Mullen describes would be unnecessary, for we would see efforts to reinforce that order similar to what was seen in the years following World War II. But it is not as if the current U.S. national security advisor and the secretaries of state and defense are spending their days working toward some updated blueprint to Bretton Woods. In fact, quite to the contrary, U.S. leaders have allowed an IMF reform deal that is nearly form-fitted to U.S. interests—notably, the deal would allow China a greater role in the institution while still protecting America's unique veto position—to languish, the United States being the only remaining holdout refusing to agree to it. As Chinese international lending has soared, Washington has moved in the opposite direction, with Congress nearly dismantling the U.S. Export-Import Bank and the financing the bank offers for overseas customers. Nor has the U.S. government proven willing to put even a fraction of the diplomatic muscle it routinely expends on political and security crises in the Middle East toward curbing China's plans to implement a multilateral alternative to the World Bank. "I've been searching for a word to describe it, and the one I use is 'withdrawal,' best I can come up with," said Edwin Truman, a former Treasury official now with the Peterson Institute for

International Economics. "We're withdrawing from the central place we held on the international stage."[31]

Of course, this neglect of geoeconomics matters only when foreign policy considerations and economic considerations advise diverging courses. As Chapter 6 noted, for the past few decades a convergence of U.S. foreign policy interests and liberal economic prescriptions has meant that such different prescriptions were rare. But as the recent TPP experience suggests, this happy moment may be coming to an end. As it does, it is reasonable to expect more and more divides between economic and geopolitical interests.

This, then, raises a crucial question: assuming geoeconomics does somehow manage to regain better standing in policy debates, how should U.S. policy makers think about what constitutes acceptable and unacceptable forms of geoeconomic statecraft?

Certainly, having a clearer baseline would help. Ironically, for all of their efforts to distance trade policy from foreign policy considerations, U.S. trade negotiators are very much working in a realm that, from its most basic component parts on up, reflects U.S. power. To paraphrase Harvard economist Dani Rodrik: Imagine it was Bangladesh or Mozambique that designed our global trading system. What are the chances that this system would look rather different from the one in effect today?[32] It is precisely because the system works to America's advantage that U.S. policy makers have all the more incentive to hold up as neutral the disciplines of trade, investment, and finance that together comprise rules-based order, vesting them with the authority of Rawlsian impartiality, blind to the national interests of any one country over any other.

However fiercely the United States (or any other country) sees fit to bind itself to this rules-based order, and however much internal authority and logic such a system might assume, the problem is that internal authority only goes so far. "Those who seek to design a free market on a worldwide scale," philosopher John Gray reminds us, "have always insisted that the legal framework which defines and entrenches it must be placed beyond the reach of any democratic legislature. Sovereign states may sign up to membership of the World Trade Organization; but it is that organization, not the legislature of any sovereign state, which determines what is to count as free trade, and what a restraint of it. The rules of the game of the market must be elevated beyond any possibility of revision through democratic choice."[33] Such, at least, has been the vision that the WTO's champions have sought to realize. But there is no escaping the fact that the WTO's authority ultimately remains derivative—loaned to it by its member states, and therefore subject to the same underlying geopolitical realities governing how these states interact in other realms.

Likewise, not only do global financial markets also depend ultimately on U.S. power, but these markets would look vastly different were it not for the shaping hand of U.S. geopolitical considerations. Gulf countries admit to the purchase of U.S. securities as the price of their U.S. security reassurance, just as Germany did before them during the Cold War. The eurozone was at least as much a geopolitical project for the United States as an economic one. And as the starkly different fates of Mexico and Argentina can attest, geopolitics certainly becomes a distinguishing factor in U.S. decisions regarding sovereign bailouts and swap lines.

Coming to a clearer understanding of how U.S. power and interests underpin the present system, though, is not to suggest that the present system works *only* to the advantage of the United States. To the contrary, the largest beneficiary of current practices may well be China. By 2011, ten years after joining the WTO, Chinese imports from other WTO members had grown substantially, with an average annual net increase of more than $100 billion.[34] China also saw its dollar GDP quadruple and its exports almost quintuple over this decade.[35] At the same time, however, the fact that China and others are working so hard to undermine the U.S.-led system ought to be a clue that there are certain system-level reforms that, if made, would better advance these countries' national interests.[36]

Beyond muddy parameters for debate and misguided baselines, a third problem impeding U.S. policy makers' overall comfort with geoeconomics centers on faulty comparisons and double standards. Arguments against geoeconomics often treat decisions as if policy makers were operating in a "first-best world," when the reality is almost always one of a second-best world (or, often, worse). Such arguments tend to fixate on the costs associated with a given geoeconomic technique of statecraft, for instance, without assessing these costs in terms of the next-best alternative, or in many instances without considering any alternative at all. Indeed, "choices are costly," David Baldwin once noted. "Choosing to use economic statecraft—or any other kind of statecraft for that matter—costs something."[37]

Moreover, where there is some effort to compare costs, the comparison is often not so much between options as between states. This line of reasoning is seen, for example, in arguments against a certain geoeconomic policy move on the grounds that "it costs us more than it costs them." Similarly, when it comes to questions of expected benefit, there is a tendency to arrive at a pessimistic view of the efficacy of a given geoeconomic policy without any attempt to consider how alternatives stack up; for example, we were told that sanctions were unlikely to work against Iran, but the alternatives—war or resignation to Tehran's nuclear ambitions—were not discussed.[38] Success is usually a matter of degree, especially in foreign policy, and a certain geoeconomic course may have a low likelihood of success, but it may still be the best option available.

Finally, criticisms of geoeconomic approaches often fall into the trap of judging geoeconomic outcomes by economic ends rather than geopolitical ones. President Carter's decision to freeze Iranian assets during the hostage crisis came despite stiff opposition from the Treasury Department and the U.S. banking community, which warned that the move would deter foreigners from maintaining deposits in American banks. As the *Wall Street Journal* wrote at the time, the freeze "reinforced a widely held opinion around the world that this administration is not as serious as it should be about the integrity of the U.S. dollar and the sanctity of private property." In fact, former Treasury official Robert Carswell, utterly convinced of the large costs that such measures would entail, argued the measures should be considered only after exhausting "every possible avenue of multilateral cooperation," even if this means "substantial modification in U.S. objectives."[39] This gets guiding objectives backward. Rejecting unilateral action may be "a fine way to protect the dollar, but it would not have been a very effective way to demonstrate resolve in the hostage crisis."[40]

Even with clearer ground rules for debating geoeconomic choices—more scrutiny of alternatives, greater burdens of proof on claims of "defending the rules-based system," and so on—these choices remain a game of linedrawing. There will still be tough cases, and it is inevitable that different people will draw different lines of acceptability. For many policy makers, it may well be that, so long as upholding the rules-based system is still seen as geopolitically advantageous for the United States, most forms of geoeconomic power, to pass as net beneficial, will need to be at least neutral in their impact on this system. Adhering to this standard will constrain the U.S. far more than many other states, especially in more coercive, shorter-term cases, but even working within this exacting standard, there remains much room for improving current U.S. geoeconomic performance.

Even though foreign policy considerations have not been leading factors in either TPP or TTIP, in both cases arguments for putting more emphasis on those considerations could meet this limited test. If successfully concluded, both TPP and TTIP could mark important geopolitical wins for the United States, but not because the U.S. government formulated them with this purpose in mind (and the geopolitical benefits for the United States could have been much greater had the administration set out to achieve them). One analysis suggests that the TPP could cost China as much as $100 billion in lost annual income and exports by excluding it from the group of countries participating in the partnership, not to mention the disadvantage of being shut out of a consortium that could evolve into the nucleus of future U.S. geoeconomic responses to the rise of Chinese power.[41] Further, in Asia more so than in any other region, economics and trade are seen as the geopolitical coin of the realm.[42] As such, U.S. failure to conclude this deal is far more likely to be seen by our allies and non-allies alike as foremostly a geopolitical failure and a negative test of U.S. staying power in the region, a point Lee Kuan Yew made repeatedly.[43]

When viewed through the same geoeconomic lens, the Transatlantic Trade and Investment Partnership between the United States and the European Union offers security benefits by creating economic partnerships that can strengthen diplomatic ties and shape the international system in favor of American national interests. The economic benefits are clear—TTIP could add as much as $223 billion to the global economy by 2025, and U.S. exports could increase by nearly $124 billion.[44] This would of course redound to the general well-being (and thus power projection capabilities) of both the United States and its closest allies. But TTIP would also have geopolitical and geoeconomic consequences around the world. "If the United States can complete the Pacific and Atlantic partnerships, it will have framed standards and market access for about two-thirds of the global economy."[45] From a national security perspective, these and other geopolitical benefits are what make agreements such as TPP and TTIP, even granting their shortcomings, of central importance to the future of U.S. power projection.[46]

Structural Limitations

If American limitations when it comes to geoeconomics are partly institutional, they are also largely structural. Certain geoeconomic tools will be simply better suited for some countries than for others. And for better or worse, given certain structural realities, the United States will probably never be capable of using trade and investment for foreign policy goals—and especially not in shorter-term, more transactional or coercive ways. Consequently, the most important question is not how inclined the United States is to engage in the geoeconomic uses of trade and investment but rather how (and how assertively) the United States sees fit to respond to the growing geoeconomic use of trade and investment by other countries.

Similarly, cyber is another geoeconomic tool that, for a mix of structural and ideological reasons—many of them compelling—is not likely to be of much use for the United States. Not only do countries such as Russia and China not face any real legal or popular constraints in committing cyberattacks against private firms, but these countries also tend to be adroit at translating the stolen data into economic and geopolitical gains without ever leaving state-controlled channels. The United States has spent billions developing offensive cyber weapons—but to date it has deployed these weapons in only one known instance (a conventional military application).[47] Underpinning this reluctance is a deeper concern about geopolitical outcomes. To put it mildly, in the context of the recent domestic controversy regarding the National Security Agency's acquisition of big data, it is difficult to imagine that Washington could ever replicate in peacetime the cyber instruments so pervasively used by certain countries, especially China and Russia. Nevertheless, President Obama told an audience of business executives in September 2015, "If we wanted to go on offense, a whole bunch of countries would have some significant problems."[48]

Considerable as the gap is between potential U.S. geoeconomic power and U.S. willingness to use that power on trade and cyber issues, nowhere is the gap larger than in the realm of financial and monetary policy. Nor, with the exception of cyber, is any realm of U.S. geoeconomic power undergoing such dramatic shifts. As Chapter 3 noted, the United States no longer enjoys a monopoly on where capital originates, how it is intermediated, and where it ends up. This fact makes U.S. financial sanctions more difficult—and more reliant on multilateral diplomacy. Even short of sanctions, it means that countries are more able to challenge the United States without exacting a toll on their borrowing costs. Finally, the emergence of swap lines and deep-pocketed central banks outside the United States means that Washington no longer owns a decisive say on whether a country receives a sovereign bailout or credit lifeline in times of crisis.

Even if the United States no longer enjoys a monopoly on these financial and monetary chokepoints, it still retains considerable leverage. Discomfort with exercising this potential for geopolitical use, however, can amount to geoeconomic blinders. It is telling that in the run-up to a potential military strike on Iran's nuclear program in the fall of 2013, there was no indication that the United States and its allies might seize on what had by that time become a full-blown foreign exchange crisis in Iran. Options of that sort—intervention in foreign exchange markets, for instance—involve real risks and are not to be taken lightly. But the same is even more true of war, especially war involving nuclear weapons programs. That the United States not only contemplated taking advantage of precisely this sort of currency weakness at multiple junctures in the twentieth century but actually did so—for example, using Lend-Lease to control the value of the pound in World War II, and then threatening to orchestrate a run on the pound amid the Suez Canal dispute in 1956 (against an ally as close as the United Kingdom, no less)—makes clear just how far norms have shifted in the decades since. Acts such as those would be deemed unthinkable today, whatever the facts and circumstances.

Again, the point is not that U.S. policy makers must move toward a more activist use of financial and monetary policy as a geoeconomic tool. It is simply that they should not delude themselves into thinking that these realms either are or can be insulated from geopolitics. The preponderance of history shows these monetary and financial tools to have been regular parts of the U.S. foreign policy arsenal. To weigh them alongside America's potent and high-risk military and diplomatic tools is the shift in debate we are advocating. To fail to consider them and then commit to a military option (especially one that exposes the United States to costly economic and military sacrifice), for example, is damning.

Even absent a clearer willingness by Washington officials to contend with the modern realities of monetary or financial statecraft, the United States still enjoys a number of geopolitical benefits arising from the dollar's global role. The fact that international financial markets tend to operate in dollars gives the United States a power that other countries do not have. That it is impossible to foresee exactly under what circumstances this geoeconomic instrument might be deployed does not mean it should be ignored.[49] Oil and commodities are priced in dollars, sparing the United States exchange rate shocks associated with sudden swings in commodity prices. The dollar's global role acts as a form of disaster insurance—in times of financial or military turmoil, money flees to dollars, boosting U.S. buying power and hence the nation's ability to respond to international crises. It also affords Washington the unique ability to run large fiscal and current account deficits while borrowing in its own currency. After more than sixty years, these privileges have so permeated American thinking as to go largely unnoticed—especially by foreign policy and defense officials. If lost, they would force the United States to confront new trade-offs between geopolitical objectives and the higher domestic financial costs required to support those external goals. And—underscoring the mutual dependencies that can exist across different geoeconomic instruments—so long as the United States seems reliant on financial sanctions, protecting the dollar's global role becomes all the more important.

All this highlights the fact that the effective constraint on geoeconomics in U.S. foreign policy today is not so much ideological discomfort or bureaucratic paralysis as basic neglect. In particular, geoeconomic tools and techniques of statecraft do not register as saliently on the minds of foreign policy officials as they once did. It is a problem that surfaces at all levels of U.S. foreign policy. In questions of overarching grand strategy, for instance, despite a widely shared belief that the rise of China constitutes the greatest challenge to American foreign policy in the coming decades, the United States has been largely unable to extract itself from an overwhelming focus on the Middle East (notwithstanding a noteworthy, if largely unrealized, attempt at precisely this in the Obama administration's Asia pivot, launched in 2011).

One might argue that events in the Middle East simply made the prospect of such an Asian pivot too difficult. Even granting this, however, it remains difficult to justify certain decisions—like the deliberate choice, however well intended, to focus intensely on the Middle East peace process at the start of the Obama administration's second term. There may have been a time when focusing on peace between Israel and Palestine could have made sense as a strategy for unlocking stability in the region. But with negotiations over Iran's nuclear program reaching the moment of decision, with Egypt in revolution and counterrevolution, and with Syria and Iraq threatening to pull the region into sectarian strife, the eighteen months between February 2013 and June 2014, when negotiations finally collapsed, was not that time. Even had a peace deal been reached, it is difficult to see how such an agreement would have meaningfully advanced any of the most pressing U.S. national interests in the region at that time: it would have offered no solution to the Syrian conflict and its destabilizing influence on Iraq, no way to answer the Iranian nuclear weapons challenge in a way that would have been both peaceful and acceptable to the United States and its allies in the region, and no clear trajectory for a stable, inclusive Egypt on terms that would lend confidence to Egypt's treaty commitments (including maintenance of the Suez Canal and recognition of Israel).[50]

Inattention to geoeconomics by U.S. foreign policy makers creates problems beyond poorly triaged priorities. As noted at the outset of this book, Washington has also been hindered by a persistent political-military bias in how it goes about pursuing its objectives, whatever they may be. Once the United States did manage to turn full diplomatic attention to the growing threat posed by ISIS in Syria and Iraq, for instance, these efforts still focused overwhelmingly on questions of tactical military advances, troop readiness, and arms flows, with only belated attention to what made ISIS different and more successful than other radical Islamic groups in the first place: money. From the beginning, ISIS had prioritized securing money, lots and lots of money. Had more U.S. military and intelligence efforts gone sooner to tracking and halting ISIS's financial gains, at least some of the considerable U.S. and allied military and intelligence efforts now being deployed against their territorial gains might not have been necessary.

Beyond ideological opposition, bureaucratic stasis, and neglect, there is another category of cases in which geoeconomic instincts are visible in the design choices of U.S. policy but executing on these instincts proves too difficult, even with the benefit of a fully engaged State Department. Take the case of the Arab Spring, where the U.S. initial responses were decidedly geoeconomic. In May 2011, President Obama outlined a suite of measures, among them establishing loan guarantees and enterprise funds for Egypt and Tunisia, swapping $1 billion of Egypt's debt into projects meant to generate jobs and education for the young people who led the revolution, and repurposing the European Bank of Reconstruction and Development to provide capital to North Africa. At the center of these efforts were two new initiatives: the region-wide Middle East/North Africa Incentive Fund (MENA-IF) and the regional Middle East/North Africa Trade and Investment Partnership (MENA-TIP). Both ideas were envisioned and designed within the administration in 2011, in the earliest days of the Arab Spring.[51] In 2013, the State Department asked Congress for $770 million in funding for MENA-IF, to "capitalize on the opportunities presented by the Arab Spring, supporting those countries that are moving to undertake the democratic and economic reforms necessary to address citizens' demands and provide lasting stability in the region."[52] But the plan asked Congress essentially to trust the administration in terms of how best to spend the proposed $700 million. Congressional authority to greenlight (or not) specific projects and uses was altogether absent.[53] Unsurprisingly, Congress proved skeptical and the bill never passed.[54]

With the Obama administration unable to overcome opposition on Capitol Hill, this particular moment of American geoeconomic opportunity has long since passed. Momentum for MENA-IF has been lost, the region has moved on, and the administration has also lost interest in the initiative.[55] And, however ambitious in design, the program involved a relatively small amount of money—certainly so compared to Saudi or Emirati standards, and too modest, skeptics have argued, to incentivize meaningful reforms.

Unlike MENA-IF, MENA-TIP contemplated no large congressional appropriation or new assistance dollars. Instead, it was to rest on active diplomacy with governments in the region to encourage trade and investment reforms—leading ultimately, or so many thought at the time, to the prospect of negotiations on a free trade agreement with the United States. Like MENA-IF, however, MENA-TIP has yielded little geopolitical benefit. Any promise of negotiations leading to eventual market access quickly fell away. What remained was never bold or visionary enough.[56]

Despite an accurate assessment of the post-Arab-uprising environment as one best suited to geoeconomic initiatives, both MENA-IF and MENA-TIP have been underwhelming in their outcomes. The Obama administration, led in this case by a fully engaged State Department, attempted to employ these geoeconomic tools but ultimately failed to engage Congress or to provide enough incentives and political will to make MENA-IF and MENA-TIP look valuable and worthwhile to regional governments.[57] Both efforts proved to be fair measures of U.S. geoeconomic attempts in response to the Arab Spring. Neither effort redounded to America's credit.

Moving past the MENA proposals, one of the Obama administration's other plans, the $1 billion debt swap proposal that would have supported projects targeting Egyptian youth, was championed primarily by the State Department and so proved a somewhat difficult sell within the interagency process. Questions of how to allocate the funds were bureaucratically contentious, and that leaves aside the difficulties of finding a consistent Egyptian counterparty with which to negotiate. The upshot was that revolution and counterrevolution swept in long before the administration could settle on a clear plan for how the money should be spent. Somewhat scarred by how difficult the debt swap ordeal had become, officials at the State Department would later advocate cash transfers in the case of Tunisia.

Finally, in some instances, the issue is not so much a matter of the United States being able or willing to mount a sufficiently geoeconomic response as it is a question of how aggressively the United States is willing to deploy geoeconomic tools, and, more fundamentally, how U.S. policy makers come to understand and weigh the relative economic and geopolitical considerations bearing on their decisions.

Consider U.S. sanctions measures in recent years. In June 1998, President Clinton famously told CBS News that the United States "seem[s] to have gotten sanctions-happy at a time when we are reducing our foreign assistance to the countries that agree with us . . . We are in danger of looking like we want to sanction everybody who disagrees with us and not help anybody who agrees with us."[58] Around the same time, Republicans in Congress, including Jesse Helms and John Ashcroft, worried that without sanctions, to quote Helms, U.S. "options would be empty talk or sending in the marines. Without sanctions, the United States would be virtually powerless to influence events absent war. Sanctions may not be perfect and they are not always the answer, but they are often the only weapon."[59] It is notable that the only geoeconomic instrument that was apparently known to Helms and his staff was sanctions.

In all, the United States as of September 2014 had twenty-six sanctions programs and thousands of designated entities—more than double the number in place during President Clinton's time—covering countries as far-flung as Cuba, Belarus, and Syria.[60] The Obama administration has sanctioned more entities than any other administration (perhaps even several combined).

Part of the reason sanctions came to occupy a larger role in U.S. foreign policy is simply that the United States got better at them. The Clinton administration channeled its doubts about sanctions into important revisions, introducing "smart sanctions" targeting individuals or entities as opposed to entire economies (Mexican and Colombian drug lords who wound up on what became known as "la lista Clinton" found it far harder to convert their ill-gotten gains into expensive toys). After the 9/11 attacks, the United States again updated its approach to targeted sanctions, this time focusing on the global financial system as a force multiplier. Washington began blocking illicit financial transfers and sought to use the prevalence of the U.S. dollar in global finance to shut out what it considered rogue banks. And, using America's central role in financial markets, U.S. officials also began effectively conscripting banks all over the world into enforcement agents, presenting them with a simple choice: either comply with U.S. sanctions, or stop doing business in US dollars.[61] This deputizing of the global financial sector in turn allowed U.S. sanctions officials to harness various technological advances that have so thoroughly reshaped finance and banking operations worldwide: the fact that almost all money trails are now virtual means that correspondent banking relationships are more easily targeted by sanctions, as are electronic payments systems.

The most important present test cases for sanctions—Iran and Russia—could not be more different. Iran is not well integrated into global financial markets, many of the sanctions emanated from the UN Security Council, and the target of the sanctions—Iran's nuclear program—spans decades and remains under the exclusive purview of Tehran. Unencumbered by economic costs and buoyed by widespread global support, the U.S. strategy was one of maximal economic denial. By contrast, Russia is far more integrated into global markets, the sanctions were mostly a U.S.-EU exercise instead of a UN Security Council matter, and the sanctions were precipitated by a military conflict involving Russia and another state. These factors called for an approach that was more attentive to U.S. and EU economic exposure and more calibrated, leaving Russia "exit ramps" in what was a fast-moving situation. To the degree that U.S. sanctions manage to succeed across cases as different as these, it should offer a fairly telling indicator of the strength and efficacy of U.S. sanctions policy more generally.

The question of what constitutes success in sanctions, though, is more varied than most observers appreciate. Sanctions, like any other geoeconomic instrument, can have multiple aims and multiple audiences—signaling seriousness to adversaries, demonstrating commitment to allies, sending deterrent signals to third parties, indicating willingness to escalate, or inflicting economic costs. And often aims such as these exist in addition to primary stated objectives, which typically center on changing regime behavior or policy in some way. Gary Samore, who served as the White House expert for arms control and weapons of mass destruction in the first term of the Obama administration, argued in 2013 that "the sanctions have worked to pressure Iran to accept temporary limits on its nuclear program. But whether the remaining sanctions and the threat of additional sanctions will be sufficient to force Iran to accept more extensive and permanent nuclear limits is unclear."[62] We now know the answer to that question.

Sanctions against Russia may have exerted some deterrent effect on Moscow's handling of the Ukraine crisis but have not thus far led to a fundamental change in Russian policy. Still, incremental progress is important, and too often overlooked. The problem is that measuring the deterrent effect would depend on a counterfactual—what Moscow would have done otherwise, were the sanctions not in place—and so is an impossible exercise.

Finally, sanctions can generate knock-on effects that, while not exactly intended, are notable all the same. Take Armenia, for example, where government officials in Yerevan are once again keener on some kind of economic agreement with the EU, in part because Russia's financial troubles have had a serious impact on the Armenian economy.[63] Or the Balkans, where Russia's financial limitations in the wake of sanctions have raised questions among its Balkan partners about Moscow's ability to deliver on energy infrastructure proposals.[64]

What success sanctions against Iran and Russia have achieved traces back to a mix of further innovations to sanctions themselves, together with basic teamwork, foreign and domestic. The United States employed novel financial instruments to moderate Iranian behavior, and across the Bush and Obama administrations has secured widespread international compliance. The Comprehensive Iran Accountability, Sanctions, and Divestment Act of 2010 authorized the Treasury Secretary to require that U.S. banks terminate correspondent banking relationships with foreign banks that knowingly engaged in significant transactions with designated Iranian banks.[65] The Treasury Department went immediately to work. By the time the United States and Iran began secret negotiations in March 2013, the Treasury had "conducted outreach to more than 145 foreign financial institutions in more than 60 countries as well as to foreign governments, regulators, and other trade groups and associations."[66]

Impressive as these strides are, they have not been easy or inevitable. What looked from the outside like a steady increase in pressure, in lock-step with allies, was far messier than headlines conveyed. On questions of escalating sanctions, arguments almost invariably lined up along predictable bureaucratic lines. Economic-minded arguments against escalating sanctions tended to cite concerns about provoking a cascade of unforeseeable and uncontrollable economic consequences. Such assertions—effectively, that one cannot know the costs or risks—are almost impossible to counter. In fact, economic analysis and predictions offered in support of such assertions often turned out to be flat wrong—time and again, various horrible consequences never came to pass. When in July 2014 Washington and Brussels were considering proposals to level so-called sectoral sanctions on Russia's banking and energy sectors, many prominent economic commentators warned simultaneously and without any hint of irony that there was no means of predicting the magnitude of economic fallout but that it was likely to be higher than anticipated.[67] And when, after all of the hand-wringing, these feared sectoral sanctions finally did come to pass, nothing much about the eurozone's economic woes changed.[68] The United States, meanwhile, went on to enjoy its lowest levels of unemployment and fastest levels of growth in years throughout the remainder of 2014. And far from spiking, oil and gas prices instead touched record lows in the months following the tougher U.S.-EU energy sanctions on Russia.

A final problem, seen in the 2014 U.S.-EU sanctions against Russia in particular, is the lack of willingness to mount meaningful pressure on allies, either to ensure effectiveness of the sanctions themselves or to curb free-riding by allies. It took nearly seven months to convince France to suspend its sale of military equipment to Russia; once France finally did, its decision had far more to do with Russia's growing military intervention into Ukraine than U.S. pressure.[69]

For the United States, strategic patience may be the largest factor in whether sanctions manage to achieve their aims. They do not work until they do. Indeed, after seven years of steadily escalating sanctions on Iran, Washington's fortunes finally changed in 2013. The economic hardships brought about by these crippling sanctions—worsened by profound economic mismanagement under Mahmoud Ahmadinejad—compounded popular dissatisfaction with the regime and played a role in the election of Hassan Rouhani to Iran's presidency. And sanctions certainly influenced the Iranian regime's willingness to begin negotiations in Geneva and to conclude the 2015 agreement.

After the International Atomic Energy Agency confirmed that Iran had "stuck to its part of the landmark deal agreed in November [2013] to freeze its nuclear ambitions," the United States and the EU decided to reward Iran by easing some sanctions.[70] The lifting of $4.2 billion worth of sanctions over six months by the United States and the European Union in January 2014 appears to have been a factor in Iran slowing down its nuclear program.[71] It thus seems as though both incentives and disincentives have influenced Iranian behavior.

The Iran experience suggests that Washington's new flair for sanctions has one major drawback: it is often easier to impose sanctions than to lift them. The 2015 nuclear accord underscores how both the enforcement *and* the removal of sanctions play a positive role in changing the actions of countries. In any case, there is no doubt that economic sanctions remain a robust—and improving—geoeconomic tool for the United States.

Like sanctions, U.S. assistance policy seems poised to take a new, more geoeconomically assertive turn, even as assistance budgets remain squeezed by the 2011–2013 budget wars in the U.S. Congress and their resulting sequestration cuts.[72] The $1 billion that Washington prepared, after agonizingly slow internal deliberations, to extend to Egypt during the past three years was hardly likely to help shape its transition trajectory, or to reinforce American influence in Cairo—especially compared to a GCC assistance plan for Egypt that looks poised to spend $40 billion over the next five years. Although it is impossible to know whether more money would have improved these outcomes, there is good reason to suggest it might have. In Egypt, unemployment worsened in the two years following Mubarak's ouster; food prices soared 50 percent between 2010 and 2013, while GDP dropped by 50 percent. FDI fell from Mubarak-era levels of $10 million to around $1.5 million in 2013. It was enough to draw millions of signatures on a petition calling for Morsi's removal on economic grounds in the weeks leading up to his eventual ouster by the military. (The petition read in part, "Because the poor still have no place, we don't want you.")[73] The degree of influence Egypt's largest GCC donors have enjoyed in Cairo, meanwhile, lends at least good circumstantial evidence that more (and more timely) U.S. assistance dollars in the early phases of Egypt's transition could well have increased U.S. geopolitical influence.

The $1 billion earmarked by the United States is not simply modest in comparison to GCC spending in the region (or, for that matter, the multibillion dollar packages in economic aid and investment that China and Russia each pledged to Egypt in 2015); it is small even by the U.S. historical standards.[74] A latter-day exception to the general departure from geoeconomics in the United States in recent decades was the $3 billion in annual aid promised each to Egypt and Israel in 1979 during the Camp David accord negotiations, a crucial pillar of the Egypt-Israel peace treaty that in turn has underpinned American Middle East policy for more than three decades.[75] However, given America's current domestic political climate and its domestic economic challenges, it is questionable whether this degree of U.S. generosity and strategic ambition will occur again anytime soon.

Even beyond steadily declining aid budgets, however, another major problem facing the United States in terms of translating assistance dollars into foreign policy leverage is credibility. The United States has a lot invested in how it spends substantial sums in countries such as Pakistan and Egypt. And—short of crises like the military coup and subsequent violence that seized Egypt during the summer of 2013—these countries well appreciate how unlikely their actions are to jeopardize these assistance dollars, no matter how disagreeable those actions are to Washington.[76]

That said, there are some signals that the United States may be more willing to consider toughening its stance on aid, more straightforwardly connecting these dollars to progress on certain U.S. foreign policy aims, especially around democratic reforms rather than geopolitical objectives. Secretary of State John Kerry, on a trip to Africa in May 2014 to discuss the Democratic Republic of Congo's steps toward democracy, offered to increase the American financial commitment to the DRC to $30 million on the one condition that President Joseph Kabila not seek reelection after his current, second term in office.[77] And despite substantial pressure from Egyptian officials, as well as mutual allies such as Saudi Arabia, the United States withheld civilian assistance dollars from Egypt for nearly a year, and certain types of military assistance for nearly two years, following the violence seen in the summer of 2013. However, several pressures—the urgings of GCC allies, concern over losing influence in the Arab world's most populous nation, and the emergence of the Islamic State in the Sinai Peninsula—prodded the administration to reinstate the full amount of annual aid to Egypt in March 2015 (without forcing any real reform commitments from Cairo in return).[78] These cases notwithstanding, ample opportunity remains for the United States to generate better geopolitical returns through its allocations of overseas aid.

Finally, no dimension of U.S. foreign policy holds more geoeconomic promise than energy. The United States is ushering the world toward more diversified and often localized energy supplies. Among its virtues, this diversification will weaken the geopolitical leverage that some energy suppliers have long sought to use to their advantage. The United States, by contrast, will find itself newly and uniquely positioned to use geoeconomic energy instruments to support its geopolitical objectives into the decade and beyond.

Sizing Up America's Geoeconomic Potential

American geoeconomic potential is inherently promising. But Washington must first face a set of questions about the country's overall comfort level with restoring geoeconomics as a more considered part of its foreign policy. Skeptics will argue that more straightforward attempts to link economic and geopolitical agendas will result in a race to the bottom. But the alternative cannot be to do nothing. In any case, the surest means of avoiding such a downward spiral may be to recognize what the United States is now dealing with: a set of states thoroughly comfortable employing most of the tools of geoeconomics to advance state power and geopolitical goals, often in ways that undermine U.S. national interests and chip away at the U.S.-led rules-based economic order.

Again, for U.S. policy makers, to recognize this is not to advocate necessarily a response in kind. On the contrary, America's long-term prosperity and security are ultimately staked upon what Benn Steil and Robert Litan call "a liberal, rules-based international economic and political order to which people around the globe aspire to be attached . . . An enlightened American financial statecraft will always be consistent with this principle."[79] It is, though, to advocate a different kind of policy debate, one where all sides begin from a clear geopolitical objective and where geoeconomic proposals are measured against that objective and in the context of viable alternatives. In extreme instances the alternative may be war. Where this is the case, U.S. officials need to ensure more appropriate standards of debate and comparison in weighing various options and their relative trade-offs.

Finally, history provides precedent for a more robust strand of economic statecraft that balances U.S. goals of openness and security; changes do not necessarily need to be dislocating ones. As noted earlier, during World War II the United States established the Office of Economic Warfare, charging it to safeguard the dollar and secure vital imports on favorable terms.[80] The United States supported these efforts with an economic intelligence-gathering infrastructure, which carried over into the Cold War period, equipping the country from the outset with the information it needed to fight that war.

To be sure, the United States should not re-create an office focused on "economic warfare." But the underlying lesson remains valid. For example, coming to terms with the uncomfortable reality that markets represented an unavoidable front in the war on terror was not easy.[81] But once this point won reluctant interagency acceptance following 9/11, the U.S. government launched a range of initiatives that have since drawn wide praise for their effectiveness in targeting terrorism without sacrificing American lives and economic liberties.[82] Paradigm-shifting approaches and tools

have often seemed impossible or sacrilegious when they were first introduced, from convincing NATO allies to adopt nuclear "flexible response"
at the height of the Cold War to proceeding with new forms of sanctions
(targeting energy and central banking, for example). But after a hard-fought
battle for acceptance, these have proven crucial in addressing the nuclear
ambitions of North Korea and Iran.

In short, vital and very important U.S. national interests are again at
stake in how we wage a very different sort of campaign. This time the goal
is to shape the behavior of states that wield substantial economic and financial muscle and are in some ways, though not in others, using this
leverage to pursue policies that could be damaging to U.S. national interests.
As one market observer summarized the task facing policy makers, "It's
[about] re-writing the rules of diplomacy to better engage" in a world
where influence "is determined by economic power."[83] The United States
has such geoeconomic assets. The abiding question is how effectively it will
use them, including, as Chapter 8 addresses, in the energy arena.

CHAPTER EIGHT

The Geoeconomics of North America's Energy Revolution

Thanks to the boom in American unconventional oil and gas production, the United States is swapping its long-suffered vulnerability to imported energy in favor of a new strategic asset.

—MEGHAN L. O'SULLIVAN, PROFESSOR AT HARVARD UNIVERSITY'S
JOHN F. KENNEDY SCHOOL OF GOVERNMENT

FOR many, many decades, energy has been a strategic liability for the United States.[1] America's ever-growing thirst for oil has shaped its foreign policy and national security strategy in ways that created sometimes incongruous alliances and complex obligations—all in the interests of securing access to reasonably priced energy.

These patterns are being upended. The United States is at the center of an energy revolution driven by the widespread use of fracking, with the result that it is poised to become the world's leading producer of crude oil and natural gas liquids as well as of natural gas.[2] For the coming decade and beyond, this presents America with a major new geoeconomic windfall.

The quest to secure energy has shaped global diplomacy and warfare for more than a century—consider the search for coaling stations to supply European fleets before World War I, the Japanese decision in 1941 to invade the Dutch East Indies, Cold War competition in the Middle East, the 1991 war with Iraq, and China's increased engagements in the Middle East, Africa, and Latin America in recent years. For much of the last hundred years, energy scarcity or the fear of it has sculpted the nature of global challenges and the response by governments to them.

The historic shift in global energy production is reshaping the geopolitical landscape as well. The United States is in the vanguard of moving the world to much more diversified and oftentimes localized supplies of energy. While renewables, coal, nuclear, and hydro will remain part of the new mix, and even as coal remains the world's fastest-growing energy source, a dramatic shift is occurring in oil and gas. In addition to its economic benefits, this diversification of supply will diminish the geopolitical leverage that some energy suppliers have enjoyed for many decades. All the great powers will be affected by these developments. Above all, the United States will remain uniquely positioned to use this new geoeconomic instrument to advance its geopolitical objectives around the globe for the foreseeable future.

The New Energy Landscape: Gas Is the New Gas, Oil Is the New Oil

In the early 2000s, headlines featured concerns about "peak oil" and potential new dependence upon imports of liquefied natural gas (LNG). Today we live in a different world.[3] During the past seven years, the locus of global energy production has begun to shift away from traditional energy suppliers in Eurasia and the Middle East. New energy resources are being tapped around the world, including in the waters off Australia, Brazil, and Africa, and, to a lesser extent, in the eastern Mediterranean (Israel and Cyprus). The United States, however, has emerged as the leader of unconventional gas and oil production. Fracking is the main driver of this transformation. During the past two decades, energy innovators in North America modernized and combined two technologies whose lineage goes back more than thirty years: the precise horizontal drilling of wells that penetrate bands of shale, and hydraulic fracturing, whereby fluid is injected under high pressure into the rock to create fractures and then release gas or oil when the fluid is extracted. The impact of this production is now defining the economic contours of the new global energy landscape.

Consider the dramatic increase in U.S. natural gas production. As fracking unlocked new energy plays, U.S. Geological Survey estimates of technically recoverable gas in the United States increased by over 680 percent between 2006 and 2013. At the rate of U.S. consumption in 2013, the United States is estimated to have enough natural gas to meet domestic demand for at least eighty-five years.[4] Shale gas production rose by over 50 percent annually between 2007 and 2014, a trend expected to broadly continue until 2040.[5] In a dramatic turnaround, shale will soon dominate U.S. gas production. Whereas in 2007 shale gas accounted for only 5 percent of U.S. production, by the end of 2013 it represented over 40 percent.[6] While terminals were previously being constructed to move foreign gas to U.S. consumers, U.S. companies are now competing to build new plants to export American LNG to the world.

Developments in oil have the potential to be just as significant. Total U.S. crude oil production has risen from 5.6 million barrels per day in 2010 to 9.4 million barrels in March 2015, nearly as high as daily oil production in Saudi Arabia.[7] Fracking has generated dramatic increases in American production of Light Tight Oil (LTO) in places such as the Bakken formation in North Dakota and the Eagle Ford and Permian formations in Texas. Between 2008 and 2014, America experienced a 56 percent increase in LTO production—an increase that, in absolute terms, is larger than the total output of each of eight of the twelve OPEC countries.[8] The Bakken alone crossed the 1-million-barrel-a-day threshold in December 2013. The long decline in U.S. oil production has been reversed: between 2008 and 2014, overall production increased by 77 percent.[9]

The United States is poised to become an energy superpower, a position it will likely retain for many years to come.[10] Fueled by unconventional gas and oil developments, the United States surpassed Russia in 2013 as the world's leading producer of oil and gas.[11]

Significantly, other countries will not easily mimic U.S. unconventional developments. Fracking took off in North America not just because of favorable geology. In addition, a distinctive convergence of factors—capital market financing that supported risk taking, a property rights regime that gives private owners outside federal lands the right to the natural resources beneath the surface, a dense network of private pipelines, a developed and competitive oilfield services industry, and an industry structure defined by over a thousand independent operators and entrepreneurs rather than a monolithic national oil company—provided an environment favorable to the unconventional revolution. While some other countries possess the right rocks, none matches the United States and Canada in this alignment of other factors. While many may well develop these resources, the path to significant production will be longer and more fraught, and most of the risks are aboveground.

Up until recent years, gas producers such as Qatar and Nigeria geared up to meet what was expected to be a burgeoning U.S. demand for LNG imports. The shale revolution is forcing these gas producers to deliver to new markets. While these exports first found a home in Europe in 2010 and 2011, they have since been partially redirected to Asia, where the thirst for gas continues to grow, especially after the Fukushima nuclear disaster. Given these opportunities, investors are now pushing forward with permits for new LNG terminals that will enable the United States to begin exporting LNG. While projections vary, most energy analysts agree that such exports would boost U.S. production of LNG within the next decade, contributing to increased global supplies.[12] While an integration of international gas markets will require years of infrastructure investments and even then will not reach the same level as global oil markets, increased liquidity and exchange between the North American, European, and Asian markets could help put further downward pressure on prices in Asia and potentially Europe in the decade ahead.

The development of unconventional oil in the United States is having similar impacts on global oil flows. U.S. oil imports have declined steadily in recent years, a result of lowered demand due to the 2008 recession, growing energy efficiency (primarily in transportation), and, importantly, increased LTO production. The United States has begun to "back out" imports, starting with those countries whose oil is closest in composition to LTO. Imports from Nigeria and Angola, for instance, are now at their lowest level since the 1990s. As this trend continues, the east-to-west transatlantic flow of oil will dwindle. Suppliers in the Middle East and Africa will thus shift to selling in Asian markets. In the coming decades, China and India are projected to more than double their current imports of Middle Eastern crude.[13] At a very practical level, the number of oil tankers transiting through the India Ocean and the Straits of Malacca to East Asia will increase two- or threefold in the next ten years, accelerated by the shale revolution. While insurers will adjust the risk premium for this altered trade, the question of who should protect the global commons and free transit in these sea-lanes will become increasingly important.

Energy Reshapes the International Geopolitical Landscape

Recent history instructs humility in predicting the future of global energy markets. That said, the North American energy revolution is transforming global energy markets, and we can see the broad outlines of how these economic forces will reshape the geopolitical landscape. Most fundamentally, the North American energy revolution will continue to increase and diversify the global supply of energy and give the United States a new and powerful geoeconomic instrument.

Many of the more dramatic geopolitical consequences of the North American energy revolution rest on the near certainty that substantial additions of U.S., Canadian, and Mexican oil to non-OPEC supply will substantially lower global pricing for oil in a sustained way. Historically, OPEC has used spare production capacity to stabilize the global price of oil. While there is much debate around OPEC's willingness and ability to use spare capacity to regulate global oil prices, spare capacity will remain an important metric closely correlated with the price of oil on the global market.[14] When the market is very tight, oil prices generally spike upward. Such spikes can undercut overall global growth, which eventually leads to reduced demand and downward price recalibrations. In recent years, when there has been a few million barrels a day of spare capacity in the international system, OPEC has been able to manage the overall price of oil around $90–110 per barrel. In mid-2014, however, it appeared that OPEC was beginning to rethink its priorities. Since mid-June 2014, the price of Brent crude oil has fallen by nearly 25 percent, going from a high of $115 to below $36 a barrel—the lowest oil price since 2009, and an unexpected decline that has led the Energy Information Administration to issue a downward revision of U.S. oil production estimates to 8.8 million barrels per day in 2016.[15]

Most analysts predict that prices will drop further before recovering—possibly dipping as low as $20 per barrel, which is the breakeven cash cost for highly levered high-cost U.S. shale producers.[16] Much of the downward pressure on oil prices traces to a shift in OPEC strategy.[17] OPEC's decision to maintain its production ceiling of 30 million barrels per day throughout 2015, even in the face of soft demand and a glut of excess supply, marked a clear shift away from prioritizing price stability in order to compete for shares in the global energy market.[18] Analysts at Goldman Sachs further suspect that OPEC production will exceed that quota of 30 million barrels per day, extending the downward pressure on prices. Indeed, Saudi Arabia, Iraq, and Russia all produced in 2015 at the highest level for many years, and this was before Iran returned to the global oil market.[19]

If oil prices remain low for a sustained period of time, every government in the world that depends upon revenue from hydrocarbons as the mainstay of public finance would be under domestic strain. Countries as diverse as Vietnam and Indonesia in Asia, Russia and Kazakhstan in Eurasia, Colombia, Venezuela, and Mexico in Latin America, Nigeria and Angola in Africa, and of course Iran, Iraq, and Saudi Arabia in the Middle East would all feel such a shock.[20] Each country has a different capacity to endure such a blow, depending on the duration of the lowered prices, the structure of its economy, and its institutions and their ability to absorb fiscal cutbacks. Some of the biggest losers from falling oil prices are countries not especially friendly to the United States and its allies, such as Venezuela, Iran, and Russia. As Harvard professor Martin Feldstein notes, "These countries are heavily dependent on their oil revenue to support their governments' spending . . . [and] even at $75 or $80 a barrel, these governments will have a difficult time financing the populist programs they need to maintain public support."[21] But when oil prices plummet, all such countries are enduring the shock at the same time, which magnifies instability throughout the international system.[22]

While policy makers should consider a scenario in which multiple energy-producing countries are experiencing fiscal strains and corresponding political instability, they should also focus in particular on the implications for countries that have used their energy to influence geopolitics, usually in ways counter to American interests.

Russia is the country that has the most to lose from the U.S. energy boom in the next decade. While it has large amounts of its own shale oil in Western Siberia that could be developed over the medium and long runs, the more immediate impact of the unconventional revolution will serve to weaken Russia across several dimensions. First, the shale revolution in the United States (and, over the very long term, perhaps in Europe) could eventually diminish Russia's ability to use its energy resources to geoeconomic ends. The unconventional revolution will not completely free Europe from Russia's influence, as Russia will remain the continent's largest supplier of energy under almost any energy scenario. Russia supplies Europe with both Urals crude, oil products, and natural gas; all three are under pressure in terms of volume (with higher U.S. exports) and price (because of excess supply). But in the decades ahead, European countries—particularly those in the east—should become less dependent on Russian energy and thus less vulnerable to Moscow's geoeconomic coercion.[23]

With the United States ending its forty-year ban on exporting crude oil in December 2015, U.S. crude oil exports could eventually develop into an important check on the longstanding Russian monopoly over European energy supplies.[24] It is not as if Washington could route U.S. crude exports toward its desired customers; like any other export, these crude exports would be sold by private companies looking to maximize profit. Still, increased access to U.S. oil by European consumers would allow these countries a potential alternative to Russian oil (currently Europe obtains about 30 percent of its oil supply from Russia). Similarly, Europe's ability to look elsewhere for oil supplies would make Russia compete harder in the global market, diminishing revenue from sales to neighboring European countries.[25]

Even if the unconventional revolution is limited to the United States and Canada, the extra gas in the market should—as it did in 2010 and 2011—give

European countries more leverage in their negotiations over price with Russia.[26] If Europe continues with its efforts to integrate its natural gas market, builds more LNG terminals capable of accepting imports of natural gas from the United States and elsewhere, and extends its transmission infrastructure, the diversification of supply alone will increase its energy security in general; it will certainly give Europe greater options for managing crises such as when Russia discontinued gas supplies to Ukraine in 2006, 2009, and 2014 in the midst of the Russian interventions in Crimea and eastern Ukraine.[27] Moreover, if divisive EU domestic politics permit, the development of indigenous shale resources in Europe—seeking to replicate the U.S. production boom—could help the continent stem its decline in overall (conventional) gas production and could further buffer countries such as Ukraine and Poland from Russia's energy-induced coercion.

Second, Russia could also face politically destabilizing consequences of a sustained drop in oil prices, and lower oil prices will also drive down Gazprom's oil-linked gas export price. With crude prices slumping below $40 at the end of 2015, hitting a seven-year low, and the ruble under severe pressure, Russia's expectations for economic growth in the period ahead are dismal.[28] Without energy largesse to maintain Russia's highly personalized political system, Putin could find his influence diminished, creating openings for new political developments. As other nations in the area observe this decline in Russian resources and perhaps domestic stability, Moscow's power and influence in its near abroad could be substantially weakened.

While this may sound like unequivocally good news to the United States and other Western governments, they must consider that a weakened Russia is not necessarily synonymous with a less troublesome Russia. The most that policy makers contemplating the longer-term face of U.S.-Russian relations should count on a surlier, more volatile Russia. Particularly if more nationalist political forces are the ones to succeed Putin or if Putin becomes even more aggressive, Russia could seek to secure its influence over its "near abroad" in more direct ways, as it did with Georgia in 2008 and Ukraine in 2014.

The unconventional revolution in energy will also have overall negative implications for Gulf energy producers and their ability to wield influence in the international system. Although less vulnerable than Russia in the short term, the Gulf monarchies, led by Saudi Arabia, must also be concerned about significant and sustained price troughs. To be sure, rising U.S. output will continue to reduce U.S. oil imports from the region, but the fact is that Middle East supply has not loomed very large in the overall U.S. petroleum picture for some time now, and it should be clear that America's geopolitical stake in the Middle East will not diminish because of the North American energy revolution.[29]

While Riyadh will most likely continue its attempts to play a stabilizing role in international energy markets, it now faces constraints on its ability to reduce production that it did not have in the past. Saudi Arabia has responded to the Arab uprisings and instability in the region with significantly increased public spending at home, combined with economic and security assistance to its neighbors. The kingdom's break-even price for oil—where its budgets would balance—was roughly $70 per barrel in 2010, then jumped to $85 per barrel a year later, and reached $104 in 2015.[30] High birth rates in earlier decades mean that an extremely young population is demanding more education, more health care, better infrastructure, and most importantly—more jobs. Absent significant changes such as plentiful natural gas discoveries or price-driven efficiency improvements, rapidly growing domestic energy demand to support such economic development means that Saudi Arabia could reach its own "peak export" scenario in the 2020s, when it begins to consume more energy than it exports.[31]

Riyadh is well aware of these demographic pressures and associated economic ones and is pushing hard to diversify its economy. Analysts warn that Saudi Arabia's long-term fiscal position is not sustainable, and prolonged slack in the price of oil will eventually test Riyadh's ability to maintain the public services that are an important basis for the regime's legitimacy. But this would take many years, given the kingdom's enormous insurance policy in the form of another geoeconomic instrument: its roughly $700 billion in holdings of foreign exchange reserves.[32] Thus, a world marked by lower oil prices, while hardly foretelling the end of the Saudi monarchy, would represent increasing domestic strains in the kingdom with uncertain outcomes. It would also render Riyadh potentially less able to compete as aggressively in contests for geoeconomic influence, especially should the Saudis no longer find themselves in a position to extend massive, predictable sums to finance their preferred regimes in Egypt and elsewhere in the region.

Even greater challenges could come to Iran's ruling regime. Iran's decision to enter nuclear negotiations might well not have happened were it not for the shale revolution which managed to replace sanctioned Iranian oil exports with U.S. LTO and avoid a spike in oil prices (although the prospect of U.S.-EU sanctions and denial of SWIFT payments may have been even more consequential).[33] With the July 2015 completion of a nuclear deal with the permanent members of the UN Security Council and

Germany, and—if the deal is implemented—the prospect of some sanctions relief within a year, Tehran intends to increase its oil production from its July 2015 level of about 3 million barrels per day to 4 million barrels per day by mid-2016.[34] And its longer-term goal is even more ambitious—by 2020, Tehran hopes to raise its production levels to roughly 6 million barrels per day, even higher than before the sanctions took effect. While these projections are probably overly optimistic and would require some $100 billion in foreign investment, Tehran will have considerable new energy revenue to enhance its power projection capabilities in the region. In addition, this surge of Iranian oil exports will be one further factor in downward pressure on global oil prices over the medium term.[35]

While the world's major energy producers, on the whole, have reasons to worry about the unconventional energy boom, energy-importing countries can look forward to benefits unexpected just a few years ago. Of course, lower energy prices would be an economic blessing for energy-importing countries. Just as the spike in the price of oil following the 1973 OPEC embargo created severe difficulties for the developing world, saddling it with debt that lasted at least a decade, a decline in the price of energy would be a boon for such economies; it is a transfer of real income from energy producers to consumers. China and India in particular, given their anticipated growth in oil demand of 40 percent and 55 percent, respectively, would find themselves better equipped to meet energy needs while simultaneously tending to other pressing fiscal challenges.[36] This is true as well of Japan and Korea, which import most of their energy.

China also stands to take advantage of the energy boom in other ways, even if we discount current efforts to access its own very substantial reserves of shale gas (there are issues with complex geology, lack of water for fracking, deep deposits, pushback from farmers, and high cost). As the world's largest importer of oil and largest consumer of energy in the world, China will benefit from the downward pressure on price that higher U.S. (and Canadian and Argentine) LTO supply will provide.[37] Less obvious but equally important, the shale revolution could compel Beijing to alter how it engages in commodity-rich states.[38] Over the long term, if China is able to pilot its own planned shale extraction programs successfully, Beijing could lessen its reliance on African and Middle East countries that provide the bulk of current energy supplies.[39] No longer would China need to offer aid or investments to backstop uninterrupted energy flows from Africa and elsewhere. But such a prospect would be in the far distant future, if it ever occurs. Both oil and gas demand will grow substantially in China, and it is an open issue whether Chinese shale gas will be significant or even competitive with Russian/Kazakh pipeline gas and LNG imports. As far as LTO is concerned, China does not seem to have the best rocks, so for the foreseeable future it will keep importing either crude from the Gulf or Russia (to be refined in joint-venture refineries) or oil products from the Gulf or Singapore.

In addition, the unconventional revolution could provide an unexpected spur to better relations between Russia and China, relations in which China has the strong upper hand. For decades, these two countries—despite the obvious rational basis for a long-term partnership between the world's largest energy producer and world's largest energy consumer, which share a 2,600-mile border—have struggled to come together for a common purpose. History, suspicion, and ideology continue to pose serious challenges. However, Russia will increasingly need to secure energy markets in the East to compensate for the unconventional energy revolution and Europe's move away from Russian gas exports, and China requires greater sources of energy to meet the burgeoning demand that underpins its domestic growth. While progress is slow, all signs point to the fact that Moscow and Beijing are moving closer together, not further apart, on long-stalled energy deals and pipelines.[40] Take the $400 billion gas deal China and Russia signed in May 2014. The contract between Gazprom and China National Petroleum Corporation runs for thirty years and requires the construction of pipelines and other infrastructure that will move 38 billion cubic meters of gas per year to China. Once implemented, such energy deals could provide the basis for a more extensive geopolitical relationship between Beijing and Moscow, with China in the dominant position and Russia making unprecedented concessions to Beijing in the context of pressure from the West.

Other friendly Asian countries, such as Japan, South Korea, and India, are also looking forward to more LTO and natural gas coming into global energy markets.[41] These Asian countries eagerly anticipate the explosion in global LNG expected in coming years. While not the main source of their enthusiasm, the potentially dramatic uptick in gas and oil being transported through the South China Sea will increase the costs of a conflict there (for China and others) and could, depending on the character of Beijing's foreign policies, provide additional incentives for cooperation. But these countries have even greater hopes that increased liquidity in the gas market and the growth of a spot market will force down the price Asian nations currently pay for gas. Similar to Gazprom's European export price, Asian LNG prices are mostly oil-linked, so higher LTO supply from the United States, lowering world oil prices, will also lower Asian LNG prices—as will U.S. LNG exports to Asia.

The Sources of American Advantage

While other countries will have to adapt to a new energy landscape, the United States will be uniquely positioned among the major powers to define and benefit from these developments. How well American leaders understand, articulate, and leverage that strength will help define the geopolitics of the coming era.

Most fundamentally, unconventional energy will make the U.S. economy stronger. The North American energy revolution will continue to boost U.S. GDP through three channels. First and most obvious, the rapid expansion of North American energy production will create new wealth and generate new jobs in the energy sector; IHS, a global energy consultancy, assesses that the unconventional energy boom supported 2.1 million jobs in the United States in 2012. Second, since the United States has one of the lowest gas costs in the world, American manufacturers are competitively advantaged in any process that relies primarily upon gas for feedstock. Energy-intensive industries such as petrochemicals and even steel—which make up over half of the U.S. manufacturing sector, measured by output—are already receiving a competitive if modest boost. In just one sign of this resurgence in U.S. petrochemicals, major players such as Dow have announced plans to build new facilities and expand current production that will increase overall U.S. ethylene production by 40 percent.[42] Third, the energy boom is fueling indirect gains in terms of infrastructure investment, construction, and services. All told, the energy boom could boost U.S. GDP between 1 to 4 percent, depending on the price of oil.[43] Naturally, some of these gains in employment and investment will fluctuate over time as higher LTO output drives world oil prices down and leads to a contraction in U.S. oil and gas drilling until a new supply-demand equilibrium is reached. (Indeed, since summer 2014, the U.S. oil industry has cut costs substantially and shed almost 86,000 jobs).[44]

U.S. policy makers will need to forge a nuanced and nonpartisan understanding of the significance of this new geoeconomic strength for America's position in the world. The North American energy revolution should help put to rest narratives of American "declinism" at home and in foreign capitals from Beijing to Berlin. The lessened requirement for overseas energy supplies—and the reduced dependence on producer countries with which the United States has prickly, volatile relations—will increase America's strategic self-confidence in addition to boosting its economy. One might already detect a new candor, for instance, in the way the United States is publicly venting its frustration over the steady financing from countries such as Saudi Arabia, Qatar, and others that lent significant early support to radical Islamists in Syria and Iraq.[45] And in the absence of the North American energy boom, it is unlikely that Washington would have felt the same leeway to move as swiftly as it did to sanction Russia in the wake of the latter's Ukraine intervention.

However, as noted earlier, declining dependence on energy imports should not be confused with full energy independence from developments beyond American shores. The United States will remain linked to globalized energy markets, and it will also have the opportunity to play a greater role. As net imports of crude oil drop, U.S. oil production will continue to climb, allowing for increased oil exports across the global energy market.[46] But any dramatic disruption of global oil supply would still ultimately impact the price at the pump in the United States and derail overall global growth. This means that U.S. interests in preserving stable international energy markets will endure. Nowhere is this truer than in the Middle East, where the United States will continue to have vital national interests, including counterterrorism, counterproliferation, and overall regional security to help protect our allies in the region (such as Israel) and ensure global flows of energy.[47]

Against this backdrop, U.S. leaders will need to explain clearly and consistently—to both the American people and audiences abroad—that the North American energy revolution will not change the national interests of the United States (a topic examined in Chapter 10). The United States will remain the most powerful country by almost any measure, yet it cannot isolate itself from shocks to the globalized economy—even if its more flexible economy and continued dollar pricing for energy will minimize the relative impact of these shocks. The United States will still have an enduring national interest, therefore, in protecting the global commons, such as the major sea-lanes upon which trade—of energy and other goods—flows. Neither the American public nor allies or adversaries overseas should mistakenly conclude that North American LTO will propel the United States to disengage from the world. Washington will have to reassure the world—and especially its partners in the Middle East—of this fact, given the coincidence of the timing of the North American energy revolution with the announced pivot toward Asia and uncertainty surrounding American policy toward the region.

At the same time, U.S. administrations will need to commit themselves to protecting this emerging energy largesse. So far it has been almost exclusively private sector players who have driven the North American energy revolution, with the vast majority of activity occurring on private rather than federal lands.[48] Nonetheless, a supportive legal and regulatory environment was critical to accelerating these developments. Leaders at the state and federal levels will be challenged to find the right balance between legitimate concerns over environmental and other risks linked to fracking and the overall economic and geoeconomic benefits.[49] Similarly, the United States will face the necessity of adapting old energy infrastructure and building new infrastructure in order to harness fully the unconventional oil and gas developments.

Sharpening Geoeconomic Instruments

The North American energy revolution promises to sharpen U.S. instruments for geoeconomic statecraft: sanctions, trade negotiations, reassurance of allies, and negotiation with rivals. Recent experience with Iran suggests how important the increased diversification of energy supplies could be in eroding energy suppliers' market leverage. Sanctions have been denigrated since the end of the Cold War as "chicken soup diplomacy"—measures taken to make the imposer of sanctions feel good about a situation that does not merit military force. The unprecedented sanctions against Iran, however, would have been nearly impossible to put in place in the absence of the North American energy boom.[50]

Unlike less successful earlier sanctions against Iran, Iraq, Sudan, and Libya that were instituted during oil gluts, the international community placed wide-ranging sanctions on Iran in the context of a tight oil market with high prices. Getting the support of allies and other countries reluctant to impose such robust geoeconomic measures on Iran required a credible case that a removal of Iranian oil from the international market would not cause a spike in oil prices. U.S. legislation even contained a provision allowing the administration to waive the implementation of certain sanctions against consumers of Iranian oil if it judged that further removal of Iranian oil supplies from the global market would cause economic distress by driving up prices. But President Obama did not have to use this provision. Steadily increasing U.S. LTO production compensated for the over 1 million barrels per day of Iranian oil that came off the market. The administration then assuaged fears of oil price spikes and ultimately won support for the rigid and exacting sanctions regime, which significantly damaged the Iranian economy and pushed Tehran first to the negotiating table and then to an agreement. It remains to be seen if this episode was a historical oddity or a talisman for the future.

The U.S. energy revival also provides U.S. trade negotiators with a new instrument. At this writing, and as discussed at length in Chapter 7, Washington is immersed in engineering two major multilateral trade deals, one with the European Union and the other with a number of Pacific countries. American law favors natural gas exports to countries with which the United States has Free Trade Agreements (FTAs). Applications for LNG terminals intended to ship gas to countries with FTAs are automatically approved, while those to all other nations require a review to determine whether such trade is in the national interest. Given the intense desire of many countries in Asia and Europe to diversify their sources of energy by including U.S. natural gas exports in their mix, achieving this special trade status holds extra value. In fact, the link between FTAs and approvals for the export of natural gas was a factor in convincing Japan—hungry for gas in the wake of the Fukushima disaster that took its entire nuclear power infrastructure offline—to join the TPP talks.

The United States has the potential to use energy diplomacy as a new geoeconomic instrument for reinforcing alliance and partner relationships. Take Poland and Ukraine—two countries that, with some help, could diversify their energy supplies and reduce their dependence on Russia by developing their shale gas and oil resources. If EU politics and regulations permit, development of Poland's huge shale gas resources could allow that country to emerge as one of the star economies of Europe—and therefore all the better equipped to push back against a newly hostile Kremlin.[51] The Polish economy, currently the sixth-largest in Europe, has been growing rapidly for the last two decades at more than 4 percent per year—a faster rate than any other EU nation.[52] In 2013, Poland produced 4.2 billion cubic meters of conventional gas while importing 9.6 billion cubic meters from Russia and 1.8 billion cubic meters from the rest of Europe. With roughly 60 percent of its gas currently coming from Russia, Poland has aggressively sought out international help to develop its shale resources, which are among the largest in Europe.[53] But, absent outside help, the outlook for both Poland and Ukraine is gloomy. As of late 2015, both countries are making little or no actual progress as far as shale developments are concerned—in Poland because the rocks are not promising, and in Ukraine because of conflict where the rocks are located.

Looking to the future, the United States could also use its shale energy edge to reassure allies under pressure from energy suppliers. Imagine situations in which Russia again attempts to obtain geoeconomic leverage over countries in Eastern Europe by restricting gas supplies or linking political positions to the free flow of energy at reasonable rates. The United States could signal support for any allies under such pressure through well-timed and public delegations of private sector energy experts and investors aimed at assisting the country to develop its own shale resources. Although results would not be immediate, the development of shale resources takes years even in the most favorable environments—their presence could nonetheless provide a public symbol of American geoeconomic support and solidarity.

Similarly, the United States will be able to tap into its unconventional energy expertise as a new element in its broader diplomatic engagement with other countries ranging from Argentina and Algeria to, most importantly, China. The United States has multiple, diverse interests with China—but, at least in the realm of energy security, Washington's and Beijing's interests are more similar than not. As massive consumers of energy, both countries have an interest in a stable and growing global economy, which depends in part on the reliable flow of energy at reasonable rates. They also share the goal of finding ways to reduce greenhouse gas emissions to minimize the impact of economic activity upon the climate. Given its vast and expanding demand for energy, Chinese energy policy is effectively "all of the above"—involving a diversified portfolio of oil, gas, hydroelectric, nuclear, coal, and renewables. As the United States has demonstrated, the retirement of coal power plants or their conversion to gas has been the single biggest driver for rapidly reducing greenhouse gas emissions. These common interests in diversifying energy supplies and reducing greenhouse gas emissions point to an energy-economics nexus that provides an avenue for U.S.-Chinese collaboration.

Onlookers in Beijing see the U.S. shale revolution as an opportunity that can, in due course, be exported to China with equally successful results. However, as noted earlier, China's rocks are not especially good, and most of the issues the PRC faces are aboveground: institutional problems to which solutions cannot be imported, as they conflict with the way the Chinese economy and society are organized.[54] Given the important role the United States plays in the Middle East and in protecting the global commons upon which China relies for the free flow of energy, future dialogues could be expanded beyond unconventional developments.[55] Such energy dialogues have already begun, in fact, yielding a joint U.S.-China announcement on climate change and clean energy cooperation at a November 2014 summit; depending on China's external behavior, these should be expanded.[56] Conversely, a hostile China would give Washington few incentives to assist Beijing in confronting its profound energy challenges.

Finally, the unconventional revolution can provide a boost to American leadership in the pursuit of more robust measures to address climate change. Natural gas, while still a hydrocarbon, emits at least 50 percent less carbon than coal. And the downward trend in emissions in the United States provides Washington with some credibility in assuming a more forceful stance toward others reluctant to rein in emissions.[57]

THESE developments represent a new chapter in the global history of energy and geopolitics. Especially as the United States moves toward becoming a net energy exporter by 2020, the world will see downward pressure on the supply side of the supply-demand balance. The geoeconomic power of traditional energy producers such as Russia, Iran, and the Gulf monarchies will diminish. OPEC will be challenged to regain its traditional role as manager of global energy prices and its consequent geoeconomic influence. Overall, most consumers will welcome this diversification of supply and the potential for lower energy prices.

The United States will be uniquely positioned to seize the geoeconomic opportunities presented by the unfolding North American energy revolution, and its foreign policy must embrace its transformed position on the energy stage. The North American energy revolution will add fuel to the U.S. economic revitalization. The steady diminishment of U.S. dependence upon energy imports and the potential power of its exports will provide greater degrees of geopolitical freedom and influence. The United States will have powerful new geoeconomic instruments to support its allies and friends and to engage with China in redefining the energy infrastructure to sustain a globalized economy in the twenty-first century. Chapter 9 addresses these energy issues and many others, while proposing specific U.S. geoeconomic policy prescriptions for the period ahead.

CHAPTER NINE

American Foreign Policy in an Age of Economic Power

There is no more difficult administrative undertaking in the United States Government than that posed by the management of the various economic assistance programs and the necessity for assuring their conformity to foreign policy objectives.

—COMPOSITE REPORT OF THE PRESIDENT'S COMMITTEE TO STUDY
THE UNITED STATES ASSISTANCE PROGRAM (DRAPER
REPORT), AUGUST 1959

THE PRECEDING chapters have sought to establish the basic instruments and requirements of geoeconomic power, explore how it is currently deployed by a variety of nations as a tool of statecraft, and consider what sort of changes these new power realities imply for the logic and conduct of U.S. foreign policy. Taken together, these explorations highlight two main points: the importance of emphasizing geoeconomics as a distinct foreign policy discipline, endowed with its own set of questions, assumptions, and organizing principles, and (the subject of this chapter) the need to reorient America's foreign policy to suit an era of geoeconomics, akin to similar reappraisals in response to the Cold War and the events of September 11, 2001.

Given the persistent use of geoeconomic instruments by China, Russia, and others, there is no reason to expect that the issue or the stakes will diminish anytime soon. Washington's focus should therefore shift to a new organizing question for U.S. foreign policy, namely: how does America maintain global leadership in an age importantly defined by geoeconomic power?

Coming up with a specific geoeconomic vision for U.S. foreign policy and translating it into initial lines of action is a complex task. It requires specific policy solutions; such recommendations are outlined at the end of this chapter. But because reasonable minds can differ on the specifics, it is worth ensuring they derive from the right framework. Accordingly, the first part of the chapter presents four lessons drawn from the previous chapters, which should help provide a foundation for specific policy choices.

LESSON 1

National power depends above all on the performance of the domestic economy and the ability to mobilize and allocate its resources.

The first set of questions that a more geoeconomic-centric U.S. foreign policy would need to confront involve how to mobilize and allocate resources. Whatever one thinks of overall spending levels and the tools we use to determine them, there are important questions of allocation. In particular, if one agrees that U.S. foreign policy has become overmilitarized in the decade following the 9/11 attacks, then a central question that should follow is what, in power projection terms, is the United States getting for all of this military spending?

After surveying a wide body of empirical research, international relations expert Dan Drezner concludes that "the fungibility of military power is more circumscribed than advocates of military primacy contend."[1] According to Drezner, the lesson for U.S. foreign and fiscal policy is clear: America's overreliance on military power is "badly misguided." To be absolutely clear, it is not that military power is useless. Rather, it is yielding diminishing returns. To quote Drezner, "Excessive reliance on military might, to the exclusion of other dimensions of power, will yield negative returns."[2] There is a mounting need to shift Department of Defense resources to the application of geoeconomic instruments to advance U.S. national interests.

LESSON 2

If the currency of power is shifting toward the geoeconomic, so too must the attention spans, competencies, and priorities of U.S. foreign policy makers.

One of the central lessons of Chapters 2–4 is that geoeconomic forces and instruments now do much of today's diplomatic work. Increasingly, this is as true for the United States as it is for, say, Russia. For example, our ability to isolate Iran economically has proven to be our best hope for realizing the aim of curbing Iran's nuclear weapons program without war. To take the Russian example, Moscow's strategy for sowing dependence among its neighbors is geoeconomic as well as military, and Moscow's calculus on how and how far to press military intervention into Ukraine has turned partially on the relative economic interests at stake between Russia and the West. But between Washington and Moscow, only the latter seems to realize the importance of geoeconomic instruments and their widespread uses. The underlying preoccupations and self-understandings of American foreign policy need to catch up to these realities. But old habits die hard, and the U.S. foreign policy apparatus still tends to fixate on crises that code as political-military in nature, while it views projecting geopolitical influence through economic means as too complicated, too slow-burning, or somehow apart from the central issues of the day.

Often only in hindsight do Washington policy makers come to appreciate the geopolitical salience of issues mistakenly perceived as narrowly economic. For years now, the U.S. government has done little to curb forced joint venture or localization rules, whereby countries mandate that Western companies seeking to enter their markets partner with local, often state-owned firms, or that they house critical infrastructure or intellectual property within the country. But when the Obama administration was forced to consider various sanctions possibilities on Russia over the Ukraine crisis, years of allowing the steady creep of these localization rules complicated U.S. options, narrowing the scope for maneuver and raising the costs of potential actions.[3]

There is also a parallel tendency to misdiagnose crises as predominantly military in nature, often neglecting substantial economic components. Compare, for instance, the number of U.S. government man-hours spent scoping the size and composition of the Afghan National Security Forces versus thinking through how to ensure Afghanistan's economic viability, or debates about arming the Iraqi Kurds rather than about promoting the long-term health of their economy.

Better responding to and projecting geoeconomic power requires a fresh look at how America's foreign policy and national security apparatus concentrates on traditional security and military challenges, and the effect on how we apportion finite diplomatic influence and, more fundamentally, how we spend the time and energies of our senior officials. It should mean more focus on rising theaters of geoeconomic power, especially the Asia-Pacific region. It should mean more willingness to take a tough approach against international economic coercion and the flouting of economic norms, including by China and Russia.

Finally, infusing U.S. foreign policy with greater geoeconomic logic should require retooling our closest security alliances for an era of geoeconomics. This is especially true of Europe and America's Asian allies. Again, certainly insofar as TTIP and TPP strengthen the economies of Europe and of Asian nations friendly to the United States, thus making for stronger U.S. allies and partners, both would be positive geopolitical steps. But domestic economic strength is not enough. It is a different thing to retrain these alliances to deal as effectively in geoeconomic power as they have done in military power for the past seventy years, to seek geopolitical benefits from their exercise of economic instruments.

Both the transatlantic and U.S.-Asian alliances were purpose-built to respond to security threats primarily through military means. As Russia's recent geoeconomic coercion and eventual military intervention into Ukraine brought into sharp relief, however, when presented with threats that are geoeconomic in nature, or when called upon to exercise geoeconomic power, the United States and EU member states are usually caught flat-footed, often with dangerous rifts exposed for the world to see. As noted earlier, why was enormous political pressure necessary to compel France to suspend military arms sales to Russia in the middle of Moscow's military thrust into Crimea? Or to pressure Germany and the United Kingdom toward sanctions when it was most immediately the security of Europe, not the United States, at stake? Worse, Washington was forced to consider sanctions against Russia on the safe assumption that any loss for American companies would almost certainly produce windfall gains for French, British, or German firms.

In short, any meaningful attempt by U.S. foreign policy officials to restore geoeconomics to a more prominent place in U.S. statecraft ought to entail an early effort to engage our allies in a deliberate, educational discussion. American officials must open more space for geoeconomics to become primary in these alliance relationships, describing to our closest allies what, in Washington's view, today's brand of geoeconomics consists of; calling out geoeconomic coercion every time it takes place and developing responses together with our allies; finding inventive ways to use geoeconomic instruments to promote Western geopolitical objectives; and more generally collaborating with these partners on the rightful role of geoeconomics in Western grand strategy.

Many of the most difficult geopolitical challenges the United
States faces are cases where states, often rising powers, are
applying geoeconomics as a tool of first resort.

Understanding the nature of the exercise one is engaged in tends to boost
one's odds of success. Surveying the global landscape, we see that geoeconomics is on the march. With Russia, China, and the Gulf states all enthusiastic exponents of geoeconomics, and with India showing similar intent,
geoeconomic-led foreign policies are unfolding across a large swath of the
world's population. And in terms of the foreign policy challenges of most
pressing concern to the United States and its allies, geoeconomics figures
prominently in nearly all of them. From revisionist and increasingly assertive tones out of China and Russia to Gulf states struggling for influence
over their tumultuous region, as varied as these challenges are, they share
at least one important feature. Each is a case where the tools of liberal economics and finance are being deployed by other nations quite apart from
the handling instructions that have traditionally guided their application.
This realization should in turn prompt the United States to revisit certain
basic foreign policy assumptions. It should also spell new policy concerns
and new margins for patience.

For one, it should mean expending more diplomatic energy and political
capital on issues that go to the core of this new appreciation of geoeconomic tools, such as cyber, economic espionage, and state capitalism. It
should also compel a fresh look at many of these tools themselves, stripped
of certain liberal (often neoclassical) economic assumptions that no longer
always apply. Would it be nice if Russia and China were not using the
World Trade Organization and International Monetary Fund as a routine
part of how they conduct geopolitics? Of course. But that is not the reality,
and the longer U.S. policy makers remain content to perceive these institutions as they were intended rather than as they are now functioning, the
more difficult it becomes to police and punish abuses. The same holds true
for the instruments and institutions of monetary and sovereign debt, pro-
curement, investment, and new forms of protectionism that can serve the
dual purpose of geoeconomic coercion.

U.S. administrations also require updated margins for patience. These
international economic institutions were meant to emit a gravitational pull
that compelled countries along a steady reform path; as such, they are the
mechanics behind the widely held assumption that investment abroad will
change China and Russia more than China and Russia will change the
global market.[4] Given enough time, enough economic growth, and enough

channeling of capital into the United States and Europe, the argument goes, places like China, Russia, and the Gulf will come to resemble their investments. State investors will transition into private investors, illiberal regimes into liberal ones. Such a Ptolemaic view of market transitions, though, requires the magnetic pull of a far healthier set of global economic institutions than the world seems to have at its disposal. (Even in the case of Russia, part of the rationale for fast-tracking Moscow's inclusion into the global economy was to use interconnections as a check upon aggression. As events between Ukraine and Russia prove, the Kremlin has figured out that this can be flipped, further bolstering the need for capacity building for the West to deal with disinformation and to track the role of Kremlin-connected influencers).[5]

When pressing rising powers for reform, in other words, what is America's margin for patience? Is China changing the rules of the game more quickly than the existing rules are changing China? And if the answer is yes, what is Washington prepared to do? What geoeconomic resources are we willing to commit to tip this ratio back toward a more favorable balance for the United States? Again, considering the scale of military operations and defense dollars spent policing perceived military or security threats to U.S. national interests, U.S. officials should show at least some more-comparable determination in policing geoeconomic incursions on those same interests.

LESSON 4

As we confront a set of powers that do not make the same distinctions between public policies and private companies, it will require more interplay between our own domestic economic decisions and national security decisions.

The United States should be prepared to air in the interagency process the delicate issues that span all the interests and competencies of the U.S. executive branch. The decision to treat currency as a trade issue, for example, or to use geoeconomic pressure on Iran beyond sanctions requires that all sides within U.S. administrations be represented. At other times, it is a matter of new issues that do not map well onto U.S. bureaucratic organizational lines. Take technology-driven issues such as cyber espionage and data privacy. In both cases, the United States faces outsized harm from cyber intrusions, including geoeconomically motivated cyberattacks, compared to emerging powers. Yet neither the U.S. government nor existing international arrangements are well suited to tackle the blend of intrusive state and nonstate actors and the prevalence of American private sector targets inherent in the cyber security and espionage threats. And in cases where a potential tougher U.S. stance on geoeconomic coercion or abuses might come into tension with security and military priorities, the latter wins virtually every time.

What, as a practical matter, would such a geoeconomic-centric U.S. foreign policy agenda specifically entail? What would it require? We believe it would be animated by the following presidential and congressional vision: U.S. foreign policy must be reshaped to address a world in which economic concerns often outweigh traditional military imperatives and where geoeconomic approaches are often the surest means of advancing American national interests. It must also systematically address the domestic economic sources of American power projection.

There will inevitably be times where our security or our democratic values lead us to act abroad. We will always face international threats. But returning geoeconomics to the helm of U.S. foreign policy means that, for these cases and indeed every foreign policy decision we make, we must ask three questions: How does this affect America's economic position in the world? How can we use geoeconomic tools to advance our strategic interests? And how can we shape emerging economic trends to produce geopolitical results beneficial to the United States, to our allies and friends, and to a rules-based global order?

U.S. Foreign Policy in an Age of Geoeconomics: A Twenty-Point Agenda

Next comes the difficult task of translating this vision into concrete lines of action. We offer twenty specific policy prescriptions—by no means an exhaustive list, but taken together, they would amount to a meaningful and self-reinforcing improvement in U.S. geoeconomic performance.

POLICY PRESCRIPTION 1

Nothing would better promote America's geoeconomic agenda and strategic future than robust economic growth in the United States.[6]

Economists are a contentious lot, but there is a wide, bipartisan consensus—further backed by the IMF—that U.S. growth over the next decade will require increased public and private investment in the near term, and a solution to the U.S. entitlement pressures over the longer term.[7] By 2016, non-defense-related discretionary spending is projected to reach its lowest level as a share of GDP since the early 1960s and to continue dropping from there. As a result, funding for U.S. science and R&D is at its lowest levels in more than forty years, with China now expected to overtake the United States as the world's leading investor in R&D within five years.[8] Both at the federal level and in most states, the United States is spending less on education in 2015 than before the 2008–2009 recession—amounting in some cases to a 10 percent drop in spending per child. And the Congressional Budget Office assesses that federal infrastructure spending is roughly 60 percent of what is needed to maintain current economic growth rates. By contrast, according to the U.S. Chamber of Commerce, citing economic analysis by the University of Maryland, a "targeted and long-term increase in public infrastructure investments from all public and private sources over the next 15 years would increase jobs by almost 1.3 million at the onset of an initial boost, and grow real GDP 1.3% by 2020 and 2.9% by 2030."[9]

Even if one's only concern were federal debt and deficits, and even if one's sole criterion for evaluating spending were long-term impact on fiscal health, there are a set of public investments—in infrastructure, in education, and in basic science and R&D—that will immediately stimulate growth while improving the U.S. debt-to-GDP picture over the longer term. Returning to more normal baseline averages in federal investments would help the United States confront its other major obstacle to long-term growth: its entitlement pressures. Recalling the Reagan-era R&D push of the 1980s, libertarian thinker and computer engineer Jim Manzi argues for a similar federal effort today, treating basic research outlays as "infrastructure" spending, akin to education, transportation, and utilities—all of which form the necessary ecosystem for an innovation economy.[10] Manzi is correct: the United States should create a capital investments column in the national budget for education, infrastructure, and science R&D funding, committing to return to more normal historical funding levels for each. The United States should also get serious about addressing spiraling entitlement costs; as Erskine Bowles, cochair of the bipartisan Simpson-Bowles Commission, pointed out, the across-the-board cuts put in place by the 2012 sequester help neither objective.

POLICY PRESCRIPTION 2

The president must speak to geoeconomic policy.

The next president should lay out an affirmative vision for a geoeconomic-centered foreign policy—backed by a mandate for the changes, big and small, it will require of her or his foreign policy establishment. Without presidential geoeconomic leadership, Pavlovian political-military responses are likely to most often carry the day in Washington, and thus drive the bureaucratic responses to America's external challenges.

POLICY PRESCRIPTION 3

The leadership of the Congress should schedule a comprehensive set of hearings on the potential of the United States to use economic tools to further U.S. geopolitical objectives.

Much of the needed U.S. geoeconomic agenda cannot be implemented without congressional approval. The Constitution gives Congress the preeminent role in U.S. trade policy, yet the last significant congressional overhaul came in the Trade Act of 1984. After thirty years, it is time for a broader legislative overhaul of the current legislative authorities governing U.S. trade policy.

POLICY PRESCRIPTION 4

Funds should be shifted from the Pentagon to be used to promote U.S. national interests through geoeconomic instruments.

The administration's State Department budget request for fiscal year 2016 was $50.3 billion, while the Department of Defense's total FY16 request was $585.2 billion.[11] The State Department figure is 8.6 percent of the Defense Department's request, a ratio that is incompatible with an era of geoeconomic power projection.

POLICY PRESCRIPTION 5

Develop a more concerted understanding of geoeconomics across all executive branch agencies with responsibilities in U.S. foreign policy and national security.

In order to discern when geoeconomics is at work and how it matters for U.S. foreign policy, the U.S. government first needs a common understanding of what geoeconomics is. Such a conceptual framework should, at minimum, be capable of distinguishing geoeconomic from non-geoeconomic instruments and influence, as well as determining what makes them more or less effective; it should also offer policy makers a means of evaluating geo-economic policy options against other policy alternatives.

POLICY PRESCRIPTION 6

Pass TPP Round 1.

Geopolitical strategy by the United States in Asia cannot succeed without delivering on TPP Round 1, bringing a "comprehensive, high-standards regional trade agreement" to the region.[12] Even though TPP began as a straightforward exercise in liberalizing trade barriers, its geopolitical stakes largely brought in as after-the-fact marketing to win the domestic support needed for its passage in Congress are now real, and were made all the more so by the Obama administration's repeated emphasis. Certainly, TPP could have better prioritized certain U.S. geopolitical interests (and again, often in ways that would have also advantaged U.S. economic interests, tougher provisions on SOEs and currency as two examples). Still, the reality remains that TPP, however imperfect, is now the overriding geoeconomic component of the Asia pivot, tying together America's friends in Asia and negotiating the terms of engagement between U.S. collaborators in the Western and Eastern Hemispheres.[13]

POLICY PRESCRIPTION 7

Conclude the TTIP agreement with America's European allies.

Nothing else will so further transatlantic geoeconomic prospects—especially if both sides seek to make this a trade agreement that prioritizes geoeconomic aims in its design choices. Like the TPP accord, any deal of this magnitude will require strong and sustained presidential leadership, but this is especially true of an agreement that attempts to move beyond the twenty-five-year-old template of free trade agreements. One could imagine in TTIP explicit commitments to develop joint responses to economic coercion by third parties for geopolitical purposes. Lessons learned from the U.S.-EU sanctions efforts could be incorporated throughout the deal. An energy chapter could help spell out preemptive safeguards and common responses to future attempts at pipeline politics on the continent. Especially given the unlikelihood of finalizing TTIP by the end of President Obama's term, there are fewer and fewer disadvantages to both sides exploring what a more sophisticated set of geoeconomic measures within TTIP might entail.

Reboot U.S. alliances for geoeconomic action focused as intensely on shared geoeconomic as on political and military challenges.

For a decade or more, America's economic relationships with many of its closest allies have lagged behind security cooperation. With the EU, we should design TTIP not just as a means of reducing market barriers bilaterally but also as a vehicle to curb geoeconomic coercion and global market abuses, and to positively promote Western geopolitical interests (again, the United States and the EU could use the agreement to develop common responses to geoeconomic coercion applied by an outside party, whether that coercion happens to be directed against a state that is party to TTIP or against some third country that is not party to the agreement). Washington and Brussels should also develop a coordinated position on whether to accord China market economy status.

To push Europe to take responsibility for its core security interests, Congress, as part of reauthorizing NATO budgets, should require the secretary of state to certify that the EU has made substantial progress toward diversifying its energy supplies and building in greater resilience to threatened shutoffs—always, of course, with a presidential waiver. The degree to which companies have filled in behind any U.S. sanctions regime should also be considered when approving countries and companies, European and otherwise, for U.S. export licenses.

The same goes for our treaty allies in Asia. As noted above, finalizing a TPP Round 1 deal that includes Japan would be a significant modernizing force for the U.S.-Japan alliance. But it should not stop there. Washington should lead collective negative responses to economic coercion in the region. Recent U.S. efforts to expand economic engagement with the member countries of ASEAN will help, but it is likely that the United States will need to invent new sources of geoeconomic leverage and influence, drawing on treaty allies.[14]

With Canada and Mexico, while we should have used NAFTA's twentieth anniversary to chart a new agenda for North American competitiveness, the case only continues to strengthen. In the words of former Mexican foreign secretary José Antonio Meade, NAFTA doesn't need to be reopened per se, but rather built upon, constructing and revitalizing "the idea of a dynamic North America."[15] Invigorating the economies of Canada, Mexico, and the United States and forging a higher level of competitiveness should include rallying public support, eliminating transportation and services restrictions, building infrastructure for new trade corridors, melding North American regulatory requirements, and making antitrust policies continental.[16]

Such deeper trade and investment ties, done well, should also come with updated standards for corporate governance, labor rights, and environmental protection (all areas where NAFTA remains well behind more recent trade agreements).[17] Certain options building upon NAFTA, such as a possible North American Investment Fund under the auspices of the World Bank, could provide much-needed funding for U.S. infrastructure through the North American Development Bank.[18] All these measures would not only strengthen the United States at home and thus improve its power projection capabilities but also ensure that America's neighborhood is stable and prosperous rather than an uncertain diversion from the indispensable U.S. role in the world.

POLICY PRESCRIPTION 9

Construct a geoeconomic policy to deal with China over the long term.

America's economic pivot to the Asia-Pacific has lagged behind our diplomatic and military investments. But more than any other region, economics is the coin of the realm in Asia. As we now work out the content of the rebalancing, our strategy must change to reflect this basic reality. Finishing the TPP is an indispensable element of this challenge, but too often TPP is couched in almost valedictory terms—touted as a "centerpiece" of America's renewed regional presence. It needs to be construed and communicated, both in Washington and in the region, as more an opening act than a finale.

Washington should also outline clear, credible security parameters for resolving maritime and territorial disputes. Secretary Clinton drew praise from Republicans and Democrats alike for inserting the United States into the maritime disputes in the South and East China Seas, outlining a code of conduct but not taking a position on the disputes themselves (as Clinton asserted in 2012, "No party should take any steps that would increase tensions or do anything that would be viewed as coercive or intimidating").[19]

But America's more recent lack of focus on the region has undone this momentum, inviting escalations by an increasingly aggressive Chinese leadership. As scholars have rightly noted, China continues to work to "Finlandize" Southeast Asia, allowing regional governments to "maintain nominal independence but in the end abide by foreign policy rules set by Beijing."[20] China has heightened its use of geoeconomic incentives, both in its neighborhood and beyond, with the goal of increasing the stake other countries have in maintaining good relations with China.[21] Little has been done—in Washington or elsewhere—to check China's geoeconomic influence.[22]

To help give teeth to the current principles for resolving the region's territorial disputes, the United States should build on recent warnings against the use of force, and make clear to Beijing that economic coercion, too, will have negative consequences. The United States should work to fortify countries, from Japan to India, against economic coercion—identifying their leading vulnerabilities and assisting with resiliency and diversification efforts to plug these exposures, as well as developing a policy across U.S. treaty allies in the region to ensure that if one ally suffers economic coercion, another doesn't take advantage by filling in behind.

There are at least some promising data points. Some experts have looked at regional instances where countries on China's periphery have realized their vulnerability to Chinese geoeconomic manipulation and have developed targeted policy responses. There is frequent discussion of the vulnerability of democracies versus nondemocracies to geoeconomic influence; Hufbauer, Schott, Elliot, and Oegg argue that democracies are fundamentally more susceptible to economic pressure than autocracies.[23] Thus for democracies on China's periphery, as is the case with democracies elsewhere around the world, there remain several frequently discussed geoeconomic defensive policy options: trading with a third party, import-substitution policy, or smuggling and resource conservation programming.[24] What remains missing in these discussions, though, is how a democracy adequately mobilizes a populace and private sector it often cannot compel.[25]

At the same time, we should outline collaborative approaches to Beijing's two largest sources of anxiety: securing China's energy needs in exchange for a PRC foreign policy that abandons its recent aggressive streak and returns to a more moderate posture, and assisting with its transition to domestic consumption.[26]

POLICY PRESCRIPTION 10

In another aspect of rebalancing to Asia, the United States should make geoeconomic investments in India's emergence as a Pacific power.

The last two U.S. administrations have rightly noted that the relationship between India and the United States is one of the defining partnerships of the twenty-first century. Washington has demonstrated commitments to help India graduate into the ranks of global actors—backing India's bid for UN Security Council membership; supporting the four multilateral non-proliferation regimes; deepening defense cooperation, including in the Indian Ocean; initiating a trilateral strategic dialogue with India and Japan; and enhancing our coordination with India in the East Asia Summit, the Asian Regional Forum, the ASEAN Defence Ministers' Meeting (ADMM-Plus), and other Asia security forums. Washington has launched all these initiatives despite the troubling fact that India is arguably the most difficult country in the world on the subject of trade. One hopes that under Prime Minister Modi this may eventually change.

Nevertheless, U.S. efforts to anchor India as part of a broader Indo-Pacific theater make sense for several reasons—they help reinforce Asia's current stabilizing balance of power, and they offer ASEAN states a crucial means of diversifying their economic and security relationships. But so far, U.S. efforts have focused primarily on security dimensions. Washington needs to make similar investments on the geoeconomic side, especially when nearly every major U.S. initiative from Central Asia to the Pacific relies on India's continued growth trajectory and cooperation: the U.S. New Silk Road vision (quite separate from China's "One Belt, One Road" initiative which also stretches into Central Asia, and, as such, is sometimes referred to as China's New Silk Road) seeks to tie Afghanistan's future stability to the markets and values of India, and the Indo-Pacific Economic Corridor concept and the U.S. Expanded Economic Engagement with ASEAN seek to do the same for our partners in Southeast and East Asia. In this context, the United States should continue support for Indian infrastructure projects, building upon the Infrastructure Collaboration Platform agreed to by President Obama and Prime Minister Modi.[27]

With so much staked on an India that is growing economically and engaged regionally, supporting India in its bid for greater multilateral clout—backing New Delhi in its long-running desire to join the Asia-Pacific Economic Cooperation (APEC), for instance—would seem a minimum ante for the United States. We should also elevate our own economic engagement with India by launching a study group akin to the effort that laid the groundwork for the U.S.-EU trade agreement. The final pillar of U.S.-India strategy should be a maturing of the Indo-Pacific Economic Corridor. This vision of an economic corridor powered by new energy and transportation infrastructure would undermine Myanmar's economic dependence on China and offer an answer to Beijing's plans for its own corridor from the Indian Ocean to southern China.

Additional recommendations for the U.S.-India geoeconomic relation-ship could begin with a look at the use of collaborative development funds abroad.[28] India is the top assistance power in its region; perhaps it is worth examining the potential for collaboration with the United States on aid to other countries of geopolitical importance. U.S. administrations should also not rule out the use of infrastructure development, modeling any such initiatives after Japan's overseas development fund for India. India lacks the capital markets that would make it even more economically attractive, a gap the United States should be instrumental in helping to fill.

POLICY PRESCRIPTION 11

Construct a geoeconomic policy to deal with Russia over the long term.

One of the central truisms shared across virtually all schools of interna-tional relations theory holds that it is dangerous to reduce analysis of a country to the personhood of its leader. If there is an exception to prove this rule, it is found in Vladimir Putin's Russia, where Putin is the best lens for understanding and predicting the country's behavior. Many long-time Russia followers consider force and threats of force to be the only languages Putin reliably understands—and certainly there is much in the empirical record, much of it supplied by Mr. Putin himself, to support that view.[29]

Undoubtedly, Putin's Russia is a case where a more robust geoeconomic approach by Washington and its European counterparts would require the backing of conventional military power in NATO. And happily, if slowly, the United States and the European Union are rallying a meaningful response to Russian aggression through NATO, centered in a new rapid reaction force expected in 2016 (a prototype of which became operational in January 2015).[30] These NATO measures, together with intensive U.S.-EU efforts around sanctions, have formed the bulk of the U.S. response. Given the nature of the challenges presented, however—German chancellor Angela Merkel and President Obama were quite correct that there are no military solutions to these problems—and indeed the heavily geoeconomic strategy that President Putin has himself employed since his 2012 return to power, a narrow focus on military power and sanctions is not sufficient.

A more geoeconomic-minded strategy is needed. This includes working closely with allies, toughening the U.S. posture on backfilling economic voids created by sanctions, reducing Europe's dependence on Russian oil and gas, increasing economic support for Russia's neighbors in former Soviet space (including ramping up support for Western private investment as an alternative to Russian and Chinese state-led investment, an alternative that many Central Asian and Eastern European leaders are desperately seeking precisely for this reason), and punishing Moscow's neoimperial behavior.[31] The market has heaped its share of opprobrium on Moscow for the country's aggressive behavior, certainly helped along by threat of U.S. and EU sanctions and the steep drop in oil prices that began in mid-2014.[32] But beyond allowing the Darwinian logic of global markets to impart its own helpful lessons, there remains plenty to be said for affirmative state responses to state provocations. Working with the EU to initiate a new standing policy of jointly policing and punishing acts of geoeconomic coercion and intimidation in Russia's "near abroad," in whatever form, would not only help habituate the Europeans into swifter actions but also send stronger signals of U.S.-EU resolve to Moscow and to other countries that may be looking to visit similar tactics on their regions.

POLICY PRESCRIPTION 12

Convert the energy revolution into lasting geopolitical gains.

The strategic premium the United States can gain from the unconventional energy boom is just as significant as the improvements seen in U.S. energy production.[33] But the geopolitical benefits to America cannot be realized if the production of U.S. unconventional energy resources is not given the priority it deserves. As Chapter 8 underscored, energy as a geoeconomic tool has massive potential, and Russia's continued insistence on using energy flows in pursuit of geopolitical objectives may have galvanized the beginning of a bipartisan U.S. political consensus supporting its use.

The United States should begin by expediting its approval process for LNG projects, which currently is unnecessarily laborious and expensive. The approvals system can and should be reshaped by, for instance, eliminating the need to review projects that involve shipping to countries with which the United States has free trade agreements.

With our allies, the United States should further the interconnectedness, productivity, and continuity of global gas markets.[34] Indeed, the unconventional energy revolution should become a pillar for core U.S. relationships with America's European and Asian allies. Closer to home, some administration policies—export bans in particular—have unintended consequences for both Canada and Mexico. Lifting these bans and approving the necessary infrastructure to link energy networks makes sense to ensure that our neighbors are able to enjoy the geopolitical benefits of the shale boom.

Long-term strategic decisions in the post-OPEC order also necessitate a reconceptualization of the Strategic Petroleum Reserve and management of the International Energy Agency's strategic reserves system. Given that energy price volatility can be as detrimental to economic growth as steady high prices, U.S. national security officials—in close collaboration with policy makers in the Departments of Energy, Treasury, and State—should consider how the existing Strategic Petroleum Reserve might be revamped to play an active balancing role should other countries become unwilling or unable to do so in the future. Similarly, a post-OPEC world will see increasing instability among regional powers. Russia, Nigeria, Venezuela, Iran, and perhaps even Saudi Arabia could be facing tough times if the emergence of shale energy production continues to put downward pressure on energy prices. The United States should actively begin to look for ways to help friendly nations deal with potential fallout as well as employing other geoeconomic instruments where appropriate in handling rogue regimes.

In addition, the United States should include energy as a key component of TTIP and should consider forging a Pacific Energy Zone designed to link North American energy supplies with customers in Asia. The United States should include an energy chapter within TTIP with the overarching aim of reducing Europe's energy dependence on Russia. In addition, the chapter should include a fast-track dispute settlement process that, even beyond its immediate function in resolving contract disagreements, might also serve as a model for similar efforts elsewhere.

The United States should also lead in the creation of a Pacific Energy Zone that would include North America (the United States, Canada, and Mexico), Japan, Korea, and perhaps China if its external policies permit. The goal would be to create a comprehensive energy framework for the region that, by bringing North American supplies to Asian markets, alleviates supply insecurities, sets norms, and begins to close the disparities in gas prices across the region. Such a plan could help to stabilize relations between the United States and China. It could defuse tensions between China and its neighbors—many of which begin with and escalate thanks to the actions of state-owned energy companies—while also providing the United States with a more direct foothold in preempting economic coercion. It would help answer the geopolitical influence of the thirty-year, multibillion-dollar gas deal signed in 2014 to supply Russian gas to China.

POLICY PRESCRIPTION 13

Meet the test of climate change.

As former head of the U.S. Pacific Command, Navy Admiral Samuel J. Locklear III was America's top military officer charged with managing hostile actions by North Korea, tensions between China and Japan, and a spike in computer attacks traced to China. And when asked what he regarded as the largest long-term security threat facing the United States in the Pacific region, his answer was climate change. Like many other issues in the geoeconomic domain, solving the problem of climate change requires harmonizing domestic and foreign policies, an objective often not currently being accomplished.[35]

A more geoeconomic approach by the United States might mean including climate provisions in key trade agreements, for instance—such as a TPP Round 2 or a U.S.-EU agreement. To date, most of our environmental provisions in trade and investment agreements are more about ensuring a level playing field based on existing U.S. environmental standards than about incentivizing strategic progress on climate change as such. Apart from including climate provisions more explicitly within trade agreements, the United States should also explore whether there is value in a new form of bilateral agreement, akin to a scaled-down free trade agreement or bilateral investment treaty.

POLICY PRESCRIPTION 14

Blunt the threat of state-sponsored geoeconomic cyberattacks.

The costs of geoeconomic-minded cyberattacks fall disproportionately on U.S. (and to a lesser extent EU) firms, as the leading suppliers of R&D and tech-intensive goods and processes. For this same reason, however, it is little secret that the United States has more to lose in any tit-for-tat escalation in cyber hostilities. This has so far caused the United States to stop short of launching geoeconomic cyberattacks, even in cases where Washington officials have managed to trace back an attack to a state sponsor. The bar for provoking a U.S. government response—generally understood to be "massive economic harm or potential loss of life"—is purposely vague but still enables states to test the upper reaches of this standard.

The United States should create more intermediate costs to geoeconomic cyberattacks through two broad lines of effort. First, Washington should better empower private U.S. companies to engage in self-help, especially clarifying the rules surrounding defensive attacks (empowering companies to make their own decisions on whether to engage in so-called hackbacks, whereby companies hack into an attacker's computer, either to ascertain the damage of the initial attack or to nullify its benefits to the attacker). Second, to help to mitigate the sort of whack-a-mole quality that remedies can often assume (where exclusion from one market is remedied simply by shifting to other markets), the United States should work diplomatically to enact coordinated cyber measures, beginning with enacting binding measures between the United States and the European Union in the context of TTIP, and then expanding toward other major economies from there.

Cooperation on cyber-related theft of intellectual property and trade secrets in the TTIP context could take a number of different forms and levels of ambition. At the most basic level, there is utility in engaging with the EU within the context of these negotiations to explore potential responses to these problems (and forced technology transfer more broadly). Specific measures could include:

- Possible uses of Section 301 of the Trade Act of 1974, authorizing countervailing duties (CVD) or CVD-like remedies for cyberattacks against private U.S. firms, jointly agreed and implemented with the EU, that would take effect in both U.S. and EU markets.
- An update of Sec. 337 (which allows the United States to keep pirated goods out of U.S. markets) to include cyberattacks and harmonize it with an EU equivalent.
- The creation of new cause(s) of action for U.S. and EU firms harmed by cyber espionage to bring suit against firms benefitting from the stolen data, allowing for variation in remedies from country to country.

Finally, the United States, the European Union, and others could enact coordinated measures targeting the ability to contract (or, more narrowly, the cost of financing) for foreign companies found to have committed cyber theft and/or to have otherwise benefitted from ill-gotten trade secrets or intellectual property. Much in the way that British crown companies in the 1700s drastically lowered their financing costs by binding themselves as subject to contracts, a set of rules targeting the ability of certain offending companies to contract could substantially increase their borrowing costs. Such restrictions could be limited to certain types of contracts and/or certain countries (e.g., those already on a designated watch list), and provisions could include a number of measures:

- Targeting the cost of financing (e.g., for any deal where a U.S. or EU firm is found to have suffered a result of cyber-related economic

espionage, contracts would not be enforceable in U.S. or EU courts, which would essentially increase borrowing costs for suspicious companies)
- Coordinating whistleblower protections designed to incentivize firms to report cyber espionage
- Anti-retaliation regime(s) that would seek to create coordinated penalties and sanctions, similar to countervailing duty remedies, for any state or state affiliate found to be retaliating against a U.S. or EU company for pursuing a claim for cyber-related theft of trade secrets or intellectual property

Finally, given the evidentiary difficulties, there may be value in shifting presumptions, burdens of proof, and evidentiary thresholds so that claims are easier to bring and to adjudicate, especially where state-backing or sponsorship is alleged. It might also be worth exploring the assignment of disproportionately large remedies, which would serve to alter the cost-benefit ratio of entering into retaliatory tactics.

POLICY PRESCRIPTION 15

Reinforce economic foundations for democracy and peace in the Middle East and North Africa.

Years after President Obama announced the creation of two new enterprise funds, one with Egypt and one with Tunisia, both funds have only just begun to cut checks. Years after the United States announced a new regional trade vision, no evidence of any progress exists. Instead, Washington has spent most of that time infighting and otherwise walking back the president's initial commitment.

The United States should move immediately to articulate a mid- to long-term economic vision for the Middle East/North Africa region in order to strengthen U.S. power and influence there and to help stabilize these societies. For the past few years, as the Arab revolt has grown darker, the United States has by necessity focused on immediate stabilization, but with paltry results; a broader, longer-term vision can no longer wait, especially as the lack of such a vision is hampering our ability to manage the short-term challenges.

Such a strategy should center on revamping the MENA Incentive Fund (MENA-IF) and the MENA Trade and Investment Partnership (MENA-TIP), elevating them to presidential-level initiatives. For the MENA-IF, the goal should be a modified proposal that allows Congress greater oversight while still maintaining enough flexibility to keep pace with fast-moving developments in the region. MENA-TIP, meanwhile, should live up to the president's initial concept: it should envisage real market access for those countries genuinely interested; it should weave together its existing bilateral free trade agreements, transforming the five separate agreements into a single, updated set of trade terms that apply between all participating states (a process known as cumulation); and it should incentivize participation through new, specially dedicated lines of economic assistance linked to incremental benchmarks.

With Egypt, the United States should rewrite the ground rules for assistance. The Egyptian government is ever hopeful that U.S. assistance flows will return with the same unflinching reliability that characterized U.S.-Egypt ties before the Arab Uprising, which would serve as a seal of approval for the country's changing political environment. Ever since the fall of Mubarak, though, Egypt has been a story of halting progress, with more fits than starts. Even should there be democratic progress, U.S. assistance to Egypt will remain choked by interference from the country's Ministry of International Cooperation—the Tammany Hall of Egypt.[36] A better use of U.S. assistance to Egypt, then, would be a push to rewrite how aid is delivered, if possible removing the Ministry of International Cooperation from the process. At the same time, the United States should increase transparency and develop a publicly accountable process for how it dispenses its aid. Large amounts of democracy aid would be counterproductive in the current climate, but Washington could discreetly support civil society initiatives within Egypt. Such geoeconomic measures would make at least a minor contribution to the stability of Egypt, a crucial objective of U.S. Middle East policy.

With Tunisia, Washington should launch negotiations on a free trade agreement. Tunisia marks the one success, the one country transitioning to democracy in the wake of the events of January 2011. The Obama administration has committed nearly $700 million to support Tunisia's transition, targeting elements of internal and external security, the promotion of democratic practices and good governance, and supporting sustainable economic growth.[37] The leadership in Tunis is taking all the right steps— ratifying a progressive constitution, hitting reform benchmarks pursuant to its IMF deal, and conducting elections.[38] Tunisian leaders are now looking to a free trade agreement with the United States as the government's top priority. Beyond the diplomatic goodwill toward the United States it would engender, a free trade agreement would, as former chairman of the House Rules Committee David Dreier aptly noted, lock in structural reforms by creating "the resources necessary for sustainable democratic development and prosperity in Tunisia."[39] And because Tunisia is a country of just 11 million people, the economic impacts of such a deal for the United States, the sum total of winners and losers, would be negligible.

Next, the United States should establish a region-wide, high-profile, private-sector-led investment initiative. This would start from a familiar premise: channel willing capital, especially surplus capital in the Gulf states and Asia, toward infrastructure investments in Egypt, Jordan, Tunisia, Yemen, and other transitioning countries in the Middle East and North Africa. The investment mechanism would have three basic elements: (1) a multisovereign trust fund (overseen by third parties, such as the World Bank or United States) with windows to attract public and private investment, (2) a project development team and assistance secretariat to help countries propose projects and coordinate third-party financing (e.g., the European Bank for Reconstruction and Development, Islamic Infrastructure Financing Facility, World Bank, and others), and (3) a policy forum, composed of representatives of investor states, that would provide a venue to discuss regional employment and transition issues, and also help set policy objectives, country allocations, and various working requirements.[40]

This plan differs from the current crowded landscape in several ways—most notably in its largely private-sector dimension. Unlike the current G8 Deauville framework, this is Arab-centered and focuses on investment rather than sovereign loans; unlike the Arab Financing Facility for Infrastructure, capital would be channeled directly to the private sector; and perhaps most important, would-be investors from the Gulf Cooperation Council would have a meaningful seat at the table. If successful, the plan should help foster a much-needed indigenous leadership presence in these countries—providing at least a partial answer to the economic leadership deficit across the region.

The plan's financial viability hinges on earning the support of GCC actors, who are prone to infighting and their own internal struggles for influence in Cairo. The primary role for the United States likely would be in publicly planting the initial call for such a plan and in offering quiet support for the plan to GCC officials—emphasizing the GCC's common strategic interest in stabilizing these economies as the best prevention against Islamic radicalism. Washington should also underscore the benefits of the plan's multiparty vehicle for the GCC (e.g., controlling shareholder status and return on investment).

Finally, the G8 Deauville Partnership should be transitioned into a permanent, APEC-like body for the Middle East and North Africa, notwithstanding the current turmoil in the region. Just as APEC provided the Asia-Pacific an organizing principle for economic integration and spurred domestic reforms, a similar organization in the very different—and much more challenging—Middle East/North Africa region could spur the reinforcement of democratic progress with economic reforms. Specifically, it would provide the means for the countries of the region to agree on a common agenda of expanding intraregional and interregional trade. APEC's Bogor Goals, which set the goal of a free trade area for the Pacific within twenty years, offers a loose model. As was noted by Egypt's finance minister, Hany Dimian, there is no need to reinvent the principles of economic integration for the Middle East and North Africa.[41] For such a body to materialize, stepped-up support from the international community should bolster the regional economic and political reform already under way. The United States and others will need to continue providing financing so that public spending can support regional economic growth.

POLICY PRESCRIPTION 16

Refocus U.S. development aid toward cultivating the next generation of emerging markets, especially in Latin America and Africa.[42]

The China Development Bank and Brazil's BNDES each now have lending portfolios that outstrip the World Bank's. More than half of global development aid comes from the EU and its member states but depends upon fulfillment of select criteria.[43] Canada has also actively sent aid and development-minded investment dollars into countries identified as having mineral resources of interest to Canadian firms, including Mongolia, Peru, Bolivia, Ghana, and even the conflict-torn Democratic Republic of the Congo; it smacks of corporate welfare for some critics, of crass commercialism for others. But they are taking Canadian standards with them.[44]

The United States should respond in six ways:

- *Explore aligning Canada and the United States with the Pacific Alliance.* The Pacific Alliance is a coalition that unites Chile, Colombia, Mexico, and Peru in support of free trade and open economies.[45] As a current observer to the alliance, the United States should pursue full membership while continuing to expand cooperation with member countries.[46]
- *Initiate a new Plan Central America.* The goal is to promote better security, governance, and economic development in the region with support from Mexico, Colombia, Panama, and Canada.[47] Furthermore, the United States should work to manage the complexities of dealing with regional governments in pursuing a Plan Central America initiative, addressing root causes of weak governance and uncertain public expectations as necessary.

- *Create a development financing institution.* As official aid sources account for an ever-smaller share of development budgets—falling from 70 percent to 13 percent in the past decade alone—achieving U.S. development goals will require greater private sector investment. Presently, only a limited share of U.S. annual development resources is devoted to private sector investment. The Overseas Private Investment Corporation (OPIC), the U.S. government's primary private sector development partner, invested $2.58 billion in 2014 and returned $269 million profit to U.S. taxpayers (providing a net resource, as opposed to net expense, to the $56 billion international affairs budget).[48] Other smaller, disparate private-sector-focused activities are spread throughout the U.S. Agency for International Development (through the Development Credit Authority), the U.S. Trade and Development Agency, the Millennium Challenge Corporation, the State Department, and the Export-Import Bank. Despite all of these various efforts, the U.S. government does not offer a comprehensive set of investment tools with the range of equity, debt, and guarantee products needed to support private investment in more challenging and risky landscapes.

This makes the United States something of an outlier among its G7 peers. Japan's Bank of International Cooperation, along with European development finance institutions such as the Dutch FMO and Germany's KfW, and multilateral mechanisms such as the International Finance Corporation (the private sector lending arm of the World Bank) are innovating new, private sector development approaches through a broad set of financial offerings, including equity. They also invest a sizeable share of their resources in businesses that are locally owned in developing countries, provided those investments are projected to have a positive development impact (in comparison, OPIC is limited to debt financing and is required to have a U.S. business involved in any investment).

China has grown foreign direct investment flows to low-income countries (primarily in Africa) an estimated twentyfold between 2003 and 2009. As Chapters 4 and 5 underscored, these flows are quickly becoming choice tools in Beijing and elsewhere for waging geopolitics and exercising influence. Once operational, the BRICS bank and the Asian Infrastructure Investment Bank will only compound these disparities.

OPIC is likely the most attractive and efficient foundation on which to build a robust U.S. development finance institution. Several changes in OPIC's mandate and structure would be required, including enabling equity investments as well as first-loss and other risk-sharing arrangements; permitting investment in a wider range of businesses that support development goals, in particular indigenous businesses in priority partner countries (which could be specified for geopolitical as well as development reasons); creating one or more new financing windows more explicitly linked to development impact targets (projects in these windows would share development as well as financial targets); congressional reauthorization for OPIC's budget on an enduring multiyear basis (as opposed to the current annual authorization cycle); and merging a meaningful share of the related programmatic activities and assets of other agencies to enable OPIC to provide a full range of financial products without interagency competition, duplication, or inefficient costs.

- *Revamp tools of U.S. power projection to play to two of our greatest national assets: technology and entrepreneurship.* In an era of unprecedented youth unemployment, American entrepreneurship remains underdeveloped as a geoeconomic instrument. We need to move beyond our current, largely programmatic approach, seeking instead to elevate technology and entrepreneurship as a fully developed tool in our diplomatic arsenal. One possibility might be partnering with Venture for America to launch a global counterpart to their U.S. operations. Modeled on Teach for America, Venture for America recruits and trains top young college graduates to spend two years in the trenches of a community-development-oriented start-up with the goal that these graduates become mobilized as entrepreneurs.[49]
- *Consider preemptive contract sanctions.* Washington should also pursue an updated spin on a long-standing concept known as "odious debt"—effectively creating a new type of sanctions regime, what we and some others call preemptive contract sanctions, that would enlist the power of credit markets in ousting the most brutal and kleptocratic regimes. The idea would be to designate contracts as unenforceable for judgment going forward from the day of designation.[50] In the case of, say, the Assad regime in Syria or Qaddafi's in Libya, the United States would designate any new commercial contracts signed after a given date as unenforceable in U.S. jurisdictions. Ideally, other major financial hubs (the United Kingdom, Singapore, and Hong Kong are perhaps the most important three) would follow suit. The result would be to force regimes subject to the sanction to pay sharp increases in borrowing rates.
- *Release the evidence packets that U.S. administrations and Congress use in making sanctions determinations.* As part of handing these packets to Congress, all information contained is usually not classi-

fied. The idea, then, would be to go one step further and provide this information to the public in certain appropriate cases. Even the threat that this could happen may have a chilling effect on certain corruption-prone leaders, offering a potential counter to President Putin and others, who are blackmailing with presumably much of the same information.

- *Treat corruption as the systematic geoeconomic weapon it often is.* Western diplomats with experience in Eastern Europe and Central Asia frequently regale one another with accounts of Russian president Vladimir Putin corrupting corporate and government officials as a reliable, cheap means of marshaling influence in Russia's near-abroad. U.S. military officials returning from forward deployments describe how terrorist groups in Afghanistan, Iraq, Nigeria, and elsewhere capitalize on endemic government corruption as a recruiting tool. Yet diplomatic priorities and defense budgets do not reflect the central role that corruption plays in the United States' toughest security challenges.[51] The next U.S. president could, for example: direct the Department of Justice to indict corrupt foreign officials with greater regularity; order various federal agencies to cooperate with foreign corruption proceedings, supplying prosecutors with evidence on a case-by-case basis; establish new requirements on contracting transparency (ensuring that noncommercially sensitive portions of resource-based contracts with foreign governments are made public); and grant victims of corruption greater ability to sue in third-party jurisdictions.

POLICY PRESCRIPTION 17

Shore up the rules governing geoeconomic playing fields.

Our current system is buckling under the weight of a host of new forces that our existing rules and institutions never contemplated—from the rise of state capitalism to a host of market distortions far more damaging and elusive than tariffs. As international trade law has substantially eliminated tariff barriers to trade between major economies, countries have turned to a host of market-distorting practices that are largely impervious to existing rules, including currency manipulation, indigenous innovation policies, the deliberate nonenforcement of intellectual property rights, and abusive regulatory regimes. Rising public awareness of these new barriers in the United States and elsewhere, meanwhile, is causing an ebb in domestic public support for a robust, liberal trade and investment agenda—creating potential long-term problems for America's ability to shape the rules governing global playing fields going forward.

Much as the General Agreement on Tariffs and Trade and the World Trade Organization offered a global solution to the problem of tariff barriers, the United States must develop a means of confronting the most salient forms of protectionism in evidence today, particularly when they are used for coercive purposes. A robust TPP Round 1 and a meaningful TTIP together would mark real momentum but still fall short of a global answer to these challenges.[52]

Fashioning such a global answer will require several fundamental changes. First, the United States must move beyond the current trade and investment framework toward an expanded geoeconomic approach that takes the full range of competitive conditions as an organizing principle and introduces dimensions of international antitrust law, currency practices, regulatory policy (including financial regulation as well as regulatory issues touching data and spectrum management), and mercantilist tax policies, such as value-added tax rebates for exporters. The single largest factor in the offshoring of U.S.-based production and millions of jobs abroad, say many economists, is the packages of financial incentives that China and others offer to global companies to encourage them to relocate production.[53] Others point to China's value-added tax rebates for exporters, which cost China the equivalent of 20 percent of annual government spending in 2010. Existing trade and investment rules simply do not address these realities and thus are entirely disconnected from America's geopolitical objectives.

The problem is not just about antiquated and insufficient rules but also about how the United States measures and enforces them. In a world of competing global supply chains and integrated capital flows, trade rules that focus largely on tariffs, national treatment, and most-favored-nation status are outdated and permit nations to pressure recalcitrant neighbors through geoeconomic means. The harmful practices tend to be fluid, and where one is struck down or becomes too controversial, governments can all too easily reintroduce it with only slight refinement.

POLICY PRESCRIPTION 18

If America is going to be effective at exploiting its geoeconomic potential, it needs the right signals and bureaucratic structures in place, many of which can only come from the White House.

Progress on all of these fronts will require a sustained and determined look by successive U.S. administrations at how Washington too often privileges security tools over geoeconomic instruments, especially in terms of how the

United States apportions finite diplomatic influence and how it allocates the time and energies of its senior officials.

U.S. foreign policy is and will remain an advocacy-based system. The reason geoeconomic approaches are not suitably reflected in recent U.S. policy is simply that there are no institutional or bureaucratic actors properly incentivized to argue for them. Under the current system, there are two White House offices with responsibility for coordinating U.S. international economic policy: the International Economics Directorate of the National Security Council (NSC), which tends to be staffed by officials with backgrounds in investment banking and finance (often coupled with substantial time at the Treasury Department or the IMF), and the National Economic Council (NEC), whose portfolio spans both domestic and international issues. The NEC, especially under the Obama administration, has tended to shrink away from its international mandate, partly to avoid overlap with the NSC, and partly owing to more than enough work to do on domestic issues alone.

A new White House entity should be created and tasked with strengthening the country's overall understanding and use of geoeconomics and, as noted earlier, the harmonization of domestic and foreign policies. Housed within the National Security Council, this office should be staffed with roughly equal numbers of officials from the State, Intelligence, Defense, Treasury, and Commerce Departments, plus the Office of the U.S. Trade Representative, and should replace the current NSC International Economics Directorate. The new office should occupy itself with two overarching responsibilities. First, it should diagnose cases of geoeconomic coercion at work in the world, and coordinate international responses wherever U.S. national interests are at stake. Second, it should make geoeconomic reflexes far more central to every element of U.S. foreign policy—in effect, helping to restore the balance lost as military approaches have steadily won out over the past three decades. Where inevitable tensions arise between certain purely economic and geopolitical interests, this new entity should be clear-eyed about these tensions, and should be charged with ensuring that the geoeconomic dimension is included in interagency deliberations (realizing that the purely economic interests, meanwhile, will continue to be well represented by the economic agencies). The NEC, meanwhile, should reclaim its international economic policy coordination responsibilities, so as to fill the void of coordinating more straightforward international economic policy matters.

Second, administrations need to build in safeguards to help senior officials balance the important alongside the urgent. There are countless small, routine processes—how trip agendas are planned, how issues get elevated up the chain of command, how certain outreach is designed and executed (high-level phone calls to foreign counterparts, congressional briefings, etc.)—that tend to occur in nearly automated channels, often with powerful cumulative effects. A Presidential Study Directive process should be established and charged with identifying ways to insert geoeconomic approaches at all stages of policy formulation, and to protect the time and attention of senior officials executing these geoeconomic policies.

Finally, the executive branch also needs to become far better at managing American defensive concerns (as with the example around crafting disciplines for state-owned enterprises mentioned earlier), and more generally at negotiating delicate issues that span foreign and domestic policy agencies and often have substantial domestic political and thus congressional implications. The decision to treat currency as a trade issue and the decision to look to forms of economic pressure on Iran beyond sanctions are examples of the crucial debates represented in this agenda that—given the trade-offs and the range of equities (including domestic interests) they often span—only the White House can broker.

Adopt new rules of engagement with Congress.

One reason U.S. officials reach so reflexively for military solutions to foreign policy challenges is because, counterintuitively, U.S. political institutions often render military solutions easier than serious geoeconomic alternatives. Military interventions such as that in Libya need not require congressional authorization, and once a country becomes an active theater for U.S. troops, funds become available from a variety of sources, typically adding to many times beyond what a country might otherwise expect absent a U.S. military presence of some kind. Thanks to the blanket Authorization of Military Force issued in 2001 and still in effect, the executive branch need not request congressional approval for ongoing military and counterterror operations in Pakistan and Yemen, for example. Compare this to the years of largely unsuccessful conversations between the Obama administration and Congress aimed at securing the necessary approvals to deliver the $1 billion debt swap to Egypt, announced by President Obama in May 2011 as the centerpiece of the U.S. response to the democratic uprisings. Funding sources for countries seen as theaters of combat for U.S. troops are also far more flexible than those for countries without an active combat presence but of high strategic value nonetheless. As the Ukraine crisis fomented in the spring of 2014, it was only after enormous effort and several precious weeks that Congress agreed to allow the State Department to draw from its Overseas Contingency Operations accounts (dedicated to Iraq, Pakistan, and Afghanistan) to finance the 2014 loan guarantee to Ukraine following the ouster of President Yanukovych.[54]

Even in the area of sanctions—the area that arguably enjoys the highest levels of cooperation between the executive branch and Congress—a lack of nuance in congressional sanctions has hindered foreign policy makers' room for maneuver. Many point to the 2013–2014 negotiations with Iran, noting that because administration officials lack authority to roll back some of the most severe, congressionally mandated sanctions, administration credibility on this score is less than what a maximal negotiating strategy would advise. Policy makers and legislators will need to devise new approaches geared toward maximizing credibility in both the application and removal of sanctions.[55]

In other areas beyond sanctions, the situation is far worse. Aid budgets continue to shrink. Real questions hang over the fate in Congress of both TPP and TTIP. The G20 issued an ultimatum to the United States to implement changes, agreed in 2010, to voting weights and operations of the International Monetary Fund.[56] Add in Congress's near refusal to renew the U.S. Export-Import Bank's license or reauthorize OPIC, and a dismaying picture emerges. Put bluntly, the U.S. Congress is often a serious impediment to implementing a coherent American geoeconomic strategy.

POLICY PRESCRIPTION 20

Increase university teaching around geoeconomics.

In order to produce the skills required over the long term to implement this ambitious geoeconomic agenda, academic preparation needs to go well beyond narrow disciplinary boundaries. Geoeconomics needs its own disciplinary language, one that joins the tools of economics with the logic of geopolitics. Only by endowing geoeconomics with its own analytic framework can policymakers approach these questions clearly. Universities need to create this interdisciplinary approach, and foundations need to fund it.[57]

THE POLICY prescriptions contained in this chapter, if implemented in a sustained way, would make the United States a powerful geoeconomic actor in the world. They would allow the United States to address seriously the growing geoeconomic coercion practiced by authoritarian governments in Asia and Europe against their neighbors. They would give the industrial democracies new positive tools to influence regional and global geopolitics. And they would strengthen the U.S. alliance systems and thus bolster the current regional and global balance of power. But these measures will, of course, not be implemented in a day or, in many cases, even a year. They will require a fundamental redefinition of how America conducts its foreign policy, including in the first instance presidential leadership and an increased and sustained realization by the Congress that geoeconomic instruments can frequently promote America's national interests, a subject we address in Chapter 10.

CHAPTER TEN

Geoeconomics, U.S. Grand Strategy, and American National Interests

Never let the other fellow set the agenda.

—JAMES BAKER, FORMER SECRETARY OF STATE

A S THE United States faces an uncertain, complex, and periodically dangerous world in the decade ahead, how should it forge its external relations? What should be its primary foreign policy objectives, and what strategies and instruments should it adopt in an era of limited resources to realize those objectives? How can the United States avoid, to paraphrase former secretary of state Warren Christopher, careening from crisis to crisis? As Arnold J. Toynbee observed, great nations die by suicide, not murder.

After Pearl Harbor, Roosevelt and Churchill adopted a grand strategy for conducting the war: defeat Germany first, and then Japan. The clarity of that grand strategy—its insistent relationship of ends to means, of resources and instruments to priorities and long-term outcomes—was apparent to all who sought defeat of the Axis, and the strategy was implemented with tactical adjustments every day until the end of the war. Crucially, the United States emerged from that conflict far stronger and more influential than when it entered it—an abiding characteristic of a successful grand strategy and perhaps the best evidence that millennial America lacks one.

The mandate staked out in 2011 by Secretary of State Hillary Clinton's Economic Statecraft agenda marks a modest beginning in this crucial endeavor.[1] As Clinton put it: "Our foreign and economic relations remain indivisible. Only now, our greater challenge is not deterring any single military foe, but advancing our global leadership at a time when power is more often measured and exercised in economic terms."[2] George Shultz and James Baker, both of whom served as both secretary of state and treasury secretary, would undoubtedly applaud the concept and its policy objectives.

Consistent with this vision, Clinton articulated four broad lines of effort: updating U.S. foreign policy priorities to take economics more into account; turning to economic solutions for strategic challenges; stepping up commercial diplomacy (or "jobs diplomacy") to boost U.S. exports, open new markets, and level the playing field for American companies; and building U.S. diplomatic capacity to execute this ambitious agenda.[3]

There was some progress during her tenure. Clinton was a strong advocate for launching a trade agreement with Europe, urging the point on precisely geoeconomic grounds, and making that case internally with the Obama White House for an agreement different in kind compared with previous trade accords—one that, among other things, would be more responsive to the strategic dimensions of the transatlantic relationship. In the wake of the Arab uprisings, Secretary Clinton noted that, to be successful, the Middle East political awakening also required an economic awakening, and she succeeded in pushing through an initial package in the early months of the uprisings that, announced by President Obama in May 2011, included over $4 billion in government financial support for the region (including $1 billion in debt relief for Egypt). And perhaps most important, it was primarily Clinton and her staff who engineered the pivot to Asia, which—not coincidentally—she launched the same week in October 2011 as her Economic Statecraft agenda. And she pushed through far more aggressive sanctions on Iran against a divided and skeptical group of agencies.

Of lesser importance, the State Department over the past several years has developed new expertise, partly through standing up new offices (including appointing a chief economist and establishing the Bureau for Energy and Natural Resources) and in part through new internal training. It created new communications tools for economic officers, allowing for better insight into problems and patterns—state-owned enterprises, for example, or Chinese influence in Latin America—that may well impact U.S. national interests similarly across far-flung posts. It introduced new commercial diplomacy requirements for senior officials. And after conducting a review of promotion rates and opportunities for midlevel and senior economic officers, it wrote new economic criteria into performance evaluations to place economics into the context of U.S. strategic objectives.

But though any progress is welcome, these efforts were clearly far from sufficient. Writing in 2013, Robert Zoellick noted that "the administration has talked about some of these topics. But it is oddly passive, as if it were hesitant to lead. State Department speeches are not enough."[4] Zoellick is right. It is unlikely that any State Department, no matter how forcefully engaged on reprioritizing geoeconomics within U.S. foreign policy, could succeed alone. Given the diverse competencies involved, such a mandate can come only from the White House. Only the president can translate the growing stock of observations and commitments by U.S. policy makers and others attesting to the need to reprioritize geoeconomics into effective geo-economic action. As efforts from the Obama administration on Egypt, Syria, Ukraine, the pivot to Asia, the TPP, and the TTIP all attest, U.S. policy has tended to fall back on old habits and fall plain short.[5]

During the four-decade-long Cold War, the U.S. strategic elite, Democrats and Republicans alike, and the American public generally accepted Washington's grand strategy. George Kennan introduced the concept of containment in a 1947 article in *Foreign Affairs*, written under the pseudonym "X," describing a U.S. approach that would block Soviet encroachment on Western territory and national interests and prevent Moscow from shaping a malignant international order, with the attendant central proposition that the internal contradictions of the Soviet empire would eventually produce its demise. It is difficult to imagine a clearer U.S. grand strategy—or one with greater success, as the USSR itself dissolved in 1991.

At the same time, it is worth stressing how much this American grand strategy became interpreted as resting fundamentally on the instruments of the U.S. military and NATO: nuclear weapons, deterrent military capability, and arms control. Economic issues entered discussions of U.S. grand strategy in the context that an America with a strong economy at home would be able to sustain a large and potent military and conduct robust security policies abroad.

It is noteworthy that Western grand strategy toward the Soviet Union had virtually no serious geoeconomic element in the years following the Gulf of Tonkin incident in 1964 and America's subsequent involvement in the Vietnam War. With the exception of intermittent sanctions against Moscow, such as the U.S. wheat embargo following the Soviet invasion of Afghanistan and strict prohibitions against technology transfer, Washington right up to the fall of the Berlin Wall continued to be largely preoccupied with the military balance between the two sides.

Thus the West's extraordinary victory in the U.S.-Soviet confrontation, abetted by Ronald Reagan's grand strategy of geopolitical offensive and concluded by George H. W. Bush's skillful diplomatic handling, was accomplished much more with political-military instruments than with geoeconomic ones, an omission that has had its consequences in the years following the collapse of the Soviet Union.

Since the 1990s, the United States has been searching without much success to find a new grand strategy to match the new era. Perhaps a robust

American grand strategy would have eventually emerged except for al-Qa'ida's attacks on New York and Washington on September 11, 2001, and the subsequent decade-long wars in Afghanistan and Iraq. Perhaps. What happened, in fact—as in World War II, the Cold War, the Korean War, the Vietnam War, and the Balkan and Desert Storm conflicts—was that U.S. administrations and the Congress became preoccupied with military instruments, both to destroy al-Qa'ida through the war on terror and to conduct the two large conventional conflicts. Washington's national security debates concentrated on the size and content of the defense budget, including missile defense; on war-fighting capabilities and strategies; and on what constituted successful security outcomes in Iraq and Afghanistan. This military mind-set also contributed to the U.S./NATO attack on Libya, triggered the debate regarding whether the United States should use force to change the balance of power on the ground in Syria and deal with ISIS, and, of course, addressed how the United States should roll back the Iranian nuclear weapons program.

Other than economic sanctions against Iran, it is striking how little of the public debate has addressed whether the United States, possessing the largest and most powerful economy in the world, could use economic instruments for geopolitical purposes. And when the administration and Congress have encountered these geoeconomic possibilities, whether in the form of economic assistance to Egypt and Jordan or the TPP and TTIP negotiations, they have been blunted by bureaucratic disputes inside the administration, by differences within a Congress largely unfamiliar with the potential of these geoeconomic tools, and by contentious U.S. domestic politics.

The post-9/11 United States faces a blizzard of international problems: the rise of Chinese power, the return of Russian systemic destabilizing policies in Eurasia and beyond, chaos in the Middle East, the continuing danger of terrorism involving weapons of mass destruction (WMD). With statesmen rare in any age, perhaps it is best to return to a compelling compass for U.S. external behavior—American national interests as a basis for U.S. grand strategy—and to examine briefly again how geoeconomic instruments, as informed by history and enumerated in this book, might promote these interests.[6]

Vital National Interests

Vital national interests are conditions that are strictly necessary to safeguard and enhance Americans' survival and well-being in a free and secure nation. *Vital U.S. national interests are:* (1) preventing a WMD, major terrorist, or cyber attack on the American homeland; (2) maintaining the global balance of power, including through America's alliance systems, and preventing the emergence of a hegemonic rival on the Eurasian landmass; (3) ensuring the survival of U.S. allies and their active cooperation with the United States in shaping an international liberal order, based on democratic values and the rule of law, in which the United States can thrive; (4) preventing the emergence of hostile major powers or failed states on America's borders; and (5) ensuring the viability and stability of major global systems (trade, financial markets, supplies of energy, and the environment).

Extremely Important National Interests

Extremely important national interests are conditions that, if compromised, would severely prejudice but not strictly imperil the ability of the U.S. government to safeguard and enhance the well-being of Americans in a free and secure nation.

Extremely important U.S. national interests are: (1) preventing, deterring, and reducing the threat of the use of nuclear, biological, and chemical weapons anywhere; (2) preventing the regional proliferation of WMD and delivery systems; (3) promoting the acceptance of international rules of law and mechanisms for resolving or managing disputes peacefully; (4) promoting the well-being of U.S. allies and friends and protecting them from external aggression; (5) promoting democracy, prosperity, and stability in the Western Hemisphere; (6) preventing, managing, and (if possible at reasonable cost) ending major conflicts in important geographic regions; (7) maintaining a lead in key military-related and other strategic technologies, particularly information systems; and (8) preventing genocide.

U.S. MILITARY primacy continues to be essential in promoting and defending these national interests. With respect to international diplomacy, the United States is, as Secretary of State Madeleine Albright stressed, "the indispensable nation." At the same time, geoeconomic tools as defined and discussed in this volume seem especially relevant to each and every one of these vital and extremely important American national interests.

America's problem today is that after many decades of being preoccupied with the security dimension of American foreign policy, Washington instinctively reaches for the military instrument when often it is largely or entirely irrelevant or inappropriate to the external challenge at hand.

As we have earlier sought to demonstrate in detail, China, in our judgment, seeks a grand strategy that will end U.S. primacy in Asia and alter the balance of power in that vast and crucial region. And although the People's Republic of China is undertaking an ambitious program of military modernization, its tools in pursuing that grand strategy for the foreseeable future are primarily geoeconomic and not military.

The strength of the economies of America's Asian allies and of India will be crucial factors in their ability to resist Chinese economic coercion and to stand strong in maintaining the current balance of power in Asia writ large.

A stable and collaborative Egypt is a linchpin of broader U.S. national interests in the Middle East. Again, however, American military power will have little to do with whether Egypt overcomes its current monumental economic problems.

Tough international economic sanctions against Iran ultimately brought it to the negotiating table and to an agreement—a classic use of a geoeconomic instrument.

The future of Jordan—based in large part on the viability of its economy—will be an important determinant of whether the Middle East can regain a degree of peace and stability in the period ahead.

Putin's Russia appears to be embarked on an effort to re-create Soviet-era spheres of dominating influence on its borders and beyond, witness its military intervention in Syria. Although NATO allies in Eastern Europe in these circumstances require reassurance through U.S. military deployments and power projection, the future of Ukraine, Georgia, Azerbaijan, and the nations of Central Asia will not be decided by American military capabilities. The only hope for Ukraine to withstand Moscow's disruptive policies is to stabilize its economy, and that in turn depends extensively on American and European use of geoeconomic tools—trade, loans, grants—and the assistance of international lending institutions.

If Mexico's economic challenges were to produce deep and prolonged instability across the border, the United States certainly would be significantly diverted from its broader international missions and responsibilities.

During World War II, during most of the Cold War period and its aftermath, and in America's immediate responses after the 9/11 attacks, the military and security dimensions of U.S. foreign policy were rightly preeminent. After all, it was U.S. military power that defeated Germany and Japan, held NATO together, animated the U.S.-Japan alliance, deterred the Soviet Union, and killed most of al-Qa'ida's leadership. But in the years ahead, U.S. military prowess is not going to ease China's economic coercion against the nations of Asia, not going to help rescue Egypt, not going to promote Ukraine's independence from Moscow, and not going to assist Mexico to thrive as a stable modern democracy.

Either the United States will begin to use its geoeconomic power with much greater resolve and skill, or its national interests will increasingly be in jeopardy. U.S. domestic economic strength in the decades ahead must have more relevance to American national interests and the identification of consequent international threats and opportunities than simply funding a huge defense budget, useful as that is to U.S. global purposes. To recall Mao, international power and the influence needed to flourish and to shape the balance of power in America's favor must derive not only from the barrel of a gun but also from the strength and geopolitical applications of the U.S. economy. Whether administrations and the Congress will understand, digest, and implement this compelling reality with focus, clarity, and a sense of geoeconomic purpose remains a preeminent issue of American grand strategy in our era.

Notes

Introduction

1. This bears emphasis. To be sure, the United States has for much of the past century pursued geoeconomic policy at the level of grand strategy by supporting free trade and investment and a rules-based international order. These twin objectives over the long term promote prosperity, democratic pluralism, and a more benign international system, all of which make the world geopolitically safer for America and bolster U.S. national interests. However, strong U.S. rhetorical adherence to these general concepts is quite different from Washington using economic instruments operationally to address current geopolitical challenges regarding the rise of Chinese power, the Ukrainian economy and Russia's neo-imperialist ambitions, Egypt's desperate economic condition, and so forth. As we argue at length in Chapter 7, we do not question the value of this rules-based order, but we see little evidence of it being robustly prosecuted by U.S. administrations in a concerted and systematic way as geoeconomic policy.

2. Leslie H. Gelb, "GDP Now Matters More than Force," *Foreign Affairs*, November/December 2010, 35.

3. Michael Mandelbaum, *The Road to Global Prosperity* (New York: Simon and Schuster, 2014), xvi–xvii.

4. David Baldwin, *Economic Statecraft* (Princeton, N.J.: Princeton University Press, 1985), 58–59.

5. Ibid.

6. Francis Fukuyama first presented the "end of history" thesis in 1989, arguing that there is a positive direction to current history, demonstrated by the collapse of authoritarian regimes of right and left and their replacement by liberal governments. In a later piece on the "future of history," he admits to having been a bit too

quick off the mark. See "The End of History," *National Interest,* Summer 1989, and "The Future of History," *Foreign Affairs,* January/February 2012.

7. Gelb, "GDP Now Matters More than Force."

8. Gelb, "GDP Now Matters More than Force." Former Secretary of State Hillary Clinton voiced similar calls as part of her "Economic Statecraft" agenda ("Economic Statecraft," speech delivered at the Economic Club of New York, October, 14, 2011, and "Delivering on the Promise of Economic Statecraft," speech delivered at Singapore Management University, November 17, 2012). These high-level comments are reverberated by a wide range of outside observers, most powerfully by Leslie Gelb ("GDP Now Matters More than Force"), Robert Zoellick ("Economics and Security in American Foreign Policy: Back to the Future?," speech delivered at Harvard University's Kennedy School of Government, October 2, 2012, and "The Currency of Power," *Foreign Policy,* October 2012), and Richard Haass (*Foreign Policy Begins at Home* [New York: Basic Books, 2013]).

9. Clinton, "Delivering on the Promise of Economic Statecraft."

10. David Baldwin's 1985 *Economic Statecraft* and Alan Dobson's 2002 *US Economic Statecraft for Survival* mark two happy exceptions to this general lack of focus on economic techniques of statecraft. Both Baldwin and Dobson themselves bemoan the same void, however, and in the intervening years since, the literature on international political economy has only grown more theoretical and less relevant to questions of how, why, and to what effect states use economic instruments to pursue geopolitical agendas.

11. See such works as Kim Holmes, *Rebound: Getting America Back to Great* (Lanham, Md.: Rowman and Littlefield, 2013) and Haass, *Foreign Policy Begins at Home.*

12. See Mandelbaum, *The Road to Global Prosperity,* and Francis J. Gavin, *Gold, Dollars, and Power: The Politics of International Monetary Relations, 1958–1971* (Chapel Hill: University of North Carolina Press, 2004).

13. Jonathan Kirshner, "Political Economy in Security Studies after the Cold War," Department of Government, Cornell University, April 1997.

14. See, for instance, Richard N. Cooper, "Economic Aspects of the Cold War, 1962–1975," February 2008, available at http://scholar.harvard.edu/files/cooper/files/chcw.rev-2.pdf.

15. Gelb, "GDP Now Matters More than Force."

16. To be sure, Cyprus made its own share of unwise investment decisions in the run-up to its 2013 banking crisis, many of them in the form of Greek bond purchases. And no doubt the allure of Cyprus's low tax rates explains much of its popularity as an offshore haven for Russian depositors. Yet at the same time, many of Russia's oligarchs and wealthy investors used Cyprus as a means of avoiding not just taxes but also "political risk at home and [as a way] to access Cyprus' relatively reliable court system to adjudicate disputes." A net $56 billion left Russia in 2012—the year that Vladimir Putin returned to the Russian presidency. Much of this belonged to Russian firms and oligarchs uneager to see their resources become "the Kremlin's tool of choice for settling domestic and foreign policy problems," *New York Times* journalist Andrew Kramer explained at the time of the Cypriot crisis. Notwithstanding the other factors in play, the rise in

Russian deposits in Cyprus maps robustly with Putin's return to power. Quotations cited in Andrew Kramer, "Protecting Their Own, Russians Offer an Alternative to the Cypriot Bank Tax," *New York Times,* March 19, 2013. For further analysis on the contributing role of Russia and its brand of geoeconomics to the Cypriot banking crisis, see also Ben Judah, "Putin's Role in Cyprus," *New York Times,* April 2, 2013, and Charles Clover and Courtney Weave, "Russian Money Streams through Cyprus," *Financial Times,* February 6, 2013.

17. Baldwin makes this point ably: "Even when economists turn their attention to economic sanctions or economic warfare," he argues, "the fixation with economic ends is likely to persist. . . . Inflicting economic harm on the target country may well be the instrumental, or intermediate, goal of the influence attempt, but it is almost never an end in itself." See Baldwin, *Economic Statecraft,* 62.

18. Graham Allison and Robert Blackwill, "America's National Interests," Commission on America's National Interests, Belfer Center for Science and International Affairs, Harvard University, 2000, http://belfercenter.ksg.harvard.edu/files/amernatinter.pdf.

19. David Baldwin, "Power Analysis and World Politics: New Trends versus Old Tendencies," *World Politics* 31, no. 2 (1979): 161–194.

20. Baldwin takes a similar approach in his *Economic Statecraft.*

1. What Is Geoeconomics?

Epigraph: Benjamin Constant, quoted in Albert O. Hirschman, *National Power and the Structure of Foreign Trade* (expanded ed. [Berkeley: University of California Press, 1980]) (Berkeley: University of California Press, 1945), 145–155.

1. Deborah Cowen and Neil Smith, "After Geopolitics? From the Geopolitical Social to Geoeconomics," *Antipode* 1 (2009): 22–48; Jean-François Gagné, "Geopolitics in a Post–Cold War Context: From Geo-Strategic to Geo-Economic Considerations?," *Étude Raoul-Dandurand* 15, University of Quebec, Montreal, 2007; Edward Luttwak, "From Geopolitics to Geoeconomics: Logic of Conflict, Grammar of Commerce," *National Interest* 20 (1990): 17–23. Other equally abstract definitions of geoeconomics are seen in David A. Baldwin, *Economic Statecraft* (Princeton, N.J.: Princeton University Press, 1985) and Renato Cruz DeCastro, "Whither Geoeconomics? Bureaucratic Inertia in U.S. Post–Cold War Foreign Policy toward East Asia," *Asian Affairs* 26, no. 4 (2000): 201–222.

2. The Brussels- and Madrid-based think tank Foundation for International Relations and Foreign Dialogue (FRIDE) defines it thus: "Geoeconomics denotes the use of statecraft for economic ends; a focus on relative economic gain and power; a concern with gaining control of resources; the enmeshing of state and business sectors; and the primacy of economic over other forms of security." Richard Youngs, "Geo-Economic Futures," in *Challenges for European Foreign Policy in 2012: What kind of geo-economic Europe?,* ed. Ana Martiningui and Richard Youngs (Madrid: FRIDE, 2011), 14.

3. Mark Thirlwell, "The Return of Geo-economics," *Interpreter,* Lowy Institute for International Policy, May 24, 2010. A similarly broad definition, offered by Brad Setser and Paul Swartz, defines geoeconomics simply as "anything that touches

on both the economy and geopolitics" ("Geoeconomics, in Pictures," *Follow the Money* [blog], Council on Foreign Relations, July 31, 2009). Still others bifurcate geoeconomics with economic competition, labeling the instruments of power to be centered around productive efficiency, market control, trade surplus, strong currency, foreign exchange reserves, and so on; see Samuel Huntington, "Why International Primacy Matters," *International Security* 17, no. 4 (1993): 68–83.

4. French political economist Pascal Lorot, for example, explains that "geoeconomics analyzes economic strategies—especially trade strategy—that are adopted by the states in certain political conditions for the protection of their economies or their exactly determined segments, so as to help their enterprises to acquire technologies or penetrate certain segments of world market for certain production or commercialization of some product." Pascal Lorot, "La geoeconomie, nouvelle grammaire des rivalites internationals," L'information géographique 65, no. 1 (2001), 43–52; Blagoje S. Babić, "Geo-Economics—Reality & Science," *Megatrend Review* 6, no. 1 (2009): 32, www.webster.ac.at/files/BlagojeBabic_2008.pdf.

5. See Ian Bremmer, *The End of the Free Market: Who Wins the War between States and Corporations?* (New York: Portfolio, 2010); David Cortright and George Lopez, eds., *Smart Sanctions: Targeting Economic Statecraft* (New York: Rowman and Littlefield, 2002); Daniel Drezner, "Trade Talk," *American Interest* 1, no. 2 (December 2005): 68–76, and his *The Sanctions Paradox: Economic Statecraft and International Relations* (Cambridge: Cambridge University Press, 1999); Richard Haass, *Economic Sanctions and American Diplomacy* (New York: Council on Foreign Relations Press, 1998); Edward Luttwak, *Turbo-Capitalism: Winners and Losers in the Global Economy* (New York: Harper Perennial, 2000); Robert A. Pape, "Why Economic Sanctions Do Not Work," *International Security* 22, no. 2 (Fall 1997): 90–136; James D. Sidaway, "Asia–Europe–United States: The Geoeconomics of Uncertainty," *Area* 37, no. 4 (2005): 373–377; Matthew Sparke, "From Geopolitics to Geoeconomics: Transnational State Effects in the Borderlands," *Geopolitics* 3, no. 2 (1998): 62–98; and Brendan Taylor, *Sanctions as Grand Strategy* (New York: Routledge, 2010).

6. "The argument was first made popular in the 1850s by Richard Cobden, who asserted that free trade 'unites' states, 'making each equally anxious for the prosperity and happiness of both.' This view was restated in *The Great Illusion* by Norman Angell just prior to World War I and again in 1933. Angell saw states having to choose between new ways of thinking, namely peaceful trade, and the 'old method' of power politics. Even if war was once profitable, modernization now makes it impossible to 'enrich' oneself through force; indeed, by destroying trading bonds, war is 'commercially suicidal.' " Dale C. Copeland, "Economic Interdependence and War: A Theory of Trade Expectations," *International Security* 20, no. 4 (Spring 1999): 5–41.

7. James Allen Smith, *Strategic Calling: The Center for Strategic and International Studies, 1962–1992* (Washington, D.C.: Center for Strategic and International Studies, 1993).

8. In recent years, calls have emanated from across the American foreign policy spectrum pointing to the strategic necessity of prioritizing U.S. domestic economic renewal, based on the assumed correlation between an orderly U.S. domestic house

and the ability to project American power abroad. In the aptly named book *Foreign Policy Begins at Home,* Richard Haass argues that the biggest threat to the security and prosperity of the United States comes from within. For Haass, this necessitates rebuilding "the foundation of [U.S.] strength to be in a better position to stave off potential strategic rivals or be better prepared for them should they emerge" (Richard Haass, *Foreign Policy Begins at Home* [New York: Basic Books, 2013], 104). Similar sentiments are echoed in comments by Zbigniew Brzezinski (*Strategic Vision: America and the Crisis of Global Power* [New York: Basic Books, 2012], 63–64), Kim Holmes (*Rebound: Getting America Back to Great* [Lanham, Md.: Rowman and Littlefield, 2013]), George Shultz ("Memo to Romney—Expand the Pie," *Wall Street Journal,* July 13, 2012), and Robert Zoellick ("American Exceptionalism: Time for New Thinking on Economics and Security," Alastair Buchan Memorial Lecture, International Institute for Strategic Studies, London, July 25, 2012).

9. The 2010 U.S. National Security Strategy, for instance, is built entirely upon the premise that national security begins at home and that American strength has domestic roots. The 2015 version further echoes these sentiments.

10. Works by the likes of David Baldwin (*Economic Statecraft*), Susan Strange ("International Economics and International Relations: A Case of Mutual Neglect," *International Affairs,* 1970), Alan Dobson (*US Economic Statecraft for Survival 1933–1991* [New York: Routledge, 2002]), Albert Hirschman (*National Power and the Structure of Foreign Trade,* expanded ed. [Berkeley: University of California Press, 1980]), Paul Samuelson (*Economics,* 10th ed. [New York: McGraw-Hill, 1976]), and Klaus Knorr (*The Power of Nations: The Political Economy of International Relations* [New York: Basic Books, 1975]); Klaus Knorr and Frank Trager (eds., *Economics Issues and National Security* [Lawrence, Kan.: National Security Education Program, 1977]) account for the various tools of economic statecraft available, but largely fail to touch upon the extent to which such tools are used. This gap in the literature review is discussed in greater detail in Chapters 2 and 3.

11. This conception of geoeconomics encompasses both purposive behavior (state actions or non-actions of some kind) as well as consequential factors (that is, the effects of other nations' economic actions on a country's geopolitical goals). This interpretation is shared by thinkers such as Gyula Csurgai and Klaus Solberg Søilen, even if the definitions themselves differ. See, for instance, Csurgai, "Geopolitics, Geoeconomics and Economic Intelligence," Strategic Datalink no. 69 (Toronto: Canadian Institute of Strategic Studies, 1998); Søilen, "The Shift from Geopolitics to Geoeconomics and the Failure of Our Modern Social Sciences," Electronic Research Archive, Blekinge Institute of Technology, 2010.

12. Similar sentiments are echoed in comments by Brzezinski (*Strategic Vision,* 63–64), Haass (*Foreign Policy Begins at Home,* 1), Shultz ("Memo to Romney—Expand the Pie"), and Zoellick ("American Exceptionalism").

13. The vast literature on "commercial peace" (essentially asking whether increased economic ties reduces incentives for conflict among trading partners) and the globalization debates of the 1990s and early 2000s (on whether the onset of a single global marketplace will reduce global conflict) mark what are perhaps international political economy's most totemic contributions to understanding how

economic phenomena can alter geopolitical incentives and outcomes. See William Domke, *War and the Changing Global System* (New Haven, Conn.: Yale University Press, 1988); Erik Gartzke, Quan Li, and Charles Boehmer, "Investing in the Peace: Economic Interdependence and International Conflict," *International Organization* 55, no. 2 (2001): 391–438; Edward D. Mansfield, *Power, Trade, and War* (Princeton, N.J.: Princeton University Press, 1994); Bruce Russett and John R. Oneal, *Triangulating Peace: Democracy, Interdependence, and International Organizations* (New York: Norton, 2001).

14. Dobson, *US Economic Statecraft for Survival.*

15. Benn Steil, "Taper Trouble," *Foreign Affairs,* October 7, 2014.

16. Ibid.

17. Ibid.

18. Robert D. Blackwill, "The Geopolitical Consequences of the World Economic Recession—A Caution," RAND Corporation Occasional Paper, 2009; Jeff Lightfoot, "The Strategic Implications of the Euro Crisis," *Fletcher Forum of World Affairs,* January 24, 2013; Simon Nixon, "EU's Next Challenges Are Geopolitical," *Wall Street Journal,* July 20, 2014; Jonathan Kirshner, "Geopolitics after the Global Financial Crisis," *International Relations and Security Network,* September 3, 2014; Alexander Mirtchev, "Europe's Strategic Future: Implications of the Eurozone Crisis," *International Relations and Security Network,* October 14, 2013.

19. Susan Strange, "International Economics and International Relations: A Case of Mutual Neglect," *International Affairs,* April 1970, 308.

20. See Gary C. Hufbauer, Jeffrey J. Schott, Kimberly A. Elliott, and Barbara Oegg, *Economic Sanctions Reconsidered* (Washington, D.C.: Peterson Institute for International Economics, 2007); Per Lundborg, *The Economics of Export Embargoes* (London: Croom Helm, 1987); Drezner, *The Sanctions Paradox,* and his "Sanctions Sometimes Smart: Targeted Sanctions in Theory and Practice," *International Studies Review* (March 2011); Jonathan Kirshner, "Currency and Coercion in the Twenty-First Century," in *International Monetary Power* (Ithaca, N.Y.: Cornell University Press, 2006); James Reilly, "China's Unilateral Sanctions," *Washington Quarterly* (Fall 2012); David Baldwin, "The Sanctions Debate and the Logic of Choice," *International Security* 24, no. 3 (1999–2000): 80–107; Richard Haass and Meghan O'Sullivan, eds., *Honey and Vinegar: Incentives, Sanctions, and Foreign Policy* (Washington, D.C.: Brookings Institution Press).

21. Edward Luttwak, *The Rise of China vs. the Logic of Strategy* (Cambridge, Mass.: Belknap Press of Harvard University Press, 2012), 40.

22. Ibid., 42.

23. As noted earlier, Baldwin's definition comes among the closest to ours, emphasizing means rather than ends and describing the "empirically undeniable fact that policy makers sometimes use economic means to pursue a wide variety of noneconomic ends" (*Economic Statecraft,* 40). Baldwin's definition differs from our use of the term *geoeconomics* in that his definition is only purposive, not a means of analysis. His use of economic statecraft thus appears more restrictive on the point of noneconomic tools in a way that may exclude cyber activity.

24. The so-called classic cases of geoeconomic statecraft often include the League of Nations sanctions against Italy, the U.S. embargo against Japan, the restrictions

on trade with Communist countries imposed by the United States and Western Europe, U.S. sanctions against Cuba, and UN sanctions against Rhodesia. See Baldwin, *Economic Statecraft,* chap. 8 and p. 373.

25. Dobson notes that economic statecraft is a neglected area of study, due in part to bias in the international relations academy but also to a sense among scholars that economic tools are not terribly effective in the realm of geopolitics. He also notes the unwillingness of liberal economists to accept economics as resting upon—and subject to—political (and geopolitical) choices and forces (see *US Economic Statecraft for Survival,* 4–5). More recently, Zoellick also argues that America's security strategists seem to have lost the ability to integrate economics and foreign policy ("Currency of Power," *Foreign Policy,* October 8, 2012).

26. Sanjaya Baru, "Introduction: Understanding Geo-economics and Strategy," presented at the seminar "A New Era of Geo-economics: Assessing the Interplay of Economic and Political Risk," IISS, October 24, 2012.

27. Baldwin, *Economic Statecraft,* 40.

28. Some have tried, although employing different definitions of geoeconomics, geopolitics, or both. According to Babić, geopolitics focuses on exercising control over territories and the populations contained therein, whereas geoeconomics focuses on exercising control over commodities, technologies, and markets. Second, geopolitical strategies rely on the deployment of military power or the threat to deploy it; geoeconomic strategies rely on economic means. And third, where geopolitics is typically conceived of as zero-sum, geoeconomics need not be. Klaus Solberg Søilen, author of a book on geoeconomics, provides another distinction: "The activities [of geoeconomics] are not undertaken chiefly by individuals representing the nation state, but by employees of private-sector organizations." Klaus Solberg Søilen, *Geoeconomics* (BookBoon: 2012), 8.

29. Graham Evans and Jeffrey Newnham, *The Penguin Dictionary of International Relations* (London: Penguin Books, 1998), 197. For a review of geopolitics that is second to none, see Gearóid Ó Tuathail, Simon Dalby, and Paul Routledge, *The Geopolitics Reader* (London: Routledge, 1998).

30. Geopolitics, as mid-twentieth-century U.S. diplomat and academic Robert Strausz-Hupé once noted, is "the struggle for space and power." Robert Strausz-Hupé, *Geopolitics: The Struggle for Space and Power* (New York: G. P. Putnam's Sons, 1942). See also Robert D. Kaplan, "Crimea: The Revenge of Geography," *Forbes,* March 14, 2014.

31. Note that "economic performance" as used here refers only to the relationship between a nation's overall economic health and military strength; it does not include the concerted use of economic tools or influence to attain specific geopolitical objectives.

32. Hillary Clinton does so in her "Economic Statecraft" speech, noting the role strong economic capabilities play in underwriting elements of smart power, namely robust diplomacy and development and the strongest military in the world. Speech delivered at the Economic Club of New York, October 14, 2011.

33. Michael Mandelbaum, *The Road to Global Prosperity* (New York: Simon and Schuster, 2014), xvi.

34. Ibid.

35. As part of her Economic Statecraft agenda, Clinton also spoke openly about the institutional changes needed to bring these policy shifts about. See, e.g., Hillary Rodham Clinton, "Economic Statecraft," remarks to the New York Economic Club.

36. See, e.g., Zoellick, "The Currency of Power"; David Rothkopf, "Hillary Clinton Ingests the Commerce Department," *Foreign Policy*, October 14, 2011; R. Nicholas Burns and Jonathon Price, eds., *The Global Economic Crisis and Potential Implications for Foreign Policy and U.S. National Security* (Washington, D.C.: Aspen Institute, 2009). One of the finest articulations of this call, however, was also one of the earliest. C. Fred Bergsten, writing in April 1971 as a young NSC staffer to his boss, national security advisor Henry Kissinger, in preparation for a meeting between Kissinger and Pete Peterson, said, "There is, however, a deeper and more philosophical point which will continuously pervade your relationship with Peterson: the relationship between foreign economic policy and overall foreign policy. It is roughly accurate to say that foreign economic policy has been the hand-maiden of overall U.S. foreign policy throughout the post-war period; all of our great 'economic' initiatives (IMF-IBRD, Marshall Plan, Kennedy Round, SDRs, etc) have been undertaken for essentially foreign policy reasons, and foreign policy considerations have dictated the U.S. position on virtually all issues of foreign economic policy. . . . There is now great and increasing pressure to change this relationship. In fact, it probably must be changed to some extent—to increase the 'economic' content of foreign economic policy—for the same reasons that we are now seeking to share our global role in political and security matters." "Memorandum from C. Fred Bergsten of the National Security Council Staff to the President's Special Assistant for National Security Affairs (Kissinger)," *Foreign Relations of the United States, 1969–1976 Volume III, Foreign Economic Policy; International Monetary Policy, 1969–1972*, Document 64, Department of State, Office of the Historian, http://history.state.gov/historicaldocuments/frus1969-76v03/d64.

37. Rothkopf, "Hillary Clinton Ingests the Commerce Department."

38. Nicholas Burns, personal communication.

39. Zoellick, "The Currency of Power."

40. Historians like Alan Dobson and Frank Gavin have offered portrayals similar to Zoellick's. By Gavin's telling, throughout much of its history, "the United States has ruthlessly exploited economic tools to reward friends and punish adversaries whenever it saw fit, and has rarely hesitated to subordinate financial gain to achieve perceived geo-political goals." F. J. Gavin, "Both Sticks and Carrots," *Diplomatic History* 28 (2004): 607–610.

41. Luttwak, "From Geopolitics to Geo-Economics"; Francis J. Gavin, *Gold, Dollars, and Power: The Politics of International Monetary Relations, 1958–1971* (Chapel Hill: University of North Carolina Press, 2004); Mandelbaum, *The Road to Global Prosperity*, xvi–xvii.

42. See, for instance, Colin S. Gray and Geoffrey Sloan, eds., *Geopolitics, Geography, and Strategy* (New York: Routledge, 1999); Jakub J. Grygiel, *Great Powers and Geopolitical Change* (Baltimore: Johns Hopkins University Press, 2006); Walter Russell Mead, "The Return of Geopolitics," *Foreign Affairs*, May/June 2014; Robert Kaplan, *The Revenge of Geography: What the Map Tells Us about Coming Conflicts and the Battle against Fate* (New York: Random House, 2012).

43. Dobson, *US Economic Statecraft for Survival*.

44. The practical stakes matter little. Because the United States and most countries have long since decoupled sanctions efforts from physical embargoes, physical embargoes are no longer of central importance in present-day sanctions debates.

45. This section owes great intellectual debt to Baldwin; he discusses at length how the ambiguity with which several distinct concepts—foreign economic policy, mercantilism, and liberal economic thought, among others—are often linked to geoeconomics (what he calls "economic statecraft") can pose hindrances to thinking about geoeconomics. See Baldwin, *Economic Statecraft*, 48–77.

46. Stephen D. Cohen, *The Making of United States International Economic Policy: Principles, Problems, and Proposals for Reform* (New York: Praeger, 1977), xvii–xxiii, cited in ibid., 34.

47. Baldwin, *Economic Statecraft*, 77.

48. Or, as Baldwin puts it, "between the study of such mean things as 'national rivalries and national power' and the 'study of national wealth'" (ibid.).

49. It is not a large leap from this reading of Adam Smith and his cohorts to the view that "the free trade doctrine . . . (as well as other intellectual descendants of liberal economic thought) denies the validity of the use of economic instruments for political ends." John Pinder, "Economic Diplomacy," in *World Politics: An Introduction,* ed. James N. Rosenau, Kenneth W. Thompson and Gavin Boyd (New York: Free Press, 1976).

50. Adam Smith, *An Inquiry into the Nature and Causes of the Wealth of Nations,* 1776, cited in Baldwin, *Economic Statecraft,* 80.

51. Smith quoted in Baldwin, *Economic Statecraft,* 81.

52. Ibid., 84, 81.

53. Robert Gilpin quoted in Baldwin, *Economic Statecraft,* 84.

54. Both David Baldwin and David Singh Grewal forcefully make this point. See Baldwin, *Economic Statecraft,* 78–85; and Grewal, *Networked Power,* 235–238, 360–361.

55. John Maynard Keynes, "National Self Sufficiency," *Yale Review* 22, no. 4 (June 1933).

56. Ibid.

57. Baldwin, *Economic Statecraft,* 79.

58. Ibid., 85.

59. See Frank M. Russell, *Theories of International Relations* (New York: Appleton-Century, 1936), 295; Edmund Silberner, *La guerre dans la pensée économique du XVIe au XVIIIe siècle* (Paris: Librairie du Recueil Sirey, 1939), 282; Hirschman, *National Power and the Structure of Foreign Trade,* 6.

60. Edward Mead Earle, "Adam Smith, Alexander Hamilton, Friedrich List: The Economic Foundations of Military Power," in *Makers of Modern Strategy: Military Thought from Machiavelli to Hitler,* ed. Fred I. Greenstein and Nelson W. Polsby (Reading, Mass.: Addison-Wesley, 1975), 123–124.

61. Frank M. Russell, *Theories of International Relations* (New York: Appleton-Century, 1936), 296, cited in Baldwin, *Economic Statecraft,* 86.

62. F. H. Hinsley, *Power and the Pursuit of Peace* (London: Cambridge University Press, 1963), 97, cited in Baldwin, *Economic Statecraft,* 86.

63. Ibid.

64. Baldwin, *Economic Statecraft,* 77.

65. Russell, *Theories of International Relations,* 179–203, 282–313; Hirschman, *National Power and the Structure of Foreign Trade,* 6–10; Silberner, *La guerre dans la pensée économique,* 125–269.

2. Geoeconomics and the International System

1. Leslie H. Gelb, "Foreign Affairs; The Asia Test for Mr. Bush," *New York Times,* October 9, 1991.

2. Reginald Dale, "Thinking Ahead: Diplomats: Don't Forget the Economy," *New York Times,* November 26, 1996. Walter Russell Mead also argues that the "end of history" in the post–Cold War world allowed in a shift of focus from geopolitics to development economics and nonproliferation. This conflation of the end of geopolitics has offered an "especially enticing prospect to the United States: the idea that the country could start putting less into the international system and taking out more. It could shrink its defense spending, cut the State Department's appropriations, lower its profile in foreign hotspots—and the world would just go on becoming more prosperous and more free" ("The Return of Geopolitics: The Revenge of the Revisionist Powers," *Foreign Affairs,* May/June 2014).

3. Thomas A. Stewart with Ricardo Sookdeo, "The New Face of American Power," CNNMoney, July 26, 1993.

4. Asma Alsharif, "Saudi, Qatar Paying Salaries to Syria Rebels: Diplomat," Reuters, June 23, 2012, http://www.reuters.com/article/us-syria-crisis-saudi-idUS BRE85M04J20120623. Lila Shetova, "Putin's Attempt to Recreate the Soviet Empire Is Futile," *Financial Times,* January 7, 2014.

5. Ibid.

6. Doug Gavel, "Linda Bilmes on U.S. Engagement in Iraq and Afghanistan: 'The Most Expensive Wars in U.S. History,'" John F. Kennedy School of Government, Harvard University, March 28, 2013; Mark Thompson, "The True Cost of the Afghanistan War May Surprise You," *Time,* January 1, 2015.

7. Recent reports suggest al-Qa'ida is making a comeback in Afghanistan. Marine general Joseph Dunford pointed out, "Where at one time al Qaeda could be isolated—as we intended to do in 2001—extremist networks have now expanded in the country" (Kristina Wong, "General: Al Qaeda Has Expanded throughout Afghanistan," *The Hill,* March 12, 2014). Other recent reports bolster this viewpoint, including Bruce Riedel, "Al Qaeda's Next Comeback Could be Afghanistan and Pakistan," *Daily Beast,* January 13, 2014; and Robert Blackwill, "Plan B in Afghanistan: Why a De Facto Partition Is the Least Bad Option," *Foreign Affairs,* January/February 2011.

8. A 2013 analysis observed that "Iraq is now seized with some of its bloodiest, sectarian violence since the darkest days of the American-led occupation. Afghanistan is threatened with internecine bloodletting the moment Western forces withdraw at the end of this year.... [T]he avowed target of the Afghan campaign—jihadism—has simply dissipated to re-form elsewhere, in Somalia, Yemen, the desert hide-outs of North Africa and the newest killing fields of Syria." Alan Cowell,

"As They Leave Afghanistan, Britons Ask, 'Why?' " *New York Times,* October 17, 2013. See also Joseph Goldstein, "Afghan Security Forces Struggle Just to Maintain Stalemate," *New York Times,* July 22, 2015.

9. Robert Kagan, "New Europe, Old Russia," *Washington Post,* February 6, 2008.

10. Peter Pomerantsev, "How Putin Is Reinventing Warfare," *Foreign Policy,* May 5, 2014.

11. As Australian foreign policy strategist Hugh White summarized this view: "American officials have also affirmed support for Japan as an ally under the United States-Japan defense treaty. But it's clear that Beijing doesn't buy that. Instead, China has concluded America would stand back in an armed conflict, which is why it increasingly courts confrontation with Japan so brazenly." Hugh White, "Sharing Power with China," *New York Times,* March 19, 2014.

12. Kissinger quoted in Alan P. Dobson, *US Economic Statecraft for Survival, 1933–1991* (New York: Routledge, 2002), 4.

13. Dobson, *US Economic Statecraft for Survival,* 4.

14. Ibid.

15. State capitalism, according to one political scientist, has four primary actors: national oil corporations, state-owned enterprises, privately owned national champions, and sovereign wealth funds. With the state acting as the leading economic actor and using markets primarily for political gain, new global competition between competing economic models is the new norm. Ian Bremmer, "State Capitalism Comes of Age: The End of the Free Market?," *Foreign Affairs,* May/June 2009.

16. Ian Bremmer, "State Capitalism and the Crisis," *McKinsey Global Insight,* July 2009; Ian Bremmer, "The Long Shadow of the Visible Hand: Government-Owned Firms Control Most of the World's Oil Reserves," *Wall Street Journal,* May 22, 2010.

17. Joshua Kurlantzick, "The Rise of Innovative State Capitalism," *Bloomberg Businessweek,* June 28, 2012.

18. United Nations Conference on Trade and Development, *World Investment Report 2013,* July 2013, http://unctad.org/en/PublicationChapters/wir2013ch1_en .pdf; Adrian Woolridge, "The Rise of State Capitalism: An Economist Special Report," *Economist,* January 21, 2012.

19. Woolridge, "The Rise of State Capitalism."

20. Estimates for total sovereign wealth fund (SWF) assets vary, at least partly based on whether data sources define SWFs to include various reserve asset management entities. According to estimates by Peterson Institute senior fellow Ted Truman, total SWF assets as of mid-2013 totaled "$4.2 trillion, including $3.6 trillion in foreign assets—increases of almost 40 percent from mid-2010." A 2014 report from KMPG estimates that sovereign wealth funds control $5.9 trillion in assets. See "Sovereign Wealth Funds, 2014," KPMG, http://www.kpmg.com/ES/es /ActualidadyNovedades/ArticulosyPublicaciones/Documents/sovereign-weath -funds-v2.pdf. On total reserves, see International Monetary Fund, "Currency Composition of Official Foreign Exchange Reserves (COFER)," data as of Q2 2015, http://data.imf.org/?sk=E6A5F467-C14B-4AA8-9F6D-5A09EC4E62A4;

Allie Bagnall and Edwin Truman, "Progress on Sovereign Wealth Fund Transparency and Accountability: An Updated SWF Scoreboard," Peterson Institute for International Economics Policy Brief PB13-19, August 2013.

21. International Monetary Fund, "Currency Composition of Official Foreign Exchange Reserves (COFER)," data as of Q1 2015.

22. China's trade surplus, for instance, has enabled Beijing to invest growing foreign exchange reserves in low-risk sovereign debt, such as U.S. Treasuries. Continued volatility in commodity prices since 2000 (measured by the standard deviation from the mean commodity price) has been roughly three times what is was in the 1990s. This trend of volatile resource prices will only be further exacerbated in years ahead, leaving individual countries more exposed to fluctuations in production. See James Manyika et al., "Global Flows in a Digital Age: How Trade, Finance, People, and Data Connect the World Economy," McKinsey Global Institute, April 2014. Richard Dobbs et al., "Resource Revolution: Tracking Global Commodity Markets," McKinsey Global Institute, September 2013.

23. Bremmer, "State Capitalism Comes of Age."

24. Hillary Rodham Clinton, "Economic Statecraft," speech at the New York Economic Club, October 14, 2011.

25. Euro-watchers such as Martin Feldstein have already labeled the euro experiment a failure, not because of "bureaucratic mismanagement, but rather the inevitable consequence of imposing a single currency on a very heterogeneous group of countries." Martin Feldstein, "The Failure of the Euro," *Foreign Affairs,* January/February 2012.

26. There is a growing discussion on the North American energy revolution. Recent noteworthy pieces include Robert Blackwill and Meghan O'Sullivan, "America's Energy Edge: The Geopolitical Consequences of the Shale Revolution," *Foreign Affairs,* March/April 2014; "The Petrostate of America," *Economist,* February 15, 2014; Christof Rühl, "Spreading an Energy Revolution," *New York Times,* February 5, 2013; Javier Solana, "The Shale Revolution's Global Footprint," Project Syndicate, November 20, 2013; Leonardo Maugeri, "The Shale Oil Boom: A U.S. Phenomenon," Belfer Center for Science and International Affairs, John F. Kennedy School of Government, June 2013; Alan Riley, "The Shale Revolution's Shifting Geopolitics," *New York Times,* December 25, 2012; Carolyn Barnett, "The New Energy Revolution and the Gulf," Center for Strategic and International Studies, Washington, D.C., November 2014; Amy Myers Jaffe and Ed Morse, "The End of OPEC," *Foreign Policy,* October 16, 2013; Edward L. Morse, "Welcome to the Revolution: Why Shale Is the Next Shale." *Foreign Affairs,* May/June 2014; Andrew Higgins, "Oil's Swift Fall Raises Fortunes of U.S. Abroad," *New York Times,* December 24, 2014.

27. The U.S. Energy Information Administration estimated "the amount of technically recoverable shale gas in the United States was 482 trillion cubic feet—an increase of 280 percent from EIA's 2008." U.S. Government Accountability Office, "Oil and Gas: Information on Shale, Resources, Development, and Environmental Public Health Risks," GAO-12-732, September 2012.

28. Saudi Arabian officials also delayed sending any new aid to Egypt until the results of the May 2014 presidential elections were announced. Al-Masry Al-Youm,

"Saudi Arabia to Provide Aid to Egypt if Sisi Becomes President," *Egypt Independent,* April 29, 2014.

29. Homi Kharas, Brian Pinto, and Sergei Ulatov, "An Analysis of Russia's 1998 Meltdown: Fundamentals and Market Signals," Brookings Papers on Economic Activity no. 1, 2001, Brookings Institution, Washington, D.C.

30. Reserves peaking at $600 billion was a short-lived success, as by October 2008 the start of the global financial crisis sent figures back down to $484 billion. Andrew Kramer, "New Anxiety Grips Russia's Economy," *New York Times,* October 30, 2008; "Russia's International Reserves Gain Five Billion Dollars in Seven Days," *Pravda.ru,* May 12, 2008.

31. Russia's use of financing power throughout the Ukraine crisis has left the United States strained to respond. "On the question of Russian money, yes, of course we are concerned about what is clearly a Kremlin strategy of trying to pick off, shall we say, the brethren who may be less committed or more vulnerable in the run-up to the June decision," said the British foreign secretary, Philip Hammond. "It will not have escaped the Kremlin's notice that this is a unanimity process and they only need one." Andrew Higgins, "Waving Cash, Putin Sows E.U. Divisions in an Effort to Break Sanctions," *New York Times,* April 6, 2015.

32. Peter Baker, "As Russia Draws Closer to China, U.S. Faces a New Challenge," *New York Times,* November 8, 2014.

33. In Angola, pro-democracy forces were gunned down, and days later the government signed a $1.52 billion contract with China's Sinopec Group for the purchase of one of Marathon Oil's offshore oil and gas fields; see Fayen Wong, "China's Sinopec Buys Marathon's Angola Oil Fields for $1.52 Billion," Reuters, June 23, 2013, and Dulce Fernandes, "Police and Military Crackdown after Women's Protest in Lunda-Norte," *Maka Angola,* June 18, 2013, http://allafrica.com/stories /201306181377.html. In Venezuela, Chavez openly remarked that Chinese assistance was enormously helpful in enabling him to pursue foreign policy ends, policy more often openly hostile to U.S. interests than not; see Evan Ellis, "China's Cautious Economic and Strategic Gamble in Venezuela," *China Brief* 11, no. 18 (September 30, 2011). Similarly, in Zimbabwe, Mugabe's dictatorship allows Beijing to make investments beneficial to China, again to the detriment of U.S. interests; see Jera, "Chinese Republic of Zimbabwe," *The Zimbabwean,* March 19, 2014, http://www.thezimbabwean.co/2014/03/chinese-republic-of-zimbabwe; Reagan Thompson, "Assessing the Chinese Influence in Ghana, Angola, and Zimbabwe: The Impact of Politics, Partners, and Petro," Center for International Security and Cooperation, Stanford University, May 21, 2012.

34. Nathan Gill, "China Loans Ecuador $1 Billion as Correa Plans First Bond Sale since 2005," *Bloomberg Business,* January 24, 2012; Naomi Mapstone, "China-Ecuador: The Love-in Continues," *Financial Times,* February 17, 2012; Felix Salmon, "How Ecuador Sold Itself to China," Reuters, July 5, 2011.

35. "China and Rio Tinto Complete Guinea Mining Deal," BBC News, July 29, 2010; Tom Burgis, Helen Thomas, and Misha Glenny, "Guinea Reignites $2.5bn Mining Tussle," *Financial Times,* November 2, 2012.

36. On commentary characterizing Qatari Airways as a diplomatic asset for Qatar, see, e.g., Elizabeth Dickinson, "Qatar Punches above Its Weight," *The*

National, September 26, 2012 ("Qatar Airways has become one of the country's most effective—if indirect—diplomatic tools"); Golnaz Esfandiari, "Qatar Conquers Iran's Airspace," Radio Free Europe/Radio Liberty, November 5, 2011; Jim Krane, "Flying High," *Foreign Affairs,* September 18, 2014.

37. Esfandiari, "Qatar Conquers Iran's Airspace."

38. Ibid.

39. Jake Rudnitsky and Stephen Bierman, "Rosneft's $270 Billion Oil Deal Set to Make China Biggest Market," *Bloomberg Business,* June 21, 2013; "China Signs $1.4bn Brazil Plane Deal to Kick Off Summit," BBC News, April 12, 2011.

40. Edward Luttwak, *The Rise of China vs. the Logic of Strategy* (Cambridge, Mass.: Belknap Press of Harvard University Press, 2012). China has been using aircraft purchases for geopolitical purposes since June 1990, when the Chinese government ordered 36 jets, totaling nearly $4 billion, from Boeing after President George H. W. Bush renewed China's most-favored-nation trade status. China has since continued to purchase Boeing aircraft alongside high-level government meetings. In 2011, 200 Boeing aircraft were purchased during President Hu Jintao's visit to the United States; in 2012, another 51 aircraft were purchased prior to the U.S.-China Strategic and Economic Dialogue in Beijing and during U.S. Treasury secretary Jack Lew's visit. Most recently, after the Xi-Obama summit at Sunnylands in June 2013, Boeing confirmed delivery of the first of ten 787s to Hainan Airlines.

41. Alison Smale, "Leaked Recordings Lay Bare EU and U.S. Divisions in Goals for Ukraine," *New York Times,* February 7, 2014; Suzanne Lynch, "Unified EU Response on Ukraine Will Not Be Simple," *Irish Times,* March 20, 2014; Naftali Bendavid, "Ukraine Wants EU to Be More Forceful," *Wall Street Journal,* March 17, 2014.

42. Andrew England and Daniel Schafer, "Standard Bank to Sell Control of London Arm for $765m," *Financial Times,* January 29, 2014.

43. Enda Curran, "Standard Bank Starts Legal Action over Suspected Qingdao Port Fraud," *Wall Street Journal,* July 10, 2014; Thekiso Anthony Lefifi, "China Syndrome May Hit Standard Bank," *BusinessDay Live,* July 13, 2014; Standard Bank Plc Consolidated Annual Report 2011, 7.

44. "Limited Partnership: The Biggest Banks in China and in Africa Team Up Again," *Economist,* February 1, 2014. (Asked why the 2008 Standard Chartered–ICBC deal "has . . . been so disappointing," the article explains that "in part it is because many big Chinese investments in Africa are negotiated government-to-government or funnelled through state development banks, says Martyn Davies of Frontier Advisory, a research firm based in Johannesburg.")

45. "Trying to Pull Together: The Chinese in Africa," *Economist,* April 20, 2011.

46. Media reports offer a similar, if still less than fully clear account of the exact circumstances that led to the forfeiture of $230 million in fraudulent tax claims by Hermitage Capital. See, e.g., Luke Harding, "Bill Browder: The Kremlin Threatened to Kill Me," *Guardian,* January 25, 2015 ("In 2005 [Browder] was deported from the country. A corrupt group of officials expropriated his fund, Hermitage Capital, and used it to make a fraudulent tax claim. They stole $230m."); cf. Andrew Kramer, "Major Investor in Russia Sees Worldwide Fraud Scheme," *New York Times,* July 30, 2009 ("Mr. Browder was expelled from Russia in a politically

tinged visa refusal in 2005, and relocated his business, Hermitage Capital Management, to London. Later, he said subsidiary companies he had formed in Russia to invest in Gazprom, the Russian gas monopoly, were used by others to acquire a fraudulent tax refund of $230 million.").

47. Andrew Kramer, "Moscow Presses BP to Sell a Big Gas Field to Gazprom," *New York Times,* June 23, 2007.

48. Anders Aslund, "Rosneft Is Foundation of Putin's State Capitalism," *Moscow Times,* October 23, 2012. To take another example, in February 2008, the China Development Bank (CDB) backed a $14 billion secret raid by Chinalco, a state-owned mining firm, to acquire stock in Australian mining giant Rio Tinto. As Sanderson and Forsythe pointed out, "The dawn purchase of Rio Tinto shares, the largest overseas purchase by a Chinese company in history at the time, was followed by more CDB-backed purchases in a rights issue in 2009" (Henry Sanderson and Michael Forsythe, *China's Superbank: Debt, Oil, and Influence—How China Development Bank Is Rewriting the Rules of Finance* [Singapore: John Wiley and Sons, 2013], 77–78). Reports suggest that the State Council apparently ordered these deals, leaving CDB's board no say. While Chinalco's 2008 and 2009 bids ultimately fell short of a takeover, Chinalco pursued a subsequent 2010 agreement that would have doubled Chinalco's stake in Rio. When those talks collapsed, China imprisoned four members of Rio Tinto's negotiating team—hinting at China's willingness to mix forms of market and state power in pursuit of a deal. Australian officials responded by insisting that the "Chinese investment must be commercial and business oriented investment and it must not be to advance strategic political ends" (Luke Hurst, "Comparative Analysis of the Determinants of China's State-owned Outward Direct Investment in OECD and Non-OECD Countries," *China & World Economy* 19, no. 4 [2011]: 75). But what the Rio Tinto episode suggests is it may not be that simple. Even when motives are primarily commercial, today's states can use bargaining tactics that are largely unique to sovereigns.

49. Elizabeth Economy and Michael Levi tackle China's quest for fuel, ores, water, and arable land, examining how Beijing deploys any and all necessary means to secure resources. They rightly note that tying up all aspects of national power in China's global resource quest will continue to have social and political ramifications within China. See their *By All Means Necessary: How China's Resource Quest Is Changing the World* (New York: Oxford University Press, 2014).

50. Rosemary Kelanic, "Oil Security and Conventional War: Lessons from a China-Taiwan Air War Scenario," Council on Foreign Relations Energy Report, October 2013.

51. Ian Bremmer, *The End of the Free Market: Who Wins the War between States and Corporations?* (New York: Portfolio, 2010), 104.

52. Charlie Zhu and Jim Bai, "Argentine Move to Seize YPF Scuppers Sinopec Deal," Reuters, April 18, 2012.

53. Even after the emergence of OPEC, energy markets were driven by private forces of supply and demand, intermediated by mostly private (not state-owned) oil companies.

54. "China to Increase Loans to Africa by $10 Billion," *Wall Street Journal,* May 5, 2014.

55. By far, the leading destinations for Chinese state-led FDI are resource-rich parts of Africa and Latin America. Behind them are major achievements, especially in Africa. Chinese-funded infrastructure projects are visible all across the continent: roads and bridges in Congo and Sierra Leone, railways in Angola and Kenya, power stations in Zambia, mass transit systems in Nigeria, a telecommunications network in Ethiopia, high-voltage power transmission lines to connect countries in southern Africa, and a $600 million dam in Ghana. By the end of 2010, China had invested some $40 billion in more than 2,000 enterprises in fifty African states. Chinese president Xi Jinping promised another $20 billion in financing to Africa in the spring of 2013. The bulk of this will be siphoned to infrastructure projects, the foundation for Africa's industrialization and economic development (Yun Sun, "China's Increasing Interest in Africa: Benign but Hardly Altruistic," Brookings Institution, April 5, 2013). China has, for instance, stepped in to help a housing shortage in Angola's capital city, Luanda. The Industrial and Commercial Bank of China, backed by oil revenues, built a million new homes twenty kilometers outside the city, fulfilling a promise Angolan president Jose dos Santos made to his people ("Kilamba City Flats Sold Out," *Agência Angola Press*, September 4, 2013); and in Latin America, China has invested heavily in hydroelectric facilities and raw materials (Fernando Menédez, "The Trend of Chinese Investments in Latin America and the Caribbean," *China U.S. Focus*, December 19, 2013).

56. China has also supplied Harare with twelve jet fighters and one hundred military vehicles, worth an estimated $240 million; see David H. Shinn, "Military and Security Strategy," in *China into Africa: Trade, Aid, and Influence*, ed. Robert Rotberg (Baltimore, Md.: Brookings Institution Press, 2008), 174. As for Venezuela, China established a $6 billion joint fund with Caracas in 2007, boosting the total reserves to $12 billion in 2009 as part of the "strategic alliance" with the Chavez government; see "Venezuela, China Boost Joint Investment Fund to $12 Billion," *Latin American Herald Tribune*, 2009.

57. Beth Walker, "China's Uncomfortable Diplomacy Keeps the Oil Flowing," *China Dialogue*, November 26, 2012. Also see Dambisa Moyo, *Winner Take All: China's Race for Resources and What It Means for the World* (New York: Basic Books, 2012); Jacques deLisle, "China's Quest for Resources and Influence," *American Diplomacy*, February 2006.

58. Sudan is China's largest oil project and home to upward of 10,000 Chinese workers; in return, China is Sudan's largest arms supplier. David Blair, "Oil-Hungry China Takes Sudan under Its Wing," *Telegraph*, April 23, 2005; Jared Ferrie, "Sudan's Use of Chinese Arms Shows Beijing's Balancing Act," *Bloomberg Business*, April 30, 2012; Peter S. Goodman, "China Invests Heavily in Sudan's Oil Industry," *Washington Post*, December 23, 2004; Yitzhak Shichor, "Sudan: China's Outpost in Africa," *China Brief* 5, no. 21 (2005).

59. Peter Brookes and Ji Hye Shin, "China's Influence in Africa: Implications for the United States," Heritage Foundation, Backgrounder #1916, February 22, 2006; United Nations Department of Peacekeeping Operations, "Troop and Police Contributors," March 2014, www.un.org/en/peacekeeping/resources/statistics /contributors.shtml; United Nations Department of Peacekeeping Operations, "UN Mission's Contributions by Country," March 31, 2014, www.un.org/en/peacekeeping /contributors/2014/mar14_5.pdf.

60. As CDB advisor Liu Kegu put it in April 2012, well before the steep drop in oil prices that occurred in late 2014: "The more important metric is the debt service capability, not necessarily the absolute amount of debt-to-GDP . . . [O]il is very simple to drill. You drill a hole, put a pipe in the ground and it comes out! And then you ship it. So Venezuela's debt service ability is very strong." Erich Arispe of Fitch Ratings came to a far different and more prophetic picture on Venezuela the very same month: "The revision of the outlook to Negative reflects Venezuela's weakening policy framework, which has resulted in increased vulnerability to commodity price shocks and deterioration in fiscal and external credit metrics as well as rising political uncertainty" (both quoted in Sanderson and Forsythe, *China's Superbank*, 123). In other cases of CDB lending, though, commercial rates are very much in evidence. CDB extended a $10 billion credit to Argentina in 2010 at the London Interbank Offered Rate (Libor) plus 600 basis points (see Kevin P. Gallagher, Amos Irwin, and Katherine Koleski, "The New Banks in Town: Chinese Finance in Latin America," *Inter-American Dialogue*, http://www.thedialogue.org/wp-content/uploads/2012/02/NewBanks_FULLTEXT.pdf). In the same year, the World Bank lent Argentina $30 million at Libor plus 85 basis points (see ZhongXiang Zhang, China's Quest for Energy Security: Why Are the Stakes So High?," *Review of Environment, Energy and Economics,* http://re3.feem.it/getpage.aspx?id=5296). See, e.g., John Rathbone, "China Lends More than $75bn to Latin America," *Financial Times,* February 15, 2012.

61. Charles Wolf Jr., Xiao Wang, and Eric Warner, "China's Foreign Aid and Government-Sponsored Investment Activities," RAND Corporation, 2013.

62. Walker, "China's Uncomfortable Diplomacy Keeps the Oil Flowing."

63. Ibid.

64. Nathan Crooks and Jose Orozco, "PDVSA Receives $1.5 Billion Housing Loan from Chinese Bank," *Bloomberg Business,* February 27, 2012; Sanderson and Forsythe, *China's Superbank,* 138; Hogan Lovells, "Latin America," http://www.hoganlovells.com/latin-america.

65. Robert Kagan, "League of Dictators," *Washington Post,* April 30, 2006.

66. Ibid.

67. Ibid.

68. Ibid.

69. Most date a change in Chinese behavior to early 2009, when Chinese ships engaged in multiple skirmishes with U.S. surveillance vessels in an effort to hinder American naval intelligence gathering efforts. See "Naked Aggression," *Economist,* March 12, 2009.

70. Former chairman of the Joint Chiefs of Staff Admiral Michael Mullen repeatedly averred that debt is the single greatest threat to national security; see Ed O'Keefe, "Mullen: Despite Deal, Debt Still Poses the Biggest Threat to U.S. National Security," *Washington Post,* August 2, 2011. Also see Robert Zoellick, "The Currency of Power," *Foreign Policy,* October 8, 2012; Regina C. Karp, *Security without Nuclear Weapons? Different Perspectives on Non-Nuclear Security* (Oxford: Oxford University Press, 1992).

71. In the wake of the 2008 financial crisis, for instance, the future of U.S.-China relations was framed as whether U.S. leaders would be willing to "double down against American national debt to facilitate the economic rise of those insistent

upon an export-led growth model." Moreover, according to some analysts, as inauspicious as traditional prospects of U.S. financing for export-led growth may sound, insecurities after the last financial crisis have left the U.S. with decreasing ability to act unilaterally. See Matthew J. Burrows and Jennifer Harris, "Revisiting the Future: Geopolitical Effects of the Financial Crisis," *Washington Quarterly* 32, no. 2 (April 2009): 27–38. Others have doubted those strategic effects; see Robert D. Blackwill, "The Geopolitical Consequences of the World Economic Recession—A Caution," RAND Corporation Occasional Paper OP-275-RC, 2009. Also see Robert Zoellick, "After the Crisis?," speech at Johns Hopkins University, Baltimore, Md., September 28, 2009, www.cfr.org/international-organizations-and-alliances/zoellicks-speech-after-crisis-september-2009/p20303.

3. Today's Leading Geoeconomic Instruments

1. Robert E. Rubin and Jacob Weisberg, *In an Uncertain World: Tough Choices from Wall Street to Washington* (New York: Random House, 2004), 25.
2. Those that realized what was going on called for a review of the Camp David accord itself. See "Muslim Brotherhood Calls for Review of Camp David Accord," *Bloomberg Business*, May 6, 2011.
3. T. J. Chisinau, "Why Has Russia Banned Moldovan Wine?," *Economist*, November 25, 2013.
4. Svante E. Cornell and S. Frederick Starr, *The Guns of August 2008: Russia's War in Georgia* (Armonk, N.Y.: M. E. Sharpe, 2009); "Russia Bans Wine Imports from Neighboring Georgia," National Public Radio, May 16, 2006.
5. Vladimer Papava, "Economic Component of the Russian-Georgian Conflict," *Geo-Economics* 6, no. 1 (2012): 66.
6. Following the NATO summit in Wales in the fall of 2014, the Georgian president continued to make strong declarations about Georgia's commitment to Eurasian integration: "I am here today in order to stand united and by means of relevant reforms, to accelerate implementation of our task—integration to EU and NATO." Speech by President Margvelashvili to the Parliament of Georgia, November 14, 2014, www.parliament.ge/en/media/axali-ambebi/the-speech-by-the-president-of-georgia-mr-giorgi-margvelashvili.page.
7. Paul Taylor, "Analysis: Russia's Phantom Pain to Hurt Ukraine in EU Pact," Reuters, November 11, 2013.
8. Russia's chief food inspector said that chocolates produced by Roshen, the Hershey of Ukraine, contained carcinogens. Roshen gave Russian officials safety documentation from European purchases and the United Nations' main food agency and invited Russian inspectors to visit the Ukrainian plant to examine it, all with no response from the Russians. Judith Miller, "Chilly Neighbors," *City Journal*, September 24, 2013.
9. Andrew Kramer, "Russia Steps Up Economic Pressure on Kiev," *New York Times*, March 23, 2014; Michael Birnbaum, "Russia Pressures Moldova and Ukraine ahead of Signing of EU Association Agreement," *Washington Post*, June 26, 2014.
10. This bullying continued when Russia told Moldovan officials that it would be a "grave mistake" to seek closer ties with Europe. Deputy Russian prime min-

ister Dmitri O. Rogozin let fly a threat about the coming winter in telling the former Soviet republic, "We hope that you will not freeze," a reference to the Moldovan dependence upon Russian gas for heat. See David M. Herszenhorn, "Russia Putting a Strong Arm on Neighbors," *New York Times,* October 22, 2013. In the case of Moldova, a 2006 ban on wine imports (grounded in claims of subpar food safety standards) has evolved into a 2014 ban on meat and a tightening of gas pipelines. Christian Oliver, "Moldovan Winemakers Struggle as Russia Vies with EU for Influence," *Financial Times,* April 8, 2014; "Russia Bans Meat Imports from Moldova," *Moscow Times,* October 27, 2014.

11. John Stevens, "How Russia Hurts UK Dairy Farmers: Sanctions Banning Import of EU Products Leads to Slump in Demand," *Daily Mail,* August 26, 2015.

12. Andrew E. Kramer, "Russia Burns Dutch Flowers Amid Netherlands' Inquiry Into Malaysia Airlines Crash," *New York Times,* August 17, 2015.

13. Pavel Feigenhauer, "Russia Preparing for Global Resource War," *Eurasia Daily Monitor,* November 14, 2013; Andrew Witthoeft, "Russia Tries to Turn Ukraine East," *National Interest,* September 9, 2013.

14. Michael Leigh, "Ukraine's Pivot to Europe?," *Real Clear World,* November 13, 2013.

15. Chisinau, "Why Has Russia Banned Moldovan Wine?"

16. According to a survey conducted by the International Foundation for Electoral Systems, 87 percent of Ukrainians are displeased with the economy and 79 percent expressed the same opinion on the political state of affairs. Thirty-seven percent of respondents indicated support for joining the EU, while 33 percent would prefer to join the Eurasian Customs Union. Low levels of confidence in major national leaders also prevail, with 69 percent of respondents expressing little or no confidence in Yanukovych. See U.S. Agency for International Development, "IFES Public Opinion in Ukraine 2013—Key Findings," December 2013; David M. Herszenhorn, "Facing Russian Threat, Ukraine Halts Plans for Deals with EU," *New York Times,* November 21, 2013; "Ukraine's Decision on Association with the EU," U.S. Department of State, Press Statement, November 21, 2013.

17. In December 2014, Ukrainian president Petro Poroshenko told his country that it should prepare to join the European Union by 2020. He stated, "Poland's signature on a document ratifying the EU-Ukraine agreement marks a historic moment that means Ukraine is entering a new reality on its way towards the EU." Ed Adamczyk, "Poroshenko: Ukraine in EU by 2020," United Press International, December 18, 2014.

18. David Herszenhorn, "Armenia Wins Backing to Join Trade Bloc Championed by Putin," *New York Times,* December 10, 2014; Benoît Vitkine, "Vladimir Putin's Eurasian Economic Union Gets Ready to Take On the World," *Guardian,* October 28, 2014.

19. At the time of the previous ban, in 2006–2007, Russia accounted for 60 percent of Moldova's wine exports. Since then Moldovan winemakers have found new markets. On the eve of the latest embargo, only 29 percent of their exports went to Russia, reflecting the limits of this sort of geoeconomic leverage. Still, the latest ban cost Moldova $6.6 million in just a few weeks, a loss equivalent to nearly one month of total goods exported from Moldova into neighboring Russia.

Razvan Hoinaru, "Analysis: Moldovan Wine. A Passage to Europe," Cartier European, October 4, 2013, http://cartiereuropean.com/2013/10/04/moldovan-wine-a-passage-to-europe/; Tessa Dunlop, "Why Russian Wine Ban Is Putting Pressure on Moldova," BBC News, November 21, 2013; Delphine d'Amora, "Russia Prepares Economic Retaliation over Moldova's EU Deal," *Moscow Times,* July 16, 2014; Chisinau, "Why Has Russia Banned Moldovan Wine?"

20. d'Amora, "Russia Prepares Economic Retaliations over Moldova's EU Deal."

21. Victor Chirila, "Moldova's Last Chance for Reform," European Council on Foreign Relations, December 9, 2014.

22. T. J. Chisinau, "A Geopolitical Hostage: The Path to European Integration Goes through Ukraine," *Economist,* November 23, 2013.

23. Thorvaldur Gylfason, "Meeting Russia's Challenge to EU's Eastern Partnership," *Vox,* January 25, 2014. The sentiment was common across Europe. "Brussels was asleep," as former Swedish foreign minister Carl Bildt bemoaned, speaking of the EU's response to Russia during the Ukraine crisis.

24. Kristi Raik, "Eastern Partnership as Differentiated Integration: The Challenges of EaP Association Agreements," *Eastern Partnership Review* 15 (December 2013).

25. Ibid.

26. Benn Steil and Robert Litan, *Financial Statecraft: The Role of Financial Markets in American Foreign Policy* (New Haven, Conn.: Yale University Press, 2006).

27. Author interview with Douglas Rediker. Also see Heidi Crebo Rediker and Douglas Rediker, "Capital Warfare," *Wall Street Journal,* March 28, 2007.

28. "The Global Financial Centres Index 15," Long Finance, March 2014, www.longfinance.net/images/GFCI15_15March2014.pdf.

29. International Monetary Fund, "Global Financial Stability Report: Moving from Liquidity- to Growth-Driven Markets," World Economic and Financial Surveys, April 2014, 71.

30. Susan Lund, Toos Daruvala, Richard Dobbs, Philipp Härle, Ju-Hon Kwek, and Ricardo Falcón, "Financial Globalization: Retreat or Reset?," McKinsey Global Institute, March 2013; James Manyika et al., "Global Flows in a Digital Age: How Trade, Finance, People, and Data Connect the World Economy," McKinsey Global Institute, April 2014.

31. China's "going out" campaign, compelled by a mix of resource insecurity and building on China's WTO membership, reflected a desire to make China's SOEs into global competitors. It was launched in 2002 under Premier Jiang Zemin as part of Beijing's tenth Five-Year Plan.

32. Lucy Hornby, Jamil Anderlini, and Guy Chazan, "China and Russia Sign $400bn Gas Deal," *Financial Times,* May 21, 2014; "BP to Sign $20 Billion LNG Supply Deal with China's CNOOC," Reuters, June 17, 2014.

33. International Monetary Fund, Currency Composition of Official Foreign Exchange Reserves (COFER) data, Q2 2015, http://data.imf.org/?sk=E6A5F467-C14B-4AA8-9F6D-5A09EC4E62A4

34. According to the IMF's Q1 2015 COFER data, total foreign exchange holdings for emerging economies totaled $7.5 trillion (see ibid.).

35. Yung Chul Park, "Reform of the Global Regulatory System: Perspectives of East Asia's Emerging Economies," presentation for the World Bank conference in Seoul, June 2009, as cited in Joshua Aizenman, "Hoarding International Reserves Versus a Pigovian Tax-Cum-Subsidy Scheme: Reflections on the Deleveraging Crisis of 2008–9, and a Cost Benefit Analysis," National Bureau of Economic Research, Working Paper No. 15484, November 2009, 5.

36. As noted in Chapter 2, SOEs account for 80 percent of China's stock market, 62 percent of Russia's, and 38 percent of Brazil's. United Nations Conference on Trade and Development, *World Investment Report 2013,* July 2013, http://unctad .org/en/PublicationChapters/wir2013ch1_en.pdf.

37. Another oft-cited problem is that Chinese SOEs fail to comply with government orders to focus on the "strategic sectors" of aviation, power, and telecommunication. "Fixing China Inc.," *Economist,* August 30, 2014.

38. And even on purely economic grounds, they do have substantial help from the government—in China, for example, the government handed out subsidies to the auto parts industry worth $28 billion from 2001 to 2011, with another $10.9 billion promised by 2020. "Perverse Advantage," *Economist,* April 27, 2013.

39. Estimates for total sovereign wealth fund (SWF) assets vary, at least partly based on whether data sources define SWFs to include various reserve asset management entities. According to estimates by Peterson Institute senior fellow Ted Truman, total SWF assets as of mid-2013 totaled "$4.2 trillion, including $3.6 trillion in foreign assets—increases of almost 40 percent from mid-2010." A 2014 report from KMPG estimates that sovereign wealth funds control $5.9 trillion in assets. See "Sovereign Wealth Funds, 2014," KPMG, http://www.kpmg.com/ES/es /ActualidadyNovedades/ArticulosyPublicaciones/Documents/sovereign-weath -funds-v2.pdf. On total reserves, see International Monetary Fund, "Currency Composition of Official Foreign Exchange Reserves (COFER)," data as of Q2 2015; Allie Bagnall and Edwin Truman, "Progress on Sovereign Wealth Fund Transparency and Accountability: An Updated SWF Scoreboard," Peterson Institute for International Economics Policy Brief PB13-19, August 2013.

40. Gregory Zuckerman, Juliet Chung, and Michael Corkery, "Hedge Funds Cut Back on Fees," *Wall Street Journal,* September 9, 2013. And see Hedge Fund Research Global Industry Report, 2013, https://www.hedgefundresearch.com/?fuse =products-irglo.

41. United Nations Conference on Trade and Development, *World Investment Report 2013.*

42. SWF Institute, "Sovereign Wealth Funds Ranking," updated January 2013, www.swfinstitute.org/fund-rankings. Some may also classify Singapore as democratic; the 2012 Freedom House survey listed Singapore as "partly democratic."

43. The four megabanks are ICBC, China Construction Bank, Agricultural Bank of China, and Bank of China. See Standard & Poor's, "China's Top 50 Banks," September 2013, 51, http://www.standardandpoors.com/spf/swf/ereports/china/China _DimSum/document/AveDoc.pdf.

44. The first SWF was established by Kuwait in 1953; SWFs grew dramatically in the first decade of the twenty-first century. See Anna Gelpern, "Sovereignty,

Accountability, and the Wealth Fund Governance Conundrum," *Asian Journal of International Law* 1, no. 1 (2011): 289–320. Edwin Truman defines SWFs as "separate pools of government-owned or controlled assets that include some international assets"; see Edwin Truman, "Do Sovereign Wealth Funds Pose a Risk to the United States?," remarks at the American Enterprise Institute, February 2008, and Edwin Truman, "Sovereign Wealth Funds: Is Asia Different?," Peterson Institute for International Economics, Working Paper 11-12, June 2011.

45. See, e.g., Michael Hagan and Heidi Johanns, "Sovereign Wealth Funds: Risks, Rewards, Regulations and the Emerging Cross-Border Paradigm," *M&A Journal* 8, no. 8 (2008), available at www.mofo.com/docs/pdf/MAJ808_SovreignWealth .pdf. They write, "Commonly referred to now as sovereign wealth funds or SWFs . . . these investment vehicles have risen from relatively recent obscurity to center stage in international finance, with a number of attendant legitimate concerns and some potentially thorny misconceptions." Anna Gelpern also offers a detailed overview of popular descriptions of perceived risks surrounding SWFs in "Sovereignty, Accountability, and the Governance Conundrum."

46. There is some evidence to suggest that political motives play a role in SWF investment. Bernstein et al. find that when politicians are involved, P/E ratios of investments are higher and that valuations fall in the year after investment, suggesting that political distortions may be the reason. See Shai Bernstein, Josh Lerner, and Antoinette Schoar, "The Investment Strategies of Sovereign Wealth Funds," *Journal of Economic Perspectives* 27, no. 2 (Spring 2013): 219–238. See also Sofia Johan, April Knill, and Nathan Mauck, "Determinants of Sovereign Wealth Fund Investment in Private Equity versus Public Equity," November 15, 2012, http://papers.ssrn.com/sol3/papers.cfm?abstract_id=2181130. Knill summarizes this work in the 2012 Sovereign Wealth Fund Annual Report as follows: "The results . . . in our research suggest that SWFs make investment decisions with regard to investing in private equity distinctly from other institutional investors. Though these results do not answer the question as to whether or not SWFs invest with geopolitical motives in mind, it certainly leaves room for the possibility. It would even perhaps make sense if geoeconomics played a role in investments. After all, the sovereign entities associated with these pools of money are charged with making decisions that are for the betterment of their nation's citizens."

47. Gelpern, "Sovereignty, Accountability, and the Governance Conundrum."

48. Ibid.

49. Steve Johnson, "Norway's Sovereign Wealth Fund Joins Exodus from Israel," *Financial Times,* February 2, 2014.

50. Kerin Hope, "Greece Seeks Investments from Libya," *Financial Times,* June 8, 2010; "Factbox—Libyan Aid and Investment Projects in Africa," Reuters, November 24, 2010; Jeffrey Gettleman, "Libyan Oil Buys Allies for Qaddafi," *New York Times,* March 15, 2011.

51. Gambia abruptly split its relations with Taiwan in late 2013; as of November 2014, formal diplomatic ties between Banjul and Beijing had not been established, but investments from China are readily found: plans for a Trans-West African highway and a hydropower dam on the Gambia River require Chinese coopera-

tion with Gambian organizations. See Jessica Drun, "China-Taiwan Diplomatic Truce Holds despite Gambia," *Diplomat,* March 29, 2014; Jamie Anderlini, "Beijing Uses Reserves Fund to Persuade Costa Rica over Taipei," *Financial Times,* September 12, 2008; Graham Bowley, "Cash Helped China Win Costa Rica's Recognition," *New York Times,* September 12, 2008.

52. A Chinese state-owned construction firm built the new African Union building in Addis Ababa, a gift costing Beijing $129.5 million but boosting diplomatic recognition of the People's Republic of China across the continent. David E. Brown, "Hidden Dragon, Crouching Lion: How China's Advance in Africa Is Underestimated and Africa's Potential Underappreciated," Strategic Studies Institute, U.S. Army War College, September 17, 2012.

53. Lucy Hornby and Luc Cohen, "No Ties? No Problem as China Courts Taiwan's Remaining Allies," Reuters, August 6, 2013; Shannon Tiezzi, "Why Taiwan's Allies Are Flocking to Beijing," *Diplomat,* November 19, 2013; Ministry of Foreign Affairs, Republic of China (Taiwan), "Diplomatic Allies" [in Chinese], www.mofa.gov.tw/EnOfficial/Regions/AlliesIndex/?opno=f8505044-f8dd-4fc9-b5b5-0da9d549c979; Audra Ang, "China Defends Dealings with Africa," *Washington Post,* October 31, 2006.

54. This correlation prompted some to speculate that Libyan SWF patronage "may be one reason why the African Union, which has emerged as a potential Libyan peace broker, refused to support coalition air strikes, even as the Arab League and Gulf Cooperation Council came out in favor." Jon Rosen, "Whither the King of Kings?," *ISN Insights,* April 2011, available at www.africanewsanalysis.com/2011/04/26/wither-the-king-of-kings-how-qaddafis-battle-for-libya-will-impact-africa-by-jon-rosen-for-isn-insights.

55. Ibid.

56. Mohsin Kahn, "The Gulf and Geoeconomics," MENA Source, Atlantic Council, March 7, 2014, available at http://www.atlanticcouncil.org/blogs/menasource/the gulf and geoeconomics.

57. Asa Fitch, "Qatar SWF Drops Flashy Deals as Foreign Policy Shifts, Report Says," *Wall Street Journal,* June 16, 2014.

58. More generally, the GeoEconomica report found that "Arab SWFs have demonstrated neither their managements' operational independence nor their economic and financial orientation, and therefore have not contributed to building confidence . . . in line with the Principles' aspirations." Sven Behrendt, "Santiago Compliance Index 2014: Assessing the Governance Arrangements and Financial Disclosure Policies of Global Sovereign Wealth Funds," GeoEconimica, October 2014, https://www.nzsuperfund.co.nz/sites/default/files/documents-sys/SCI%20 2014%20October%202014_final.pdf.

59. Ashley Lenihan, "Sovereign Wealth Funds and the Acquisition of Power," *Journal of New Political Economy,* April 2013.

60. As one group of authors summarizes these structural differences, "Put simply, SWFs are unconstrained investors, which affects (or should affect) the nature of the risks that they are willing to bear, the time horizon of investment, the benchmarks (if any) used to evaluate performance, the demand for innovation in investment

management, as well as the nature of 'products' offered to SWFs by investment companies." Gordon L. Clark, Adam D. Dixon, and Ashby H. B. Monk, *Sovereign Wealth Funds: Legitimacy, Governance, and Global Power* (Princeton, N.J.: Princeton University Press, 2013), 9.

61. China and Russia are two such examples. India's multibrand retail ban is another important limit on FDI, which goes well beyond the national security screening mechanisms seen in many countries, including the United States.

62. Committee on Foreign Investment in the United States, Annual Report to Congress, December 2013, 3; also see Jonathan Masters, "Foreign Investment and U.S. National Security," Council on Foreign Relations backgrounder, September 27, 2013.

63. According to the IMF, at the end of 2011 Iran held $106 billion in official foreign reserves, mainly deposits in euros and other European currencies, enough to cover thirteen months' worth of imports of goods and services into Iran. But these declined rapidly, such that by November 2012, Iran announced it plans to stop holding dollars and euros in reserves. Amir Paivar, "Iran Currency Crisis: Sanctions Detonate Unstable Rial," BBC News, October 2, 2012; "Iran Plans to Phase Out Dollar, Euro in Foreign Trade," PressTV, January 15, 2013, www.presstv.ir /detail/2013/01/14/283517/iran-to-phase-out-euro-dollar-in-trade; Thomas Erdbrink and Colum Lynch, "New Sanctions Crimp Iran's Shipping Business as Insurers Withhold Coverage," *Washington Post,* July 21, 2010.

64. Aside from the initial bulletin (Lloyd's Market Bulletin Ref. Y4463, "Iran-EU Sanctions," January 20, 2011), Lloyd's also conducted extensive sanctions due diligence, issuing a longer report in February 2012 ("Sanctions Due Diligence Guidance for the Lloyd's Market").

65. In the most recent report to Congress, released February 2015 and covering CY 2013, CFIUS undertook 193 investigations from 2009 to 2013. The report is available at http://www.treasury.gov/resource-center/international/foreign-investment /Documents/2014%20CFIUS%20Annual%20Report%20for%20Public%20Re lease.pdf.

66. Geoff Dyer, "Sanctions: War by Other Means," *Financial Times,* March 30, 2014.

67. Daniel W. Drezner, "Serious about Sanctions," *National Interest,* Fall 1998, 67–68.

68. Ibid.

69. David Wessel, "From South Africa to Iran, Economic Sanctions Evolve," *Wall Street Journal,* December 11, 2013.

70. Betty Glad, *An Outsider in the White House: Jimmy Carter, His Advisors, and the Making of American Foreign Policy* (Ithaca, N.Y.: Cornell University Press, 2009), 208.

71. "Russia's Gazprom Neft to Sell Oil for Rubles, Yuan," *Ria Novosti,* August 27, 2014; Jack Farchy, "Gazprom Looks to Drop the Dollar to Avoid Sanctions' Bite," *Financial Times,* April 7, 2014.

72. Certainly there is enough "new" about the geopolitical struggles now playing out in the cyber domain to warrant treating cyber as among the newest geoeconomic tools. Still, there remains an interesting question about the extent to which

cyber issues, rightly understood, actually belong within a larger tradition in Anglo-American statecraft of prizing control over global information flows—dating back, for example, to the United Kingdom's efforts to have the world telegraph and cable lines under its sway in the nineteenth century; U.S. government efforts in the Cold War to support global distribution lines for content, such as *Reader's Digest*; and, perhaps, pre-Internet telecom satellite policy in the United States. This question strikes us as still unsettled and worth further thought; we are grateful to one of our anonymous readers for Harvard University Press for raising it.

73. The November 2011 NCIX report, as characterized by the *Financial Times,* "directly names the Chinese and Russian governments as being behind many efforts to steal technology." Geoff Dwyer, "U.S. Takes Aim at China and Russia over Cyber Attacks," *Financial Times,* November 3, 2011. See also the 2012 Breach Report, available at www.wired.com/images_blogs/threatlevel/2012/03/Verizon-Data-Breach -Report-2012.pdf. The report breaks down 620 data breaches documented by various organizations such as the U.S. Secret Service and European Cyber Crime Center. Among its findings, the report states: "Ninety-six percent of espionage cases were attributed to threat actors in China and the remaining 4 percent were unknown."

74. Tony Capaccio, "China Most Threatening Cyberspace Force, U.S. Panel Says," *Bloomberg Business,* November 5, 2012.

75. Adam Segal, "Shaming Chinese Hackers Won't Work," *Guardian,* May 30, 2013.

76. "It is now evident that intellectual property and commercially strategic information stored on IT systems are being accessed and infiltrated, perhaps to a degree that affects America's economic position." Richard Danzig, "Surviving on a Diet of Poisoned Fruit: Reducing the National Security Risks of America's Cyber Dependencies," Center for a New American Security, July 2014, 8.

77. Ian Traynor, "Russia Accused of Unleashing Cyberwar to Disable Estonia," *Guardian,* May 16, 2007.

78. Joshua Davis, "Hackers Take Down the Most Wired Country in Europe," *Wired,* August 21, 2007.

79. Ibid.

80. What evidence is available suffers from an enormous observation bias—especially in terms of what companies voluntarily disclose—which should not be underestimated.

81. Evan Osnos, "China's 863 Program: A Crash Program for China's Clean Energy," *New Yorker,* December 20, 2009.

82. Ellen Nakashima, "U.S. Said to Be Target of Massive Cyber-Espionage Campaign," *Washington Post,* February 10, 2013. See also David Sanger, David Barboza, and Nicole Perlroth, "China's Army Is Seen as Tied to Hacking against U.S.," *New York Times,* February 18, 2013.

83. This point was initially raised by a cyber expert for a private security firm in a not-for-attribution meeting. Cyber expert James Lewis also makes this point: "It also takes time for an acquirer to turn stolen IP into a competitive product. In some cases, the damage may not be visible for years." James Lewis, "Raising the Bar for Cyber Security," Center for Strategic and International Studies, Washington, D.C., February 2013.

84. As one *Economist* piece explains, "Other victims of hacking attacks included the International Olympic Committee and the World Anti-Doping Agency after the 2008 Beijing Olympics; Tibetan and Uighur activists and Chinese dissidents; think-tanks that analyze China (including its hacking capabilities); and NGOs operating in China. None of these seemed to have any commercial value." "Masters of the Cyber Universe," *Economist,* April 6, 2013.

85. Although, in the case of the 2010 Google attacks, experts later reported that hackers did obtain sensitive data pertaining to U.S. government surveillance targets. See, e.g., Charlie Osborne, "U.S. Officials Report Chinese Cyberattack on Google Exposed Spy Data," *ZDNet,* May 21, 2013.

86. Nicole Perlroth, David Sanger, and Michael Schmidt, "As Hacking against U.S. Rises, Experts Try to Pin Down Motive," *New York Times,* March 3, 2013.

87. Author interview.

88. Including Bloomberg, the cyber security firm Mandiant, the Project 2049 Institute, the *Washington Post,* and the *New York Times,* among others. These investigative efforts have linked the preponderance of attacks back to PLA Unit 61398, formally known as the 2nd Bureau of the People's Liberation Army's General Staff Department's 3rd Department.

89. Ellen Nakashima, "U.S. Decides against Publicly Blaming China for Data Hack," *Washington Post,* July 21, 2015.

90. Ellen Nakashima, "U.S. Said to Be Target of Massive Cyber-Espionage Campaign," *Washington Post,* February 10, 2013. Also see Mandiant, "APT 1: Exposing One of China's Cyber Espionage Units," April 2013, http://intelreport.mandiant .com.

91. Adam Segal, "Curbing Chinese Cyber Espionage," *Global Public Square* blog, CNN, May 9, 2011. And see Mark Thompson, "Execs Say Cyber-Attacks a Top Threat," CNBC Online, February 6, 2013. One Economist Intelligence Unit survey found that roughly 70 percent of senior executives believed cyberattacks "occurred regularly or are rampant." A separate February 2013 survey of CEOs found that cyberattacks topped their list of concerns. Of the 258 executives surveyed, 85 percent said they were very or somewhat concerned about cyberattacks on their organizations—topping concerns over income loss, property damage, and securities and investment risk.

92. Jesse Riseborough, "Rio Tinto, BHP Billiton, Fortescue Hit by China Computer Hackers, ABC Says," *Bloomberg Business,* April 19, 2010; Ben Elgin, Dune Lawrence, and Michael Riley, "Coke Gets Hacked and Doesn't Tell Anyone," *Bloomberg Business,* November 4, 2012.

93. Mark Clayton, "US Hacking Charges against China for Economic Cyber-Spying: Why Now?," *Christian Science Monitor,* May 21, 2014.

94. He revealed that one "major London listed company" was estimated to have lost around £800 million following a hostile-state cyberattack. Tom Whitehead, "Cyber Crime a Global Threat, MI5 Head Warns," *Telegraph,* June 26, 2012.

95. Daniel Schearf, "North Korea's 'World Class' Cyber Attacks Coming from China," *Voice of America News,* November 21, 2013.

96. According to a 2014 report by McAfee, "a conservative estimate would be $375 billion in losses, while the maximum could be as much as $575 billion."

See "Net Losses: Estimating the Global Cost of Cybercrime" (report presented at the Center for Strategic and International Studies, Washington, D.C., June 2014), available at www.mcafee.com/us/resources/reports/rp-economic-impact-cybercrime2.pdf. In 2012, NSA chief Keith Alexander estimated U.S. losses to be closer to $114 annually; Josh Rogin, "NSA Chief: Cybercrime Constitutes the 'Greatest Transfer of Wealth in History,'" *Foreign Policy,* July 9, 2012.

97. McAfee "Net Losses."

98. Ibid.

99. Zain Shauk, "Malware on Oil Rig Computers Raises Security Fears," *Houston Chronicle,* February 22, 2013.

100. Mark Clayton, "Energy Sector Cyberattacks Jumped in 2012. Were Utilities Prepared?," *Christian Science Monitor,* January 7, 2013.

101. The 2012 virus Shamoon erased data on three-quarters of Aramco's corporate PCs—documents, spreadsheets, emails, files—replacing the files with an image of a burning American flag; see Nicole Perlroth, "In Cyberattack on Saudi Firm, U.S. Sees Iran Firing Back," *New York Times,* October 23, 2012. Just a week later, Qatar's RasGas was targeted with, many suspect, the same virus; see Camilla Hall and Javier Blas, "Qatar Group Falls Victim to Virus Attack," *Financial Times,* August 30, 2012, and Kim Zetter, "Qatari Gas Company Hit with Virus in Wave of Attacks on Energy Companies," *Wired,* August 30, 2012.

102. Blake Clayton and Adam Segal, "Addressing Cyber Threats to Oil and Gas Supplies," Council on Foreign Relations Energy Brief, June 2013, 2.

103. Ibid.

104. Ibid.

105. Ellen Nakashima, "Iran Blamed for Cyberattacks on U.S. Banks and Companies," *Washington Post,* September 21, 2012. Daniel Fineren and Amena Bakr, "Saudi Aramco Says Most Damage from Computer Attack Fixed," Reuters, August 26, 2012.

106. Perlroth, "In Cyberattack on Saudi Firm, U.S. Sees Iran Firing Back."

107. Clayton and Segal, "Addressing Cyber Threats to Oil and Gas Supplies." Citing interviews with anonymous U.S. cyber-security specialists, Clayton and Segal report that "some security experts believe the [Aramco] attack could have been damaging had it penetrated further into the network." Abdullah Al Sa'adan, Aramco's vice president for corporate planning, stated, "The main target in this attack was to stop the flow of oil and gas to local and international markets and thank God they were not able to achieve their goals" (quoted in "Shamoon Was an External Attack on Saudi Oil Production, *Infosecurity,* December 10, 2012, http://www .infosecurity-magazine.com/news/shamoon-was-an-external-attack-on-saudi-oil/).

108. Clayton and Segal, "Addressing Cyber Threats to Oil and Gas Supplies."

109. Nakashima, "Iran Blamed for Cyberattacks on U.S. Banks and Companies." These were "probes that suggest that someone is looking at how to take control of these systems," as one official put it.

110. David E. Sanger and Nicole Perlroth, "New Russian Boldness Revives a Cold War Tradition: Testing the Other Side," *New York Times,* October 30, 2014.

111. Ellen Nakashima, "U.S. Rallied Multinational Response to 2012 Cyberattack on American Banks," *Washington Post,* April 11, 2014. U.S. officials considered

the possibility of hacking into the attacker's network in Iran before dismissing the idea as too confrontational. Support also briefly cohered around another option, forwarded by NSA director and head of U.S. Cyber Command Keith Alexander, that would, through a series of covert NSA actions, permanently shut down the process responsible for the cyberattack without risking collateral damage. Ultimately, U.S. officials chose neither.

112. Nakashima, "U.S. Rallied Multinational Response to 2012 Cyberattack on American Banks."

113. Ibid.

114. Associated Press, "Dollar May be Next Screw for U.S. to Tighten on North Korea," *New York Times*, April 9, 2015.

115. Hugh Son, "JPMorgan Assailed by Russia as Bank Blocks Payment," *Bloomberg Business*, April 2, 2014; Michael Riley and Jordan Robertson, "FBI Examining Whether Russia Is Tied to JPMorgan Hacking," *Bloomberg Business*, August 27, 2014.

116. Jessica Silver-Greenberg, Matthew Goldstein, and Nicole Perlroth, "JPMorgan Chase Hacking Affects 76 Million Households," *New York Times*, October 2, 2014; Matthew Goldstein, Nicole Perlroth, and David Sanger, "Hackers' Attack Cracked 10 Financial Firms in Major Assault," *New York Times*, October 3, 2014.

117. Silver-Greenberg, Goldstein, and Perlroth, "JPMorgan Chase Hacking Affects 76 Million Households."

118. Michael Corkery, Jessica Silver-Greenberg, and David Sanger, "Obama Had Security Fears on JPMorgan Data Breach," *New York Times*, October 8, 2014.

119. Chris Strohm, "JPMorgan Hack May Be Warning, Says Former NSA Chief," *Bloomberg Business*, September 3, 2014. See also Gerry Smith, "Vladimir Putin Employs an Army of Skilled Hackers, Report Finds," *Huffington Post*, October 28, 2014.

120. McAfee, "Net Losses."

121. "While Warning of Chinese Cyberthreat, U.S. Launches Its Own Attack," National Public Radio, April 2, 2014. Others, like Greg Gilligan, have echoed similar sentiments. Responding to a recent Pentagon report, Gilligan said, "The salient point [is] . . . that there is some organized effort by some group attacking business interests" (referring to the Chinese government's persistent campaign against U.S. companies). "This is not government to government. It's not military to military. It's [someone] attacking the economic interests of United States companies." Tom Gjelten, "U.S. Turns Up Heat on Costly Commercial Cybertheft in China," National Public Radio, May 7, 2013.

122. Jane Perlez, "Xi Jinping Pledges to Work with U.S. to Stop Cybercrimes," *New York Times*, September 22, 2015.

123. "Will China Keep its Cyber Promises?," *Washington Post*, October 21, 2015.

124. "While Warning of Chinese Cyberthreat, U.S. Launches Its Own Attack."

125. "Foreign Military Financing Account Summary," U.S. Department of State, Under Secretary for Arms Control and International Security, Office of Plans and Initiatives, www.state.gov/t/pm/ppa/sat/c14560.htm. Also see recent pieces chroni-

cling U.S. military aid to Egypt, such as Ernesto Londoño, "U.S. to Partially Resume Military Aid to Egypt," *Washington Post,* April 22, 2014.

126. Anne Barnard, "Saudis' Grant to Lebanon Is Seen as Message to U.S.," *New York Times,* January 6, 2014.

127. Ibid.

128. Ibid.

129. Ibid.

130. Ibid.

131. Michael P. Croissant, *The Armenia-Azerbaijan Conflict: Causes and Implications* (Santa Barbara, Calif.: Praeger, 1998); RIA Novosti, "Russia Shipping Arms Worth $1 Bln to Azerbaijan—Report," *Sputnik International,* June 18, 2013.

132. Judith Miller, "Clintons Urge Ukraine to Spurn Russian Pressure, Sign Deal with European Union," *Newsmax,* September 21, 2013.

133. Andrew Jacobs, "Asia Rivalries Play Role in Aid to the Philippines," *New York Times,* November 14, 2013 (arguing that the outpouring of aid to the hundreds of thousands of homeless Filipinos has been a show of "one-upmanship" directed at Asia's rising power, China).

134. The United States and China took two starkly different responses to Haiyan. The United States sent its navy and marines, pledging $20 million in disaster assistance. China, on the other hand, sent an initial $100,000 in government assistance until it folded before the badgering of the international community, increasing its contribution to a paltry $1.6 million. Walter Lohman, "What Typhoon Haiyan Taught Us about China," *National Interest,* November 18, 2013.

135. Claire Provost "Foreign Aid Reaches Record High," *Guardian,* April 8, 2014.

136. Ibid.

137. "Qatar's Aid to Egypt Raises Fears on Motives," *Wall Street Journal,* May 17, 2013.

138. Of the $18 billion pledged, $8 billion is for gas/power/iron/steel plants at the northern entrance to the Suez Canal; $10 billion is for a giant tourist resort on the Mediterranean coast. Marwa Awad, "Qatar Says to Invest $18 Billion in Egypt Economy," Reuters, September 6, 2012. Provost, "Foreign Aid Reaches Record High."

139. Iyad Dakka, "How the U.S. Can Capitalize on a Budding Egypt-Saudi Alliance," *World Politics Review,* September 10, 2015.

140. Dana Halawi, "Choucair: Firms Must Hire More Lebanese," *Daily Star Lebanon,* January 29, 2014.

141. Blake Hounshell, "The Qatar Bubble," *Foreign Policy,* April 23, 2012.

142. Mehreen Zahra-Malik, "Saudi Arabia Loans Pakistan $1.5 Billion to Shore Up Economy," Reuters, March 13, 2014.

143. Farhan Bokhari, "Saudi Arabia Gives Financial Aid to Pakistan," *Financial Times,* March 14, 2014. "The Saudi support to Pakistan follows a mid-February visit by Salman bin Abdul Aziz al-Saud, Saudi crown prince, amid suggestions that Saudi Arabia is seeking an expansion of its security ties with Pakistan. In February a senior Pakistani intelligence official told the *Financial Times* that Saudi Arabia was seeking "a large number of [Pakistan] troops to support its campaign along the Yemeni border and for internal security."

144. "Pakistan Defends $1.5b Aid from Saudi Arabia," *Gulf News,* March 19, 2014.

145. As Gulf expert and head of the Carnegie Foundation's Middle East Center, Lena Khatib, explains these regional struggles, "Qatar's foreign policy decisions and their repercussions have been tightly connected to its long-standing rivalry with Saudi Arabia over the two Gulf countries' degree of regional influence. Doha had long been a minor regional actor in the shadow of Riyadh. Qatar's desire to increase its political clout led it into confrontation with the Kingdom over the Syria and Egypt files." Lina Khatib, "Qatar and the Recalibration of Power in the Gulf," Carnegie Middle East Center, September 11, 2014, http://carnegie-mec.org/2014/09/11/qatar-and-recalibration-of-power-in-gulf/hofm.

146. Jodi Rudoren, "Qatar's Emir Visits Gaza, Pledging $400 Million to Hamas," *New York Times,* October 23, 2012.

147. Claire Provost, "The Rebirth of Russian Foreign Aid," *Guardian,* May 15, 2011.

148. Sarah Teo, Bhubhindar Singh, and See Seng Tan, "South Korea's Middle-Power Engagement Initiatives: Perspectives from Southeast Asia," S. Rajaratnam School of International Studies, Singapore, November 28, 2013.

149. Nackhoon Han, "South Korea & ASEAN: To the Next Phase," *Fair Observer,* March 26, 2012.

150. "National Security Strategy, December 17, 2013 (Provisional Translation)," Government of Japan, Cabinet Secretariat, www.cas.go.jp/jp/siryou/131217an zenhoshou/nss-e.pdf.

151. Reflecting the post–Cold War zeitgeist, Japan's ODA Charter, established in 1991, bluntly prohibited the use of foreign aid for security purposes. Widely seen in Japan as a necessary counter to Chinese geoeconomic influence in the region, Abe's reforms will do away with this prohibition on foreign aid for geopolitical purposes, and will direct more assistance dollars to "seed support for overseas activities by Japanese firms in regions of vital importance." Ibid.

152. "But Belarus, too, although on a far lesser scale, has been punished in the recent past for seeking economic aid from China." Peter Beaumont, "Russia Makes Latest High-Risk Move to Keep Pieces of Its 'Near Abroad' in Check," *Guardian,* March 1, 2014.

153. As Moscow was applying some of its heaviest trade sanctions on Ukraine, President Putin presented proposals including a $15 billion financing program for Ukraine, reduced natural gas prices, and promises to continue cooperation on joint projects in nuclear energy and technology as well as the manufacturing sectors. See David Herszenhorn and Andrew Kramer, "Russia Offers Cash Infusion for Ukraine," *New York Times,* December 17, 2013; Darina Marchak and Katya Gorchinskaya, "Russia Gives Ukraine Cheap Gas, $15 Billion in Loans," *Kyiv Post,* December 17, 2013; "Kiev Testing 'Pause' in EU Integration," Kiev Ukraine News Blog, November 15, 2013, http://news.kievukraine.info/2013/11/kiev-testing-pause -in-eu-integration.html.

154. For a discussion of a smart, strategic approach to the Eastern Partnership, including how Russia's increasingly assertive tactics should be balanced alongside

the long-standing ties binding the Eastern Partnership countries to the EU, see Richard Youngs and Kateryna Pishchikova, "Smart Geostrategy for the Eastern Partnership," Carnegie Foundation Europe, November 14, 2013.

155. Henry Sanderson and Michael Forsythe, *China's Superbank: Debt, Oil and Influence—How China Development Bank is Rewriting the Rules of Finance* (New York: John Wiley & Sons, 2012), 41; Pruden Ho, "Chinese Bank Takes Great Leap Forward," *Wall Street Journal*, September 4, 2012.

156. Sanderson and Forsythe, *China's Superbank*, preface.

157. According to Martyn Davies, CEO of Johannesburg-based Frontier Advisory, "The deepest rationale for the BRICS is almost certainly the creation of new Bretton Woods–type institutions that are inclined toward the developing world. There's a shift in power from the traditional to the emerging world . . . there is a lot of geopolitical concern about this shift." Mike Cohen and Ilya Arkhipov, "BRICS Nations Plan New Bank to Bypass World Bank, IMF," *Bloomberg Business, ness*, March 26, 2013.

158. Barry Eichengreen, "Do the Brics Need Their Own Development Bank?," *Guardian*, August 14, 2014. For analysis of the AIIB, see Andrew Higgins and David E. Sanger, "3 European Powers Say They Will Join China-Led Bank," *New York Times*, March 17, 2015; and see Sebastian Heilmann, Moritz Rudolf, Mikko Huotari, and Johannes Buckow, "China's Shadow Foreign Policy: Parallel Structures Challenge the Established International Order," Mercator Institute for China Studies, *China Monitor* 18 (October 28, 2014).

159. Eichengreen, "Do the Brics Need Their Own Development Bank?"; see also Dingding Chen, "3 Reasons the BRICS' New Development Bank Matters," *Diplomat*, July 23, 2014.

160. Jeremi Suri, "State Finance and National Power: Great Britain, China, and the United States in Historical Perspective," Tobin Project discussion paper on "Sustainable National Security Strategy," January 2014.

161. Ibid.

162. Jeremi Suri noted that Paul Kennedy examines this history in depth, reaffirming the necessity of sound finance for sustenance and preservation of great powers (see "State Finance and National Power"). In his controversial text, Paul Kennedy asserts that nations can grow and expand without sound finance, but they cannot sustain that growth and expansion if they confront capital shortages resulting from burdensome foreign military or occupation expenses. See Paul Kennedy, *The Rise and Fall of the Great Powers: Economic Change and Military Conflict from 1500 to 2000* (New York: Random House, 1987), xv–xxv, 73–139. Also see Michael J. Mazarr, "The Risks of Ignoring Strategic Insolvency," *Washington Quarterly* 35, no. 4 (2012): 7–22; David Landes, *The Wealth and Poverty of Nations: Why Some Are So Rich and Some So Poor* (New York: W. W. Norton, 1998).

163. Suri's reference here is to Kennedy, *The Rise and Fall of the Great Powers*, 76–86.

164. Paul Kennedy is, yet again, a prime example. His *Rise and Fall of the Great Powers* links sound finances to great-power preservation, but without an update for recent evolutions in the global financial and monetary landscape. Daniel Drezner

looks at global economic governance in the wake of the financial crisis in *The System Worked: How the World Stopped Another Great Depression* (New York: Oxford University Press, 2014), 184–185, and notes that the relative influence of the United States declined on some dimensions but remained resilient in many others. He specifically points to Washington's control of the global reserve currency, capital markets, and asset ownership.

165. Charles P. Kindleberger, *Power and Money: The Economics of International Politics and the Politics of International Economics* (New York: Basic Books, 1970), 204.

166. Daniel Dăianu, "Re-discovering the Values of Bretton Woods," *Europe's World,* October 1, 2013; George Melloan, "The Euro Has Been a Smashing Success," *Wall Street Journal,* March 8, 2010; Russell Shorto, "In Praise of the Euro: A Case for the World's Most Hated Currency," *New Republic,* November 8, 2011.

167. Romano Prodi, former president of the European Commission, quoted in David Fairlamb, "Euros in Hand, Europe Expects a New Era," *Bloomberg Businessweek,* January 1, 2002. Also see Strobe Talbott, "Monnet's Brand & Europe's Fat," *Brookings Essay,* February 11, 2014.

168. Bundesbank Council meeting with Chancellor Schmidt (assurances on operation EMS), November 30, 1978, Bundesbank Archive, declassified 2008.

169. Richard Milne, "Latvia Sees Joining Euro as Extra Protection against Russia," *Financial Times,* December 30, 2013.

170. Ibid.

171. Jonathan Kirshner, an international political economy historian at Cornell University, takes a fresh look at the link between the dollar's international status and U.S. ability to project power in the aftermath of the 2008–2009 global financial crisis, arguing that the crisis has reduced the dollar's global status and with it the geopolitical standing of the United States. Jonathan Kirshner, "Bringing Them All Back Home: Dollar Diminution and U.S. Power," *Washington Quarterly,* Summer 2013.

172. As Kirshner explains in earlier work, safe haven flows into the United States during global political confrontation have meant that the United States generally has not had to worry about a simultaneous political and financial crisis. See Jonathan Kirshner, "The Inescapable Politics of Money" in Jonathan Kirshner, ed., *Monetary Orders: Ambiguous Economics, Ubiquitous Politics* (Ithaca, N.Y.: Cornell University Press, 2003). Also see generally Jonathan Kirshner, *Currency and Coercion: The Political Economy of International Monetary Power* (Princeton, N.J.: Princeton University Press, 1995).

173. From 2000 to 2005, the dollar share of global reserves as indicated by the IMF COFER data has decreased by 4.4 percentage points on a value basis and 2.2 percentage points on a quantity basis. Anna Wong and Ted Truman, "Measurement and Inference in International Reserve Diversification," Peterson International Institute for Economics, Working Paper 07-06, July 2007.

174. Arvind Subramanian, "The Inevitable Superpower: Why China's Dominance Is a Sure Thing," *Foreign Affairs,* September/October 2011; Kirshner, "Bringing Them All Back Home"; Sebastian Mallaby and Olin Wethington, "The

Future of the Yuan," *Foreign Affairs,* January/February 2012; Robert Zoellick, "The Currency of Power," *Foreign Policy,* October 8, 2012.

175. Alan Wheatley, *The Power of Currencies and Currencies of Power* (London: International Institute for Strategic Studies, 2013), 13.

176. "The financial crisis . . . let us clearly see how unreasonable the current international monetary system is," said Li Ruogu, head of China Ex-Im Bank (Geoff Dyer, David Pilling, and Henny Sender, "A Strategy to Straddle the Planet," *Financial Times,* January 17, 2011). Former World Bank chief economist Justin Yifu Lin echoed these sentiments, reportedly telling an audience at Bruegel, a Brussels-based economic think-tank, "The dominance of the greenback is the root cause of global financial and economic crises." See Michael Barris, Fu Jing, and Chen Jia, "Replace Dollar with Super Currency: Economist," *China Daily USA,* last updated January 29, 2014.

177. Dyer, Pilling, and Sender, "A Strategy to Straddle the Planet."

178. "[A] self-serving Washington has abused its superpower status and introduced even more chaos into the world by shifting financial risks overseas . . . the cyclical stagnation in Washington for a viable bipartisan solution over a federal budget and an approval for raising debt ceiling has again left many nations' tremendous dollar assets in jeopardy and the international community highly agonized. . . . The developing and emerging market economies need to have more say in major international financial institutions including the World Bank and the International Monetary Fund, so that they could better reflect the transformations of the global economic and political landscape. What may also be included as a key part of an effective reform is the introduction of a new international reserve currency that is to be created to replace the dominant U.S. dollar, so that the international community could permanently stay away from the spillover of the intensifying domestic political turmoil in the United States." "Commentary: U.S. Fiscal Failure Warrants a De-Americanized World," Xinhua, October 13, 2013. See also Mark Landler, "Seeing Its Own Money at Risk, China Rails at U.S.," *New York Times,* October 15, 2013.

179. A 2010 paper coauthored by Asian Development Bank chief economist Dongyun Park casts the issue in even stronger terms, suggesting that the growing presence of SWFs and more activist management and investing of central bank reserves will also contribute to a diminished global role for the dollar, and in so doing, will accelerate reforms to the global monetary system. Donghyun Park, "Asia's Sovereign Wealth Funds and Reform of the Global Reserve System," Nanyang Technological University, 2010.

180. See generally "Beijing Symposium on the Future of the International Monetary System and the Role of the RMB," organized by Council on Foreign Relations, November 2011, conference papers available online at www.cfr.org/thinktank/cgs /beijingpapers.html. See also Sebastian Mallaby and Olin Wethington, "The Future of the Yuan," *Foreign Affairs,* January/February 2012.

181. While some would point to the global monetary system prior to World War I (dominated by the British pound, the German deutschmark, and the U.S. dollar), all systemic reserve currencies in the first half of the twentieth century were effectively pegged to gold, in contrast to today's fiat system.

182. Benn Steil elaborates on this point in "The End of National Currency," *Foreign Affairs*, May/June 2007. See also Barry Eichengreen, "The Once and Future Dollar," *American Interest*, May/June 2012.

183. Barry Eichengreen reflects on this point in his remarks at the conference "Internationalization of the Renminbi: Its Implications for China's Domestic Reform and the International System," University of San Diego, June 7–8, 2012, noting that "throughout history all reserve currencies were managed by democratic governments." Conference summary available at http://china.ucsd.edu/_files/renminbi/pdf -rmb-report.pdf.

184. See note 41 in this chapter and the IMF's Currency Composition of Official Foreign Exchange Reserves (COFER) Report. When updated in December 2014, the 2014Q2 estimate for total foreign exchange holdings was $12 trillion. By comparison, in March 2006, reserves held by monetary authorities worldwide totaled $4.9 trillion, equivalent to 11 percent of world GDP at the time. According to the Bank of International Settlements Quarterly Review in September 2006, "Between 1995 and 2005, all industrial countries reported to COFER but only 80–90 developing countries did, accounting for between 51 and 66% of total developing countries' reserves. The IMF does not identify the contributing countries but, considering the size of the gap, China appears to be among those missing. Furthermore, changes in reporting practices make comparisons over time difficult." Available online at http://bis.hasbeenforeclosed.com/publ/qtrpdf/r_qt0609e.pdf.

185. "Security considerations also drive reserve management in parts of Asia, where Japan, South Korea, and Taiwan are under the U.S. diplomatic and military wing. Even if there is no explicit *quid pro quo*, it is hard to conceive that they would jeopardize relations with the U.S. by abandoning the dollar. Limited diversification into other currencies would be understandable, but a public threat by Japan in 1998 to sell U.S. bonds, for example . . . has not been repeated." Wheatley, *The Power of Currencies and Currencies of Power*.

186. Min Zeng, "Big Drop in Foreigners' Treasury Holdings at Fed Stirs Talk," *Wall Street Journal*, March 14, 2014; Patrick Jenkins, Daniel Schäfer, Courtney Weaver, and Jack Farchy, "Russian Companies Withdraw Billions from West, Say Moscow Bankers," *Financial Times*, March 14, 2014.

187. Michael Mackenzie and Philip Stafford, "Belgium Packs Punch in U.S. Treasury Market," *Financial Times*, April 15, 2014; Martin Wolf, "Debt Troubles within the Great Wall," *Financial Times*, April 1, 2014.

188. See data from U.S. Treasury at www.treasury.gov/ticdata/Publish/mfh .txt as well as Mackenzie and Stafford, "Belgium Packs Punch in U.S. Treasury Market."

189. Mackenzie and Stafford, "Belgium Packs Punch in U.S. Treasury Market."

190. "The 'Shocking' Buying Spree of America's Mysterious Third Largest Treasury Holder Ramps Higher," *Zero Hedge*, April 15, 2014.

191. Citing analysis from David Yoo, a foreign exchange trader from the Bank of America/Merrill Lynch, journalist Jeff Cox finds that China most likely bought U.S. treasuries in 2014Q1 given its relatively large reserves inflows and its preference to keep a large share of FX reserves in U.S. Treasuries. Jeff Cox, "As everyone else sells, China buys U.S. debt," *CNBC*, April 29, 2014.

192. As several economists have noted, Tokyo has more financial maneuvering room than might seem apparent, thanks to what Carmen Reinhart, from the Harvard Kennedy School, and Vincent Reinhart, chief economist at Morgan Stanley, have called a "war chest of liquid assets at its disposal." Japan's citizens, not foreign hedge funds, own 95 percent of the country's debt, thus making it "unlikely the public would dump their bond holdings if the government takes on more debt to rebuild." In addition, Japanese authorities have been stockpiling foreign exchange reserves for years, nearing totals of $1 trillion (or slightly below 20 percent of total GDP). See Carmen Reinhart and Vincent Reinhart, "Japan Must Dip into Its Rainy Day Fund," *Financial Times*, March 24, 2011; Marcus Noland, "Will the Crisis Create a New Japan?," *Washington Post*, March 16, 2011.

193. Kirshner, "Bringing Them All Back Home," 39.

194. Washington has renewed its enthusiasm for loan guarantees in recent years—and guarantees to Jordan, Tunisia, and Ukraine have served crucial geopolitical interests for Washington, although these cases were more about ensuring against state insolvency and instability in crucial moments than about achieving any single diplomatic aim.

195. John Goshko, "Baker Firm on Guarantees as Mideast Talks Resume," *Washington Post*, February 25, 1992. GAO reports paint a different story, however, describing how loan guarantees had no discernible effect on Israeli housing policies and did not influence the Israeli government's decisions on where to build new housing or on how much settlement activity to undertake in occupied territories. General Accounting Office, National Security and International Affairs Division, Report B-247481 to Robert C. Byrd, Chairman of Committee on Appropriations, February 12, 1992, available at http://gao.justia.com/department-of-the-treasury /1992/2/israel nsiad-92-119/NSIAD-92-119-full-report.pdf.

196. Bonds were issued in euros with the aim of helping alleviate the consequences of Ukraine's critically low foreign exchange reserves at the time. Concerns surrounding the eurobonds resurfaced in September 2014, as a clause in the original bail-bond may enable the Kremlin to demand immediate repayment, forcing Western leaders to scramble up more cash for Kiev or, in the worst-case scenario, forcing payment on all Ukraine's remaining dollar bonds if Moscow is not paid on time. Sujata Rao, "As Ukraine's Debt Tangle Unwinds, Russia Holds Key Thread," Reuters, September 24, 2014.

197. Anna Gelpern, "Russia's contract arbitrage," *Capital Markets Law Journal* 9, no. 3 (2014): 308–326. First published online June 25, 2014.

198. Ibid.

199. "The Asian Financial Crisis of 1997–1998," *China Daily*, June 7, 2012.

200. Robert E. Rubin and Jacob Weisberg, *In an Uncertain World: Tough Choices from Wall Street to Washington* (New York: Random House, 2004), 25.

201. Under the country's obligations to NAFTA, Mexican president Carlos Salinas de Gortari implemented a strong economic adjustment program to liberalize trade with Canada and the United States, a decision that boosted Mexican FDI by 40 percent and staved off ripple effects of the currency crisis. Daniel Lederman, William F. Maloney, and Luis Serven, *Lessons from NAFTA for Latin America and the Caribbean* (Washington, D.C.: World Bank, 2005); M. Angeles

Villarreal, "NAFTA and the Mexican Economy," Congressional Research Service, June 3, 2010, 7.

202. Germany, the EU's paymaster, has been at the heart of the euro zone crisis. In the words of Chancellor Merkel, "The progress of [Germany] is as dependent as ever on making headway in Europe and on enduringly overcoming the sovereign debt crisis in earnest." Erik Kirschbaum, "Merkel Says Permanently Fixing Euro Zone Crisis Vital for Germany," Reuters, December 30, 2013; also see Sebastian Dullien and Ulrike Guérot, "The Long Shadow of Ordoliberalism: Germany's Approach to the Euro Crisis," European Council on Foreign Relations, Policy Brief No. 49, February 2012.

203. See Alexander Reisenbichler and Kimberly J. Morgan, "How Germany Won the Euro Crisis," *Foreign Affairs,* June 20, 2013; Jack Ewing, "German Court Validates Participation in Euro Zone Bailout Fund," *New York Times,* March 18, 2014.

204. It is worth emphasizing again that the impetus leading to the European Monetary Union and the euro was geopolitical, not economic. According to economist Martin Feldstein, "European politicians reasoned that the use of a common currency would instill in their publics a greater sense of belonging to a European community and that the shift of responsibility for monetary policy from national capitals to a single central bank in Frankfurt would signal a shift of political power." Feldstein, "The Failure of the Euro," *Foreign Affairs,* January/February 2012.

205. Ernst and Young, "Foreign Investment into Europe Rises despite Eurozone Crisis," June 2012, http://www.ey.com/GL/en/Newsroom/News-releases/News_Foreign-investment-into-Europe-rises-despite-Eurozone-crisis.

206. Take market economy status, for example. At various points in the eurozone crisis, China has rather explicitly conditioned any purchases of European distressed sovereign debt or other investment meant to ease Europe's debt crisis on the EU's willingness to confer market economy status on China. Justin McDonnell, "China-EU Relations: Trade and Beyond," *Diplomat,* April 24, 2014; European Parliament Directorate-General for External Policies, "Trade and Economic Relations with China," Policy Briefing, 2013, 23.

207. Dan Alexander, "The World's Largest Debtor Governments, 2013," *Forbes,* November 8, 2013; Charles Riley, "Even Abenomics Can't Ignore Japan Debt," CNN Money, April 23, 2013.

208. According to U.S. Treasury International Capital Survey data covering June 30, 2011, through June 30, 2012, 58.6 percent of all foreign official holdings of U.S. Treasuries will mature in a period of between one and five years. Multiplying this percentage by the stock of foreign official holdings of all treasures for the same period ($3.489 trillion), total foreign official holdings for the one-to-five-year segment of the U.S. Treasury curve equals $2.5 trillion, which amounts to 55.9 percent of the $3.57 trillion in outstanding one-to-five-year Treasury notes as of the end of June 2012. As Keith Bradsher explained the growing spread between 2-year and 10-year Treasuries: "China has been buying more Treasury bills with a maturity of a year or less, [giving] China the option of cashing out its positions in a hurry, by not rolling over its investments into new Treasury bills as they come due should inflation in the United States start rising and make Treasury securities

less attractive." Keith Bradsher, "China Grows More Picky about Debt," *New York Times,* May 20, 2009.

209. U.S. Treasury International Capital Survey Data, accessed March 2013, www.treasury.gov/resource-center/data-chart-center/tic/Pages/index.aspx.

210. According to former Treasury secretary Hank Paulson, the Russians made a "top-level approach" to the Chinese "that together they might sell big chunks of their GSE [government-sponsored enterprise] holdings to force the U.S. to use its emergency authorities to prop up these companies." Hank Paulson, *On the Brink* (New York: Business Plus, 2010), 161. Paulson declined to offer evidence for his claims; however, coordinated or not, China and Russia did sell off sizeable portions of their GSE debt at the same time. "Nonetheless," write Benn Steil and Paul Swartz, both economic analysts with the Council on Foreign Relations, "both countries dumped GSE debt that summer. Russia sold $170 billion during 2008, while China sold nearly $50 billion between June 2008, when its holdings peaked, and the end of 2008." See Swartz and Steil, "The Dangers of Debt: Chinese and Russian GSE Dumping," *CFR Geo-graphics,* June 15, 2010.

211. Putin walked this back within a few days. As of March 2013, IMF estimates found that roughly 43 percent of Russia's €537 billion of foreign exchange reserves were euro-denominated. *IMF Global Markets Monitor,* March 21, 2013.

212. A withdrawal on this scale is nearly unprecedented; see Matt Phillips, "And Now, It Looks Like Russia May Be Messing with the Fed," *Quartz,* March 14, 2014. While these assets were pulled from the U.S. Federal Reserve holdings, they were not necessarily sold; experts suggest that Russia retained its Treasury holdings but relocated them or registered them under a different name ("Financial Mutually Assured Destruction Keeps Bonds Stable in Crimea Standoff," *Moscow Times,* March 20, 2014). If the $100 billion in bonds has indeed been relocated, analysts further warn that Russia could sell off to the detriment of U.S. financial markets without interference from U.S. authorities; see Patrice Hill, "Economic Cold War?: Weapons in Russia Standoff More Likely to Shed Treasure than Blood," *Washington Times,* March 31, 2014.

213. For detailed descriptions, see Chapter 4.

214. Keith Johnson, "Putin's Gas Gambit Backfires," *Foreign Policy,* December 12, 2013.

215. Jack Farchy, "Russia's Neighbours: Primary Colours," *Financial Times,* June 9, 2014.

216. Rushydro and Inter RAO, the Russian state electricity companies, are both building hydroelectric power plants in Kyrgyzstan.

217. Chen Kane and Miles A. Pomper, "Russia Becomes the Middle East's Preferred but Flawed Nuclear Partner," *World Politics Review,* April 23, 2015.

218. Ibid. Sources suggest that, at least in the case of the Turkey deal, the Russian firms involved do not expect a profit.

219. Ibid.

220. Farchy, "Russia's Neighbours."

221. As China's ambassador to Kazakhstan put it in a June 2014 interview with the *Financial Times,* "The cooperation of one or another country with Kazakhstan is not a zero-sum game. No one stole anyone else's cheese." Ibid.

222. Authors' private conversations in the region.

223. Brian Spegele and Wayne Ma, "For China Boss, Deep-Water Rigs Are a 'Strategic Weapon,'" *Wall Street Journal,* August 29, 2012.

224. "The World in Their Hands: State Capitalism Looks Outward as Well as Inward," *Economist,* January 21, 2012.

225. Approximately 84 percent of Japan's crude oil imports in 2014 came from the Middle East, whereas U.S. imports from the region reached 20 percent. See U.S. Energy Information Administration, "Japan: International Energy Data and Analysis," last updated January 30, 2015, http://www.eia.gov/beta/international /analysis_includes/countries_long/Japan/japan.pdf; "Oil and Gas Emergency Policy— Japan 2013 Update," International Energy Agency, 2013; Florence Tan and James Topham, "Japan to Import Less Oil from Middle East as Demand Peaks," Reuters, August 19, 2013; U.S. Energy Information Administration, "How Much Petroleum Does the United States Import and from Where?," September 14, 2015, http://www .eia.gov/tools/faqs/faq.cfm?id=727&t=6.

226. For details, see Chapter 4.

227. Jack Fahy, "European Supplies in Jeopardy as Putin Warns of a Shut-Off," *Financial Times,* April 11, 2014.

228. Marc Fisher, "Qatar Is Suddenly Investing Heavily in the U.S., Bank-rolling D.C.'s City Center, Other Projects," *Washington Post,* December 17, 2013.

229. Mohsin Khan, "The Gulf and Geoeconomics," *MENASource* blog, Atlantic Council, March 7, 2014.

230. China was one of the few countries not on Washington's list of exemptions from U.S. sanctions over Iran. Eleven countries—including India, South Korea, Turkey, Taiwan, South Africa, Sri Lanka, Malaysia, and Japan—have received exemptions after the administration determined that each country sufficiently reduced, or agreed to reduce, its consumption of Iranian oil. Tennille Tracy, "7 Buyers of Iran Oil Will Avoid Sanctions," *Wall Street Journal,* June 11, 2012; "India and China Ignore U.S. Sanctions against Iran," OilPrice.com, August 20, 2013.

231. Chapter 4 describes how state-bank assets and foreign exchange reserves become ready financing as part of a "going-out" strategy meant to help Chinese SOEs venture abroad (typically in industries labeled "strategic" by Beijing.

232. In some cases, Chinese SOEs have themselves been forthcoming: in an annual 20-F filing with the SEC, China Southern Airlines acknowledged that the "Company is indirectly majority owned by the Chinese government, which may exert influence in a manner that may conflict with the interests of [shareholders]." Andrew Szamosszegi and Cole Kyle, "An Analysis of State-Owned Enterprises and State Capitalism in China," U.S.-China Economic and Security Review Commission, October 26, 2011.

233. In the words of Yang Jiechi, "China is a big country and other countries are small countries, and that's just a fact." John Pomfret, "U.S. Takes a Tougher Tone with China," *Washington Post,* July 30, 2010.

234. For commentary on how the geographies of capital, land, and labor shape Singapore (and neighboring Malaysia and Indonesia), see Matthew Sparke, James D. Sidaway, Tim Bunnell, and Carl Grundy-Warr, "Triangulating the Border-less World: Geographies of Power in the Indonesia-Malaysia-Singapore Growth

Triangle," *Transactions of the Institute of British Geographers* 29, no. 4 (2004): 485–498. As illustrative commentary touting the geoeconomic prowess of Qatar, see, for instance, press reports surrounding the June 2014 prisoner exchange between the U.S. government and the Taliban, including Mark Mazzetti, Eric Schmitt, David E. Sanger, and Helene Cooper, "Behind P.O.W.'s Release, Urgency and Opportunity: Concern for Health of Bowe Bergdahl Drove Prisoner Exchange," *New York Times,* June 4, 2014: "At the same time, much of the fate of the administration's strategy was now in the hands of Qatar, the tiny wealthy emirate that in recent years has used its riches to amass great influence in the Middle East and Central Asia."

235. Devadas Krishnadas, "Sovereign Wealth Funds as Tools of National Strategy: Singapore's Approach," CIWAG Case Study on Irregular Warfare and Armed Groups, U.S. Naval War College, 2013; Jeremy Grant, "Singapore Leads the Pack in Sovereign Wealth Deals," *Financial Times,* November 3, 2014; Jon Grevatt, "Singapore Announces SGD12.56 Billion Defense Budget," *HIS Jane's 360,* February 24, 2014; Dhara Ranasinghe, "Singapore, the Tiny State with Military Clout," CNBC, February 9, 2014.

236. Qatar was an early supporter of Morsi and the Muslim Brotherhood, providing $8 billion in grants and loans to the short-lived Morsi government in Egypt. See, e.g., Khan, "The Gulf and Geoeconomics."

237. Selina Williams, "BP Says North America Shale Oil Boom Will Pressure OPEC," *Wall Street Journal,* January 16, 2013; Clifford Krauss, "OPEC Split as Oil Prices Fall Sharply," *New York Times,* October 13, 2014; "The Future of OPEC," *Forbes,* December 5, 2013.

238. As new financial hubs emerge, financial centers are becoming capable of transacting large-scale deals without requiring dollars or touching U.S. banks. Mike Bird, "Putin's Revenge: Russia and China Try to End the Dominance of the Dollar," *Business Insider,* November 10, 2014; Paoala Subachi and Helena Huang, "The Connecting Dots of China's Renminbi Strategy: London and Hong Kong," Briefing Paper, Chatham House and RUSI, September 2012.

239. "International Finance System and Development, Report of the Secretary-General," United Nations General Assembly, July 2014, www.un.org/csa/ffd/documents/69GA_SGR_IFSD_AUV_250714.pdf.

240. See Scott Snyder, "Sony Hack: North Korea's Toughest Counteraction to Obama's Proportional Response," *Asia Unbound* blog, Council on Foreign Relations, December 24, 2014.

241. David A. Baldwin, *Economic Statecraft* (Princeton, N.J.: Princeton University Press, 1985), 63.

242. Harvard professor and former NSC official Meghan O'Sullivan makes this point aptly with respect to sanctions, cautioning that "sanctions regimes should have different structures to them depending on what objectives they're meant to address. If you want to bring about a change in behavior by a government, you should have a sanctions regime that creates a flexible framework for working through a set of issues and where incremental progress can be acknowledged by the lifting of partial sanctions. If you want to contain a regime, your premium will be on getting multilateral support for your efforts in order to maximize the economic impact of the sanctions regime. "The Limits of New Iran Sanctions," interview with

Meghan L. O'Sullivan, Council on Foreign Relations, July 8, 2010, www.cfr.org /iran/limits-new-iran-sanctions/p22607?cid=rss-iran-the_limits_of_new_iran _sanctio-070810.

4. Geoeconomics in Chinese Foreign Policy

1. James Reilly, "China's Economic Statecraft: Turning Wealth into Power," Lowy Institute, November 2013. For a look at how the United States should rethink its strategy toward China, also see Robert D. Blackwill and Ashley J. Tellis, "Revising U.S. Grand Strategy toward China," Council on Foreign Relations Special Report, April 2015.

2. Leslie Gelb, "GDP Now Matters More than Force," *Foreign Affairs*, November/December 2010.

3. People's Republic of China, "The One-China Principle and the Taiwan Issue," Taiwan Affairs Office and Information Office of the State Council, February 21, 2000.

4. Bruce Gilley, "Not So Dire Straits: How the Finlandization of Taiwan Benefits U.S. Security," *Foreign Affairs*, January/February 2010.

5. Ibid.

6. Reilly, "China's Economic Statecraft."

7. Ross Anthony, Sven Grimm, and Yejoo Kim, "South Africa's Relations with China and Taiwan: Economic Realism and the 'One China' Doctrine," Centre for Chinese Studies, Stellenbosch University, November 2013.

8. Chris Barker, "What Implications Does Rising Chinese Influence Have for Latin America?," E-International Relations Studies, August 13, 2013.

9. "Diplomatic Allies," Ministry of Foreign Affairs, Republic of China (Taiwan), http://www.mofa.gov.tw/en/AlliesIndex.aspx?n=DF6F8F246049F8D6&sms =A76B7230ADF29736.

10. "China Threatens U.S. Firms with Sanctions over Taiwan Arms," *Ria Novosti*, January 30, 2010; Keith Bradsher, "U.S. Deal with Taiwan Has China Retaliating," *New York Times*, January 30, 2010; Andrew Browne and Jay Solomon, "China Threatens U.S. Sanctions over Arms Sale to Taiwan," *Wall Street Journal*, January 31, 2010; James Reilly, "China's Unilateral Sanctions," *Washington Quarterly*, Fall 2012.

11. Reilly, "China's Unilateral Sanctions," 125.

12. Business in Taiwan's IT sector notably slowed around this time, and China opted not to send a delegation to the 2004 Computex IT fair in Taipei. See Murray Scot Tanner, *Chinese Economic Coercion against Taiwan: A Tricky Weapon to Use* (Santa Monica, Calif.: RAND Corporation, 2007), 17. See also Austin Ramzy, "Concession Offered, Taiwan Group to End Protests," *New York Times*, April 7, 2014.

13. Tanner, *Chinese Economic Coercion against Taiwan*, xiv; Jason Dean, "Wikileaks: Singapore's Lee Rates China's Leaders," *Wall Street Journal*, November 30, 2010.

14. Kastner, *Political Conflict and Economic Interdependence across the Taiwan Strait and Beyond*, 79.

15. "Prepared Testimony of David N. Laux, President, USA-ROC Economic Council, before the House Banking and Financial Service Committee," Federal News Service, March 20, 1996; Eric Gartzke and Quan Li, "How Globalization Can Reduce International Conflict," in *Globalization and Armed Conflict*, eds. Nils Petter Gleditsch, Gerald Schneider, and Katherine Barbieri (New York: Rowman & Littlefield, 2003), 123–140.

16. "NT$1.5 Trillion Wiped off Stock Market in Past Week," *Taiwan Economic News*, July 19, 1999; "Cash-Rich State Funds Strive to Staunch Market Decline," *Taiwan Economic News*, July 20, 1999; "Political Uncertainties Cloud Taiwan's Stock Market," *Taiwan Economic News*, July 26, 1999.

17. Lien Chan, "Government Work Report to the Legislative Yuan," Taipei, September 1996.

18. Mark Landler, "Taiwan Lifts Restrictions on Investment in China," *New York Times*, November 8, 2001.

19. Ibid. See also Lin Chieh-yu, "Chen Wants to Lift Direct Links Ban," *Taipei Times*, September 17, 2000.

20. Xin Ming, "Pros and Cons of 'Three Direct Links' between Mainland China and Taiwan," *Epoch Times* (English edition), December 27, 2008; "China's Policy on 'Three Direct Links' across the Taiwan Straits," Xinhua News Agency, December 17, 2003.

21. Reilly, "China's Economic Statecraft."

22. Cindy Sui, "Taiwan at Crossroads in Relationship with China," BBC News, May 21, 2010; "Chinese Mainland, Taiwan Sign Landmark Economic Pact," Xinhua, June 29, 2010.

23. Only in the LED and solar battery manufacturing industries are Chinese companies prohibited from holding controlling power. All other Taiwanese sectors are fair game for mainland investment. See J. Michael Cole, "No Missiles Required: How China Is Buying Taiwan's 'Re-Unification,'" *Diplomat*, August 23, 2013.

24. William Wan, "Taiwan's President, Ma Ying-jeou, Plans to Expand Relations with China," *Washington Post*, October 24, 2013.

25. "Full Transcript: Interview with Taiwanese President Ma Ying-jeou," *Washington Post*, October 24, 2013.

26. "Taiwan Economic and Political Background Note," U.S. Department of State, Bureau of East Asian and Pacific Affairs, February 8, 2012; Reilly, "China's Economic Statecraft."

27. Rachel Rosenthal, "The Burden of Taiwan's Stalled Trade Deal with China," *Wall Street Journal*, May 8, 2015.

28. Ibid.

29. Jean-Pierre Cabestan and Jacques deLisle, *Political Changes in Taiwan under Ma Ying-jeou: Partisan Conflict, Policy Choices, External Constraints and Security Challenges* (New York: Routledge, 2014), 86.

30. "The Name-Change Fever," *China Post*, February 11, 2007.

31. Cheng Chih-yu, Chi-yuan Liang, and Chu-chia Lin, "An Evaluation of Taiwan's Economic Performance after 2000," *Taiwan Development Perspectives 2003* (Taipei: National Policy Foundation, 2003), 73–91.

32. "Taiwan Gov't Halves Daily Slide Limit to Stabilize Stock Market," *Taiwan Economic News,* March 27, 2000.

33. Kastner, *Political Conflict and Economic Interdependence across the Taiwan Strait and Beyond,* 84. Commentary from *People's Daily* verbally attacked "green" (pro-independence) Taiwanese businessmen, calling Chi Mei founder Hsu Wenlung a "shameless" anti-Chinese bigot, for instance. Tanner, *Chinese Economic Coercion,* 127–129.

34. Tanner, *Chinese Economic Coercion,* 127–129.

35. "China Attacks Chi Mei over 'Ideology,'" *Taipei Times,* June 1, 2004.

36. "Back to the Kowtow," *Wall Street Journal,* June 2, 2004; "Pro-Independence Investors Not Welcome," *China Daily,* June 22, 2004.

37. "Pro-Independence Investors Not Welcome."

38. Chi-hung Wei, "China's Economic Offensive and Taiwan's Defensive Measures," *China Quarterly* 215 (September 2013): 644.

39. Ibid., 645.

40. Keith Bradsher, "Election Outcome in Taiwan Buoys Stock Market," *New York Times,* March 25, 2008.

41. Beijing has offered its official support on multiple occasions, including in 2003 and again in 2005, when Chinese President Hu Jintao reassured the Taishang that the business leaders have an important part to play in strengthening cross-strait relations. Tanner, *Chinese Economic Coercion against Taiwan.*

42. Sofia Wu "Taiwan Eyes Currency Swap Pact with China," *Focus Taiwan,* November 11, 2013.

43. Jing Song, "Taiwan Nears Formosa Bonds Landmark," *Finance Asia,* December 4, 2013; Kathryn Chiu, "Formosa Bonds of Mainland's State-Owned Banks Hit GreTai," *China Post,* December 10, 2013. Note: While *renminbi* (or RMB) is the formal term most often used by the Chinese government for China's currency, the term "yuan" refers to the actual unit and is also frequently used interchangeably with RMB. The two are used interchangeably in this book.

44. RMB deposits in Taiwan are the second-largest among foreign currency deposits on the island, ranking behind the U.S. dollar but ahead of the yen and euro. RMB settlements handled by the Taipei branch of the Bank of China alone, for instance, amounted to RMB 700 billion at the end of 2013, while remittances surpassed RMB 290 billion. See "Taiwan Eyes Currency Swap Pact with China."

45. Debby Wu, "Taiwan Dives into the Competition for 'Hub' Status," *Asian Review,* December 4, 2014.

46. "Chinese Firm Signs Tainan Milkfish Deal," *Taipei Times,* March 5, 2011.

47. Du Yu, "Chinese Delegation Comes Fishing," *Taipei Times,* February 25, 2012.

48. Ibid.

49. The Investment Commission of Taiwan's Ministry of Economic Affairs announced in 2013 stricter rules for investment projects by Chinese companies, including the right to refuse any investments that are politically sensitive. Justina Lee and Argin Chang, "Taiwan Restricts Chinese Investment amid Trade Pact Review," *Bloomberg Business,* November 13, 2013.

50. For an overview of these events, see Jonathan Spangler, "Taiwan and the Future of the Cross-Strait Service Trade Agreement," *Diplomat,* March 27, 2014;

Jenny Hsu, "Thousands Protest Taiwan's Trade Pact With China," *Wall Street Journal,* March 30, 2014; Austin Ramzy, "Concession Offered, Taiwan Group to End Protests," *New York Times,* April 7, 201; Michael Gold and James Pomfret, "Over 100,000 Protest in Taiwan over China Trade Deal," Reuters, March 30, 2014.

51. The agreement's many opponents worry it will leave Taiwan vulnerable to increased political pressure from Beijing if Chinese state-owned companies are able to own Taiwanese hospitals, supermarkets, and taxi companies. "The Chinese Communist party's 'united front' policy emphasizes the use of money to buy loyalty," as Michael Anti, a prominent political commentator on China, explained to the *Financial Times* in June 2014. Anderlini, "Thousands of Taiwanese Rally against Closer Ties with China."

52. "Army Says Mainland Cyberattacks Thwarted," *Liberty Times,* March 14, 2000; John Leyden, "Taiwanese Engineer 'Assisted Mainland Hackers,'" *Register* (UK), May 27, 2004; "Hackers Attack Taiwan Military News Agency Ahead of Drill," Agence France-Presse, July 20, 2000.

53. Russell Hsiao, "Critical Node: Taiwan's Cyber Defense and Chinese Cyber-Espionage," *China Brief* 13, no. 24 (December 2013).

54. Ibid.

55. Sarah Mishkin, "China Rejects Allegations It Hacked Taiwan Networks," *Financial Times,* April 29, 2013.

56. Tanner, *Chinese Economic Coercion against Taiwan,* xvi.

57. Where Chinese attempts to capitalize on this interdependence are coercive, it will mean costs for both sides. To take one example, both countries would suffer if China were to withhold rare earths, which are extracted in China and sent to electronics manufacturers in Taiwan (and it would likely spell an end to Apple products that are "assembled in China" and "designed in California"). But the dependencies are far greater for Taiwan. Taiwan's economic livelihood, as well as its national security, requires that Taipei secure the surrounding waters and have access to global sea-lanes. The island's population is almost entirely dependent on imports for energy and highly vulnerable on food imports. China's desire for regional maritime dominance and Taiwan's recent rejection of cooperation with China to advance Chinese maritime territorial claims could put Taiwan's access to global sea-lanes in jeopardy. See, e.g., Dean Cheng, "Taiwan's Maritime Security: A Critical American Interest," Heritage Foundation, March 19, 2014.

58. In 2012, Taiwan's trade represented 140 percent of GDP and was valued at over $650 billion, making it the world's nineteenth-largest trader even though it is only the twenty-eighth-largest economy in the world. Joshua Meltzer, "Taiwan's Economic Opportunities and Challenges and the Importance of the Trans-Pacific Partnership," East Asia Policy Paper Series no. 2, Brookings Institution, January 2014.

59. Gordon G. Chang, "Fatal Attraction: China's Strengthening Partnership with North Korea," *World Affairs Journal,* May/June 2011; Evan Osnos, "Lips and Teeth," *Letter from China* blog, *Atlantic,* November 24, 2010.

60. Jaewoo Choo, "Mirroring North Korea's Growing Economic Dependence on China: Political Ramifications," *Asian Survey* 48, no. 2 (March/April 2008): 344–345.

61. Dick K. Nanto and Mark E. Manyin, "China–North Korea Relations," Congressional Research Service, December 28, 2010.

62. Choo, "Mirroring North Korea's Growing Economic Dependence on China," 348; Bates Gill, "China's North Korea Policy," United States Institute of Peace Special Report, July 2011.

63. Beina Xu and Jayshree Bajoria, "The China–North Korea Relationship," CFR Backgrounder, Council on Foreign Relations, August 22, 2014. Estimates for North Korea's trade dependence range dramatically, with some South Korean statistics stating that China accounts for 90 percent of North Korea's global trade. However, Bonnie Glaser, an expert on China at the Center for Strategic and International Studies (CSIS), reasons this figure is likely too high. Transcript, "China and Japan's Perspectives on North Korea," Council on Foreign Relations meeting, October 21, 2014.

64. Fertilizers dataset (2002–2010), Food and Agriculture Organization of the United Nations, http://data.fao.org/dataset?entryId=d1a87a6c-37a8-43be-bfdc-c5cb398a1956; "China Sends Aid to North Korea despite Sanctions," Radio Free Asia, May 14, 2013; Choo, "Mirroring North Korea's Growing Economic Dependence on China," 351; Seong Yeon-cheol and Park Hyun, "China to Resume Food Aid to North Korea," *Hankyoreh,* May 16, 2013; "2012 Food Aid Flows," World Food Program, http://documents.wfp.org/stellent/groups/public/documents/newsroom/wfp262299.pdf.

65. "朝鲜向中国售大量黄金, 金正日曾要求打死都不卖 [North Korea Sells Large Amount of Gold to China, Kim Jong Un Demands Sales]," China Sougou News, December 12, 2013; Huang Shurong, "Gold Sales Raise Questions over Possible N Korean Economic Crisis," *Want China Times,* December 12, 2013.

66. Doug Bandow, "The Complex Calculus of a North Korean Collapse," *National Interest,* January 9, 2014; Frank Sampson Jannuzi, "Can the United States Cause the Collapse of North Korea? Should We Try?," Council on Foreign Relations, January 13, 1999.

67. Tania Branigan, "China's Patience with North Korea Wears Thin after Latest Nuclear Tests," *Guardian,* February 12, 2013; Jeremy Page, "China Builds up Its Links to North Korea," *Wall Street Journal,* June 6, 2013; Jane Perlez, "China Says It Won't Forsake North Korea, despite Support for U.N. Sanctions," *New York Times,* March 9, 2013.

68. Jonathan Watts, "China Cuts Oil Supply to North Korea," *Guardian,* March 31, 2003.

69. "China Didn't Export Crude Oil to North Korea in Q1," Yonhap News Agency, April 24, 2014; Dean Cheng, "The Odd Couple: China and North Korea," *National Interest,* May 12, 2014.

70. Koichiro Ishida, "China Holding Up Shipment of Iranian Petroleum to North Korea," *Asahi Shimbun,* October 20, 2013.

71. Choo, "Mirroring North Korea's Growing Economic Dependence on China," 349.

72. Bonnie S. Glaser et al., *Reordering Chinese Priorities on the Korean Peninsula* (Washington, D.C.: CSIS, November 2012).

73. Miles Yu, "China Wins 50-Year Control of Strategic North Korea Port in $3-Billion Deal," *World Tribune,* February 28, 2012.

74. These will include high-speed rail links running from Yanji to the North Korean border; Dandong and Sinuiju; and Beijing and Kaesong via Pyongyang. See Page, "China Builds Up Its Links to North Korea"; Christopher Green, "Hong, Jang, and the Mysterious Railroad Deal," *Sino-NK,* December 12, 2013.

75. Lee Jong-Heon, "N. Korea Deal Would Barter Major Mines for China-Funded High-Speed Rail Network," *East Asia Intel,* November 29, 2013.

76. Page, "China Builds Up Its Links to North Korea"; Green, "Hong, Jang, and the Mysterious Railroad Deal."

77. Nathaniel Aden, "North Korean Trade with China as Reported in Chinese Customs Statistics: 1995–2009 Energy and Minerals Trends and Implications," NAPSNet Special Reports, Nautilus Institute for Security and Sustainability, June 7, 2011.

78. Jane Perlez, "China-Korea Tensions Rise after Failed Venture," *New York Times,* October 20, 2012; Elizabeth Economy, "Beijing's North Korea Problem," *Diplomat,* February 14, 2013.

79. Shannon Tiezzi, "China Keeping Close Eye on North Korea," *Diplomat,* December 13, 2013; Drew Thompson, "Silent Partners: Chinese Joint Ventures in North Korea," U.S.-Korea Institute report, February 2011, 4.

80. Choo, "Mirroring North Korea's Growing Economic Dependence on China," 367.

81. Stephan Haggard and Weiyi Shi, "Chinese Investment in North Korea: Some Data (Part I)," *North Korea: Witness to Transformation* blog, Peterson Institute for International Economics, June 30, 2014.

82. Page, "China Builds Up Its Links to North Korea."

83. This is, of course, supplementing the Chinese role in development of these SEZs. See Park Seong Guk, "Chinese RMB to Be Legal Tender in SEZs," *DailyNK,* September 27, 2012.

84. "China Aims to Kickstart N. Korea Talks," *China Daily,* October 17, 2004; Mark Magnier, "Chinese Visitor Gives a Boost to North Korea," *Los Angeles Times,* October 30, 2005.

85. "Classified documents seen by The Daily Telegraph show that Beijing has failed to act when confronted with evidence that Chinese companies are breaking UN Resolution 1874 and helping North Korea to build long range missiles" (Julian Ryall, "Chinese Firms Breaking UN Embargo on North Korea," *Telegraph,* June 8, 2012); Malcolm Moore, "China Breaking UN Sanctions to Support North Korea," *Telegraph,* April 13, 2013.

86. Hugh Griffiths and Lawrence Dermody, "Loopholes in UN Sanctions against North Korea," 38 North, May 6, 2014.

87. Neil MacFarquhar, "North Korean Military Parts Were Intercepted, U.N. Says," *New York Times,* February 26, 2010.

88. "A Glance at Seizures of North Korea Weapons Shipments," CNN, July 16, 2013; Jay Solomon, "North Korea's Illegal Weapons Pipeline Flows On," *Wall Street Journal,* November 29, 2012.

89. Moore, "China Breaking UN Sanctions to Support North Korea"; Megha Rajagopalan, "China Says Banned Exports to North Korea Not Meant as Punishment," Reuters, September 24, 2013; "North Korean Account Closed by Bank of China," China.org.cn, May 8, 2013.

90. Moore, "China Breaking UN Sanctions to Support North Korea."

91. Page, "China Builds Up Its Links to North Korea." As Asia expert Max Fisher put it, '"And it also uses the trade as leverage to reign in North Korea a bit; without that leverage, China worries North Korea's provocations could go too far, leading to war. The regime's collapse would likely end with Korea's reunification under the South Korean government, which currently hosts tens of thousands of US troops. China doesn't want that on its border." Max Fisher, "This Chart Shows How North Korea Gets Away with Such Bad Behavior," Vox, December 17, 2015.

92. Zhu Chao, "Unwavering China-Japan Economic Relations Hardly Do without Political Trust," China Daily, November 22, 2013; "Geo-political Disputes and Economic Links Mark Sino-Japanese Relations," China Post, January 8, 2014.

93. "Latest China-Japan Spat: Who's Voldemort?," New York Times, January 9, 2014; Keiichi Hayashi, "China Risks Becoming Asia's Voldemort," Telegraph, January 5, 2014; Liu Xiaoming, "China and Britain Won the War Together," Telegraph, January 1, 2014.

94. "Who Really Owns the Senkaku Islands?," Economist, December 3, 2013.

95. Robert Marquand, "Why the Past Still Separates China and Japan," Christian Science Monitor, August 20, 2001; "China Reported to Cut Car Import Quota from Japan," China Daily, June 4, 2001.

96. Jonathan Watts, "Violence Flares as the Chinese Rage at Japan," Guardian, April 16, 2005.

97. "China Tells Citizens Not to Hold Anti-Japan Protests," Kyodo, September 19, 2012.

98. "Further on Firms Saying China Tightens Customs Inspections from Japan," Agence France-Presse, September 21, 2012; "Japanese Businesses Booted from Major China Trade Fair," Japan Times, September 27, 2012; "Japan Tossed from Trade Fair," Investor's Business Daily, September 27, 2012.

99. Phred Dvorak, Atsuko Fukase, and Dinny McMahon, "China Banks Pull out of Meetings in Japan," Wall Street Journal, October 2, 2012, cited in Reilly, "China's Economic Statecraft."

100. "News Summary: Island Standoff Hits Japan Business," Associated Press, October 9, 2012; Richard Katz, "Mutual Assured Production: Why Trade Will Limit Conflict between China and Japan," Foreign Affairs 92, no. 4 (2013): 22.

101. Keith Bradsher, "Amid Tension, China Blocks Vital Exports to Japan," New York Times, September 22, 2010; Daniel Drezner, "Three Ways of Looking at Chinese Economic Statecraft," Foreign Policy, October 20, 2010; Paul Krugman, "Rare and Foolish," New York Times, October 17, 2010.

102. According to some reports, Japan was smart and able to circumvent China's retaliatory measures. Beijing interfered with customs to prevent products made with rare earths or requiring rare earths from being shipped, forcing Japan to look to its neighbors and request that they purchase rare earths on Japan's behalf and ship directly to Tokyo. Bradsher, "Amid Tension, China Blocks Vital Exports to

Japan"; Keith Bradsher, "China Is Said to Resume Shipping Rare Earth Minerals," *New York Times*, October 20, 2010; Bonnie S. Glaser, "China's Coercive Economic Diplomacy," *Diplomat*, July 25, 2012.

103. Keith Bradsher, "Specialists in Rare Earths Say a Trade Case against China May Be Too Late," *New York Times*, March 14, 2012; Clayton Bradley Doss III, "Coercive Levers in Chinese Economic Statecraft: Attributed across Earth, Rarely Apparent," Naval Postgraduate School, Monterey, Calif., 2012; Yuko Inoue and Julie Gordon, "Analysis: Japanese Rare Earth Consumers Set Up Shop in China," Reuters, August 12, 2011; "Toyota to Make Hybrid Car Parts in China to Boost Sales," BBC, September 5, 2011.

104. Ian Johnson, "China Takes a Sharper Tone in Dispute with Japan," *International New York Times*, September 22, 2010.

105. Doss, "Coercive Levers in Chinese Economic Statecraft."

106. Yun Zhang, "China's Economic Statecraft and the Diaoyu/Senkaku Dispute," *Harvard Asia Quarterly* 16, no. 1 (Spring 2014).

107. Ibid.

108. Jane Perlez, "China Accuses Japan of Stealing after Purchase of Group of Disputed Islands," *New York Times*, September 11, 2012.

109. "Poll: Two-Thirds of Chinese Boycotted Japanese Goods over Senkakus Dispute," *Japan Times*, January 6, 2013.

110. Tensions with China were an important contributing factor, although not the sole culprit, behind Japan's deteriorating export performance in 2012; weak demand from Europe, for example, weighed on Japan's worldwide export levels. See Ben Mclannahan, "Japanese Exports Hit by China Dispute," *Financial Times*, October 22, 2012.

111. "Japan Reports Worst September Trade Figures in 30 Years," *Telegraph*, October 22, 2012; "Japan Nears Recession amid China Boycott," Sky News, November 12, 2012.

112. "China Cuts Rare-Earths Mine Permits 41% to Boost Control," *Bloomberg Business*, September 14, 2012; "China Uses Its Control of Rare Earth Minerals to Punish Japan," *Ottawa Citizen*, September 23, 2012.

113. "China-Japan Dispute Takes Rising Toll on Top Asian Economies," *Bloomberg Business*, January 9, 2013.

114. Jin Baisong, "Consider Sanctions on Japan," *China Daily*, September 17, 2012; Ambrose Evans-Pritchard, "Beijing Hints at Bond Attack on Japan," *Telegraph*, September 18, 2012.

115. World Trade Organization, Article XXI, "Security Exceptions"; Jin, "Consider Sanctions on Japan."

116. Shen Hong, "Japan-Linked Shares Tumble in Shanghai, Hong Kong," *Wall Street Journal*, September 17, 2012.

117. Li Jiabao, "Chinese Investment in Japan Drops 9 Percent," *China Daily*, July 17, 2013.

118. Ibid., 12.

119. "Cyber-attack Stole Mitsubishi Warplane, Nuke Plant Data," *Asahi Shimbun*, October 24, 2011; "Japan Defence Firm Mitsubishi Heavy in Cyber Attack," BBC News, September 20, 2011.

120. Reilly, "China's Economic Statecraft," 10.

121. "With Eye on China, India and Japan to Bolster Defence Ties," *Times of India*, January 7, 2014; Toko Sekiguchi and Yoshio Takahashi, "Japan, Asean Pledge to Work More Closely Together," *Wall Street Journal*, December 15, 2013; Carl Thayer, "Vietnam's Extensive Strategic Partnership with Japan," *Diplomat*, October 14, 2014.

122. J. Berkshire Miller, "With Eye on China, Japan Ramps Up Pacific Island Security Ties," *World Politics Review*, June 4, 2015.

123. Reilly, "China's Economic Statecraft," 10.

124. Ibid.

125. Ibid.

126. Ibid.

127. "The Dragon's New Teeth," *Economist*, April 7, 2012; "China's Aggressive Stance Reveals Lack of Coordination," *Yale Global*, December 5, 2012.

128. Analyses view the exclusive economic zone as part of either a "salami-slicing" strategy, whereby Beijing employs incremental actions to gradually change the regional status quo in China's favor, or as part of a "cabbage strategy," where control over disputed islands is consolidated—like the leaves of a cabbage—in successive layers of occupation and protection. Ronald O'Rourke, "Maritime Territorial and Exclusive Economic Zone (EEZ) Disputes Involving China: Issues for Congress," Congressional Research Service, August 5, 2014.

129. James Hardy, "China Expands Runway, Harbor at Woody Island," *IHS Jane's 360*, August 29, 2014; Shannon Tiezzi, "China Discovers Gas Field in the South China Sea," *Diplomat*, September 16, 2014.

130. Extending from the coast of mainland China through the South China Sea, the Strait of Malacca, across the Indian Ocean, and eventually on to the Arabian Sea and Persian Gulf, these geopolitical way markers would advance Chinese forward deployment and power projection capabilities along crucial sea lines of communication.

131. John J. Mearsheimer, "Can China Rise Peacefully?," *National Interest*, October 25, 2014.

132. Ibid.; Patrick M. Cronin, "The Strategic Significance of the South China Sea," (paper submitted for the CSIS "Managing Tensions in the South China Sea" conference, Washington, D.C., June 5–6, 2013).

133. Cronin, "The Strategic Significance of the South China Sea."

134. Pierre Tran, "Vietnam Has Much at Stake in S. China Sea," *Defense News*, March 28, 2015; Minnie Chan, "Southern Air Defence Zone 'Crucial for China in Long Term,' PLA Expert Says," *South China Morning Post*, February 22, 2014; "Announcement of the Aircraft Identification Rules for the East China Sea—Air Defense Identification Zone of the PRC," Xinhua News Agency, November 23, 2013.

135. Glaser, "China's Coercive Economic Diplomacy."

136. "China Attempts to Raise Electricity Price, Vietnam under Hard Pressure," *Vietnam Breaking News*, March 16, 2011; "Inside the China-Philippines Fight in the South China Sea," *International Herald Tribune*, May 15, 2012; James Reilly, "China's Unilateral Sanctions," *Washington Quarterly*, Fall 2012, 121–133; "Phil-

ippines Feels the Economic Cost of Standing Up to China," *Christian Science Monitor,* May 15, 2012; "South China Sea: China, Vietnam Clash over Oil Exploration, Fishing," *International Business Times,* December 6, 2012.

137. Anders S. Corr and Priscilla A. Tacujan, "Chinese Political and Economic Influence in the Philippines: Implications for Alliances and the South China Sea Dispute," *Journal of Political Risk* 1, no. 3 (July 2013).

138. "Vietnam Weighs Sea Rights against China Business," *Bloomberg Business,* May 28, 2014.

139. Association of Southeast Asian Nations External Trade Statistics, http://www .asean.org/resources/2012-02-10-08-47-55/asean-statistics/item/external-trade -statistics-3; "Chinese Ambassador—China Values President Sang's Visit," *Asia News Monitor,* June 19, 2013; "Indonesia Expresses Interest in New Shanghai Free Trade Zone," *Asia News Monitor,* October 8, 2013; "Indonesia Signs Investment MOU with China's Anhui Province," Xinhua News Agency, April 24, 2013; Bao Chang, "China Playing a Rising Role in ASEAN Business," *China Daily* (Asia), October 11, 2013; Yantoultra Ngui, "China Elevates Malaysia Ties, Aims to Triple Trade by 2017," *Reuters,* October 4, 2013.

140. Author interview with Bonnie Glaser, August 2014.

141. In Vietnam, imports from China doubled in value between 2009 and 2013. Chinese goods accounted for 28 percent of imports and are expected to account for more than half by 2020. Tran, "Vietnam Has Much at Stake in S. China Sea."

142. Ibid.

143. Madhu Sudan Ravindran, "China's Potential for Economic Coercion in the South China Sea Disputes: A Comparative Study of the Philippines and Vietnam," *Journal of Current Southeast Asian Affairs,* March 2012, 119.

144. Christopher Johnson, comments at Asia Forecast 2014, CSIS, January 29, 2014; Fareed Zakaria, "Southeast Asia Ponders What Is Going On in China," *Washington Post,* October 24, 2013.

145. Reilly, "China's Economic Statecraft"; Milton Osborne, "New Numbers on China's Cambodia Aid," *Interpreter,* Lowy Institute for International Policy, September 19, 2012.

146. Glaser, "China's Coercive Economic Diplomacy."

147. Ravindran, "China's Potential for Economic Coercion in the South China Sea Disputes," 118.

148. Reilly, "China's Economic Statecraft."

149. Paul Mooney, "South East Asia Faces Renewed Unity Test as South China Sea Tensions Spike," Reuters, May 9, 2014.

150. Andrew Higgins and David E. Sanger, "3 European Powers Say They Will Join China-Led Bank," *New York Times,* March 17, 2015; "China's $50 Billion Asia Bank Snubs Japan, India," *Bloomberg Business,* May 12, 2014.

151. "Now that the United States has lost the battle, it has softened its position, saying that it will encourage the World Bank and the Asian Development Bank to cooperate with the new bank, provided projects meet certain standards. Yet the shift to a more constructive position was viewed as late, and the repercussions of what many considered poor handling by Washington were on display at the Boao Forum for Asia." Jane Perlez, "Stampede to Join China's Development Bank Stuns

Even Its Founder," *New York Times*, April 2, 2015; also see Gabriel Wildau, "China Backs Up Silk Road Ambitions with $62bn Capital Injection," *Financial Times*, April 20, 2015.

152. "China-Led Asia Infrastructure Bank Gains Support from 21 Countries," Reuters, September 28, 2014; "Canberra Set to Sign for China-Led Bank," *Australian*, October 13, 2014.

153. Jane Perlez, "U.S. Opposing China's Answer to World Bank," *New York Times*, October 9, 2014.

154. Reilly, "China's Economic Statecraft."

155. Ibid.

156. Ibid.

157. Ibid.

158. China's geographic vulnerabilities have not escaped the notice of U.S. war planners. A 2015 Department of Defense report to Congress on China mapped out choke points for Chinese energy imports, a move likely to have caught attention in Beijing. While the U.S. Navy retains uncontested supremacy over the open ocean, resource constraints—and the risks posed by China's increasing anti-ship capabilities in its near seas—make it likely that U.S. forces would concentrate on blocking the choke points in the event of hostilities. Office of the Secretary of Defense, "Annual Report to Congress: Military and Security Developments Involving the People's Republic of China 2015," April 2015.

159. Jane Perlez, "China Looks to High-Speed Rail to Expand Reach," *New York Times*, August 8, 2014.

160. Ibid.

161. "China, Laos Ready to Launch Negotiations on Railway Cooperation," Xinhua News Agency, April 8, 2014; David Eimer, "China's 120mph Railway Arriving in Laos," *Telegraph*, January 14, 2014.

162. Eimer, "China's 120 mph Railway Arriving in Laos." For China, a strong relationship with Laos would also prove a conduit for developing greater access to shorter land trade routes to Southeast Asia.

163. Geoff Wade makes this point capably in Perlez, "China Looks to High-Speed Rail to Expand Reach." Additionally, China has been struggling to build a similar cross-continental railway in South America, where long-held fears that America may one day try to restrict China's access to the Panama Canal have prompted it to start working with its South American partners on a series of "dry canals" across the region. While China has promised hundreds of billions of dollars to countries involved in the projects, a combination of environmental concerns, red tape, and unease over the future of the Chinese economy after its stock market plunged in August 2015 have all caused delays in the projects. See Simon Romero, "China's Ambitious Rail Projects Crash Into Harsh Realities in Latin America," *New York Times*, October 3, 2015.

164. The latter bid was made alongside two local partners; China's State Grid emerged with 40 percent ownership of total shares, marking the first time a Chinese grid company has won a franchise for operating national power in a foreign country. Roel Landingin and Richard McGregor, "China State Grid Group Wins Philippine Auction," *Financial Times*, December 12, 2007; "State Grid Invested

Transmission Networks in the Philippines," Invest in China website, Investment Promotion Agency, Ministry of Commerce, Beijing, February 16, 2009.

165. "Philippine National Grid Denies Claims China Could Shut off Power," *South China Morning Post*, March 26, 2014.

166. Wu Jiao and Zhang Yunbi, "Xi in Call for Building of New 'Maritime Silk Road,'" *China Daily*, October 10, 2013. While the claim may be minor, it is definitely a claim: Beijing's line includes waters that Indonesia claims. "The Natuna waters . . . are part of Riau Islands Province in Indonesia, located along the southern part of the strategic Strait of Malacca. They are part of the South China Sea" (Zachary Keck, "China's Newest Maritime Dispute," *Diplomat*, March 20, 2014). "With 80% of its oil imports traversing through the strait—and this [statistic] continues to increase—China has an obvious reason to be worried about the threat that piracy and maritime terrorism pose to the security of its oil supply" (Caroline Vavro, "Piracy, Terrorism and the Balance of Power in the Malacca Strait," *Canadian Naval Review* 4, no. 1 [Spring 2008]: 16). Hu Jintao also warned at one point that certain major powers were attempting to control Malacca, but PRC has not asked to be involved in the security provisions for the Strait. As such, China's diplomatic initiatives in the region (sometimes called its "maritime silk road" or its "string of pearls strategy") matter; China's development of ports, cultivation of diplomatic ties with littoral states along vital sea lanes, and so on, offer Beijing a means of being involved without being involved (see Shi Hongtao, "China's 'Malacca Dilemma.'" *China Youth Daily*, June 15, 2004).

167. Wildau, "China Backs Up Silk Road Ambitions with $62bn Capital Injection"; "The Grand Design of China's New Trade Routes," *Stratfor Global Intelligence*, June 24, 2015.

168. Gregory B. Poling, "Dynamic Equilibrium: Indonesia's Blueprint for a 21st Century Asia Pacific," CSIS, March 8, 2013.

169. "Indonesia Expresses Interest in New Shanghai Free Trade Zone"; "Indonesia Signs Investment MOU with China's Anhui Province."

170. Reilly, "China's Economic Statecraft."

171. Ibid.

172. Fareed Zakaria, "With an Absent United States, China Marches On," *Washington Post*, July 2, 2015.

173. Ibid.

174. Glaser, "China's Coercive Economic Diplomacy." (According to Glaser, "Beijing has provided over $10 billion in aid to Cambodia. In 2011 alone the amount of foreign investment pledged to Phnom Penh by China was 10 times greater than that promised by the United States.") In the latest available statistics from the Cambodia Investment Board, released in 2012, Chinese investment pledged in Cambodia has totaled $9.1 billion since 1994, including almost $1.2 billion in 2011—eight times more than the United States. See "Economic Overview of Cambodia," Cambodia Investment Board, 2013 Guidebook, https://docs.google.com/viewer?url=https://dl.dropboxusercontent.com/u/17527828/cdc_guide_book2013/2014/03/2.ECONOMIC-OVERVIEW-OF-CAMBODIA_eng.pdf.

175. Andrew R. C. Marshall and Prak Chan Thul, "Insight: Cambodia's $11 Billion Mystery," Reuters, February 13, 2013.

176. "Myanmar: Earthquake 2011, List of All Commitments/Contributions and Pledges as of 19 December 2014," Financial Tracking Service, United Nations Office for the Coordination of Humanitarian Affairs, March 2011, http://fts.unocha .org/reports/daily/ocha_R10_E16053_asof__1411251426.pdf.

177. "China Offers Humanitarian Aid of 500,000 USD to Quake-Hit Myanmar," Xinhua, March 26, 2011; "China Provides Aid for Resettlement of Myanmar Homeless," Xinhua, December 31, 2012.

178. "China Provides Aid for Resettlement of Myanmar Homeless."

179. "Sino-Myanmar Gas Pipeline Becomes Fully Operational," *The Hindu,* October 20, 2013.

180. Aung Shin, "Contested Sino-Myanmar Oil Pipeline Nears Completion," *Myanmar Times,* November 17, 2013.

181. Sophie Song, "Myanmar Copper Mine Will Receive $997 Million from Chinese Investor Following Local Protests," *IBI Times,* July 31, 2013.

182. "Authorities Open Fire on Myanmar Copper Mine Protesters," Radio Free Asia, November 15, 2013; "Myanmar to Get Bigger Slice of Profits at China-Backed Copper Mine," *South China Morning Post,* October 3, 2013.

183. Seamus Martov, "Myitsone Dam Project on Hold, but Far from Dead," *The Irrawaddy,* November 6, 2013. See also, Thomas Fuller, "Resentment of China Spreading in Myanmar," *New York Times,* May 19, 2014.

184. Zin Linn, "Burma: Will the Myitsone Dam Project Resume?," *Asia Correspondent,* September 10, 2013.

185. Perlez, "China Looks to High-Speed Rail to Expand Reach."

186. Paul Mooney, "ASEAN Faces Renewed Unity Test as South China Sea Tensions Spike," Reuters, May 10, 2014.

187. Ely Ratner, "China Undeterred and Unapologetic," *War on the Rocks,* June 24, 2014; Ely Ratner, "A Plan to Counter Chinese Aggression," *Wall Street Journal,* June 10, 2014.

188. IMF, Direction of Trade Statistics, IMF e-Library, Myanmar, http://data.imf .org/?sk=253a4049-e94d-4228-b99d-561553731322&sId=1390030109571.

189. Leon T. Hadar, "U.S. Sanctions against Burma," Trade Policy Analysis, Cato Institute, March 26, 1998; "China to Ignore U.S. Sanctions on Myanmar," Al-Jazeera, July 16, 2003.

190. Perlez, "China Looks to High-Speed Rail to Expand Reach."

191. "Li Raises Four-Point Proposal on Upgrading China-Vietnam Business Cooperation," Xinhua News Agency, October 15, 2013.

192. Chun Han Wong, "Beijing, Singapore in Currency Pact," *Wall Street Journal,* October 22, 2013.

193. "China's 'All-Weather' Threat to India," *Diplomat,* August 8, 2013.

194. Christina Wagner, "Soft Power and Foreign Policy: Emerging China and its Impact on India," in *Emerging China: Prospects for Partnership in Asia,* ed. Sudhir T. Devare, Swaran Singh, and Reena Marwah (New Delhi: Routledge, 2012).

195. As Husain Haqqani, former Pakistani ambassador to the United States, once put it, "For China, Pakistan is a low-cost secondary deterrent to India," while "for Pakistan, China is a high-value guarantor of security against India." Ra-

mananda Sengupta, "Evaluating a Rocky India-China-Pakistan Relationship," February 2010, Al Jazeera Centre for Studies.

196. Jamal Afridi and Jayshree Bajoria, "China-Pakistan Relations," Backgrounder, Council on Foreign Relations, July 6, 2010.

197. As if to telegraph just how delicately China treats its ongoing military cooperation with Pakistan, during a May 2013 visit by Chinese premier Li to Pakistan, China's Xinhua state news agency said Beijing was looking for "pragmatic" military cooperation with Pakistan, "which is in the front line of the fight against international terrorism," and reiterated that "the military exchanges are not directed against any third party and contribute to peace and stability in both the region and the whole world." Nick Macfie, "China's Li Offers to Help End Pakistan Energy Crisis," Reuters, May 22, 2013.

198. Khurram Shahzad, "Pakistan Turns to China for Development Aid," *China Post,* December 9, 2013.

199. Jane Perlez, "China Gives Pakistan 50 Fighter Jets," *New York Times.*

200. See, e.g., James Crabtree and Victor Mallet, "India Confident of Overtaking China's Growth Rate, *Financial Times,* May 17, 2015. See also James Gruber, "Why India Will Soon Outpace China," *Forbes,* May 4, 2014. "First," Gruber explains, "it's highly probable that China's GDP growth rate is slowing much more than the fraudulent figures put out by the government. . . . Second, credit tightening in China will almost certainly take years rather than months given the boom which preceded it."

201. With plans to establish a new development bank, the BRICS grouping is widely seen as a counter to existing Western financial and political institutions such as the World Bank, the International Monetary Fund, and the G7. (See the "Financial and Monetary Policy" section of Chapter 3.)

202. "U.S. Relations with Pakistan," U.S. Department of State, September 10, 2014, http://www.state.gov/r/pa/ei/bgn/3453.htm.

203. Rajshree Jetly, "Sino-Pakistan Strategic Entente: Implications for Regional Security," Institute of South Asian Studies, National University of Singapore, Working Paper No. 143, February 14, 2012.

204. Susan B. Epstein and K. Alan Kronstadt, "Pakistan: U.S. Foreign Assistance," Congressional Research Service, July 1, 2013.

205. Ibid.

206. Farhan Bokhari, "China's Growing Influence on Pakistan Worries U.S.," CBS News, December 19, 2010; Jane Perlez, "One Place Where the U.S. Can Rest Easy about China's Influence?," *New York Times,* November 4, 2013; Chris Buckley, "Behind the Chinese-Pakistani Nuclear Deal," *New York Times,* November 27, 2013.

207. Rosheen Kabraji, "The China-Pakistan Alliance: Rhetoric and Limitations," Asia Programme Paper ASP PP 2012/01, Chatham House, London, December 2012.

208. Ibid.

209. "Hagel in New Delhi on the U.S.-Strategic Partnership," U.S. Department of State, August 9, 2014.

210. Ashley J. Tellis, "Kick-Starting the U.S.-Indian Strategic Partnership," Carnegie Endowment, September 22, 2014.

211. Frank Jack Daniel and Rajesh Kumar Singh, "With Wary Eye on the U.S., China Courts India," Reuters, May 21, 2013.

212. Saibal Dasgupta, "Thousand Links: China Ties Pak to Xinjiang Terror," *Times of India*, March 8, 2012.

213. Raffaello Pantucci, "Break Up Time for Pakistan, China?," *Diplomat*, June 7, 2012.

214. M. Aftab, "Pak-China Economic Corridor May Attract $70b Investment," *Khaleej Times*, July 7, 2014.

215. Meena Menon, "Pakistan's First Solar Power Project Launched," *The Hindu*, May 9, 2014.

216. Aftab, "Pak-China Economic Corridor May Attract $70b Investment."

217. Charles Clover and Lucy Hornby, "China's Great Game: Road to a new empire," *Financial Times*, October 12, 2015.

218. Jane Perlez, "Xi Jinping Heads to Pakistan, Bearing Billions in Infrastructure Aid," *New York Times*, April 19, 2015; "China to Invest $50bn in Uplift Projects by 2017," *Daily Times*, September 12, 2014; "China's Ambitious Silk Road Vision," *Strategic Comments*, International Institute for Strategic Studies, October 26, 2015.

219. Jeremy Page, "Pakistan Looks to China for Big Energy and Infrastructure Projects," *Wall Street Journal*, February 18, 2014.

220. See, e.g., "The Grand Design of China's New Trade Routes."

221. Kamran Haider and Khurrum Anis, "Heat Wave Death Toll Rises to 2,000 in Pakistan's Financial Hub," *Bloomberg Business*, June 24, 2015; "China's Ambitious Silk Road Vision."

222. Page, "Pakistan Looks to China for Big Energy and Infrastructure Projects."

223. Dan Markey, "Reorienting U.S. Pakistan Strategy: From Af-Pak to Asia," Council Special Report no. 68, Council on Foreign Relations, January 2014.

224. Pir Zubair Shah, "What Are the Implications of Growing Pakistan-China Commercials for the United States?," Ask CFR Experts, Council on Foreign Relations, May 24, 2013.

225. Jane Perlez, "Rebuffed by China, Pakistan May Seek I.M.F. Aid," *New York Times*, October 19, 2008. And see Kabraji, "The China-Pakistan Alliance."

226. David Blair, "China Blocks £2 Billion in Aid to India," *Telegraph*, May 19, 2009.

227. "China Blocks ADB Indian Loan Plan," *Financial Times*, April 10, 2009.

228. Dhruva Jaishankar, "Eeny, Meeny, Miney, Modi: Does India's New Prime Minister Actually Have a Foreign Policy?," *Foreign Policy*, May 19, 2014.

229. Dániel Balázs, "Monsoons on the New Silk Road," *Foreign Policy*, June 23, 2015.

230. "Wary of Chinese Advances, Narendra Modi Woos Neighbours," *Economic Times*, June 13, 2014.

231. Jayanth Jacob, "'Look East' Policy Is Now 'Act East,'" *Hindustan Times*, October 4, 2014.

232. Niranjan Sahoo, "Decoding Modi's Foreign Policy," Carnegie Endowment for International Peace, September 23, 2014.

233. Ibid.

234. And as an editorial in the *Economic Times* put it, "Mr. Modi, who is keen on strengthening economic links with China, is clearly alert to reactions in Beijing were Tokyo to be his first port of call." "Wary of Chinese Advances, Narendra Modi Woos Neighbours."

235. Kabraji, "The China-Pakistan Alliance."

236. Manish Chand, "Why China Is Wary of India-US Statement on South China Sea," *India Writes*, www.indiawrites.org/diplomacy/why-china-is-wary-of-india-us -statement-on-south-china-sea.

237. Modi's May 2015 visit to China came with business deals estimated at more than $20 billion, but there were no public remarks on China's Belt and Road initiative. As one press report summarized the omission, "Apparently, the significant shortcomings of China's current approach towards India's maritime aspirations and Indian concerns about the security implications of the [Belt and Road initiative] have resulted in Modi's reluctance to praise the project as it is presently conceived. The [Belt and Road initiative] would project Chinese power in the Indian Ocean in ways that Indians could view as undermining their country's security." Dániel Balázs, "Monsoons on the New Silk Road," *Foreign Policy*, June 23, 2015. See also C. Raja Mohan, "Chinese Takeaway: Not So Coy," Carnegie Endowment for International Peace, October 8, 2014.

5. Geoeconomic Strength in Beijing and Beyond

1. Christopher Bodeen, "Norway Snub Shows Sharp Edge of Chinese Diplomacy," Associated Press, October 28, 2013. As of spring 2014, relations are still frozen. See Ben Blanchard, "China Approves of Norwegian Leaders Not Meeting Dalai Lama," Reuters, April 28, 2014.

2. Isaac Stone Fish, "Kow-towing to Beijing and Stiff-Arming the Dalai Lama," *Foreign Policy*, May 10, 2014. "Of course I would meet the Dalai Lama," Thorning-Schmidt said in a 2007 book written by Noa Redington. And two years later, when Danish prime minister Lars Løkke Rasmussen met the Dalai Lama, Thorning-Schmidt criticized her predecessor for taking the meeting in a "private" capacity and not an official one. "He should meet with the Dalai Lama as prime minister," Thorning-Schmidt said after the May 2009 meeting. "Dalai Lama Stiffed by Danish Leaders," *Local DK*, February 9, 2015.

3. Ibid.; Andreas Fuchs and Nils-Hendrik Klann, "Paying a Visit: The Dalai Lama Effect on International Trade," paper presented at Silvaplana, July 2010, http://www .econ.cam.ac.uk/dae/repec/cam/pdf/cwpe1103.pdf.

4. Louis Charbonneau, "U.N. Nations Condemn Syria; Russia, China Seen Isolated," Reuters, August 3, 2012. After the vote at the UN, as if to reward countries that voted in a manner consistent with China's stance on Syria, Beijing agreed to finance and build the $30 billion Great Canal of Nicaragua, awarded more oil-backed loans for construction projects in Angola, and in Central Asia opened a pipeline running through Turkmenistan, Uzbekistan, and Kazakhstan into China's northwestern Xinjiang province.

5. See, e.g., Chapter 3, which discusses restrictions Riyadh placed on military aid to Lebanon prohibiting Lebanon from purchasing American products. Mark Mazzetti, Eric Schmitt, and David D. Kirkpatrick, "Saudi Oil Seen as Lever to Pry Russian Support from Syria's Assad," *New York Times*, February 3, 2015.

6. See Simone Orendain, "Philippines Aims to Drill in South China Sea," Voice of America News, January 23, 2013. As Orendain explains, British-based Philippine energy company "Forum began preliminary work to assess the area's potential reserves, but in early 2011 workers said they were chased away by Chinese vessels. . . . Manuel Pangilinan, chair of Philex Petroleum, which has a 65 percent stake in Forum Energy, is eyeing a partnership with the state-owned China National Offshore Oil Corporation (CNOOC) to drill in Reed Bank. 'There are no oil rigs in this country that are owned by Filipinos. So your options are only two: one, damn the torpedoes and send the [foreign] vessel in and see what happens,' Pangilinan said . . . [or] have a commercial arrangement with a Chinese company." In June 2012, Pangilinan told reporters, "We really need someone with experience and technology—someone who has done it before like CNOOC, Shell, or Exxon Mobil. . . . We really need a foreign partner to develop the gas field so I guess the most logical is a Chinese company." See Doris Dumlao, "Pangilinan Brings in Chinese to Disputed Recto Bank Oil Exploration Group," *Philippine Daily Inquirer*, June 24, 2012. See also "Filipino Group Says China Firm Vital for Gas Project," AFP News, January 23, 2013: "The consortium opened talks with state-run China National Offshore Oil Corp. (CNOOC) last year, and its head insisted on Thursday that it was negotiating solely with the Chinese group to be a partner in the megaproject. 'I think at the moment, the discussion would have to centre between the two of us,' tycoon and consortium leader Manny Pangilinan told reporters. 'We don't want to be talking to anyone apart from CNOOC at this stage. We want to make that clear,' he said, adding that it was 'because of China. That is the reality we have to deal with.' He said: 'I believe China will employ all sorts of tactics—to charm you, to bully you.' He added groups, including those from the US, have expressed 'soft interest' to jointly explore Reed Bank, though he stressed the inquiries were not being given serious consideration."

7. While BNDES primarily invests domestically, in 2013 $1.3 billion of BNDES's $88.1 billion in lending was allocated for foreign infrastructure projects. See "Increased BNDES Lending for Projects Abroad Draws Criticism," Murray Advogados, São Paulo, Brasil, April 14, 2014, http://murray.adv.br/en/383/increased-bndes-lending-for-projects-abroad-draws-criticism.

8. Author interview, April 2014.

9. Peter Baker and Steven Erlanger, "Russia Uses Money and Ideology to Fight Western Sanctions," *New York Times*, June 7, 2015. "Russia appears to be getting some traction lately in countries like Greece, Hungary, the Czech Republic, and even Italy and France. Not only is it aligning itself with the leftists traditionally affiliated with Moscow since the Cold War, but it is making common cause with far-right forces rebelling against the rise of the European Union that are sympathetic to Mr. Putin's attack on what he calls the West's moral decline."

10. Mark Mazzetti, C. J. Chivers, and Eric Schmitt, "Taking Outsize Role in Syria, Qatar Funnels Arms to Rebels," *New York Times*, June 20, 2013.

11. Blake Hounshell, "The Qatar Bubble," *Foreign Policy,* April 23, 2012.

12. Elizabeth Dickinson, "The Case against Qatar," *Foreign Policy,* September 30, 2014.

13. Ibid.

14. Ibid; Anne Gearan, "Egypt and UAE Strike Islamist Militias in Libya," *Washington Post,* August 25, 2014; David Kirkpatrick and Eric Schmitt, "Arab Nations Strike in Libya, Surprising U.S.," *New York Times,* August 25, 2014.

15. "The Case Against Qatar," *Foreign Policy,* September 30, 2014, http://foreignpolicy.com/2014/09/30/the-case-against-qatar/.

16. Andrew Gilligan, "How Our Allies in Kuwait and Qatar Funded Islamic State," *Telegraph,* September 6, 2014.

17. Ibid.

18. An agreement made during Anastasiades's trip to Moscow allowed Russian warships to dock in Limassol, while Cypriot officials suggested that Russia may also win offshore drilling rights in a hotly contested bidding process. Andrew Higgins, "Waving Cash, Putin Sows E.U. Divisions in an Effort to Break Sanctions," *New York Times,* April 6, 2015. Jon Rosen, "Wither the 'King of Kings?' How Qaddafi's Battle for Libya Will Impact Africa," The International Relations and Security Network, April 26, 2011, http://www.isn.ethz.ch/Digital Library/Articles/Detail/?lang=en&id=128561.

19. Graham Allison and Robert D. Blackwill, *Lee Kuan Yew: The Grand Master's Insights on China, the United States and the World* (Cambridge, Mass.: MIT Press, 2013), 4–6.

20. See Chapter 4 for details, particularly the discussion on cross-strait trade agreements.

21. Here it is important to note an equally strong link between China's economic tendencies and domestic issues. Amid talk of economic reforms under President Xi Jinping, a report addressing human rights and rule of law in China highlights that "China is no closer to granting its citizens basic human rights than when China entered the World Trade Organization nearly 12 years ago." Congressional-Executive Commission on China, "2013 Annual Report," October 10, 2013.

22. "Desperately Seeking Space," *Economist,* July 13, 2013.

23. "Japan Reports Worst September Trade Figures in 30 Years," *Telegraph,* October 22, 2012. At the time, Toyota, Japan's biggest automotive company, and others were the target of this political fomentation. "Toyota said sales of new vehicles in China dropped 48.9% in September [2012] from a year earlier to 44,100 vehicles. Honda said that September sales plunged 40.5% to 33,931 vehicles. China sales for Nissan slid 35% last month to 76,100 vehicles." Associated Press, "Japanese Car Sales Plunge in China after Islands Dispute," *Guardian,* October 9, 2012.

24. Emphasis added. "China-Japan Trade Volume Drops after Dispute on Islands," *World Bulletin,* January 22, 2014.

25. Ibid. It is unclear how the foreign firm obtained the license.

26. Alec Luhn, "Russia Closes McDonald's Restaurants for 'Sanitary Violations,'" *Guardian,* August 20, 2014; Carol Matlack, "Putin's Latest Target: More than 200 Russian McDonald's," *Bloomberg Businessweek,* October 20, 2014; Anthony Cuthbertson, "Apple iPhone and iPad 'Banned in Russia,' from 2015," *International Business Times,* November 5, 2014.

27. Simon Denyer, "U.S. Companies Feel a Chill in China, Even as Many Still Rake in Profits," *Washington Post,* July 4, 2014; Mark Schwartz, "A BIT of Help for the U.S. and China," *Wall Street Journal,* April 2, 2014.

28. Paul Eckert and Anna Yukhananov, "U.S., China Agree to Restart Investment Treaty Talks," Reuters, July 12, 2013; Schwartz, "A BIT of Help for the U.S. and China."

29. "Ease of Doing Business in China," data collected by International Finance Corporation and the World Bank, 2014, http://www.doingbusiness.org/data/exploreeconomies/china.

30. Jamil Anderlini, "China: Red Restoration," *Financial Times,* November 4, 2013.

31. The CIC is responsible for $575.2 billion of China's total foreign-exchange reserves. The CIC has made substantial investments in a variety of asset classes, including direct investments, institutional real estate and infrastructure. "China Investment Corporation," SWF Institute, April 2013; Daniel Galvez, "China's Increased Presence in the Developed World," *The China Analyst* blog, The Beijing Axis, September 2013; see also Ashley Thomas Lenihan, "Sovereign Wealth Funds and the Acquisition of Power," *New Political Economy,* April 29, 2013.

32. In January of 2008, SAFE was used "to buy $300 million in Costa Rican government bonds . . . in return for Costa Rica's severing diplomatic ties with Taiwan and establishing them with Beijing." Jamil Anderlini, "Beijing's Shadowy Pool for Buying Up Best Assets," *Financial Times,* September 12, 2008.

33. David E. Brown, "Hidden Dragon, Crouching Lion: How China's Advance in Africa Is Underestimated and Africa's Potential Underappreciated," Strategic Studies Institute, U.S. Army War College, September 17, 2012, 37.

34. The Chinese geoeconomic decision-making process is often understood as an "opportunistic search to lock in oil assets . . . [whereby] Beijing has paved the way for its NOCs by deepening comprehensive relations with countries such as Iran, Sudan, Venezuela, while Western governments have been attempting to isolate regimes in these countries." John Lee, "China's Geostrategic Search for Oil," *Washington Quarterly* 35, no. 3 (Summer 2012): 75–92.

35. "China's New Courtship in South Sudan," International Crisis Group, April 4, 2012.

36. Realizing that Sudanese oil reserves were much more substantial than expected, American oil companies blamed the U.S. government for depriving them of a lucrative oil market, consequently pressuring the Clinton administration to change its policies so U.S. companies could operate in Sudan. Ismail S. H. Zaida, "Oil in Sudan: Facts and Impact on Sudanese Domestic and International Relations," Universidad Autónoma de Madrid, January 27, 2007.

37. "China and Russia Veto Zimbabwe Sanctions," *Guardian,* July 11, 2008.

38. "Zimbabwe Now a Full-Fledged Chinese Colony," *Zimbabwe Mail,* November 4, 2011. Lamido Sanusi argues that "Africa must recognize that China—like the US, Russia, Britain, Brazil and the rest—is in Africa not for African interests but its own." Lamido Sanusi, "Africa Must Get Real about Chinese Ties," *Financial Times,* March 11, 2013.

39. In providing such funding to the Zimbabwe Defence Forces, PLA chief of staff Lieutenant General Qi Jianguo also noted that Beijing "admires the ZDF . . .

who has managed to stand against the Western machinations [who seek] to destabilize the African continent." Oscar Nkala, "Chinese Army Donates $4.2 Million to Zimbabwe Defence Forces," *Defence Web Zimbabwe,* May 8, 2014.

40. "China-Zimbabwe-Relations," *Mainstream Weekly* 49, no. 26 (June 2011); "In Zimbabwe, Chinese Investment with Hints of Colonialism," *Atlantic,* June 24, 2011.

41. Tim Johnson, "China Opposes Sanctions against Iran," McClatchy DC, January 26, 2006.

42. Chen Aizhu, "China Reiterates Opposition to U.S. Sanctions on Iran," Reuters, August 2, 2013.

43. "Case Studies in Sanctions and Terrorism," Peterson Institute for International Economics, 2006, http://www.piie.com/research/topics/sanctions/sanctions -timeline.cfm.

44. Ariel Farrar-Wellman and Robert Frasco, "China-Iran Foreign Relations," AEI Iran Tracker, July 13, 2010.

45. "Report: China Agrees to Use Oil Money for Iran to Finance $20B of Development Projects," Associated Press, November 2, 2013; Wayne Ma, "Sanction Side-Step: Iranian Oil Flows Back Into China," *Wall Street Journal,* October 24, 2013.

46. Philippa Brant, "Charity Begins at Home: Why China's Foreign Aid Won't Replace the West's," *Foreign Affairs,* October 13, 2013.

47. Emmanuel Barranguet, "China the Master Stadium Builder," *Africa Report,* July 2, 2010.

48. Axel Dreher et al., "Aid on Demand: African Leaders and the Geography of China's Foreign Assistance," AidData Working Paper 3, November 2014.

49. Mark Anderson, "African Presidents 'Use China Aid for Patronage Politics,' " *Guardian,* November 19, 2014.

50. Sebastian Mallaby, "A Palace for Sudan," *Washington Post,* February 5, 2007.

51. "Olympic Boycott Calls 'Will Fail,' " BBC News, May 18, 2007; "China Defends Oil Trade with Africa," *New York Times,* March 12, 2007.

52. Mallaby, "A Palace for Sudan."

53. Pew Global Attitudes Project, *America's Global Image Remains More Positive than China's: But Many See China Becoming World's Leading Power* (Washington, D.C.: Pew Research Center, July 18, 2013), http://www.pewglobal.org/files /2013/07/Pew-Research-Global-Attitudes-Project-Balance-of-Power-Report -FINAL-July-18-2013.pdf.

54. Larry Hanauer and Lyle Morris, "China in Africa: Implications of a Deepening Relationship," RAND Corporation, 2014, http://www.rand.org/pubs/research _briefs/RB9760.html.

55. Elizabeth Economy and Michael Levi, *By All Means Necessary* (New York: Oxford University Press, 2014); Abdoulaye Wade, "Time for the West to Practice What It Preaches," *Financial Times,* January 23, 2008.

56. The World Bank committed $31.5 billion in lending in 2013; "Lending Data," World Bank, 2013, http://siteresources.worldbank.org/EXTANNREP2013/Re sources/9304887-1377201212378/9305896-1377544475343 1/Lending_Data.pdf. See

also Henry Sanderson and Michael Forsythe, *China's Superbank: Debt, Oil and Influence—How China Development Bank is Rewriting the Rules of Finance* (New York: John Wiley and Sons, 2012), 41.

57. See Ian Taylor, *China's New Role in Africa* (Boulder, Colo.: Lynne Rienner, 2009). Also see Audra Ang, "China Defends Dealings with Africa," *Washington Post*, October 31, 2006; and Xinhua, "China Africa Development Fund Hits $5 billion" *China Daily*, December 5, 2015, http://www.chinadaily.com.cn/business /2015-12/05/content_22634863.htm.

58. Sanderson and Forsythe, *China's Superbank*, 97.

59. Ibid., 99.

60. Arthur Brice, "Iran, Hezbollah Mine Latin America for Revenue, Recruits, Analysts Say," CNN, June 3, 2013; Adam Kredo, "The Iran, Hezbollah, Venezuela Axis," *Washington Free Beacon*, March 22, 2013.

61. Shih Hsiu-chuah, "Analysts See China behind Gambia Loss," *Taipei Times*, November 17, 2013; Eva Dou, "Gambia Cuts Taiwan Ties, Raising Stakes with China," *Wall Street Journal*, November 15, 2013.

62. Shannon Tiezzi, "Why Taiwan's Allies are Flocking to Beijing," *Diplomat*, November 19, 2013.

63. "The One-China Principle and the Taiwan Issue," Government of the People's Republic of China, Taiwan Affairs Office and the Information Office of the State Council, 2000.

64. The degree of RMB undervaluation is always more art than science for economists, requiring triangulating between several imperfect summary statistics. IMF estimates for 2014 suggest the RMB is moderately undervalued by 5–10 percent, compared to a level consistent with fundamentals and desired policies. Subsequent IMF estimates, released in May 2015, suggested that the RMB is no longer undervalued; however, these findings came prior to large scale devaluations that China undertook during the summer of 2015. Another favored measure of currency restraint, China's current account surplus, has come down substantially since its 2007 peaks, but the most recent IMF forecasts expect it to widen again over the next twelve to twenty-four months. International Monetary Fund, "People's Republic of China: Staff Report for the 2014 Article IV Consultation," IMF Country Report No. 14/235, July 2014.

65. Arvind Subramanian, "The Inevitable Superpower: Why China's Dominance Is a Sure Thing," *Foreign Affairs*, September/October 2011.

66. Ibid.

67. Alan Wheatley, "Introduction," in *The Power of Currencies and the Currencies of Power*, ed. Alan Wheatley (New York: Routledge, 2013), 13.

68. Sebastian Mallaby and Olin Wethington, "The Future of the Yuan," *Foreign Affairs*, January/February 2012.

69. Ibid.

70. These remarks trace historical precedents of the rise of other currencies, namely the dollar (from 1913 to 1945), the deutsche mark (from 1973 to 1990), and the rise of the yen (from 1978 to 1991). For additional analysis, see Jeffrey Frankel, "Historical Precedents for Internationalization of the RMB," Council on Foreign Relations, November 2011.

71. Fred Bergsten, "The Dollar and the Deficits: How Washington Can Prevent the Next Crisis," *Foreign Affairs* 88, no. 6 (November/December 2009).

72. Chang Shu, Dong He, and Xiaoqiang Cheng, "One Currency, Two Markets: The Renminbi's Growing Influence in Asia-Pacific," Bank of International Settlements, BIS Working Paper No. 446, April 2014.

73. "The renminbi internationalisation project could even be a tool to help force through tricky reforms at home by opening the country's capital account. The recently announced equity market link-up between Shanghai and Hong Kong is a significant step in that process, allowing investors from all over the world to buy Chinese assets without a license for the first time." Josh Noble, "Grand Global Ambitions for Renminbi Sow Domestic Risk," *Financial Times*, September 30, 2014. Also see James Kynge, "Emerging Markets Eye Renminbi Trading Alternative to Dollar," *Financial Times,* September 30, 2014.

74. Chinese scholars do not seem to shy away from this point. Dr. Zha Xiaogang, research fellow at the Shanghai Institutes for International Studies, made this point in public remarks at a fall 2012 conference on the RMB organized by the International Institute of Strategic Studies, saying, "On the geopolitics/geoeconomics side, the internationalization of renminbi, especially in East Asia, will strengthen China's economic links with its neighbors and its influence on regional economic and financial cooperation (intraregional trade, Asian regional capital markets, crisis prevention and management), which is critical for stability in China's backyard." Zha Xiaogang, "Currencies of Power and the Power of Currencies: The Geopolitics of Currencies, Reserves and the Global Financial System," IISS Seminar, October 2, 2012, https://www.iiss.org/-/media/Images/Events/conferences%20from%20import/seminars/papers/69658.pdf.

75. Shu, He, and Cheng, "One Currency, Two Markets."

76. Andrew Batson, "China Takes Aim at Dollar," *Wall Street Journal*, March 24, 2009.

77. Shawn Donnan, "IMF Staff Say Renminbi Should Join Elite SDR Basket of Currencies," *Financial Times*, November 13, 2015.

78. Josh Noble, "Grand Global Ambitions for Renminbi Sow Domestic Risks," *Financial Times*, September 30, 2014.

79. "If implemented successfully, internationalization efforts will reduce the domestic political tension as the level of real taxation falls sharply over time. Despite wishful thinking in the West, this will likely help to consolidate the CCP's power rather than ushering in democratization." Di Dongsheng, "The Renminbi's Rise and Chinese Politics," in *The Power of Currencies and Currencies of Power.*

80. Ibid.

81. Ibid.

82. Some within China's leadership ranks have suggested that ending U.S. dominance of the monetary system is "as important as New China's becoming a nuclear power." Jiang Yong quoted in Geoff Dyer, David Pilling, and Henry Sender, "A Strategy to Straddle the Planet," *Financial Times*, January 17, 2011.

83. "Taiwan Eyes Currency Swap Pact with China," *Focus Taiwan*, November 11, 2013; "Taiwan's Yuan Deposits Down in July on Mainland Woes," *China Post*, August 19, 2015. http://www.chinapost.com.tw/taiwan/business/2015/08/19/443620/Taiwans-yuan.htm.

84. "Taiwan Eyes Currency Swap Pact with China."

85. Di, "The Renminbi's Rise and Chinese Politics."

86. Henny Sender, "Iran Accepts Renminbi for Oil," *Financial Times*, May 5, 2012. This article explains the move to begin settling the transactions in renminbi rather than U.S. dollars as "partly . . . a consequence of U.S. sanctions aimed at limiting [Iran's] nuclear program," and quotes sources describing how, "as a result of U.S. pressure, domestic [Chinese] banks . . . stopped dealing with Iran. Instead . . . much of the money is transferred to Tehran through Russian banks, which take large commissions on the transactions."

87. See, e.g., Jack Farchy and Kathrin Hille, "Russian Companies Prepare to Pay for Trade in Renminbi," *Financial Times*, June 8, 2014.

88. Bernard O'Connor, "Market-Economy Status for China Is Not Automatic," Centre for Economic Policy Research, November 27, 2011, http://www.voxeu.org /article/china-market-economy.

89. Chris Gelken, "When Is a Market Economy Not a Market Economy?," *Asia Times Online*, June 5, 2004; Cassandra Sweet and Ryan Tracy, "Solar Firms Seek Duties in China Dumping Case," *Wall Street Journal*, October 20, 2011.

90. Nicola Casarnini, "China's Geoeconomic Strategy: China's Approach to US Debt and the Eurozone Crisis," LSE Ideas SR012, London School of Economics, 2012.

91. As three such examples, an August 2007 article in the *Telegraph* cited interviews with officials from two leading Chinese government think tanks who reportedly stated that China had the power to make the dollar collapse (if it chose to do so) by liquidating large portions of its U.S. Treasury securities holdings if the United States imposed trade sanctions to force an appreciation of the RMB, and that the threat to do so could be used as a "bargaining chip." See Ambrose Evans Pritchard, "China Threatens Nuclear Option of Dollar Sales," *Telegraph*, August 7, 2007. Second, according to August 2010 reports by Reuters and the *New York Times*, Chinese army Major General Luo Yuan, in an interview with Xinhua, stated that Beijing could "attack by oblique means and stealthy feints" to make its point in Washington. Luo continued, "For example, we could sanction them using economic means, such as dumping some U.S. government bonds." See, e.g., Chris Buckley, "China PLA Officers Urge Economic Punch Against U.S." Reuters, February 9, 2010. Finally, Ding Gang, a senior editor with China's *People's Daily*, wrote in an editorial in August 2011 that China should directly link the amount of U.S. Treasury holdings with U.S. arms sales to Taiwan, stating that "now is the time for China to use its 'financial weapon' to teach the United States a lesson if it moves forward with a plan to sell arms to Taiwan. In fact, China has never wanted to use its holdings of U.S. debt as a weapon. It is the United States that is forcing it to do so . . . to defend itself when facing threats to China's sovereignty." "China Must Punish U.S. for Taiwan Arm Sales with 'Financial Weapon,'" *People's Daily*, August 8, 2011.

92. Wayne M. Morrison and Mark Labonte, "China's Holdings of U.S. Securities: Implications for the U.S. Economy," *Congressional Research Service*, August 19, 2013. For a dissenting view, see Benn Steil and Paul Swartz, "Dangers of U.S. Debt in Foreign Hands," Council on Foreign Relations, June 14, 2010.

93. Henny Sender, "China to Stick with U.S. Bonds," *Financial Times*, February 11, 2009.

94. David Singh Grewal, "What Keynes Warned about Globalization," *Seminar* 601 (March 2009): 54–59.

95. "Don't Take Peaceful Approach for Granted," editorial, *Global Times,* October 25, 2011.

96. John Murray, Bank of Canada, remarks to the Peterson Institute, April 2, 2013, transcript available at www.piie.com/publications/papers/transcript -20130402-3.pdf.

97. Jonathan Kirshner, "Bringing Them All Back Home: Dollar Diminution and U.S. Power," *Washington Quarterly* 36, no. 3 (Summer 2013): 41.

98. As *New York* Times reporter Keith Bradsher explained the growing spread between two-year and ten-year Treasuries: "China has been buying more Treasury bills, with a maturity of a year or less, than Treasuries with longer maturities." Bradsher, "China Becomes More Picky about Debt," *New York Times,* May 20, 2009.

99. In late May 2009, the spread between two-year and ten-year bond yields widened to a record 2.75 percentage points. According to some, Beijing's public questioning (together with other factors) tempered market enthusiasm about the Fed's quantitative easing program and about the general economic outlook. See Alester Bull, "Federal Reserve Puzzled by Yield Curve Steepening," Reuters, May 31, 2009. The yield on the ten-year Treasury note rose even further in subsequent days, touching a yield of 3.67 percent. See "Treasuries—U.S. 10-Year Note Falls Point as Selloff Deepens," Alibaba.com, June 4, 2009, http://news.alibaba.com/article/detail /markets/100113817-1-treasuries-us-10-year-note-falls-point.html.

100. Beginning around 2000, states such as China, Japan, and Korea began acquiring so many U.S. Treasuries that when the U.S. Federal Reserve raised interest rates in 2004–2005 in an attempt to cool the U.S. economy, their efforts had no upward, cooling impact on the prices of long-term bonds, including mortgage securities. In effect, China, Japan, and others proved themselves price-insensitive demanders of U.S. Treasury bills, actually increasing their purchases as bond prices went up—and thereby interfering with a fundamental channel through which the United States executes monetary policy. This phenomenon, labeled the "great conundrum," remains the subject of intensive exchange among economists. Speaking at a G20 event in France in 2011, Federal Reserve chairman Ben Bernanke pointed to a role for net capital inflows in pushing longer-term interest rates below macroeconomic fundamentals. "Why was the United States, a mature economy, the recipient of net capital inflows that rose to as much as 6 percent of its gross domestic product prior to the financial crisis? A significant portion of these capital inflows reflected a broader phenomenon that, in the past, I have dubbed the global saving glut. Over the past 15 years or so, for reasons on which I have elaborated in earlier remarks, many emerging market economies have run large, sustained current account surpluses and thus have become exporters of capital to the advanced economies, especially the United States. These inflows exacerbated the U.S. current account deficit and were also a factor pushing U.S. and global longer-term interest rates below levels suggested by expected short-term rates and other macroeconomic fundamentals." Full transcript available at www.federalreserve.gov/newsevents/speech /bernanke20110218a.htm. Daniel Thornton, in "Greenspan's Conundrum and the Fed's Ability to Affect Long-Term Yields," Research Division, Federal Reserve

Bank of St. Louis, Working Paper 2012-036A, September 2012, takes issue with the traditional explanation—that global savings glut is to blame for the great conundrum—advanced by Ben Bernanke (prior to his appointment as chairman of the Federal Reserve) as well as by others. But Daniel O. Beltran, Maxwell Kretchmer, Jaime Marquez, and Charles P. Thomas, "Foreign Holdings of U.S. Treasuries and U.S. Treasury Yields," Board of Governors of the Federal Reserve System, International Finance Discussion Paper No. 1041, January 2012, argues the opposite case: "Longer-term bond yields are increasingly determined in international markets. This calls into question the ability of central banks to influence longer-term interest rates by the setting of short-term rates. For example, Greenspan . . . was concerned about the failure of the longer-term interest rates to rise after the Fed began tightening monetary policy starting in mid-2004. During this period, foreign purchases of Treasury notes and bonds were particularly strong and some studies . . . found evidence that these purchases contributed to lower bond yields. Such a decoupling of long-term interest rates from the short-term interest rate, which is set by the monetary authority, has important implications for the effectiveness of monetary policy. In addition, unexpected shifts in foreign demand for U.S. Treasuries could cloud the signals extracted from movements in long-term interest rates." For a more accessible synopsis of this issue, see Chris Isidore, "Interest Rates: The New Conundrum" CNN Money, February 25, 2008.

101. In the words of Robert D. Kaplan, "China's hunger for natural resources . . . means that Beijing will take substantial risks to secure them." "The Geography of Chinese Power," *Foreign Affairs,* May/June 2010. See recent examples of Chinese strategic geoeconomic endeavors in Central Asia: "China Courts Central Asia," *Diplomat,* October 4, 2013, and "China Is Pivoting to Central Asia—but Is Washington Paying Attention?," *Atlantic,* October 28, 2013.

102. Jeff Himmelman, "A Game of Shark and Minnow," *New York Times Magazine,* October 27, 2013.

103. Recent Chinese energy deals throughout Central Asia could, for instance, lessen over time China's concern that the United States could use its superior naval power to enforce a sea blockade. Jane Perlez and Bree Feng, "China Gains New Friends in Its Quest for Energy," *New York Times,* September 23, 2013.

104. Morena Skalamera, "Pipeline Pivot: Why Russia and China Are Poised to Make Energy History," Belfer Center for Science and International Affairs, Harvard University, May 2014.

105. "China Pivots towards Central Asia," *International Affairs News Weekly,* November 9, 2013.

106. Brian Spegele and Wayne Ma, "For China Boss, Deep-Water Rigs Are a 'Strategic Weapon,'" *Wall Street Journal,* August 29, 2012.

107. Jane Perlez and Keith Bradsher, "In High Seas, China Moves Unilaterally," *New York Times,* May 9, 2013.

108. Ibid.

109. Ibid.

110. "Philippines Aims to Drill in South China Sea," Voice of America, January 24, 2013; "Filipino-UK Firm to Drill for Gas in Disputed Sea," Associated Press, September 26, 2014.

111. Simon Hall, Edward Welsch, and Ryan Dezember, "China Push in Canada Is Biggest Foreign Buy," *Wall Street Journal,* July 24, 2012; Euan Rocha, "CNOOC Closes $15.1 Billion Acquisition of Canada's Nexen," Reuters, February 25, 2013; "Oilsands Investment from China Shrinks after Nexen Deal," CBC News, May 2, 2014.

112. "Beijing Steps Up Effort to Diversify FX Reserves," Reuters, January 13, 2013; "China to Use Forex Reserves to Finance Overseas Investment Deals," *Bloomberg Business,* January 14, 2013.

113. See George Chen, "Central Bank Eyes New Agency for Forex Investment," *South China Morning Post,* August 7, 2013.

114. According to August 2013 press reports, People's Bank of China governor Zhou Xiaochuan "has assigned a division head of the foreign exchange regulator to lead a team to study the plan . . . . The new agency would be in addition to the China Investment Corp., the nation's sovereign wealth fund, and may report to the central bank directly." "China's PBOC May Plan FOREX Unit, South China Post Says," *Bloomberg Business,* August 6, 2013. Beyond searching for higher returns, such a move is also intended to broaden foreign exchange reserves beyond the U.S. dollar, tapping more instead into the euro, the Japanese yen, the British pound, and others.

115. Gabriel Wildau, "China Backs Up Silk Road Ambitions with $63bn Capital Injection," *Financial Times,* April 20, 2015.

116. Martin Wolf, "In the Grip of a Great Convergence," *Financial Times,* January 4, 2011.

117. Ibid.

118. These two goals are often referred to as the "centennial goals" in China. Broadly, the Chinese strive to "complete the building of a moderately prosperous society and become a modern socialist country that is prosperous, strong, democratic, culturally advanced, and harmonious." Robert Lawrence Kuhn, "Xi Jinping's Chinese Dream," *International Herald Tribune,* June 5, 2013; Chen Yonglong and Xue Junyin, "A Proper Path Will Help China through Its Growing Pains," *China-U.S. Focus,* April 26, 2013.

119. One of the longest-running sticking points in the negotiations centered on whether China would receive equity stakes in the "upstream" projects that would be sourcing much of the gas for the deal. China will receive equity under the terms agreed in May 2014, reflecting how bargaining power shifted toward Beijing as the negotiations wore on. This shift is the result of several factors, especially sharp increases in gas supplies globally, and a desire by Moscow to diversify its own customer base, as European purchasers signal seriousness on reducing their dependence on Russian gas.

120. In May 2014, Beijing and Moscow signed an agreement for Russia to export 38 billion cubic meters of natural gas annually, a little more than half of the 65 billion cubic meters of natural gas that is expected to flow annually from Turkmenistan to China by 2020. See Abdujalil Abdurasulov, "China's growing demand for Turkmenistan's gas," *BBC News,* November 20, 2014; and Meghan L. O'Sullivan, "New China-Russia Gas Pact Is No Big Deal," *Bloomberg View,* November 14, 2014.

121. Marat Gurt, "China Secures Larger Turkmen Gas Supplies," Reuters, September 3, 2013.

122. Heriberto Araújo and Juan Pablo Cardenal, "China's Economic Empire," *New York Times*, June 1, 2013.

123. In mid-2012, the government of Argentina moved to nationalize Spanish energy firm Repsol's Argentine assets on rumors that Repsol was in talks with Chinese state oil major Sinopec.

6. U.S. Foreign Policy and Geoeconomics in Historical Context

1. The authors thank Robert Zoellick and Philip Zelikow for their helpful feedback. This chapter also owes a profound debt to the historical craftsmanship of Alan Dobson and David Baldwin.

2. Michael Schuman, "State Capitalism vs the Free Market: Which Performs Better?," *Time*, September 30, 2011.

3. Gilpin, as quoted in David A. Baldwin, *Economic Statecraft* (Princeton, N.J.: Princeton University Press, 1985), 209.

4. U.K. House of Lords, Transatlantic Trade and Investment Partnership, European Union Committee, summarizing the views of Daniel J. Hamilton; see http://www.publications.parliament.uk/pa/ld201314/ldselect/ldeucom/179/17905.htm#note38. U.S. trade representative Miriam Sapiro echoed similar reservations during a panel at the 2013 Transformational Trends Conference, co-hosted by the Foreign Policy Group and U.S. Department of State Policy Planning Staff; a video of her remarks is available at https://www.youtube.com/watch?v=cranPeN9FSc.

5. U.K. House of Lords, views of Daniel J. Hamilton.

6. Underscoring this point, law professor Anna Gelpern observes how "the [global economic] system is set up as if market finance and political patronage were distinct." Gelpern, "Russia's Contract Arbitrage," Georgetown University Law Faculty Publication 1448, June 4, 2014.

7. Samuel F. Wells Jr., *The Challenges of Power: American Diplomacy, 1900–1921* (Lanham, Md.: University Press of America, 1990), 63.

8. "Foreign Economic Trends: The Separation between Foreign Economic and Political Policy," *Foreign Relations of the United States, 1969–1976, Volume III, Foreign Economic Policy; International Monetary Policy, 1969–1972*, Document 26, U.S. Department of State, Office of the Historian, https://history.state.gov/historicaldocuments/frus1969-76v03/d26.

9. Ibid. Cooper goes on to warn that while "by and large, international trade negotiations and international monetary discussions have proceeded in their own way and at their own pace," certain "complications" may make it "more difficult to preserve this semi-separation between economic and political relations with other countries in the next decade than it has been in the past two decades."

10. Alan P. Dobson, *US Economic Statecraft for Survival 1933–1991* (New York: Routledge, 2002). Franklin also advocated land acquisition as a means of strengthening the new nation's security. He fantasized with his friend the evangelical preacher George Whitefield about their being "jointly employ'd by the Crown to settle a

Colony on the Ohio . . . What a glorious Thing it would be, to settle in that fine country a large Strong Body of Religious and Industrious People! What a Security to the Other Colonies: and Advantageous to Britain, by Increasing her People, Territory, Strength, and Commerce." Gordon S. Wood, *The Americanization of Benjamin Franklin* (New York: Penguin, 2005), 81, cited in Lehrman Institute, "The Founders and the Pursuit of Land," http://lehrmaninstitute.org/history/founders-land.asp.

11. Baldwin, *Economic Statecraft.*

12. Felix Gilbert, *To the Farewell Address: Ideas of Early American Foreign Policy* (Princeton, N.J., Princeton University Press, 1970).

13. Lawrence S. Kaplan, *Thomas Jefferson: Westward the Course of Empire* (Wilmington, Del.: SR Books, 1999); Letter from Thomas Jefferson to Robert R. Livingston, U.S. Minister to France, April 18, 1802, http://www.let.rug.nl/usa/presidents/thomas-jefferson/letters-of-thomas-jefferson/jefl146.php.

14. Dobson, *US Economic Statecraft for Survival*, 93.

15. In 1861 U.S. secretary of state William Seward bluntly warned his White-hall counterparts that if the United Kingdom was "tolerating the application of the so-called seceding States, or wavering about it, [it could not] remain the friends of the United States." It might as well "prepare to enter into alliance with the enemies of this republic." Linus Pierpont Brockett, *The Life and Times of Abraham Lincoln, Sixteenth President of the United States* (Philadelphia: Bradley, 1865), 269.

16. Walter Stahr, *Seward: Lincoln's Indispensable Man* (New York: Simon and Schuster, 2012), 4.

17. "Annual Report of Maj. Gen. Arthur Macarthur, U.S.V., Commanding Division of the Philippines, Military Governor in the Philippine Islands," in *Annual Reports of the War Department for the Fiscal Year Ended June 30, 1901* (Washington, D.C.: Government Printing Office, 1901), 114.

18. Viscount Grey of Fallodon, *Twenty Five Years 1892–1916* (London: Hodder and Stoughton, 1923), 103.

19. Dobson, *US Economic Statecraft for Survival*, 15.

20. Ibid.

21. Woodrow Wilson, "The Meaning of Liberty," address at Independence Hall on July 4, 1914, available at http://www.presidency.ucsb.edu/ws/?pid=65381.

22. Richard N. Rosecrance and Arthur A. Stein, eds., *No More States? Globalization, National Self-determination, and Terrorism* (Lanham, Md.: Rowman and Littlefield, 2006), 81.

23. "Milestones: 1921–1936: Interwar Diplomacy," U.S. Department of State, Office of the Historian, https://history.state.gov/milestones/1921–1936; "Milestones: 1921–1936: Interwar Diplomacy," United States Department of State, Office of the Historian, available at https://history.state.gov/milestones/1921-1936.

24. "Milestones: 1921–1936: The Dawes Plan, the Young Plan, German Reparations, and Inter-Allied War Debts," United States Department of State, Office of the Historian, available at https://history.state.gov/milestones/1921-1936/dawes.

25. Frank Whitson Fetter, "The Role of Governmental Credit in Hemispheric Trade," *Law and Contemporary Problems*, Autumn 1941, 724.

26. Ronald W. Cox and Daniel Skidmore-Hess, *U.S. Politics and the Global Economy* (Boulder, Colo.: Lynne Rienner, 1999), 29.

27. Barbara W. Tuchman, *Stillwell and the American Experience in China, 1911–45* (New York: Grove Press, 2001), 190.

28. William Hardy McNeill, *America, Britain and Russia: Their Co-operation and Conflict, 1941–1946* (New York: Johnson Reprint, 1970), 778; "One War Won," *Time*, December 13, 1943.

29. H. L. Stimson and McGeorge Bundy, *On Active Service in Peace and War* (New York: Harper, 1947), 171.

30. Dobson, *US Economic Statecraft for Survival*, chap. 2, esp. 72.

31. Ibid, esp. 20.

32. David L. Dangerfield and Royden Gordon, *The Hidden Weapon: The Story of Economic Warfare* (New York: Harper and Brothers, 1947), 44.

33. Dobson, *US Economic Statecraft for Survival*, 48.

34. For a detailed history, see Jeremy Atack and Peter Passell, *A New Economic View of American History: From Colonial Times to 1940*, 2nd ed. (New York: Norton, 1994).

35. Cordell Hull, *The Memoirs of Cordell Hull* (New York: Macmillan, 1948), 1:81.

36. Baldwin, *Economic Statecraft*, 207.

37. *New York Times*, July 16, 1944, pt. 4, p. 7 (cited in Baldwin, *Economic Statecraft*, 208).

38. Letter from Harry S. Truman to James Byrnes, January 5, 1946, http://teachingamericanhistory.org/library/document/letter-to-james-byrnes.

39. George C. Marshall, "Marshall Plan" speech at Harvard University as prepared for delivery on June 5, 1947, available at www.oecd.org/general/themarshallplanspeechatharvarduniversity5june1947.htm.

40. John Gimbel, *The Origins of the Marshall Plan* (Stanford: Stanford University Press, 1976), 267.

41. Anne R. Pierce, *Woodrow Wilson and Harry Truman: Mission and Power in American Foreign Policy* (New Brunswick, N.J.: Transaction, 2007), 83.

42. Diane B. Kunz, "The Marshall Plan Reconsidered: A Complex of Motives," *Foreign Affairs*, May/June 1997, 166.

43. Pierce, *Woodrow Wilson and Harry Truman*, 193.

44. John Lewis Gaddis, *George F. Kennan: An American Life* (New York: Penguin, 2011), 283.

45. Dobson, *US Economic Statecraft for Survival*, 97.

46. Eisenhower went on to argue that "the solidarity of the free world and the capacity of the free world to deal with those who would destroy it are threatened by continued unbalanced trade relationships—the inability of nations to sell as much as they desire to buy. By moving boldly to correct the present imbalance, we shall support and increase the level of our exports of both manufactured and agricultural products. We shall, at the same time, increase the economic strength of our allies. Thus shall we enhance our own military security by strengthening our friends abroad. Thus shall we assure those sources of imports that supplement our domestic production and are vital to our defense." Dwight D. Eisenhower, Special

Message to the Congress on Foreign Economic Policy, March 30, 1954, www .presidency.ucsb.edu/ws/?pid=10195.

47. Dobson, *US Economic Statecraft for Survival,* 146–147.

48. Ibid., 168: "Rostow believed trade controls had become an 'important symbol of our cold war resolve' and 'moral disapproval' of the Soviet Union." For further discussion of Rostow's "flexible response" policy, see David A. Welch, James G. Blight, and Bruce J. Allyn, "The Cuban Missile Crisis," in *The Use of Force: Military Power and International Politics,* ed. Robert J. Art and Kenneth N. Waltz, 6th ed. (Lanham, Md.: Rowman and Littlefield, 2004), 225–226; David Milne, *America's Rasputin: Walt Rostow and the Vietnam War* (New York: Farrar, Straus and Giroux, 2008), 81; Dobson, *US Economic Statecraft for Survival,* 154–155.

49. As first leaked to the *New York Times* in January 1962, the Ball Report urged increased trade with the Communist bloc. It reportedly recommended that Kennedy "persuade other free enterprise countries . . . that we are genuinely prepared to recognize the potential economic advantage of East-West trade." See James A. Bill, *George Ball: Behind the Scenes in U.S. Foreign Policy* (New Haven: Yale University Press, 1997), 59–60; "Washington Report," *Reading Eagle,* September 26, 1963, 2nd section, 22; Dobson, *US Economic Statecraft for Survival,* 155–160.

50. Eisenhower Library, CFEP Records, Policy Paper Series box 1, folder: CFEP 501 East-West Trade Action Papers 1955 (3), "Review of Economic Defense Policy and Program: The Background," January 20, 1955, cited in Dobson, *US Economic Statecraft for Survival,* 143; Dobson, *US Economic Statecraft for Survival,* 143–144.

51. Dobson, *US Economic Statecraft for Survival,* 159; John F. Kennedy library, NSF box 176, folder: USSR General, US Economic Relations with the Soviet Bloc 5/25/61, May 25, 1961, Edwin Martin to McGeorge Bundy, subject "Review of United States Economic Relations with the Soviet Bloc," paper prepared under authority of George Ball, cited in Dobson, *US Economic Statecraft for Survival,* 159–162.

52. Lyndon Baines Johnson, *The Vantage Point: Perspectives of the Presidency, 1963–1969* (Dumfries: Holt, Rinehart and Winston, 1971), cited in Dobson, *US Economic Statecraft for Survival,* 172.

53. Lyndon B. Johnson Library, NSF Committee File, box 16, folder: Miller Committee Meetings March 4–5/18–19/25–26, 1965, presentation by Llewellyn Thompson, ambassador at large, assisted by Trezise et al., March 18, 1965, cited in Dobson, *US Economic Statecraft for Survival,* 175; Dobson, *US Economic Statecraft for Survival,* 332n96.

54. "In sum, trade with the European Communist countries is politics in the broadest sense," the Miller Commission declared in its final report. "In this intimate engagement men and nations will in time be altered by the engagement itself. We do not fear this. We welcome it. We believe we are more nearly right than they about how to achieve the welfare of nations in this century." Lyndon B. Johnson Library, NSF Committee File, box 25, folder: Miller Committee Report to the President, and Miller Committee members to Johnson, April 29, 1965, cited in Dobson, *US Economic Statecraft for Survival,* 176.

55. "The Role of Foreign Aid in Development: South Korea and the Philippines," Congressional Budget Office Memorandum, September 1997.

56. X [George Kennan], "The Sources of Soviet Conduct," *Foreign Affairs,* July 1947; Telegram, George Kennan to George Marshall ("Long Telegram"), February 22, 1946, available at www.trumanlibrary.org/whistlestop/study_collections /coldwar/documents/pdf/6-6.pdf.

57. *NSC 68: United States Objectives and Programs for National Security,* April 14, 1950.

58. Dobson, *US Economic Statecraft for Survival,* 30.

59. Ibid.

60. Ibid.

61. It is not as if geoeconomics was entirely lacking in the U.S. approach to Vietnam. Walter Rostow called for foreign aid into Vietnam, and supported a plan to develop South Asia's economy by setting up something that resembled the Tennessee Valley Authority in the Mekong Delta. Rostow had no doubt that "one can champion foreign aid and the bombing of communist-infected nations at the same time." It was also in this period that Washington targeted economic assistance in its fight to contain communism around the world, but the amounts were palpably different than the efforts undertaken two and a half decades earlier, and in any case, these measures were decidedly secondary to the military elements of the Vietnam strategy. Milne, David, *America's Rasputin: Walt Rostow and the Vietnam War* (New York: Macmillan, 2008), 7.

62. Dobson, *US Economic Statecraft for Survival,* 181–213.

63. Henry Kissinger, *White House Years* (New York: Little, Brown, 1979), 153–154.

64. In his memoirs, Nixon attributed a U.S.-Soviet summit to a cunning military and political strategy. The account is telling in his omission of any economic variables: "A U.S.-Soviet summit was at last possible because of two achievements: progress in the SALT talks before the China overture was revealed, and progress on a Berlin settlement after the China announcement had been made." Richard Milhous Nixon, *Memoirs* (New York: Grosset and Dunlap, 1978), 523.

65. Walter Russell Mead, *Special Providence: American Foreign Policy and How It Changed the World* (New York: Alfred Knopf, 2001), 73.

66. Ibid., 36.

67. I. M. Destler, *Making Foreign Economic Policy* (Washington, D.C.: Brookings Institution, 1980).

68. Ibid.

69. Kissinger, *White House Years,* 154, cited in Dobson, *US Economic Statecraft for Survival,* 199.

70. Robert L. Paarlberg, "Using Food Power: Opportunities, Appearances, and Damage Control," in *Dilemmas of Economic Coercion: Sanctions in World Politics,* ed. Miroslav Nincic and Peter Wallensteen (New York: Praeger, 1983), 127 as cited in Dobson, *US Economic Statecraft for Survival.*

71. For a detailed account of the "Great Grain Robbery" and its historical importance, see Dobson, *US Economic Statecraft for Survival,* 206–210.

72. Ibid., 206.

73. Nixon Project, Ezra Solomon Papers, box 5, folder: CIEP Task Force Draft Report, November 22, 1971, study memo 3 prepared by Robert McLellan, Department of Commerce; also see ibid., folder: CIEP 1, W. De Vier Pierson memo on

Task Force Report, January 3, 1972, which indicates that it embodies established view of the Commerce Department.

74. Dobson, *US Economic Statecraft for Survival,* 217.

75. Ibid., 220–221; Executive Order 11808, September 30, 1974.

76. Zbigniew Brzezinski, *Power and Principle: Memoirs of the National Security Adviser, 1977–1981* (New York: Farrar, Straus and Giroux, 1983), 461; Gerry Argyris Andrianopoulos, *Kissinger and Brzezinski: The NSC and the Struggle for Control of US National Security Policy* (Basingstoke, England: Palgrave Macmillan, 1991), 181; Thomas J. McCormick, *America's Half-Century: United States Foreign Policy in the Cold War and After* (Washington, D.C.: Johns Hopkins University Press, 1995), 205.

77. Samuel P. Huntington, "Trade, Technology, and Leverage: Economic Diplomacy," *Foreign Policy* 32 (Autumn 1978): 63.

78. Ibid.

79. Dobson, *US Economic Statecraft for Survival,* 216; for a broader perspective, refer to Daniel Yergin, *The Prize: The Epic Quest for Oil, Money, and Power* (London: Simon and Schuster, 1991).

80. Huntington, "Trade, Technology, and Leverage," 65.

81. Ibid., 79.

82. Baldwin, *Economic Statecraft,* 251.

83. Philip Hanson, *Western Economic Statecraft in East-West Relations: Embargoes, Sanctions, Linkage, Economic Warfare, and Détente* (New York: Council on Foreign Relations, 1988), 43.

84. Mead, *Special Providence,* 76.

85. Ibid.

86. Dobson, *US Economic Statecraft for Survival.* See also Henry Bienen and Robert Gilpin, "An Evaluation of the Use of Economic Sanctions to Promote Foreign Policy Objectives, with Special Reference to the Problem of Terrorism and the Promotion of Human Rights," (report prepared for the Boeing Corporation, April 2, 1979).

87. Ibid.

88. Charles Krauthammer, "The Unipolar Moment," *Foreign Affairs* 70, no. 1 (1990–1991).

89. See Mead, *Special Providence* on this point.

90. "A National Security Strategy for a New Century," National Security Council, May 1997, http://nssarchive.us/NSSR/1997.pdf, 2–3.

91. "A National Security Strategy of Engagement and Enlargement," National Security Council, July 1994, http://nssarchive.us/NSSR/1994.pdf, i.

92. William Kristol and Robert Kagan, "Toward a Neo-Reaganite Foreign Policy," *Foreign Affairs,* July/August 1996.

93. That is not to suggest this advice was coming only from outsiders. Indeed, often neglected in the historical retelling of 1990s Russian economic reforms is just how much of this "shock therapy" advice was originating from within Yeltsin's Russia. If anyone deserves credit as chief architect of shock therapy, it is Yegor Gaidar, who rotated through several top posts under President Yeltsin, including brief stints as minister of finance and as acting prime minister in 1991 and 1992.

94. See Juan Zarate, *Treasury's War: The Unleashing of a New Era of Financial Warfare* (New York: PublicAffairs, 2013); Maurice Greenberg, William Wechsler, and Lee Wolosky, "Terrorist Financing," Council on Foreign Relations Task Force Report, October 2002.

95. U.S. foreign policy commentator Fareed Zakaria recounts meeting a friend who was a well-connected member of the Chinese Communist Party for lunch in January 2007, not long after George W. Bush announced his surge of troops into Iraq. Asked how the news was being received in Beijing, the CCP official replied to the effect of, "We would hope that you would send the entire American Army into Iraq and stay for another 10 years. Meanwhile, we will keep building up our economy." Fareed Zakaria, "With an Absent United States, China Marches On," *Washington Post,* July 2, 2015.

96. Remarks by Robert M. Gates at the U.S. Military Academy, West Point, N.Y., February 25, 2011.

97. Interview with Robert Zoellick.

98. These measures included an end to the system of import quotas, the deregulation of natural gas prices, and incentives to expand domestic energy production. Michael L. Ross, "How the 1973 Oil Embargo Saved the Planet," *Foreign Affairs,* October 15, 2013.

99. Attended by thirteen industrial and oil-consuming nations, the meeting was meant to send a clear signal to producers that consuming countries could also organize themselves for collective action. That said, there is no record of panic among OPEC governments regarding what was largely a rhetorical exercise by Washington.

100. Richard Nixon, "Address to the Nation about Policies to Deal with the Energy Shortages," November 7, 1973.

101. Leading up to formal relations with Beijing, Nixon announced that he had asked for a "list of items of a nonstrategic nature which can be placed under general license for direct export to the People's Republic of China. Following [his] review and approval of specific items on the list, direct imports of designated items from China will then be authorized." His decision was met with an overwhelmingly favorable public reaction; not even one month later the various economic departments implemented Nixon's new policy, and by June, the president formally ended the twenty-one-year export embargo and lifted import control. Nixon Project, WHCF CO box 19 folder: CO 34-2 PRC (Red China) 1/1/71–5/31/71, Nixon Statement April 14, 1971, and Theodore L. Elliot Jr. to Kissinger on April 17, 1971.

102. Whereas economic incentives embedded in détente significantly moderated Soviet behavior. See Jean-Marc F. Blanchard, Edward D. Mansfield, and Norrin M. Ripsman, eds., *Power and the Purse: Economic Statecraft, Interdependence and National Security* (London: Routledge, 2000), 33.

103. China's economic integration has produced asymmetric relative gains even with its larger trading partners, such as the United States, thus creating the awkward situation where Washington contributes toward sustaining Beijing's economic growth and, by extension, accelerates its rise as a geopolitical rival. See Robert D. Blackwill and Ashley J. Tellis, "American Grand Strategy toward China," Council on Foreign Relations special report, 2015.

104. Robert Zoellick, "The Currency of Power," *Foreign Policy,* October 8, 2012.

105. See also Daniel Sargent, *A Superpower Transformed: The Remaking of American Foreign Relations in the 1970s* (New York: Oxford University Press, 2015); Dobson, *US Economic Statecraft for Survival;* Francis Gavin, *Gold, Dollars and Power: The Politics of International Monetary Relations, 1958–1971* (Chapel Hill: University of North Carolina Press, 2007).

106. Destler, "Foreign Economic Policy Making under Bill Clinton," in *After the End: Making U.S. Foreign Policy in the Post-Cold War World,* ed. James M. Scott (Durham, N.C.: Duke University Press, 1998), 92.

107. Ibid.

108. In Grewal's account—from the time of Adam Smith roughly up to 1945—there is a tension between the positive-sum logic of neoclassical economics, which favors liberalization, and the logic of politics, which generally tends toward the zero-sum. He examines this tension in David Singh Grewal, *Network Power: The Social Dynamics of Globalization* (New Haven, Conn.: Yale University Press, 2008), 235–237.

109. David Singh Grewal, e-mail message to author, August 22, 2015.

110. Ibid.

111. See David Allen Baldwin, *Economic Statecraft* (Princeton, N.J.: Princeton University Press, 1985); Dobson, *US Economic Statecraft for Survival;* and Grewal, *Network Power,* 235–237, 361. Certainly, Keynes was acutely aware of this interplay between economic thought and underlying realities of state power. In 1933 Keynes squarely rejected the classical economic views of Normal Angell and others who, right to the very onset of World War I, remained convinced that economic interdependence would assuage threats of war. For Keynes, this "age of economic internationalism was not particularly successful in avoiding war; and if its friends retort that the imperfection of its success never gave it a fair chance, it is reasonable to point out that a greater success is scarcely probable in the coming years." John Maynard Keynes, "National Self-Sufficiency," *Yale Review* 22, no. 4 (June 1933): 755–769.

112. Dobson, *US Economic Statecraft for Survival.*

113. Zarate, *Treasury's War.*

114. Grewal, e-mail message to author.

115. This point, along with this chapter's broader arguments around the evolving relationship between neoclassical economics and American foreign policy, owes much to exchanges with Sasha Post.

116. Granted, the term *neoclassical* was only coined after Keynes's time, as a synthesis of Keynesian and classical economics. Keynes did not deny the economic logic espoused by Angell and other classical economists; he only cautioned that it might depart from "the cause of peace." He wrote, "There may be some financial calculation which shows it to be advantageous that my savings should be invested in whatever quarter of the habitable globe shows the greatest marginal efficiency of capital or the highest rate of interest. But experience is accumulating that remoteness between ownership and operation is an evil in the relations among men, likely or certain in the long run to set up strains and enmities which will bring to nought the financial calculation." Better, thought Keynes, to be "our own masters" rather than "at the mercy of world forces working out, or trying to work out, some uniform

equilibrium according to the ideal principles, if they can be called such, of laissez-faire capitalism." Keynes, "National Self-Sufficiency." For Keynes, the creation of the Bretton Woods system, far from eliding prevailing global power realities, was precisely aimed at taming these "world forces," or at least embedding them within the prevailing power realities of the time (what international political economist John Ruggie calls "embedded liberalism"). For a detailed account of Keynes's views, as well as those of Harry Dexter White, on the degree to which Bretton Woods should be understood as answering geopolitical (in addition to economic) imperatives, see Benn Steil, *The Battle of Bretton Woods* (Princeton, N.J.: Princeton University Press, 2013).

7. America's Geoeconomic Potential

1. For instance, G. John Ikenberry, "The Rise of China and the Future of the West," *Foreign Affairs,* January/February 2008; Carl Minzer, "The Rise of China and the Interests of the U.S.," *Ripon Forum* 41, no. 2 (April 2007); Michael D. Swaine, *America's Challenge: Engaging a Rising China in the Twenty-First Century* (Washington, D.C.: Carnegie Endowment for International Peace, 2011); Kira Zalan, "The Rise of China and the Global Future of the U.S.," *U.S. News and World Report,* January 3, 2013. Robert D. Blackwill and Ashley J. Tellis, *Revising U.S. Grand Strategy toward China* (New York: Council on Foreign Relations, 2015).

2. Henry A. Kissinger, "Rebalancing Relations with China," *Washington Post,* August 19, 2009.

3. Leslie H. Gelb, "Hillary Hits the Mark," *Daily Beast,* October 14, 2011.

4. Ibid.

5. See, e.g., Michael Froman, "The Geopolitical Stakes of America's Trade Policy: Why Trade Matters More than Ever for U.S. National Security," *Foreign Policy,* February 17, 2015. Froman wrote the piece in his official capacity as the U.S. top trade representative, and its February 2015 release came as part of a broader Obama administration push to secure Congressional fast-track authority necessary to conclude both trade deals; borrowing from similar efforts on past trade deals, the Obama Administration put national security arguments at the center of its push. See generally Mary Circincione, "Kerry: Trade Accords Enhance National Security," *Military Times,* April 23, 2015; Patrick Cronin, "A Matter of National Security: America Must Support TPP," *Real Clear Defense,* March 17, 2015; Daniel W. Drezner, "The Trans-Pacific Partnership Is about More than Trade," *Washington Post,* May 7, 2015.

6. Guy Molyneux, "NAFTA Revisited: Unified 'Opinion Leaders' Best a Reluctant Public," *Public Perspective,* January/February 1994, 2.

7. See, e.g., Zhonghe Mu, "TPP's Impacts and China's Strategies in Response," Stanford Center for International Development Working Paper, January 2014.

8. Among trade experts, this dynamic is known as "competitive liberalization."

9. Ian F. Fergusson, William H. Cooper, Remy Jurenas, and Brock R. Williams, "The Trans-Pacific Partnership (TPP) Negotiations and Issues for Congress," Congressional Research Service, December 13, 2013.

10. See Chapter 5 for more discussion on the rise of the renminbi.

11. Noel Quinn, "China's RMB Liberalisation: The Growing Influence of the Currency on Asean Markets," *International Business Times,* November 6, 2013. See also "Yuan for the Money," *Economist,* February 9, 2013.

12. Barry Eichengreen, "Renminbi Internationalization: Tempest in a Teapot," Institute for New Economic Thinking, July 2013.

13. Robert Zoellick, "The Trans-Pacific Partnership: New Rules for a New Era," lecture, Wilson Center, Washington, D.C., June 19, 2013. According to Zoellick, geopolitically "TPP and TTIP could be America's economic bridges to eastern and western boarders of Eurasia." Therefore, "the need to strengthen trans-Pacific ties is pretty apparent." See also Fred Bergsten, "Submission to the USTR in Support of a Trans-Pacific Partnership Agreement," speech, Peterson Institute for International Economics, Washington, D.C., January 25, 2010.

14. See, e.g., C. Fred Bergsten and Joseph E. Gagnon, "Time for a Fightback in the Currency Wars," *Financial Times,* September 3, 2012; C. Fred Bergsten, "Addressing Currency Manipulation through Trade Agreements," Policy Brief 14-2, Peterson Institute for International Economics, January 2014; "Currency Wars: Economic Realities, Institutional Responses, and the G-20 Agenda," Peterson Institute for International Economics, April 2, 2013. Another frequently cited counterargument against including currency provisions in a trade agreement like TPP is it would be difficult to distinguish undesirable practices of currency manipulation from other, more desirable monetary policy interventions, notably the quantitative easing measures enacted by the U.S. Federal Reserve, which, while not targeting any particular currency value, nonetheless have the effect of weakening the value of a given currency. These objections seem less founded, however, as there are a number of ways to distinguish stimulative monetary policy from currency manipulation. At the most basic level, the two have different aims: unlike the explicit exchange rate targets that some countries maintain, neither the U.S. Federal Reserve's nor the Bank of Japan's quantitative easing policies target specific exchange-rate values. Second, not only are these quantitative easing aims not about currency values, they are fundamentally demand stimulating—in a sense, growing the pie for everyone—which stands in marked contrast to the zero-sum nature of currency manipulation. Finally, the two use different tools. In particular, the Bank of Japan and the U.S. Federal Reserve are confining their efforts to monetary policy tools. That is, a central bank's decision to purchase a country's own long-term bonds, while no doubt unconventional monetary policy, is still monetary policy.

15. The cover pages of the Treasury's reports to Congress on International and Economic and Exchange Rate Policies explicitly state that each report "is submitted pursuant to the Omnibus Trade and Competitiveness Act of 1988." See, e.g., www .treasury.gov/resource-center/international/exchange-rate-policies/Documents /2014-4-15_FX%20REPORT%20FINAL.pdf.

16. "State Firms Barred from Vietnam Contract Bids," *South China Morning Post,* June 9, 2014.

17. Xu Liping, an expert on China's relations in Southeast Asia at the Chinese Academy of Social Sciences, told reporters at the *South China Morning Post* that Beijing may be trying to put economic pressure on Vietnam's government. "Any measure to enhance China's investment in Vietnam is inappropriate with the current

political tension," said Xu. "This is a sign that China is playing the economic card. How effective will it be? We will have to wait and see." Ibid.

18. "SINGAPORE—Trans-Pacific Partnership (TPP) ministers during a four-day meeting here agreed to scale back the scope of proposed disciplines on state-owned enterprises (SOEs) so that they do not apply to services provided by an SOE in its home country market. The SOE decision was one of several rules issues on which ministers made progress here, U.S. Trade Representative Michael Froman told reporters, without addressing the specifics." "U.S., Other TPP Countries Agree to Narrow Scope of SOE Chapter," *Inside U.S. Trade,* February 28, 2014. See also "Open Letter from Rep. Michael Michaud (D-ME) to U.S.T.R. Michael Froman," expressing concern that the TPP SOE chapter "will not in practice level the playing field for American companies, particularly our small and medium-sized enterprises, trying to compete against SOEs." Michaud goes on to cite "several components of the SOE disciplines that will be critical to the disciplines' effectiveness and accessibility to American companies." He "urge[s] the United States Trade Representative (USTR) to ensure any SOE disciplines are subject to a dispute settlement mechanism that will provide accessible, timely, and effective relief for American businesses and workers." Available at http://michaud.house.gov/press-release/rep-michaud -presses-ustr-state-owned-enterprises-tpp.

19. Michael Froman, "Strategic Importance of TPP," Office of United States Trade Representative, remarks delivered on September 18, 2014. Transcript available at https://ustr.gov/about-us/policy-offices/press-office/speeches/2014/September /Remarks-by-Ambassador-Froman-at-US-Chamber-CSIS-TPP-Event.

20. Hillary Clinton's remarks at *Foreign Policy*'s "Transformational Trends" forum in Washington, D.C., November 2012, http://foreignpolicy.com/2012/11/30 /hillary-clintons-remarks-at-fps-transformational-trends-forum; also see Clinton, "The Transatlantic Partnership: A Statesman's Forum with Secretary of State Hillary Clinton," speech delivered at Brookings Institution, November 2012. Transcript available at http://www.brookings.edu/~/media/events/2012/11/29-clinton /20121129_transatlantic_clinton.pdf.

21. David Ignatius, "A Free-Trade Agreement with Europe?," *Washington Post,* December 5, 2012.

22. Robert Zoellick is perhaps the most notable exception.

23. William Mauldin, "U.S., U.K. Politicians Eye Strategic Aims of Trans-Atlantic Trade Talks," *Wall Street Journal,* September 25, 2013.

24. Ibid.

25. See discussion by Benn Steil and Robert Litan on tools of American financial statecraft, include value of economic rules-based system and structures in their *Financial Statecraft: The Role of Financial Markets in American Foreign Policy* (New Haven, Conn.: Yale University Press, 2008).

26. James Roberts, research fellow for Economic Freedom and Growth at the Heritage Foundation, summed it up well: "The U.S. isn't losing soft power," he said. "The Bretton Woods institutions serve a purpose, but not on such a grand scale as in previous decades." Ian Talley, "In Democrats' Eyes, Republicans Are Helping Foster Chinese Power," *Wall Street Journal,* March 27, 2015.

27. Ibid. Sebastian Heilmann and colleagues argue that "while current crises in the Ukraine, Syria, Iraq and West Africa have moved to the centre of global atten-

tion, China is advancing with a restructuring of the international order. While Beijing remains an active player within existing international institutions, it is simultaneously promoting and financing new parallel structures. The goal of these efforts is a greater autonomy primarily vis-à-vis the U.S. and an expansion of the Chinese sphere of influence beyond Asia. Some of these parallel structures . . . may also come to compete directly with existing institutions." Sebastian Heilmann, Moritz Rudolf, Mikko Huotari, and Johannes Buckow, "China's Shadow Foreign Policy: Parallel Structures Challenge the Established International Order," *China Monitor* 18 (October 28, 2014). "China," Theresa Fallon said, was offering a "whole economic and political package that provides an alternative to the creaking international structures shaped by the U.S. in the postwar period." Others see the point underscored by the faltering TTIP, once hailed as "the marquee project of trans-Atlantic solidarity," but which "has lost much of its momentum in the face of fierce hostility from European politicians and activists opposed to American-style capitalism." Andrew Higgins and David E. Sanger, "3 European Powers Say They Will Join China-Led Bank," *New York Times*, March 17, 2015.

28. Higgins and Sanger, "3 European Powers Say They Will Join China-Led Bank."

29. Ibid. In the same piece, Higgins and Sanger later note that the decision by "Germany, France and Italy that they would follow Britain and join the Chinese led venture delivered a stinging rebuke to Washington from some of its closest allies. It also called into question whether the World Bank and International Monetary Fund . . . will find their influence diminished."

30. Author communication with Admiral Michael Mullen.

31. Jonathan Weisman, "At Global Economic Gathering, U.S. Primacy Is Seen as Ebbing," *New York Times*, April 17, 2015.

32. Dani Rodrik, "The Global Governance of Trade as if Development Really Mattered" (paper submitted to the United Nations Development Programme, New York City, July 2001), http://www.giszpcnc.com/globalciv/rodrik1.pdf. See also, Dani Rodrik, "How to Make the Trade Regime Work for Development," working paper, Kennedy School, Harvard University, 2004; and David Singh Grewal, *Network Power: The Social Dynamics of Globalization* (New Haven, Conn.: Yale University Press, 2008), 240–246.

33. David Singh Grewal, *Network Power*, 241.

34. Sun Zhenyu, "Joining WTO Was a Positive Move," *China Daily*, June 1, 2011.

35. "China's Economy and the WTO: All Change," *Economist*, December 10, 2011.

36. There is ample evidence that China's grand strategy is designed to undermine the U.S.-led system and to replace the United States as the primary power in Asia. Summarizing examples cited elsewhere in this book, PRC officials have been explicit about their goals to weaken the U.S. alliance system in Asia (see, e.g., Chapter 4). They also seek to undermine the confidence of Asian nations in U.S. credibility, reliability, and staying power—seen in efforts to stand-up multilateral alternatives to the Bretton Woods institutions—the Chinese-led BRICS Bank and the Asian Infrastructure Bank, moves that, according to U.S. officials and a wide consensus of experts, are aimed in no small part at weakening U.S. global economic

leadership. PRC officials also use China's economic power to pull Asian nations closer to PRC geopolitical and policy preferences, as Chapter 4 details. Increases in PRC military capability, meanwhile, are specifically tailored to strengthen deterrence against U.S. military intervention in the region. In its bilateral diplomacy, Beijing has long sought to ensure that U.S. democratic values do not diminish the CCP's economic potential or its hold on domestic power (see, e.g., discussions of Chinese efforts in Angola, Venezuela, Sudan, and Zimbabwe in Chapters 2 and 3). And more recently, they have begun to stand up multi-lateral alternatives to the Bretton Woods institutions—the Chinese-led BRICs Bank and the Asian Infrastructure Investment Bank—moves that, according to U.S. officials and a wide consensus of experts, are aimed in no small part at weakening U.S. global economic leadership (see Chapter 3).

37. David Allen Baldwin, *Economic Statecraft* (Princeton: Princeton University Press, 1985), 191.

38. See, e.g., Bijan Khajehpour, Reza Marashi, and Trita Parsi, "Why the Sanctions Don't Work," *National Interest*, April 3, 2013 (criticizing U.S. sanctions against Iran for failing to "achiev[e] their stated objective: shifting Iran's nuclear stance" without considering whether there are more desirable alternatives).

39. Quotes from "The Chill from Frozen Assets," *Wall Street Journal*, December 4, 1979; and Robert Carswell, "Economic Sanctions," 248, as cited in Baldwin, *Economic Statecraft*.

40. Baldwin, *Economic Statecraft*, 191, 257.

41. Ashley J. Tellis, *Balancing without Containment: An American Strategy for Managing China* (Washington, D.C.: Carnegie Endowment for International Peace, 2014), n. 117.

42. Robert Zoellick, "The Currency of Power," *Foreign Policy*, October 8, 2012. And see Braz Baracuhy, "The New Geo-economics of Global Trade: The WTO's Perspective," International Institute for Strategic Studies, September 13, 2014 ("The centrality of Asia in intra- and inter-regional trade flows is a key geo-economic development of recent years"); Jeremy Page, "China Sees Itself at Center of New Asian Order," *Wall Street Journal*, November 9, 2014.

43. Conversation with author.

44. David Ignatius, "The U.S. Is Still Indispensable when It Comes to Free Trade," *Washington Post*, April 3, 2014.

45. Ibid.

46. "U.S., U.K. Politicians Eye Strategic Aims of Trans-Atlantic Trade Talks," *Wall Street Journal*, September 25, 2013. See generally Daniel Hamilton and Steven Blockmans, "The Geostrategic Implications of TTIP," Centre for European Policy Studies, April 2015.

47. David Sanger, "Obama Order Sped Up Wave of Cyberattacks against Iran," *New York Times*, June 1, 2012.

48. David E. Sanger, "U.S. and China Seek Arms Deal for Cyberspace," *New York Times*, September 19, 2015.

49. John Williamson, "The Dollar and U.S. Power," in *The Power of Currencies and the Currencies of Power*, ed. Alan Wheatley (New York: Routledge, 2013), 82–84.

50. "President Prepares to Meet King as U.S.-Saudi Divisions Deepen," National Public Radio, March 27, 2014.

51. There was no budget request for MENA-IF in FY12.

52. Josh Rogin, "State Department Tries Again to Create Arab Spring Support Fund," *Foreign Policy*, April 10, 2013.

53. The Senate bill approved $1 billion for MENA-IF; the House bill, however, zeroed out the request such that no funds were appropriate for the MENA-IF for FY13.

54. See Danya Greenfield, Amy Hawthorne, and Rosa Balfour, "U.S. and EU: Lack of Strategic Vision, Frustrated Efforts toward the Arab Transitions," Atlantic Council, September 2013.

55. Assessments of the FY15 budget request suggest that the current Obama administration continues to distance itself from the MENA-IF model in particular, but continues to prioritize transition and reform programs in the region (totaling $1.575 billion) in pursuit of the same geopolitical objectives. "Analysis of the President's FY15 International Affairs Budget Request," U.S. Global Leadership Coalition, March 4, 2014, 8.

56. Author interviews with former administration officials.

57. The authors are indebted to several former government officials for a series of discussion on MENA-IF and MENA-TIP.

58. Joseph J. Collins and Gabrielle D. Bowdoin, *Beyond Unilateral Economic Sanctions: Better Alternatives for U.S. Foreign Policy* (Washington, D.C.: Center for Strategic and International Studies, 1999).

59. Jesse Helms, "What Sanctions Epidemic? U.S. Business' Curious Crusade," *Foreign Affairs*, January/February 1999; Helms, *Empire for Liberty: A Sovereign American and Her Moral Mission* (Raleigh, N.C.: Jesse Helms Center, 2001), 96.

60. U.S. Department of the Treasury, Resource Center on Sanctions Programs and Country Information, available at www.treasury.gov/resource-center/sanctions /Programs/Pages/Programs.aspx.

61. Geoff Dyer, "Sanctions: War by Other Means," *Financial Times*, March 30, 2014.

62. Baldwin, *Economic Statecraft*; John Cassidy, "Iran Nuke Deal: Do Economic Sanctions Work after All?," *New Yorker*, November 25, 2013.

63. Richard Youngs, "Armenia as a Showcase for the New European Neighborhood Policy?," Carnegie Europe, April 2, 2015.

64. See Stephen Blank, "Russia's Unending Balkan Intrigues," *Eurasia Daily Monitor* 12, no. 108 (June 10, 2015); Stephen Blank, "Putin Sets His Eyes on the Balkans," *Newsweek*, April 17, 2015; Andrew Byrne, "Serbia Caught between Russia and West," *Financial Times*, December 3, 2014.

65. Government Accountability Office, *Iran: U.S. and International Sanctions Have Adversely Affected the Iranian Economy*, February 2013, summary section.

66. Ibid., 18.

67. Wolfgang Münchau warned that "even the current list of sanctions could be macroeconomically significant in a way not captured by forecasts or sentiment surveys. My guess is that the cumulative global effect of the sanctions will be much stronger than estimated but that it might be a while before they kick in fully. In

short: we should not see this as a decimal point disturbance." Wolfgang Münchau, "The West Risks Collateral Damage by Punishing Russia," *Financial Times,* July 27, 2014. A Deutsche Bank research piece from March 2014 claimed that potential spillover effects from further financial sector sanctions on Russia are impossible to quantify: "Note that beyond asset freezes or deterioration in credit worthiness, the international financial system may have to deal with the potential disruptions stemming from a possible ban on trading with Russian financial institutions. This could have implications for liquidity and profits, but data on this type of relationship is too patchy to make any attempt at quantification worthwhile." Gilles Moec and Marco Stringa, "Who Is Exposed to Russia?," Deutsche Bank Research, March 20, 2014. Daniel Gilbert argues that additional energy sector sanctions would threaten one of Exxon's "best chances to find and tap valuable—and much needed—crude oil reserves; "Sanctions over Ukraine Put Exxon at Risk," *Wall Street Journal,* September 11, 2014. Finally, another bank report predicts that commodity market shocks could ensue from energy sector sanctions: "So far, commodity markets have been relatively untouched by the crisis. However, there is a risk that new sanctions on Russia may constrain the country's exports, as has been the case with the sanctions on Iran. In such a scenario, the above-mentioned markets could face a supply disruption, which could push up prices significantly." Danske Bank, "Research Global: Russian-Ukrainian Crisis Takes a Tragic Turn," July 18, 2014. Additional sanctions were leveled later that summer, and by fall global oil and gas touched their lowest prices in years.

68. Indeed, revised estimates issued roughly twelve months after the sanctions took effect suggest the more aggressive sanctions negatively impact European GDP growth by less than half a tenth of a percentage point. Laurence Norman, "EU Projects Impact of Sanctions on Russian Economy," *Wall Street Journal,* October 29, 2014; Vauhini Vara, "Hurt Putin? Hurt Yourself?," *New Yorker,* August 19, 2014.

69. Dan Lamonthe, "France Backs off Sending Mistral Warship to Russia in $1.7 Billion Deal," *Washington Post,* September 3, 2014: "The decision marks a turn-around for France, which signaled as recently as Monday that it intended to complete the sale. Pressure had been building on Paris to hold the ship back, however, especially after NATO said it had determined that Russia has sent troops and military equipment into Ukraine. French officials have spent years defending the arms sale, in which France beat out rival nations like Germany and Spain to sell ships to the Russians." See also Kate Brannen, "France's Ship Sale to Russia Latest Example of Commerce and Policy Clash," *Foreign Policy,* July 23, 2014: "State Department spokeswoman Marie Harf called the French sale 'completely inappropriate. We obviously don't think the Mistral should go ahead. . . . We don't think anyone should be providing arms to Russia.' "

70. Sam Jones and Geoff Dyer, "Iran Sanctions Eased as Deal Stick," *Financial Times,* January 20, 2014.

71. Jason Rezaian and Anne Gearan, "U.S., Europe Lift Some Iran Sanctions under Nuclear Deal," *Washington Post,* January 20, 2014.

72. Susan B. Epstein, "The Budget Control Act, Sequestration, and the Foreign Affairs Budget: Background and Possible Impacts," Congressional Research Service, December 20, 2013.

73. Ursula Lindsey, "Rebels without a Pause," *New York Times,* May 21, 2103; Tarek Masou, *Counting Islam: Religion, Class, and Elections in Egypt* (Cambridge: Cambridge University Press, 2014), 210. "Economic grievances pose the greatest threat to Mursi's rule," warned Yasser el-Shimy, a Cairo-based analyst with the International Crisis Group, just ten days prior to his removal. Mariam Fam and Alaa Shahine, "Egypt's Unemployed Target Mursi after Toppling Mubarak: Jobs," *Bloomberg Business,* June 24, 2013.

74. "The Great Well of China," *Economist,* June 20, 2015.

75. It is worth noting that the original terms of the 1979 Camp David accord promised only to give funds to Israel and Egypt for three years. With this aid still flowing some three and a half decades later (and on terms largely unchanged), it is a reminder that once a geopolitical issue finds a toehold in the U.S. Congress, it can prove difficult to pull back.

76. Consider the Israeli government's reaction to the violence that seized Egypt during the summer of 2013. As the violence worsened, sparking doubts about whether the United States would continue aid in the face of a bloody crackdown by the Egyptian military, Israeli prime minister Benjamin Netanyahu expressed confidence in continued American support, noting that "peace was premised on American aid to Egypt, and I think that for us is the most important consideration. And I'm sure that's taken under advisement in Washington." Michael R. Gordon and Mark Landler, "In Crackdown Responses, U.S. Temporarily Freezes Some Military Aid to Egypt," *New York Times,* October 9, 2013.

77. Nolan Feeney, "U.S. Offers Congo $30 Million, on Condition President Steps Down," *Time,* May 4, 2014.

78. Geoff Dyer, "US Restores $1.3bn Military Aid to Egypt," *Financial Times,* April 1, 2015.

79. Benn Steil and Robert Litan, "International Financial Statecraft," Council on Foreign Relations Special Report, August 2006.

80. Board of Economic Warfare, later renamed the Office of Economic Warfare. For a detailed history, see Jeremy Atack and Peter Passell, *New View of American Economic History,* 2nd ed. (New York: Norton, 1994).

81. Members of the National Commission on Terrorist Attacks on the United States (9/11 Commission) gave the campaign against terrorist financing an A- in the commission's 2005 review of the implementation of its recommendations. That was the highest grade it gave for any aspect of the war on terrorism. For a discussion, see Council on Foreign Relations, "Terrorist Finance," 2002, http://www.cfr.org/publication.html?id=5080.

82. Ibid.

83. Author exchange with private sector commentator, May 2012.

8. The Geoeconomics of North America's Energy Revolution

1. This chapter is drawn from Robert D. Blackwill and Meghan L. O'Sullivan, "America's Energy Edge," *Foreign Affairs,* March/April 2014, and has profited from recent work by Dr. O'Sullivan on the subject. It also has benefitted from multiple insights on the draft by Dr. Drew Erdmann and Dr. Panos E. Cavoulacos.

2. As some expert analyses note, it is not just the United States that happens to have a lot of shale gas; rather, it is the United States that is the first major economy to start exploiting the geopolitical advantages of shale on a large scale. Matthew Lynn, "Shale Gas Revolution Will Create Winners, Losers," MarketWatch, August 7, 2013; Ed Crooks and Anjli Raval, "US Poised to Become World's Leading Liquid Petroleum Producer," *Financial Times,* September 29, 2014.

3. We have witnessed a transformation from resource scarcity to resource abundance, thanks to the U.S. oil and gas industry's technological and entrepreneurial prowess. The resulting surge in supply means that the global energy sector will began to behave like a "more normal market, in which demand and supply are in better balance and less power is concentrated in the hands of producers." Ian Bremmer and Kenneth A. Hersh, "When America Stops Importing Energy," *New York Times,* May 22, 2013.

4. "How Much Natural Gas Does the United States Have and How Long Will It Last?," U.S. Energy Information Administration, December 3, 2014.

5. "Market Trends: Natural Gas," Annual Energy Outlook 2014, U.S. Energy Information Administration, May 7, 2014.

6. "Shale Gas Provides Largest Share of U.S. Natural Gas Production in 2013," U.S. Energy Information Administration, November 25, 2014.

7. Stanley Reed, "Oil Prices Drop as Production Hums Along despite a Brimming Supply," *New York Times,* March 13, 2015; Henry Srebrnik, "Will American Self-Sufficiency in Oil Affect Its Foreign Policy?," *Journal Pioneer,* March 29, 2015.

8. Daniel Yergin, "The Global Impact of US Shale," Project Syndicate, January 8, 2014.

9. Bakken, Eagle Ford, and Permian are the names of shale formations. Such formations typically cover several counties, states, or sometimes countries. "U.S. Field Production of Crude Oil," data set from U.S. Energy Information Administration, November 26, 2014; Wood Mackenzie, "Global Geopolitics Reshaped by North American Energy Independence," press release, September 26, 2013.

10. Also see "Shale Oil: The Next Energy Revolution," PricewaterhouseCoopers, February 2013.

11. The combination of U.S. oil and gas production is projected to outpace Russia's by 5 billion BTU in 2013, according to EIA forecasts cited in John Waggoner, "Report: U.S. to Be Top Energy Producer This Year," *USA Today,* November 12, 2013.

12. EIA and NERA use 6 billion cubic feet per day in many scenarios and reports: http://energy.gov/fe/downloads/lng-export-study-related-documents. Also see Meghan L. O'Sullivan, "A Better Energy Weapon to Stop Putin," *Bloomberg View,* March 11, 2014; Zain Shauk, "U.S. Natural Gas Exports Will Fire Up in 2015," *Bloomberg Businessweek,* November 6, 2014; "Effect of Increased Levels of Liquefied Natural Gas Exports on U.S. Energy Markets," U.S. Energy Information Administration, October 29, 2014; Roger Howard, "How Shale Energy Reshapes American Security," *National Interest,* May 3, 2013.

13. International Energy Agency, *World Energy Outlook 2013,* 564.

14. Meghan L. O'Sullivan, "'Energy Independence' Alone Won't Boost U.S. Power," *Bloomberg View,* February 14, 2013. Robert McNally and Michael Levi, "Vindicating Volatility," *Foreign Affairs,* November 4, 2014.

15. Matt Clinch, "Oil Falls below $45 as OPEC Plays Hardball," CNBC, January 13, 2015; "A U.S. Oil Production Slowdown Eases OPEC's Mind," Stratfor Global Intelligence, December 12, 2014; "Lower Oil Prices Carry Geopolitical Consequences," Stratfor Global Intelligence, November 3, 2014; U.S. Energy Information Administration, "Short-term Energy and Winter Fuels Outlook," October 6, 2015; Nicole Friedman, "U.S. Oil Prices Hit Fresh Six-Year Low, Dipping Below $40 a Barrel," *Wall Street Journal,* August 21, 2015; " 'The New Oil Order': Making Sense of an Industry's Transformation," Goldman Sachs, December 2015.

16. Ben Sharples, "Goldman Sees Oil at $45 by October after 'Self-Defeating Rally,' " *Bloomberg Business,* May 19, 2015.

17. John Baffes, M. Ayhan Kose, Franziska Ohnosrge, and Marc Stocker, "The Great Plunge in Oil Prices: Causes, Consequences, and Policy Responses," World Bank Group, March 2015.

18. "OPEC: Monthly Oil Market Report," June 10, 2015; "OPEC Refuses to Cut Oil Production," CNN Money, June 5, 2015; Summer Said, "Saudi Arabia, Iraq Push OPEC over Its Ceiling," *Wall Street Journal,* June 10, 2015.

19. "New Oil Order: Energy and Utilities Investment Strategy. Rise of Shale Pushing OPEC from Cut to Grow; Stay Selective Post Meeting," Goldman Sachs Equity Research, June 8, 2015.

20. Indonesia, a net energy importer, is perhaps the one exception.

21. Martin Feldstein, "The Geopolitical Impact of Cheap Oil," Project Syndicate, November 26, 2014. Also see "When Oil Prices Drop, Some Countries Lose," Stratfor Global Intelligence, November 4, 2014.

22. Many of these countries have regimes that could potentially collapse if the economy—spurred by oil price shock—runs into serious trouble. Lynn, "Shale Gas Revolution Will Create Winners and Losers."

23. While experts argue that neither U.S. LNG nor domestic European shale gas production will supplant Russian gas imports, given how cheap piped Russian gas is, the U.S. unconventional energy boom can affect Russian revenue streams by putting pressure on oil indexation, which has been Russia's preferred basis for pricing gas sales to Europe and has helped keep prices high. Meghan L. O'Sullivan, "North American Energy Remakes the Geopolitical Landscape: Understanding and Advancing the Phenomenon," Goldman Sachs, May 31, 2014; Morena Skalamera, "Booming Synergies in Sino-Russian Natural Gas Partnership," Belfer Center for Science and International Affairs, Harvard University, May 2014; Ariel Cohen and Anton Altman, "U.S. Shale Gas: The Geopolitical Impact," Heritage Foundation, July 28, 2011.

24. Keith Johnson, "U.S. Mulls Lifting Oil Export Ban, but a Tough Sell on the Hill," *Foreign Policy,* October 2, 2015.

25. See European Commission, "EU Crude Oil Imports," http://ec.europa.eu/energy/en/statistics/eu-crude-oil-imports; and Elizabeth Rosenberg, David Gordon, and Ellie Maruyama, "Crude Oil Export and U.S. National Security," Center for a New American Security, May 14, 2015.

26. After the United States took Russia's spot as the world's largest gas producer in 2013, Moscow quickly began to focus beyond Europe in boosting exports to energy-hungry Asia. Alexandra Hudson, "U.S. Shale Gas Revolution Throws down the Gauntlet to Europe," Reuters, February 3, 2013.

27. Ukraine's gas company, Naftogaz, signed a deal with Gazprom in December 2014, transferring $378 million to the Russian gas giant as an up-front payment for 1 billion cubic meters of gas, a delivery that resumes Russian supplies of gas to Kiev. Natalia Zinets, "Ukraine Expects Russian Gas Supplies to Resume Monday," Reuters, December 7, 2014.

28. Russia's central bank projected the economy could shrink by 4.7 percent in 2015 if the low oil prices of late 2014 persist. See Neil MacFarquhar and Andrew Kramer, "As the Ruble Swoons, Russians Desperately Shop," *New York Times,* December 16, 2014; Friedman, "U.S. Oil Prices Hit Fresh Six-Year Low, Dipping Below $40 a Barrel."

29. Zachary C. Shirkey, "America Can't Escape the Middle East," *National Interest,* July 29, 2013.

30. "EM Oil Producers: Breakeven Pain Thresholds," Deutsche Bank Research, October 16, 2014. Also see Institute of International Finance, "IFF: Lower Oil Prices Present Challenges and Opportunities for MENA Region," March 16, 2015. KSA's break-even price a decade ago was $20–25, and today Iraq, Iran, and UAE have break-even prices in the $80–100 range, according to IMF estimates; Javier Blas and Guy Chazan, "Saudi Arabia Targets $100 Crude Price," *Financial Times,* January 18, 2012. It should be noted that although fiscal break-even oil prices give a useful overview of a country's fiscal standing, there can be significant variability between estimates from different analysts. Inconsistencies can arise from a number of factors, including different forecasts for oil production and fiscal outturns. Standard and Poor's, "How Do Middle Eastern Sovereigns' Fiscal Breakeven Oil Prices Affect Credit Ratings and Oil Prices?," February 1, 2013.

31. Anjli Raval, "Saudi Arabia Keeps the Oil Market Guessing," *Financial Times,* October 20, 2014. Also see Meghan O'Sullivan, "The Saudis Won't Let Oil Free-Fall," *Bloomberg View,* December 3, 2014.

32. International Monetary Fund, "Saudi Arabia: International Reserves and Foreign Currency Liquidity," November 6, 2015, https://www.imf.org/external/np/sta/ir/IRProcessWeb/data/sau/eng/cursau.htm.

33. Daniel Yergin, "The Global Impact of US Shale," Project Syndicate, January 8, 2014.

34. Syed Rashid Husain, "Iran Nuke Deal Sends Ripples in Oil Markets," *Saudi Gazette,* July 19, 2015.

35. Meghan O'Sullivan, "The Energy Implications of a Nuclear Deal between the P5+1 and Iran," Geopolitics of Energy Project workshop report, June 23–24, 2015.

36. Calculations based on the table in International Energy Agency, *World Energy Outlook 2013,* 505. Since China and India spend heavily on oil subsidies each year, a prolonged decline in oil prices could translate into lower costs on oil subsidies and therefore greater budget space for Beijing and New Delhi to spend on other priorities, such as sorely needed social safety nets or intensified military modernization.

37. See U.S. Energy Information Administration, "China—Analysis," February 4, 2014.

38. O'Sullivan, "North American Energy Remakes the Geopolitical Landscape."

39. Africa experienced decreases when the United States took to fracking, losing $1.5 billion in gas revenues and $32 billion in oil revenues over a period of five years. Renee Lewis, "China Shale Gas Boom Will Hit Poor African Exporters Hard," Al Jazeera America, May 7, 2014. Also see Zhenbo Hou et al., "The Development Implications of the Fracking Revolution," Overseas Development Institute working paper, April 2014; Lucy Hornby and Ed Crooks, "China's Shale Revolution: Will It Take Off?," ChinaDialogue, January 17, 2014.

40. Keith Johnson, "Russia, China Finally Ink Landmark Energy Deal," *Foreign Policy,* May 21, 2014; Richard Martin, "Russia-China Gas Deal Narrows Window for U.S. Exports," *Forbes,* May 30, 2014; Jane Perlez, "China and Russia Reach 30-Year Gas Deal," *New York Times,* May 21, 2014.

41. Along with Taiwan and China, these countries—which collectively purchase around two-thirds of the world's LNG—met in 2013 to discuss ways of using their aggregate market power to drive down prices of LNG in Asia. O'Sullivan, "North American Energy Remakes the Geopolitical Landscape."

42. IHS, "America's New Energy Future: The Unconventional Oil and Gas Revolution and the US Economy, Volume 3: A Manufacturing Renaissance," September 2013, Executive Summary, 1; McKinsey Global Institute, "Game Changers: Five Opportunities for US Growth and Renewal," July 2013; U.S. Energy Administration, "Growing U.S. HGL Production Spurs Petrochemical Industry Investment," January 19, 2015, http://www.eia.gov/todayinenergy/detail.cfm?id=19771.

43. McKinsey Global Institute, "Game Changers." IHS estimates that by 2025 total contributions to GDP will approach $533 billion. This report also estimates that the unconventional oil and natural gas value chain and energy-related chemicals activity will support almost 3.9 million jobs by 2025. IHS, "America's New Energy Future."

44. Matt Egan, "Oil Crash Cut My Pay and Killed over 86,000 Jobs," *CNN Money,* September 3, 2015.

45. Vali R. Nasr, "Diplomacy Can Still Save Iraq," *New York Times,* July 14, 2014.

46. According to the U.S. Energy Information Administration's Short-Term Energy and Summer Fuels Outlook, April 2015, net imports of crude oil to the United States declined by 31 percent between 2005 and 2014, even as crude oil production grew by 68 percent over the same time period.

47. Bremmer and Hersh, "When America Stops Importing Energy."

48. IHS, "America's New Energy Future," Executive Summary, 6.

49. Blackwill and O'Sullivan, "America's Energy Edge."

50. The oil and gas boom in the United States and elsewhere has meant that international sanctions and U.S.-allied efforts against the Iranian nuclear program removed over 1 million barrels per day of Iranian oil while minimizing the burdens on the rest of the world. See remarks by former U.S. national security advisor Tom Donilon delivered at the launch of Columbia University's Center on Global Energy Policy, April 24, 2013. Energy expert Michael Levi argues that U.S. leverage with Iran hinged on the surprise factor of its newfound oil production: "The entire premise of talk about enduring geopolitical advantage, however, is that future production gains will no longer be surprising. Anticipating those gains, some producers

will preemptively curb investment. . . . In that world, suddenly removing two million barrels a day from world markets through sanctions will send prices rapidly upward. Unexpected U.S. gains won't be able to offset unexpected losses from sanctions because U.S. gains will not be unexpected." Michael Levi, *The Power Surge: Energy, Opportunity, and the Battle for America's Future,* reprint ed. (New York: Oxford University Press, 2014), 215. Also see Dan Eberhart, "Strong Arm or Upper Hand: The Shale Revolution and US Geopolitics," *Canary,* May 1, 2014.

51. Lynn, "Shale Gas Revolution Will Create Winners, Losers."

52. Mitchell A. Orenstein, "Six Markets to Watch: Poland," *Foreign Affairs,* January/February 2014.

53. Marek Strzelecki and Isis Almeida, "Fracking Setback in Poland Dims Hope for Less Russian Gas," *Bloomberg Business,* October 10, 2014; O'Sullivan, "North American Energy Remakes the Geopolitical Landscape." A 2013 report from the U.S. Energy Information Administration downgraded its estimates of Polish gas reserves from 187 trillion cubic feet (2011) to 148 trillion cubic feet (2013). This reduction of estimates from Poland's Lubin Basin was due to the more rigorous application of the requirement that a shale formation have at least a 2 percent minimum total organic content. U.S. Energy Information Administration, "Technically Recoverable Shale Oil and Shale Gas Resources: An Assessment of 137 Shale Formations in 41 Countries Outside the United States," June 2013.

54. Erica S. Downs, "Implications of the U.S. Shale Energy Revolution for China," Brookings Institution, November 8, 2013.

55. One of the major geopolitical benefits of the shale revolution vis-à-vis U.S.-China relations is that it provides China's national oil companies with incentives to curb their business in countries less friendly to U.S. interests, such as Iran. See ibid.

56. "Fact Sheet: U.S.-China Joint Announcement on Climate Change and Clean Energy Cooperation," White House, Office of the Press Secretary, November 11, 2014.

57. Michael Porter, David Gee, and Gregory Pope, "America's Unconventional Energy Opportunity: A Win-Win Plan for the Economy, the Environment, and a Lower-Carbon, Cleaner-Energy Future," Harvard Business School, June 2015.

9. American Foreign Policy in an Age of Economic Power

1. Realists argue that force is a fungible tool of statecraft; their liberal critics see power resources as harder to strategically deploy across issue areas. Daniel Drezner, "Military Primacy Doesn't Pay," *International Security* 38, no. 1 (Summer 2013): 78–79. Also see Robert Keohane and Joseph Nye, *Power and Interdependence* (Boston, Mass.: Scott Foresman, 1978); Kenneth Waltz, *Theory of International Politics* (Long Grove, Ill.: Waveland Press, 2010); David Baldwin, *Paradoxes of Power* (New York: Blackwell, 1989); Robert Art, "American Foreign Policy and the Fungibility of Force," *Security Studies* 5, no. 4 (Summer 1996): 7–42.

2. Drezner, "Military Primacy Doesn't Pay." Also see Michael J. Mazarr, "The Risks of Ignoring Strategic Insolvency," *Washington Quarterly* 35, no. 4 (2012): 7–22. Unsurprisingly, Iran's foreign minister, Mohammad Javad Zarif, echoed these sentiments: "Due to a number of factors—the substantially changed global envi-

ronment, changes in the nature of power, and the diversity and multiplicity of state and nonstate actors—competition these days mostly takes a nonmilitary form. . . . [M]ajor powers and emerging powers alike are now loath to use military means to resolve rivalries, differences, or even disputes. This has led to the gradual rise of a revisionist approach to foreign policy." Mohammad Javad Zarif, "What Iran Really Wants: Iranian Foreign Policy in the Rouhani Era," *Foreign Affairs,* May/June 2014.

3. Localization requirements meant that there were far more U.S. and European corporate assets in Russia and thus potentially vulnerable to seizure in any tit-for-tat escalation. In some cases, these assets were jointly owned with potentially sanctionable Russian entities (Gazprom's joint ventures with Shell or Exxon, for example). Matthew Philips, "Post Crimea, Exxon's Partnership with Rosneft Feels Weird," *Bloomberg Businessweek,* March 20, 2014; Jack Farchy and Ed Crooks, "Shell Suspends Russian Shale Oil Venture with Gazprom Neft," *Financial Times,* October 3, 2014.

4. See, e.g., Robert Wright, "Is China Democratizing?," *New York Times,* April 17, 2009; Suisheng Zhao, ed., *China and Democracy: The Prospect for a Democratic China* (New York: Routledge, 2000); Kevin J. O'Brien and Lianjiang Li, "Accommodating 'Democracy' in a One-Party State: Introducing Village Elections in China," in *Elections and Democracy in Greater China,* ed. Larry Diamond and Ramon H. Myers (Oxford: Oxford University Press, 2000). Cf. Mary Gallagher, *Contagious Capitalism: Globalization and Labor Politics in China* (Princeton, N.J.: Princeton University Press, 2007); James Mann, *The China Fantasy: Why Capitalism Will Not Bring Democracy to China* (New York: Viking, 2007).

5. Peter Pomerantsev, "How Putin Is Reinventing Warfare," *Foreign Policy,* May 5, 2014.

6. David Petraeus and Paras D. Bhayani, "North America: The Next Great Emerging Market? Capitalizing on North America's Four Interlocking Revolutions," John F. Kennedy School of Government, Harvard University, June 2015.

7. See, e.g., Ben Bernanke, in his final speech as chairman of the Federal Reserve, "The Federal Reserve: Looking Back, Looking Forward," delivered at the annual meeting of the American Economic Association in Philadelphia, January 3, 2014. Richard Fisher, a conservative-leaning member of the U.S. Federal Reserve Board, argues, "The only thing holding the nation back from an economic boom was muddled fiscal policy"; Rob Curran, "Fisher Says Fed Has Overshot Mark on Stimulus," *Wall Street Journal,* October 10, 2014. See also "Global Financial Stability Report," International Monetary Fund, October 2014. Erskine Bowles, cochair of the bipartisan Simpson-Bowles Commission, reiterated that the 2011 sequester cuts to discretionary spending were counterproductive to the task of long-term debt and deficit reduction: "Instead of enacting a thoughtful, comprehensive fiscal plan that gradually reduced the deficit and put the budget on a fiscally sustainable long-term path, Washington allowed abrupt cuts from sequestration to take effect, harming the economic recovery and cutting important investments that could jeopardize future prosperity. And, for all that pain, the sequester does almost nothing to deal with the long-term drivers of our growing debt"; Erskine Bowles, "Urgency of Federal Deficit Remains," *USA Today,* October 27, 2014. See also Lawrence Summers, "Why Public Investment Really Is a Free Lunch," *Financial Times,* October 6, 2014.

8. See, e.g., American Association for the Advancement of Science, "AAAS Report XXXVIII: Research and Development FY 2014," June 13, 2013.

9. Michael Leachman and Chris Mai, "Most States Funding Schools Less than before the Recession," Center on Budget and Policy Priorities, May 20, 2014. Sheryll Poe, "The High Cost of Doing Nothing on Infrastructure Investment," U.S. Chamber of Commerce, September 23, 2014.

10. Jim Manzi, "The New American System," *National Affairs,* n. 19 (Spring 2014).

11. U.S. Department of State, "The Department of State and USAID FY 2016 Budget," Bureau of Public Affairs fact sheet, February 23, 2015; Office of the Undersecretary of Defense (Comptroller), "United States Department of Defense Fiscal Year 2016 Budget Request: Overview," February 2015.

12. These high aspirations were echoed by national security advisor Susan Rice at a White House press briefing: "White House Briefing on Obama Asia Trip with Questions on Ukraine," White House, Office of the Press Secretary, April 18, 2014.

13. Stephen Grenville, "The Trans-Pacific Partnership: Where Economics and Geopolitics Meet," *Interpreter,* March 4, 2014; Samuel Rines, "Trans-Pacific Partnership: Geopolitics, Not Growth," *National Interest,* March 31, 2014.

14. ASEAN's Expanded Economic Engagement (E3) initiative began in 2013 under the directive of identifying specific cooperative activities that further facilitate U.S.-ASEAN trade and investment, increase efficiency and competitiveness of trade flows throughout Southeast Asian nations, and build greater awareness of economic opportunities in the U.S.-ASEAN relationship. Cooperation on E3 initiatives is seen as laying the groundwork for all ASEAN countries to join other trade agreements, including the TPP. "The U.S.-ASEAN Expanded Economic Engagement E3 Initiative," U.S. Department of State Office of the Spokesperson, October 9, 2013.

15. Cris Arcos, "Keep NAFTA's Momentum Going," *Miami Herald,* February 22, 2014.

16. Details on these recommendations can be found in Robert A. Pastor, "Shortcut to U.S. Economic Competitiveness: A Seamless North American Market," Council on Foreign Relations, Policy Innovation Memorandum no. 29, Renewing America Initiative, March 5, 2013.

17. Testimony of Eric Farnsworth, Vice President, Council of the Americas, in U.S. Congress, Senate Committee on Foreign Relations, *Doing Business in Latin America: Positive Trends but Serious Challenges,* 112th Congress, 2nd session, July 31, 2012, S.Hrg. 112-607.

18. Robert A. Pastor, *The North American Idea: A Vision of a Continental Future* (Oxford: Oxford University Press, 2011), 169–172.

19. Ben Bland and Geoff Dyer, "US Warns China over Disputed South China Sea," *Financial Times,* September 3, 2012.

20. Robert Kaplan quoted in "Sea Change," *New York Times,* April 17, 2014.

21. For one such assessment, see Bonnie Glaser, "China's Coercive Economic Diplomacy," *Diplomat,* July 25, 2012.

22. The authors are grateful to Bonnie Glaser for an exchange expounding on this point.

23. Gary Clyde Hufbauer, Jeffrey J. Schott, Kimberly Ann Elliott, and Barbara Oegg, *Economic Sanctions Reconsidered,* 3rd edition (Washington, D.C.: Peterson

Institute for International Economics, 2007). Brief available at http://www.iie.com /publications/briefs/sanctions4075.pdf.

24. For further discussion of these defensive geoeconomic options, see Albert O. Hirschman, *National Power and the Structure of Foreign Trade* (Berkley: University of California Press, 1945), 14–16; Zachary Selden, *Economic Sanctions as Instruments of American Foreign Policy* (Westport, Conn.: Praeger, 1999); Jean-Marc F. Blanchard and Norrin M. Ripsman, "Asking the Right Question: When Do Economic Sanctions Work Best?," *Security Studies* 9, nos. 1–2 (1999): 219–220.

25. As noted by Chi-hung Wei, can the state implement these geoeconomic defensive policies without institutional connections to society? Can the state mobilize society, in a democratic setting, to garner support for the use of these instruments? See Chi-hung Wei, "China's Economic Offensive and Taiwan's Defensive Measures," *China Quarterly* 215 (September 2013): 644.

26. According to James McGregor, the middle-income trap "can occur when export-led fast-growth through cheap labor and easy technology adoption runs out of steam." The remedy is simple: the economy has to turn to domestic consumption and innovation. James McGregor, *No Ancient Wisdom, No Followers: The Challenges of Chinese Authoritarian Capitalism* (Westport, Conn.: Prospecta Press, 2012), 9.

27. U.S.-India Joint Statement, White House Office of the Press Secretary, September 30, 2014.

28. Author interview with Dr. Alyssa Ayres, April 2014.

29. "Putin's War of Words," *New York Times,* December 4, 2014.

30. Some are of the view that NATO should be more assertive in its response than it has been to date. Regardless of one's view on this question, the point here is simply that, based on a survey of the response the United States and European Union have mounted to date, the overwhelming focus has been limited to NATO activities, together with sanctions coordination efforts.

31. At a November 2014 exhibition of armored personnel carriers in Moscow, Mr. Putin observed how "you can do a lot more with weapons and politeness than just politeness," an unsubtle reference to the "polite" Russian soldiers who appeared in Crimea earlier that year. Central Asian and Eastern European nations are increasingly aware of the potential repercussions if Putin's Novorossiya is realized, and they are looking to the United States as an alternative to Russian and Chinese investment. For instance, securing closer trade and investment ties with the United States has been a primary focus of Kazakh foreign minister Erlan Idrissov's portfolio. "Putin's War of Words," *New York Times,* December 4, 2014 (quoting Putin). For more on Kazakhstan's efforts to increase economic ties with the United States, see generally "Joint Statement of the Third U.S.-Kazakhstan Strategic Partnership Dialogue," U.S. Department of State, December 10, 2014; Robert Guttman, "Kazakhstan Foreign Minister and U.S. Senior Officials Reaffirm and Strengthen Strategic Partnership," *TransAtlantic Magazine,* July 14, 2013.

32. One of the clearest examples came in December 2014, as Russia found itself in the grip of a full-blown currency crisis. Despite stunning interventions by the Russian central bank—including hiking deposit rates from 10 percent to 17.5 percent in the course of a single overnight period—the ruble continued a steep slide, losing more than half of its value since the start of 2014. See, e.g., David Herzenshorn and Neil

Irwin, "Interest Rate Raised to 17% in Russia," *New York Times,* December 15, 2014.

33. Many of these recommendations are from Meghan L. O'Sullivan, "North American Energy Remakes the Geopolitical Landscape: Understanding and Advancing the Phenomenon," Goldman Sachs, May 31, 2014.

34. Energy ties should, as Elizabeth Rosenthal aptly notes, be used alongside trade as leverage to strengthen regional relationships. Elizabeth Rosenthal, "Energy Rush: Shale Production and U.S. National Security," Report of the Unconventional Energy and U.S. National Security Task Force, Center for a New American Security, February 2014.

35. As Locklear put it, upheaval from a warming planet "is probably the most likely thing that is going to happen . . . that will cripple the security environment, probably more likely than the other scenarios we all often talk about." Continued Locklear, "I'm into the consequence management side of it. I'm not a scientist, but the island of Tarawa in Kiribati, they're contemplating moving their entire population to another country because [it] is not going to exist anymore." Bryan Bender, "Chief of U.S. Pacific Forces Calls Climate Biggest Worry," *Boston Globe,* March 9, 2013.

36. Overviews of problems the United States has encountered with Egypt's Ministry of International Cooperation include Thalia Beaty, "U.S. Aid and Egypt: It's Complicated," Carnegie Endowment for International Peace, October 23, 2012; Max Strasser, "Can USAID Be a Force for Good in Egypt?," *Nation,* July 22, 2011.

37. For a brief overview of recent developments in the U.S.-Tunisia relationship, see U.S. Department of State, Bureau of Near Eastern Affairs, "U.S. Relations with Tunisia," fact sheet, August 22, 2013.

38. Riddhi Dasgupta, "An Arab Spring Success Story: Tunisia's New Constitution," CNN Money, February 19, 2014; Tarek Amara, "Tunisia Sees Elections in 2014, Despite Delays," Reuters, March 26, 2014.

39. Allison Good, "Could the Next U.S. Free Trade Agreement Be with Tunisia?," *Foreign Policy,* July 12, 2012.

40. "Arab Stabilization Plan: Expanded White Paper," Stimson Center, 2012, http://www.stimson.org/images/uploads/arab_stabilization_plan_final_expanded _white_paper.pdf.

41. Adopted in 1994, the Bogor goals aim for free and open trade and investment first by 2010 for industrialized economies and by 2020 for developing economies in the Asia-Pacific region. Member countries agreed to pursue these goals by reducing barriers to trade and investment and by promoting the free flow of goods, services, and capital. See Asia-Pacific Economic Cooperation, "Bogor Goals," fact sheet, www.apec.org/About-Us/About-APEC/Fact-Sheets/Bogor%20Goals.aspx. Citing the value of learning from the experiences of other countries, Hany Dimian said: "We are not going to reinvent the wheel—countries have diagnosed the economic problems and they know the solutions and the measures that need to be taken. The safest way . . . is to implement what has been tested elsewhere." "IMF Promotes Debate on Economic Change in the Middle East," *IMF Survey Magazine,* April 16, 2014.

42. The current deficiencies of the U.S. Agency for International Development are explored in Christopher Holshek, "Why Is the United States Letting Its Best Foreign Aid Tool Fall Apart?," *Foreign Policy,* June 22, 2015.

43. Mirjam Gehrke, "New Era Possible in EU Development Aid," Deutsche Welle, February 3, 2014.

44. Kim Mackrael, "Commercial Motives Driving Canada's Foreign Aid, Documents Reveal," *Globe and Mail,* January 8, 2014.

45. David Petraeus and Robert Zoellick, "Perfect Partners: North America's Shared Future," *Foreign Affairs,* February 18, 2014.

46. The United States currently has FTAs with every country of the alliance except Ecuador. Canada has stepped up its engagement with the alliance by establishing a Trade and Development Facility to negotiate, implement, and benefit from trade and investment agreements between Canada and the member countries. Membership will help both countries to integrate the Pacific Alliance countries more quickly into the TPP or other multilateral agreements. "Join the Club," *Economist,* April 29, 2013; "Baird Announces New Trade Initiative at Pacific Alliance Meeting," Canadian Office of Foreign Affairs—Trade and Development, press release, June 20, 2014.

47. Robert Zoellick, "A Presidency of Missed Opportunities," *Wall Street Journal,* August 10, 2014.

48. OPIC has returned money to U.S. taxpayers for thirty-seven straight years. See Overseas Private Investment Corporation, "OPIC 2014 Annual Report," www .opic.gov/sites/default/files/files/opic-fy14-annual-report.pdf. The Annual Management Report of the Overseas Private Investment Corporation for Fiscal Year 2014 put OPIC's 2014 investments at $2.96 billion with $358 million returned to the taxpayer. See, "Annual Management Report of the Overseas Private Investment Corporation for Fiscal Year 2014," OPIC, November 17, 2014, https://www.opic .gov/sites/default/files/files/fy2014-management-report.pdf.

49. See Venture for America's website, ventureforamerica.org.

50. See David Gordon and Stephen Krasner, "How to Bring Bashar Assad to the Table," *Politico,* May 29, 2012; Charles Kenny, "Odious Obligations," *Foreign Policy,* March 19, 2012.

51. For a compelling account of the central role that corruption plays in virtually all of America's top national security challenges, see Sarah Chayes, *Thieves of State* (New York: W.W. Norton, 2015). See also, Rachel Kleinfeld, "The Corruption Connection," *The Hill,* July 24, 2013.

52. Akin to the way the GATT offered a global solution to the problem of tariffs, we might consider a new present-day counterpart—an agreement, binding among parties, that would seek to confront the most salient forms of protectionism skewing playing fields today. This agreement would function similarly to existing trade agreements, complete with binding negotiations and agreed-upon enforcement mechanisms and remedies, but rather than liberalizing tariffs and investment as a principal aim, it would instead focus on addressing government market distortions and other competitiveness issues. Open to all comers who meet the standards, and offering a set of norms and disciplines for non-tariff-related market distortions, such an agreement could grow to function as a near-counterpart to the GATT.

53. See, e.g., Clyde Prestowitz, "China's Not Breaking the Rules. It's Playing a Different Game," *Foreign Policy,* February 17, 2012.

54. OCO funding was later expanded for fiscal year 2015 to include uses pertaining to Yemen and Syria. See Julian Pecquet, "Congress Balks at War on Terror

Funding for Syria," *Al-Monitor,* April 16, 2014; "Analysis of the President's FY15 International Affairs Budget Request," U.S. Global Leadership Coalition, March 4, 2014.

55. See, e.g., Daniel Byman and Matthew Waxman, *The Dynamics of Coercion: American Foreign Policy and the Limits of Military Might* (Cambridge: Cambridge University Press, 2002).

56. The changes would double the IMF's quota to $720 billion, shift six percentage points of total quota to emerging markets, and move two of the twenty-four IMF directorships from European to developing countries. See Robin Harding, "G20 Gives U.S. Ultimatum over IMF Reform," *Financial Times,* April 11, 2014.

57. Richard N. Haass, *Foreign Policy Begins at Home: The Case for Putting America's House in Order* (New York: Basic Books, 2014).

10. Geoeconomics, U.S. Grand Strategy, and American National Interests

1. In disclosure, one of this book's authors was a chief architect of the Clinton Economic Statecraft agenda.

2. Hillary Rodham Clinton, "Economic Statecraft," speech at the Economic Club of New York, October 14, 2011.

3. See "Delivering on the Promise of Economic Statecraft," remarks by Hillary Rodham Clinton at Singapore Management University, November 17, 2012.

4. Robert Zoellick, "A New U.S. International Economic Strategy," *Wall Street Journal,* February 5, 2013.

5. Jonathon Weisman, "At Global Economic Gathering, U.S. Primacy Is Seen as Ebbing," *New York Times,* April 17, 2015.

6. Graham Allison and Robert Blackwill, *America's National Interests: A Report from the Commission on America's National Interests,* July 2000.

Index